Union At All Costs:
From Confederation to Consolidation

John M. Taylor

Acknowledgements

Projects such as this require considerable influence, sacrifice, and commitment. From the start, having parents and grandparents who cared about both family and Southern history sparked my own interests. In addition, when I first began writing short articles about the South and its history, I received considerable support, and one of my most enthusiastic supporters was the late Doris "Dee" Callahan, who strongly encouraged me to write a book.

I would like to acknowledge those who assisted with this project. First of all, John Sophocleus, a man with a strong knowledge of history, economics, and the U.S. Constitution, has provided both advice and insight into many of the subjects covered in the text.

Cassy Gray, formerly of Stainless Banner Publishing Company, worked through this text several times, saw the importance of its message, and stressed the importance of concrete documentation of the material covered.

I would also like to recognize Sandra Harris, who proofread the text and made many suggestions for improvement, and William "Porkchop" Adair, who assisted with ideas for an appropriate front and back cover. In addition, I would like to thank Tyrone Crowley and Douglas Wilkerson for their diligence and assistance in bringing more clarity to this revised edition. Other influences and sources are documented throughout the text.

I want to acknowledge Susan, Seth, and Will for their support and for understanding my reactions to historically inaccurate commentary through the years (and also to Will for valuable suggestions relative to subject matter).

Finally, thanks to BookLocker.com for their help in completing this effort.

Contents

Foreword

Forward to John M. Taylor's "**Union at All Costs**"
John P. Sophocleus
(Economist, Auburn University)

This book is purposefully designed not to be yet another addition to the standard fare compiled in most histories of the life and times of Abe Lincoln. It is intended to display how Lincoln was indeed different from the man oft characterized in American lore focusing on his pivotal role in changing the very nature of the Union. Mr. Taylor's goal is to show how Lincoln's view of the Declaration of Independence, State sovereignty, and understanding of a voluntary coalition of governments were vastly different from most of the Founding Fathers. Lincoln's baffling insistence the 1774 Articles of Association created an unbreakable Union (before the colonies were known as States) is in contravention of documented history. As this flawed logic has grown increasingly more pervasive, so have the resulting problems... this **is** Lincoln's legacy.

Taylor provides a brief overview of Lincoln's family background. Descended from a reputable family lineage, Lincoln's father (Thomas Lincoln) appeared to have fallen into a moral abyss. Despite these influences in his formative years, Lincoln possessed a desire for power and set out to make connections early in his life. Almost from day one, Lincoln identified with the Whig Party, the political party with the greatest economic and political power. As the protectionist wing of the Whig Party morphed into the Republican Party we observe today, it is little surprise Mr. Lincoln would be a central figure in the power struggle among rivals. Aligned with the corporate welfare recipients (especially railroads, such as the Illinois Central) it was clear Lincoln would champion special interests over the general welfare of the nation. Mr. Lincoln was a natural for playing the political game.

Mr. Taylor charts Lincoln's rise in political power, shepherding support from a wide array of factions, including the

"Wide Awake" paramilitary organization, the Free Soilers, European turned American Marxists, and most abolitionists. Buttressed with traditional Whig/Republican support (corporations, banks, etc.) these various groups provided fierce and often unyielding support. After successful coalition building and his exceptional political legerdemain when 'wheeling and dealing' at the 1860 Republican Convention in Chicago, Lincoln became the party's nominee, literally outfoxing William Seward, the presumptive favorite. It is not a stretch to opine Lincoln is the greatest politician this nation has ever produced given accomplishments of this sort in one of the more critical moments in US history. Southerners were aware of the corporate welfare interests Lincoln represented—which largely included banks in the Northeast and Upper Midwest. Behind the veil of 'Anti-slavery rhetoric' most Southerners saw the Republicans as the next generation of virulent protectionists setting a course for disaster in an agrarian economy. Aided by an ongoing schism in the Democratic Party, Lincoln was elected triggering the exodus of Southern States by a newly elected President with 39.8% of the votes cast; his name did not appear on the ballot in most Southern States where the newly formed political party had no presence.

Once in office, Lincoln expressed "surprise" Southerners viewed his presidency with trepidation, although the economic consequences to follow were well known in the South and Border States when the Republicans' triumph of protectionism is imposed on the nation. It was also known Republicans did not want any expansion of slavery outside the South and Border States; each new State allowed into the Union which preferred competition over protectionism made a 'veto-proof' result much more difficult when a protectionist was not in the executive office. The more concentrated and powerful manufacturing interests had the "whip hand" in the agrarian versus industrial battle; with an avowed extremist on protectionism in the White House, the Southern States rationally decided it was time to leave rather than return to a colonial existence under the hegemony of a mercantilist power as was England.

Once certain Lincoln was unwilling to compromise (other than complete capitulation) the reality of a severed Union was complete. This is one rare instance Lincoln parted philosophically with one of his heroes, Henry Clay (the so-called "Great Compromiser") as the Lincoln Administration rejected all attempts for peace—Southern or otherwise—i.e., increasing the certainty some level of conflict would evolve. From Colonel John Baldwin's plea to end the schism, to the Corwin Amendment, ostensibly for pacification of Southern and Border States, Lincoln remained steadfast in his assertion that the Union could not fiscally operate without the Southern States to provide tariff revenue and lower priced agricultural inputs to accomplish the desired wealth transfer.

Once hostilities began, the Lincoln Administration consistently trod on the edge of constitutional law, several times going well beyond its granted, enumerated powers. Taylor explores the numerous times the Lincoln Administration crossed the constitutional line, from calling for 75,000 volunteers from each State to invade the seceded States, to blockading ports, to suspending habeas corpus, imposing the first federal income tax/fiat money, etc. The Lincoln Administration worked diligently to frame their efforts as requirements to put down a 'rebellion.' These draconian tactics drove four more Southern States out of Lincoln's hegemonic Union. One of the more vulgar violations the book addresses was Lincoln's massive suppression of free speech, most notable the arrest of Ohio "Copperhead" Clement Vallandigham for expressing his First Amendment rights, the invasion (explicit treason) of Maryland, violations of the Fugitive Slave Act, the creation of a State in contravention of the wording of the U.S. Constitution, and even a violation of International law through the arrests of two Southerners traveling on a British Mail Ship.

As military efforts to impose his hegemonic Union failed and Northern morale attenuated, Lincoln issued the two-part Emancipation Proclamation in an attempt to coax the return of the Southern States, i.e., return to the Union and it is business as usual or remain in "rebellion" and have your slaves freed without compensation. The South was given 100 days to decide. The timing and analysis of the proclamation gives insight into Lincoln's cunning and political prowess relative to the inevitable break of the federal blockade and creating a "moral" illusion to discourage foreign intervention and/or re-establishing regular commerce with the agricultural States.

Despite strong resistance in his own party as well as outside of it, Lincoln managed to be re-nominated as the 1864 Republican candidate. Along with acknowledgement of the well-documented advantages on the side of the North, Taylor looks at the Confederate States' self-inflicted wounds through the loss of Atlanta (as if 'King Cotton' embargo policy empowering the federal blockade was not enough) and other strategic blunders which gave hope to the North an end was in sight. Once Lincoln achieved re-election, it was certain the war would continue until the South (unable to endure another four years) was forced to return to the Union.

In the war's aftermath, Taylor examines the entire context of preservation of the Union, questioning if force and Total War were compatible with what was initially created as a voluntary coalition of sovereign States. Taylor further questions the oft-repeated view the South is actually better off these past several score having suffered invasion, destruction and subjugation.

Confederate President Jefferson Davis insisted to the end Southerners had a God-given right to establish their independence. Davis' December 1864 approval of the ill-fated Kenner Mission demonstrated the true goal of the South was independence. From a historical and philosophical angle, Robert E. Lee and Lord Acton lamented the consolidation of power through the lens of prior history. Both made dire yet prophetically insightful predictions about the course of these united States then recently established as a forced coalition.

Taylor also examines the war from the standpoint of the Christian Just War Theory, questioning who was on the defensive and who was the aggressor. Before and during the war, there was heavy resistance in the North, including noted Massachusetts' Pro-South abolitionist Lysander Spooner. There was also bewilderment as to why war was necessary from Northerners such as Nathaniel

Hawthorne. In addition, the New York Draft Riots are covered for those unfamiliar with this dark episode among the many war tragedies to obtain victory over independence.

The old adage "to the victor go the spoils" is manifest in the analysis of the war, what led up to it and what followed. Taylor includes an examination of Lincoln's political philosophy relative to democracy (versus the Constitution's established representative republic) and secession. Along with the ground breaking explanation for the timing of the Emancipation Proclamation (s) the author also addresses the under-publicized religious beliefs of Lincoln through the words of relatives and friends. The truth about Mr. Lincoln has been carefully shielded from the public for obvious reasons. Taylor finds, "His sudden death at the hands of John Wilkes Booth almost instantly transformed his strongest detractors into his most ardent eulogizers."

Mr. Taylor's work is one of the best I've read (on par with Prof. Charles W. Adams - e.g., **"When in the Course of Human Events,"** or **"Those Dirty Rotten Taxes"** and **"For Good and Evil: the Impact Taxes on the Course of Civilization"** to name a few) to illustrate the degree to which Lincoln would go—i.e., his oath of office meant nothing. I find it most encouraging exemplary scholars like John Taylor are picking up where Prof. Adams' work ended. If you want to understand Lincoln's playbook (still used by politicos today) to set our nation on the course and outcomes we observe today—read Taylor's **"Union at All Costs."** The legacy costs of Lincoln remain profound today; we ignore them at our own peril. If our nation does not learn from works of this sort, then the only rational forecast is we will be cast upon junk heap of history along with all the other failed strongly centralised despotic command and control economies, which made government their god. Lincoln's more recent iteration is nothing new since the days of Nimrod. Without the efforts of modern authors like Messrs Adams and Taylor, we are certain to find many more iterations of this sort as Shakespeare penned in Julius Caesar (Act 3, Scene 1) until these lessons are re-learned well and not forgotten. How can one not think Lincoln, our modern American Caesar, one of those forecasted in

Shakespeare's text, "How many ages hence shall this lofty scene be acted over, in states unborn and accents yet unknown!"

In the closing chapter, "The Apotheosis of Abraham Lincoln," Mr. Taylor enumerates the underlying reasons northerners found it necessary to deify and propagandize the Lincoln mythos still alive and well today. Simply stated, the North needed a 'hero' as the 'front man' to proffer the Republican Party program of high taxes, big coercive centralised government, and corporate welfare.

This book more than any other I've read reaffirms Lincoln as the greatest politician our nation has and probably ever will produce. It is difficult to imagine any politician who may again be so deleterious to liberty and the general welfare because there was so much increasing freedom to take when Lincoln set us on our Soviet path of coercing free and sovereign States into his revised Union. The biggest contribution to the plethora of Lincoln books in my opinion is Mr. Taylor's courage to expose the 'Judas rhetoric' mastered by Lincoln which has become page one of every modern politicos' playbook today. Fain concern for the poor to hide one's own avarice was effective for Judas except among those with character, integrity, intelligence, and most of all courage, to expose and endeavor to stop it. "Union At All Costs" unambiguously shows our American Caesar in this light for anyone who wants to see Lincoln the man instead of wanting to read more mythos.

If you're looking for another Rushmore-type monument to morph the Spirit of independence embodied in Washington and Jefferson with the hegemony championed by Lincoln and Roosevelt (logically impossible to any rational thinker) John Taylor's work will be a disappointment. To those wanting a concise collection of documents and events to directly show the polar opposites, prepare for a very enlightening and satisfying read…

John Sophocleus is a columnist for the **Alabama Gazette** *and economist who worked for Ford Motor Company about a decade before devoting most of his time to teaching (Clemson then Auburn University) for 27 years. His most cited professional research addresses the deleterious impact of redistributive activity in the US economy.*

Preface

A seemingly endless number of books have been written about Abraham Lincoln, The War Between the States (Civil War), the events leading up to the war, and what transpired after the last Southern army surrendered. One might think every conceivable angle has been discussed, analyzed, theorized, and put out for public consumption.

Relative to the aforementioned events, those who read this text will determine if this book falls into a unique niche. I hope my perspective will add a degree of balance concerning the tragic events that helped shape the present day United States of America.

Having grown up in rural East Central Alabama, I have an indelible link to the past as provided by my family lineage. My parents, John Will Taylor and Mary Alford Taylor, were both born in the early 1900s. Like most rural Southerners of that era, they lived on farms in largely self-sufficient families, and, of course, they picked cotton. Both also had strong Southern family roots and numerous Confederate ancestors. My father was a carpenter, and my mother raised six children and briefly worked for Russell Mills in Alexander City, Alabama. Many relatives still live in or near Tallapoosa and Clay counties in Alabama.

As a child, my mother often proudly referred to her Great-Grandfather, Henry Hodnett (for whom her father, Henry Lafayette Alford, was named). In July 1861, Henry enlisted at Almond, Alabama, as a Confederate Private with Company K of the 14th Alabama Infantry Regiment. In April 1862, he was discharged and sent home suffering from measles and typhoid fever. Regaining his health, on January 1, 1863, Henry reenlisted with Company G of the 46th Alabama Infantry Regiment. He served until his capture at Vicksburg on July 4, 1863. He was paroled on July 10th and fought until he was again captured on July 30, 1864, near Atlanta. This time, Henry was sent to Camp Chase (pictured on the cover) in Columbus, Ohio, where he remained until war's end. After signing the dreaded Oath of Allegiance, Henry was released from the Ohio

"Hell Hole" on May 15, 1865. After suffering through war, sickness, and imprisonment, Henry walked home to East Alabama to put his life back together as best he could.

My mother was thirteen in 1928 when Henry Hodnett died in what is now Clay County, Alabama. She was greatly influenced by Henry, a Christian man and devoted agrarian, and much of this wisdom was passed on to my siblings and me. I am fortunate to have such a close personal link to the Southern side of the war.

Given the era in which I grew up, the public education system was still somewhat balanced relative to the issues on both sides of the conflict. Political correctness had not fully taken root. Some of my teachers had similar family connections, having parents or grandparents with intimate knowledge of the war. They knew fact from fiction and taught accordingly.

After receiving a B.S. Degree in Transportation from Auburn University, I worked for over thirty years with Russell Corporation, a one-time Fortune 500 textile apparel company that eventually felt the industry-killing effects of (the pseudo-free trade deal) NAFTA, combined with a few managerial missteps. When I joined the company's Traffic Department in 1978, one of the first things my boss, T.L. "Tommy" Griffin, spoke about was how anti-Southern discrimination in the transportation freight rate system lasted well into the twentieth century. One of the most historically egregious means of punishing the South was the discriminatory Pittsburgh Plus Pricing system, instituted at the behest of the Northern steel industry. Since Southern coal and iron ore were usually geographically close to processing locations, freight costs were relatively low, giving the South a tariff advantage. The federal government invented and imposed a phony increase in freight rates (Pittsburgh Plus fee) to effectively destroy the freight cost advantage in the South. This rate manipulation was also a remnant of Reconstruction.

In 1937, a group of Southern politicians complained to the ICC about unfair rates and requested an end to economic discrimination. They received a degree of support from President Franklin D. Roosevelt, who had become familiar with the South during his treatment for paralysis in Warm Springs, Georgia. Over time, the laws of economics helped evaporate most of this biased system, but it provided me with first-hand knowledge of the way transportation pricing could be and had been manipulated to benefit a specific group of people, an industry, or a geographic region.

From a cultural standpoint, in the 1970s and 1980s, I witnessed the seemingly intentional efforts to reshape the thinking of American citizens via the media, academia, and in the political realm. I stopped watching *network television* in 1981 because it was so clear where things were headed. (It has become full-blown propaganda and thought manipulation in much of the modern media.) Part of this program included an increasingly intense anti-Southern, anti-Confederate, and anti-Christian agenda. My knowledge of the patent falsification of many things being said and written became a source of concern. Troubled by the disinformation and encouraged by then boss and fellow history-buff, Wendell White, I joined the Sons of Confederate Veterans (SCV) in 1989. As a genealogical, historical, and educational non-profit organization, it seemed to be the best vehicle for me to document what I had been taught, especially via access to primary sources. After joining the SCV, I have read over seventy books on the pre-war, war, and post-war eras. I had no intention of joining a political organization; I often remembered my mother's threat to disown me if I ever got into politics.

It was not until later in life that I realized many of my beliefs are considered libertarian in modern vernacular and a mixed bag of "Old Right," "classical liberal," and "Jeffersonian" in prior times. Most of this realization began to make sense after discovering the writings, speeches, etc., of individuals connected to the Ludwig von Mises Institute, advocates of Austrian free market economics. My friendship with the late O.P. Alford was significant as is my continued friendship with John Sophocleus. (I met Mr. Alford and John after being contacted by the former Norma Jennings [now Willock]; in the early 1990s she invited me to visit the Mises Institute in Auburn, Alabama, on behalf of Mr. Lew Rockwell.) This perspective meshed with my traditional beliefs and an increased awareness of the insightful and timeless observations of writers such as Frederick Bastiat, John Locke, Patrick Henry, Thomas Jefferson, John Taylor of Caroline, Lord Acton, etc., and Confederates such as Raphael Semmes, E.P. Alexander, Richard Taylor, Patrick Cleburne, Jefferson Davis, and Robert E. Lee. The realization of the motives of Abraham Lincoln and the Radical Republicans was eye-opening as was the astoundingly prophetic writings and warnings of the agrarians.

My intention is to present this material in a logical, readable, and historically accurate form. As someone who strives to be fair-minded, the final judgment of my efforts will lie in the reader's eyes. I do know one thing for sure: during the past twenty-five plus years, I have re-educated myself, dramatically increased my historical knowledge, documented my findings, and learned the issues (pre-war, during the war, and post-war) were much more complicated than what is generally taught in government schools. The typical modern broad-brush interpretation of the war as well as its prelude and aftermath, is extremely simplistic.

After developing a desire to put my perspective on paper, it is my sincere hope that the subjects (some surely controversial) I have written about will stimulate the reader to delve deeper into this most fascinating and tragic time in American history.

Chapter One
The Declaration of Independence

WHEN in the Course of human Events, it becomes necessary for one People to dissolve the Political Bands which have connected them with another, and to assume among the Powers of the Earth, the separate and equal Station to which the Laws of Nature and of Nature's God entitle them, a decent Respect to the Opinions of Mankind requires that they should declare the causes which impel them to the Separation.[1]

Prior to the ratification of the U.S. Constitution, the States operated under the Articles of Confederation and Perpetual Union. Adopted on November 17, 1777, it was not until March 1, 1781, that all colonies had joined the confederation. Most of the creators of this new government were not far removed from either living under or having intimate knowledge of governments that were not voluntary, so the description of *Perpetual Union* was perhaps a bit optimistic. Article II expressly spelled out that each State retained its sovereignty and independence as well as all powers not specifically delegated to the central government.

The push to abandon the Articles of Confederation was initiated by those who desired a stronger central government. Once those efforts came to fruition, the States left the Articles of Confederation and voluntarily agreed to join the U.S. Constitution. The new coalition became official when nine States voted to join; this was accomplished with the addition of New Hampshire on June 21, 1788. March 4, 1789, became the official date of commencement. Two of the original thirteen colonies did not join until after the constitution became official—North Carolina became part of the

---

[1] "The Declaration of Independence," *ConstitutionFacts.com*, http://www.constitutionfacts.com/us-declaration-of-independence/read-the-declaration/, (Accessed April 17, 2016).

compact November 21, 1789, and Rhode Island agreed to join May 29, 1790.

Another document predated both the Articles of Confederation and the Constitution and served as the platform for liberation from Great Britain. That document was the Declaration of Independence, often considered the blueprint for government by consent. The Declaration was a direct response to taxation without representation and various acts of oppression initiated by the British government against the thirteen colonies.

Massachusetts Senator Timothy Pickering served under George Washington as Adjutant General, Secretary of War, and Secretary of State. He briefly served under John Adams before being dismissed for his opposition to Adams' desire for peace with France. Having worked within the government and realizing the motivation of the colonists, Pickering "once said that secession was 'the' principle of the American Revolution—the very right that the revolutionaries fought for."[2]

As the primary author of the Declaration of Independence, Thomas Jefferson of Virginia was charged with putting the philosophy of the American Revolution into words.[3] Knowing the depth of Jefferson's intellect, John Adams of Massachusetts asked

---

[2] Thomas J. DiLorenzo, "Rewriting History, American Style," L.M. Schwartz, *The Virginia Land Rights Coalition*, March 1, 2002, http://www.vlrc.org/authors/59.html, (Accessed April 17, 2016).

[3] Many have argued that Thomas Paine provided the true inspiration for the Declaration of Independence. Paine, born in England in 1737, moved to Britain's American colonies (Philadelphia) in 1774. His no nonsense approach to independence was embodied in his January 1776 revolutionary pamphlet *Common Sense*. Immensely popular, it was published anonymously and sold approximately 500,000 copies. Paine also published sixteen issues of his pamphlet series, *The American Crises*, between 1776 and 1783, each with a steady drumbeat advocating colonial independence. Though he may not always receive the recognition he deserves, Paine's efforts provided powerful impetus for the colonies to sever their relationship and role as underlings to Great Britain.

his friend to write the first draft. Once the initial draft was finished, "Adams and Ben Franklin made slight alterations to it before the committee presented it to the whole Congress."[4]

Adams had long been an advocate for independence of the colonies. That desire was equally strong in Virginia, a leader in the liberty movement, having declared its independence on May 15, 1776. During an early meeting of congress, Richard Henry Lee expressed the wishes of Virginia: "these United Colonies are, and of right ought to be, free and independent states, that are absolved of all allegiance to the British Crown..."[5] adding that political connections between the colonies and Great Britain should be dissolved. In early American vernacular a colony or State was essentially the same as a country, e.g., England, France, Spain, etc.

The underlying tenet of the American Revolution was essentially threefold: rights are God-given and unalienable or beyond repute; legitimate governments are created to protect these very rights; and any time government fails to live up to its charge of protecting the rights of the people, "men have a right and even a duty to overthrow that government and create a new one."[6]

Aside from the beliefs of atheists, agnostics, secular humanists, etc., it is generally accepted that rights come from God. God is not only the Creator but also the owner of everything within the realm of earth and humanity. Therefore, if God does not grant our rights, then one would have to assume some form of government grants rights, be it State, Federal, or other. The ideology that rights come from government is generally connected to various forms of collectivism, e.g., socialism, communism, fascism, etc. Though some Founders were Deists, most were Christian, and the

---

[4] Kevin R.C. Gutzman, J.D., Ph.D., *The Politically Incorrect Guide to the Constitution* (Washington, D.C.: Regnery Publishing, Inc., 2007), 11.

[5] Ibid., 10.

[6] Charley Reese, "We Are Revolutionaries," *LewRockwell.com*, September 19, 2005, https://www.lewrockwell.com/2005/09/charley-reese/were-revolutionaries/ - September 19, 2005, (Accessed April 17, 2016).

Declaration was based on individual liberty, a cornerstone of Judeo-Christian theology. They understood the tenets of Christianity relative to what constitutes legitimate government.

Second, legitimate government is created to protect the rights of individuals. If it fails to protect these rights, that government forfeits its legitimacy. This was the central argument expressed by Confederate States' President Jefferson Davis in his Farewell Address in the Senate Chamber at the U.S. Capitol on January 21, 1861. Davis claimed the central government had abandoned its charge, "I hope the time may come again, when a better comprehension of the theory of our Government, and the inalienable rights of the people of the States, will prevent any one from denying that each State is a sovereign, and thus may reclaim the grants which it has made to any agent whomsoever."[7] Davis went on to say:

> Then, Senators, we recur to the compact which binds us together; we recur to the principles upon which our Government was founded; and when you deny them, and when you deny to us the right to withdraw from a Government which thus perverted threatens to be destructive of our rights, we but tread in the path of our fathers when we proclaim our independence, and take the hazard. This is done not in hostility to others, not to injure any section of the country, not even for our own pecuniary benefit; but from the high and solemn motive of defending and protecting the rights we inherited, and which it is our sacred duty to transmit unshorn to our children.[8]

---

[7] "Jefferson Davis' Farewell Address," Senate Chamber, U.S. Capitol, January 21, 1861, *The Papers of Jefferson Davis, Rice University*, https://jeffersondavis.rice.edu/Content.aspx?id=87, (Accessed April 17, 2016).

[8] Ibid.

Conversely, Lincoln referenced the Declaration in the Gettysburg Address and various speeches; however, his interpretation was in a completely different context. Lincoln claimed the Declaration referenced a nation instead of a confederation of sovereign States. Noting the pervasiveness of this ideology within his thinking, he stated: "I have never had a feeling politically that did not spring from the sentiments embodied in the Declaration of Independence...."[9]

The third point is that when a government does not uphold its role, it is the duty of the people to either alter the existing government or create a new one. The exact wording from the Declaration is as follows:

> That whenever any Form of Government becomes destructive of these ends, it is the Right of the People to alter or to abolish it, and to institute new Government, laying its foundation on such principles and organizing its powers in such form, as to them shall seem most likely to effect their Safety and Happiness...But when a long train of abuses and usurpations, pursuing invariably the same Object evinces a design to reduce them under absolute Despotism, it is their right, it is their duty, to throw off such Government, and to provide new Guards for their future security.[10]

The Declaration is not technically the law; however, it is the foundation of the original American ideology of liberty and independence of the Thirteen Colonies. The colonies departed (or seceded) from the British Empire as separate nation-states with their

---

[9] "Lincoln, Independence Hall, February 22, 1861," *ushistory.org*, http://www.ushistory.org/independencehall/history/lincoln.htm, (Accessed July 14, 2016).

[10] Thomas Jefferson, "The Declaration of Independence," *ushistory.org*, http://www.ushistory.org/declaration/document/, (Accessed April 17, 2016).

own individual governments. As the Revolutionary War came to a close, Great Britain and these *united States* began negotiating a peace treaty in April 1782. Representing the Continental Congress from the colonies were American Peace Commissioners John Adams, Benjamin Franklin, and John Jay, with Henry Laurens joining them later. Richard Oswald represented Great Britain in the initial negotiations. Each signed the preliminary articles of peace on November 30, 1782. The final version of the Treaty of Paris of 1783, which officially ended the war, was signed in Paris, France, on September 3, 1783. American signers included Adams, Franklin, and Jay along with David Hartley, representing King George III. On January 14, 1784, the Continental Congress ratified the treaty.

Article I of the Treaty of Paris specifically describes the parties involved in the agreement: "His Britannic Majesty acknowledges the said United States, viz., New Hampshire, Massachusetts Bay, Rhode Island and Providence Plantations, Connecticut, New York, New Jersey, Pennsylvania, Delaware, Virginia, North Carolina, South Carolina, and Georgia, to be free, sovereign, and independent States." [11] The peace treaty was not made with a centralized authority, but rather with the thirteen individual Colonies.

The general view in most of the South and much of the North was the Declaration of Independence set an American precedent relative to government by consent, and the States joined both the Articles of Confederation and the U.S. Constitution voluntarily. This is often referred to as the Jeffersonian point of view and was prevalent within the Democratic Republican Party of the early 1800s. Lincoln essentially assumed the role of Great Britain, insisting the States of the South did not have the right to break away and create their own republic. He claimed the Union existed before the constitution; it was not a contractual association of States; and it is unbreakable. Lincoln contended the Union originated with the

---

[11] John S. Tilley, *Facts The Historians Leave Out*, Twenty-Second Printing (Nashville, Tennessee: Bill Coats, Ltd., 1991), 25-26.

1774 Articles of Association, which was an agreement among the Colonies to boycott most British imported goods.

It is indisputable that these united States were born out of revolution. One major difference is the South contended it was leaving a *voluntary union,* whereas the thirteen colonies left an *involuntary union* known as the British Empire. As Davis said: "[Our situation] illustrates the American idea that governments rest on the consent of the governed, and that it is the right of the people to alter or abolish them whenever they become destructive of the ends for which they were established." [12] Also, planting a seed for the legitimacy of voluntary government, he said: "A question settled by violence, or in disregard of law, must remain unsettled forever."[13] As committed as Davis was to his point of view, Lincoln was just as committed to his belief that an unbreakable Union existed before the colonies began identifying themselves as sovereign States in 1776.

---

[12] "Jefferson Davis Quotes," *Thinkexist.com,* http://thinkexist.com/quotes/jefferson_davis/, (Accessed April 17, 2016).
[13] "Jefferson Davis quotes," *AZ Quotes,* http://www.azquotes.com/quote/658598, (Accessed April 17, 2016).

Chapter Two
States' Rights

"The Secession of a state from the union depends on the will of the people of such state."[14]

William Rawle, LL. D, Philadelphia, PA

The issue of States' Rights has a life dating at least back to the founding of the Original American Republic. As the thirteen independent Republics or States entered into the Articles of Confederation and Perpetual Union, they delegated specific powers to the central government and retained the rest. Article II stated the arrangement: "Each State retains its sovereignty, freedom and independence, and every power, jurisdiction, and right which is not by this Confederation expressly delegated to the United States."[15]

After leaving the Articles of Confederation, the States joined the U.S. Constitution and granted additional power to the central government. These enumerated powers are listed in Article I, Section 8 and include power to lay and collect taxes, to borrow money on U.S. credit, to regulate commerce with foreign nations, to coin money, to provide and maintain a navy, etc. The States or the people retained the powers not expressly delegated to the federal government—these are States' Rights. The Ninth Amendment of the Bill of Rights reaffirms that un-enumerated rights are retained by the people and the clearly written Tenth Amendment states: "The powers not delegated to the United States by the Constitution, nor prohibited by it to the States, are reserved to the States respectively,

---

[14] William Rawle, LL.D, *A View of the Constitution — Secession as Taught at West Point, 1825* (Baton Rouge, Louisiana: Land and Land Publishing Division and Simsboro, Louisiana: Old South Books, 1993), 238.

[15] John S. Tilley, *Facts The Historians Leave Out,* Twenty-Second Printing (Nashville, Tennessee: Bill Coats, Ltd., 1991), 25.

or to the people."[16] During the Constitutional Convention, emphasis was placed on State sovereignty and individual rights. This was pivotal to reaching an agreement.

In this system of dual sovereignty the people of the States have supreme power over their own affairs. This arrangement was intended to provide a bulwark to keep the central government in check. The significance of State sovereignty emphasized in the Articles of Confederation was carried over to the new alliance. "No one was ever required by the Constitution to swear allegiance to the Federal government or the United States."[17]

After the Revolutionary War, Great Britain made peace with thirteen sovereign, independent States. During the Constitutional Convention, this designation did not change. For example, the State's representatives identified themselves as in the following examples: "The State of Georgia, by the grace of God, Free, Sovereign, and Independent."[18] Delegates from New York closed by saying, "This 9th day of May, in the 11th year of the Independence of the said State."[19] Also, "New York voted to accept the Constitution giving certain powers to Congress, but it added: 'That the powers of government may be reassumed by the people, whensoever it shall become necessary to their happiness.'"[20] On Virginia's acceptance, they stated: "The powers granted under the Constitution, being derived from the people of the United States, may be resumed by them, whensoever the same shall be perverted to their injury or oppression."[21] Rhode Island's agreement to join the constitution contained a similar stipulation. When Virginia, New York, and

---

[16] Ibid., 27.

[17] Lyon Gardner Tyler, *The Gray Book: A Confederate Catechism* (Wiggins, Mississippi: Crown Rights Book Company, Wiggins, Mississippi, 1997), 32. Originally printed in *Tyler's Quarterly*, Volume 33, January and February, 1935.

[18] Tilley, *Facts the Historians Leave Out*, 26.

[19] Ibid.

[20] Ibid.

[21] Ibid., 27.

Rhode Island reserved the right of secession in their respective ratifications of the constitution, "this reservation, according to the rules of law, enured to the benefit of the other States as well."[22] The voluntary nature of the compact was made clear; without this guarantee to the States, a new agreement was very unlikely.

As the new constitution was being debated, there was strong pressure to include a Bill of Rights. The most intense pressure came from Anti-Federalists such as Patrick Henry and George Mason of Virginia and Elbridge Gerry and Sam Adams of Massachusetts as well as from the lessons of history. "The Magna Carta, the English bill of rights, Virginia's 1776 Declaration of Rights, and the colonial struggle against tyranny provided inspiration and direction for the Bill of Rights." [23] Henry strongly opposed the adoption of the Constitution. He was skeptical of the secret nature of the Constitutional Convention, and he feared the new arrangement would lead to a consolidated central government. Henry was aware of historical precedent illustrating the propensity of central governments to become oppressive and abusive of power. Henry, Mason, and others felt it was necessary to list basic *God-given* or natural rights that the federal government could not constitutionally interfere with. For example, they did not want a central state run by a national church to trample on their individual rights as had happened repeatedly in the history of Europe and Great Britain.

Hamilton and other Federalists wanted a strong central government and looked favorably on a king-like ruler and/or a monarchical style of government. Also, Federalist Chief Justice John Marshall claimed the Union lost its character as a compact under the new constitution although there was no expressed provision or

---

[22] Tyler, 32.

[23] Secession Crisis: "States' Rights Powers Reserved To The States," The War for States' Rights, *Civil War Bluegrass,* http://civilwar.bluegrass.net/secessioncrisis/statesrights.html, (Accessed April 17, 2016).

revocation to indicate this occurred. This thinking echoed that of Daniel Webster and, later, Lincoln.

Most early colonists wanted to be left alone to conduct their own affairs at the State or local level. Despite the desires of the more liberty-minded citizens in the early Republic, there was a faction intent on diluting the power of the States. For example, in the 1790s, the Federalist Supreme Court ruled that the State of Georgia must submit to the authority of the federal court in court case *Chisholm vs. Georgia.* "The Georgia legislature passed a bill ordering that any federal agent attempting to execute the court's order should '...suffer death, without benefit of clergy, by being hanged.'"[24] This case led to the Eleventh Amendment that protects State sovereignty and limits the federal court's involvement with hearing a suit brought by an individual against a State.

The Federalists' Alien and Sedition Acts of 1798 were direct attacks on the Bill of Rights. In reaction, States' Rights were asserted and explained in the Virginia Resolutions of 1798 and the Kentucky Resolutions of 1798/1799. Written by Madison and Jefferson, respectively, "these resolutions...declared alien and sedition acts unconstitutional."[25] They made three basic points: (1) When the States formed the Constitution, by common agreement they created a central or national government and gave it only specific and defined powers. (2) The central or national government was created as an agent of the States, "which were the real sovereigns, and to do only those things which were specifically granted to it in the compact of the Constitution."[26] (3) Since the States created the central government, it was they who should decide if the national government acted within its delegated authority. The central

---

[24] James Ronald Kennedy and Walter Donald Kennedy, *The South Was Right!* (Gretna, Louisiana: Pelican Publishing Company, 1994), 230.

[25] Captain S.A. Ashe, *A Southern View of the Invasion of the Southern States and War of 1861-1865* (Crawfordville, Georgia: Ruffin Flag Company, published from the 2nd (1938) edition, 1997), 17.

[26] Ibid.

government was not granted authority to determine the limits of its own power.

States' Rights is also linked to Nullification, a Jeffersonian concept used by John C. Calhoun in South Carolina's opposition to the Tariffs of 1828 and 1832. Calhoun's standoff with Andrew Jackson ultimately led to a compromise that resulted in gradual decreases in import duties. However, it served as a harbinger of future disagreements of a similar nature.

When the treaty with Great Britain was signed in Paris in 1783, the independence of each sovereign State was recognized. The colonies had the option of remaining independent or joining an alliance where defined, specific powers would be delegated to the federal government. When the Constitution was adopted, there was belief in some States that they had the right to nullify any laws created by the central government if those laws were created in contravention of their granted powers. Another tactic designed to protect the States from the central government was a watered-down version of nullification known as interposition, which called for a State to interpose itself between the central government and the people of the State, essentially to block the enforcement of a federal law deemed to be unconstitutional.

Fast-forwarding to the 1860s, concerns were raised in both North and South relative to the consolidation of power in the Executive Branch. Even those connected to Lincoln observed the post-war change in the Federal-State relationship as reflected in Supreme Court Justice Salmon P. Chase's ominous comment, "State sovereignty died at Appomattox." [27] In modern times, Maine Professor Jay Hoar's commentary mirrors Chase: "The worst fears of those boys in Gray are now a fact of American life—a Federal government completely out of control." [28] Despite these dismal observations, waging and winning the war did not establish centralized government in perpetuity, i.e., the citizenry cannot

---

[27] Kennedy and Kennedy, 219.
[28] Ibid.

morally or legally be placed at the mercy of an omnipotent central government, without any recourse.

Many Southerners recognized the trend toward centralization. For example, Alabama's Senator Clement C. Clay offered the prognosis: "When they get control of the Federal government, which they vauntingly predict, the Southern States must elect between independence out of the Union or subordination within it."[29]

Calhoun also saw the handwriting on the wall, observing:

> That the Government claims, and practically maintains, the right to decide in the last resort as to the extent of its powers, will scarcely be denied by anyone conversant with the political history of the country. That it also claims the right to resort to force to maintain power she claims, against all opposition, is equally certain. Indeed, it is apparent, from what we daily hear, that this has become the prevailing fixed opinion of a great majority of the community. Now, I ask, what limitation can possibly be placed upon a Government claiming and exercising such rights?...It follows that the character of the Government has been changed, in consequence, from a Federal Republic, as it originally came from the hands of the framers, and that it has been changed into a great national consolidated Democracy.[30]

The Founders' goal of confining Article 1 powers of the central government was changed by the War Between the States. The expansion of centralized power before, during, and after the war left clear results. Lincoln's forced program of nationalism was triumphant, and the federal government became the master, rather than the agent, of the States in both North and South. Post-war, Southern influence in government became largely insignificant as

---

[29] Ibid., 233.
[30] Ibid., 233-234.

Northern corporate and financial interests took control. The late journalist, writer, and syndicated columnist Joe Sobran asserted the three greatest consolidators of centralized government power in history were Bismarck, Lenin, and Lincoln.

The defeat of the Confederate States of America dealt a near deathblow to States' Rights. As H.L. Mencken, the sage of Baltimore, noted, "The American people, North and South, went into the [Civil] war as citizens of their respective states, they came out as subjects, and what they thus lost they have never got back."[31] Not only were States' Rights diminished, the program of centralization and consolidation of power became more solidified. Most presidents after Lincoln have taken advantage of this fact. However, as Jefferson Davis said: "The principle for which we contend is bound to reassert itself, though it may be at another time and in another form."[32]

---

[31] "H.L. Mencken Quotations," *FreedomWriter.com*, http://www.freedomwriter.com/quotes.htm, (Accessed April 17, 2016).

[32] "Jefferson Davis quotes," *AZ Quotes*, http://www.azquotes.com/quote/658598, (Accessed August 5, 2016).

Chapter Three
Conflict on the Horizon

"The Union is an association of the people of republics; its preservation is calculated to depend on the preservation of those republics...Governments of dissimilar forms and principles cannot long maintain a binding coalition."[33]

William Rawle, LL. D, Philadelphia, PA

Though they possessed similarities, the early British and European immigrants in the North and South were different people who adapted to the strengths of their respective areas of settlement. Agriculture was extremely important to both regions. The milder Southern climate was more conducive to an agrarian-dominated society; thus, the early South was mainly agricultural with relatively little industry. This would have been the case even if slavery had never been introduced in the region. Along with agriculture, the North diversified and developed manufacturing, transportation, and banking interests. Over time, the regions became more and more divided relative to economic interests. Three major issues were dominant: the tariff, slavery, and banking.

In the early days, revenue in the form of import duties accounted for over ninety percent of Treasury funding. In general terms, there were two main philosophies on this subject— Hamilton's and Jefferson's. Hamilton advocated the creation of government debt and high import duties to protect American industry from foreign competition and supply the Treasury with an abundance of funds to be used to assist domestic industry. Jefferson advocated a more frugal government and import duties only high enough to cover the actual costs of operating the government,

---

[33] William Rawle, LL. D, *A View of the Constitution, 1825* (Baton Rouge, Louisiana: Land and Land Publishing Division—Kennedy and Kennedy, 1993), 234-235.

leaving economic development primarily to the free enterprise system. As a free trader, in 1786 Jefferson communicated his philosophy to French aristocrat Marquis de Lafayette: "It [is] for our interest, as for that also of all the world, that every port of France, and of every other country, should be free."[34] Thus you have the protectionist Hamiltonians and the free trading Jeffersonians. Political parties literally grew out of these two philosophies.

The Tariff Act of 1789 created the initial tariff under the U.S. Constitution. Recognizing a source of revenue was needed to facilitate the operation of the central government, Hamilton and James Madison were two of the most enthusiastic supporters. Madison offered a resolution before Congress in April 1789 to adopt an impost, stating, "that the object of the measure was to raise revenue, that it was to be a temporary expedient, to remain in force only till a comprehensive system could be arranged."[35] Section I of the Act described its purpose as a means of paying government debts and encouraging protection of certain industries. As the first legislation passed by Congress, the act provided funds to operate the government and pay Revolutionary War debt. Additionally, "The 5% duty charged on most imported goods (some higher) also helped to protect US manufacturing...."[36] The net legislative effect was the maritime and manufacturing regions gained a slight advantage over the agricultural regions.

---

[34] "Thomas Jefferson on Politics & Government," Foreign Commerce—Eliminating International Duties and Regulations, Jefferson to Marquis de Lafayette, 1786. ME 5:346, *famguardian.org*, http://famguardian.org/Subjects/Politics/ThomasJefferson/jeff1450.htm, (Accessed April 17, 2016).

[35] "Protective Purpose of the Tariff Act of 1789," from *Early Journal Content on JSTOR*, Internet Archive, http://archive.org/stream/jstor-1819831/1819831_djvu.txt, (Accessed April 17, 2016).

[36] "First Tariff Act, Approved July 4, 1789," Impact of Congress, *The Center on Congress at Indiana University*, http://tpscongress.indiana.edu/impact-of-congress/key-impacts.html, (Accessed April 17, 2016).

Building on the 1789 Act, increases in duties came about as a result of the Tariff of 1790 and the Tariff of 1792, both driven by the efforts of Hamilton, but never to the level he desired. The 1816 Tariff or Dallas Tariff was considered protectionist for the time period, with an average rate of about twenty percent. Named after Secretary of the Treasury, Alexander J. Dallas, it was sold as temporary—a three-year increase—to pay the costs of the War of 1812 and even received support from some Southerners. Northern efforts in 1820 to make the increase permanent were met with strong Southern resistance. This battle went back and forth until 1846; the South Carolina nullification crisis and the Tariffs of Abomination in the 1820s and 1830s marked the times that came closest to actual sectional conflict. The Walker Tariff of 1846 and the Tariff of 1857 were more favorable to the South, and the Morrill Tariff of 1860-61 was essentially a return to the Tariffs of Abominations.

Slavery also affected both regions. The lucrative slave trade, operated out of New England, was a source of tremendous profit; great fortunes were amassed by many of those involved. "The effects of the New England slave trade were momentous. It was one of the foundations of New England's economic structure; it created a wealthy class of slave-trading merchants, while the profits derived from this commerce stimulated cultural development and philanthropy."[37] Virginia and Georgia sought to end the slave trade in the late 1780s, but powerful Northern shipping interests used their influence to help delay its demise to 1808. Seeking an assist from the government while looking out for their own self-interests, they sought time to develop new business for reallocation of their assets. Most slaves were eventually sold to the South and Border States. Economic reality proved slave labor was largely impractical in the North but highly valuable in the South, especially for labor-

---

[37] Douglas Harper, "Northern Profits from Slavery," from *Slavery in the North*, Lorenzo Johnston Greene quote from *The Negro in Colonial New England, 1620-1776*, 319, http://slavenorth.com/profits.htm, (Accessed April 17, 2016).

intensive crops such as tobacco and cotton. The development of Eli Whitney's cotton gin increased production and helped satisfy the voracious desire for cotton by manufacturers in the North as well as in Great Britain and Europe. At least in the short run, the need for slave labor was greatly increased, and this had a significant long-term impact on the Southern States.

From the colonial beginnings not only did tariffs and slavery cause disagreement, there were also periodic ebbs and flows concerning centralized banking. The national bank was advocated by the Federalist Hamilton, and in 1791, the Bank of the United States was created, with its charter expiring in 1811. The Second National Bank was created in 1816 with a twenty-year charter. Henry Clay was one of its strongest supporters, and in 1832, he tried to get the bank re-chartered. Democratic President Jackson's aversion to central banking was heightened by his enmity and distrust toward Clay. He vetoed the bill, and Clay was unable to muster enough support to override the veto. Thus, 1832 marked the demise of the Second National Bank, and State governments took over banking. The defeat of central banking was a political blow to Clay. Sharing the defeat was Lincoln, the Clay admirer and central banking supporter.

The Jeffersonian tradition of opposition to central banking was ended during Lincoln's first presidential term. As the war raged between North and South, "Congress passed the National Currency Act in 1863. In 1864, President Lincoln signed a revision of that law, the National Bank Act."[38] A system of national banks was created and federal oversight and regulations were instituted. The implementation of this key element of Clay's American System helped appease those who supported consolidation of federal

---

[38] "A Brief History of U.S. Banking," "http://www.factmonster.com/ipka/A0801059.html" Fact Monster. © 2000–2013 Sandbox Networks, Inc., publishing as *Fact Monster*. 18 Apr. 2016 <http://www.factmonster.com/ipka/A0801059.html>. (Accessed April 18, 2016).

power. "Until Lincoln's inauguration in 1861, the Jeffersonian tradition was dominant in the United States."[39] Lincoln's actions were also a precursor to those of the immigrant Paul Warburg, "from a distinguished banking family in Germany."[40] As a proponent of European-styled central banking, Warburg reflected the visions of Lincoln and was a major force behind the Federal Reserve Act. This act was passed in December 1913 and created centralized United States banking known as the Federal Reserve System.

Working through the 1800s, numerous controversies arose relative to tariffs, slavery, and banking. Clay helped broker the Missouri Compromise of 1820 where States below 36 degrees 30 minutes parallel allowed slavery and those above the line prohibited it. The Compromise of 1850, which included the incendiary Fugitive Slave Act, stoked emotions on both sides. The Kansas-Nebraska Act of 1854 instituted popular sovereignty, allowing the people of these States to decide the slavery issue themselves. It effectively neutralized the Missouri Compromise. Also, the 1857 Tariff became a lightning rod of controversy, primarily in the North.

By 1860, regional animosity had become more intense. The Republican Platform called for a return to high import duties and confinement of slavery to the Southern and Border States. One school of thought contends the rise of the sectional Republican Party was simply a quirk of fate as a result of fighting within the Democratic Party. However, the former Northern protectionist Whigs, often bitter enemies of the Jeffersonians and later the Jacksonians, largely controlled this fledgling party, and they were destined to re-surface at some point.

---

[39] Gary North, "Abraham Lincoln and the Federal Reserve System: A Forgotten Connection," *Gary North's Specific Answers*, September 24, 2013, http://www.garynorth.com/public/11585print.cfm, (Accessed April 18, 2016).

[40] Ibid.

From the beginning, there were different regional interpretations of the Declaration of Independence and States' Rights. Thrown into this mix were the tariff, slavery, and banking issues—the conflict between agrarian and industrial interests—and even the very nature of what the republic was intended to be. Animosities approached a boiling point. Robert E. Lee lamented, "The war...was an unnecessary condition of affairs, and might have been avoided if forebearance and wisdom had been practiced on both sides."[41] This volatile mixture eventually led to a conflict that devastated the Original Republic.

---

[41] "Robert E. Lee Quotes," *Brainy Quote*, http://www.brainyquote.com/quotes/quotes/r/robertele169541.html, (Accessed April 18, 2016).

Chapter Four
Mr. Lincoln's Background and Motivation

"A huckster in politics...a first-rate second rate man."[42]
Abolitionist Wendell Phillips' description of Lincoln

As the central figure in this narrative, Abraham Lincoln deserves to be examined, beginning with his family heritage and his personal motivation. The name Lincoln, denoting one of the largest counties in England, is of ancient origins with connections to honorable associations, including "one of the colleges of Oxford University where John Wesley and John Morley pursued their studies with distinction."[43] Lincoln seldom spoke of his family, either through indifference or simply knowing little about their origins in Norfolk County, England.

Samuel Lincoln left Hingham, England, and landed in Hingham, Massachusetts, in 1637. He had four sons who went on to successful and honorable careers. The Lincolns were considered a first class family, much like the Washingtons, Randolphs, and Lees. The following offers insight as to the influence Lincoln received from his father Thomas.

Thomas Lincoln seemed to have lost something over time in that he failed to live up to the standards of a proud family lineage, which included successful businessmen, public servants, and an attorney general who served under President Jefferson. Thomas Lincoln's father, Abraham, was a principled man and good provider

---

[42] David Herbert Donald, *Lincoln Reconsidered* (New York, New York: Vintage Books, A Division of Random House, Inc., 2001), 3.

[43] Edgar Lee Masters, *Lincoln The Man* (Columbia, South Carolina: The Foundation for American Education, 1997), 6. Reprinted from 1931 original and 1959 renewal by permission of Hilary Masters.

for his family. Despite being properly reared, Thomas was considered to be of poor character, with the appearance of an individual who sprang from the dregs of society. "He was unmoral, shiftless, bound down in poverty, in spite of the fact that he inherited enough from his father Abraham to have made him well circumstanced, if he had possessed ambition and prudence." [44] Biographer Edgar Lee Masters speculated that new and peculiar genetic traits were somehow introduced through intermarriage, and Thomas took on these undesirable traits.

Thomas married Nancy Hanks, daughter of Joseph Hanks, in 1806 and settled in Elizabethton, Kentucky. In 1850, Lincoln told his law partner, William H. Herndon, that Nancy Hanks (his mother) was the daughter of Lucy Hanks and an unnamed Virginia planter of superior breeding. Lincoln viewed with pride the mere possibility that his mother had been illegitimate. He claimed, "For certain reasons, illegitimate children are oftentimes sturdier and brighter than those born in lawful wedlock."[45]

In a March 1870 letter to Ward Hill Lamon, Lincoln's bodyguard and friend, Herndon described a childhood accident Lincoln suffered. In 1818, ten-year old Lincoln and his friend, David Turnham, took corn to grind at Gordon's gristmill in Southern Indiana. The mill was located a couple of miles from the Lincoln cabin near Little Pigeon Creek, Indiana. The custom of the day required individuals to furnish their own power. Lincoln hitched the mare to the arm of the machine; as the animal walked around the circle, the machinery moved at a corresponding pace. He sat atop the arm, frequently using the whip to encourage the mare. After several strikes from the whip, the mare finally had had enough encouragement and proceeded to kick Lincoln in the head and send him sprawling to the ground, where he lay bleeding and unconscious. Fearing the blow was deadly, his friend and neighbor,

---

[44] Ibid., 9.

[45] Webb Garrison, *The Lincoln No One Knows* (Nashville, Tennessee: Rutledge Hill Press, 1993), 5.

Noah Gordon, ran to him while Turnham rushed to get Lincoln's father. Thomas arrived, placed his son in a wagon, and drove him home where he lay unconscious all night. The next morning neighbors gathered at Lincoln's cabin whereupon, after going through a series of jerking motions, Lincoln woke up and blurted out—"You old hussy" [46]—as he completed the sentence started before receiving the blow to the head.

Due to the number of hours Lincoln remained unconscious, it is likely the sheer power of the blow caused a severe concussion. These types of concussions can have long-term effects and produce symptoms like Parkinson's disease; in extreme cases they can cause death. In a modern context, we sometimes witness concussions severe and frequent enough to end careers in collision sports such as football. This often creates an adverse effect in cognitive functions. The present controversy concerning the condition known as CTE (Chronic traumatic encephalopathy) is a prime example of the brain damage caused by multiple blows to the head. Along with the trauma associated with concussions, there is often a scarring of the brain that results in a condition called *petit mal*, which is a form of epilepsy. This condition, which is not typically life threatening, includes "brief, unannounced lapses in consciousness." [47] In layman's terms, this is often referred to as a staring spell. Combined with a brief loss of awareness, there may be seizures that include blinking or a twitch in the mouth. With modern diagnosis, a unique electroencephalogram (EEG) is produced.

According to Lincoln's contemporaries, his left eye sometimes "drifted upward independently of his right eye, a condition now termed strabismus. Lincoln's smaller left eye socket

---

[46] Roger J. Norton, "Lincoln's Brush with Death!," *Abraham Lincoln Search Site*, December 29, 1996, http://rogerjnorton.com/Lincoln19.html, (Accessed April 17, 2016).

[47] "Definition of Petit Mal," *MedicineNet.com*, http://www.medicinenet.com/script/main/art.asp?articlekey=4854, (Accessed April 17, 2016).

may have displaced a muscle controlling vertical movement."[48] One symptom is double vision, which Lincoln occasionally complained about. Though the option was unavailable in the nineteenth century, this condition can be corrected with modern surgery. Lincoln's face was noticeably asymmetrical, far beyond the average person. His appearance was routinely mocked by political enemies and noted even by supporters such as author Nathaniel Hawthorne. There is some debate as to the cause of the physical maladies. "Laser scans cannot settle whether the kick or a development defect–or neither– contributed to Lincoln's lopsided face."[49]

Whatever the actual cause may have been, there is a distinct possibility that for the rest of his life Lincoln suffered "transient aphasia—inability to deal with words and memories"[50] Transient aphasia is a form of brain damage resulting from a ruptured blood vessel in the brain. This may have been a contributing factor toward Lincoln's bouts of depression, long periods of silence, and the periodic spells of seemingly sinking into another world, oblivious to his surroundings. His moods swung from one extreme to the other. "He was naturally cheerful and loved pleasant conversation, wit, anecdote and laughter. Beneath all this, however, ran a current of sadness and he was frequently subject to hours of depressed silence and introspection."[51] Among his friends and associates, Lincoln's erratic behavior was often noted.

---

[48] Dr. Ronald Fishman, "Abraham Lincoln had a Lopsided Face and Strabismus—Development defect or horse kick?," *Softpedia.com,* http://archive.news.softpedia.com/news/Abraham-Lincoln-Had-a-Lopsided-Face-And-Strabismus-62674.shtml, (Accessed April 17, 2016).

[49] Ibid.

[50] Garrison, 18.

[51] "Abraham Lincoln's Health," *Lincoln Financial Foundation Collection,* http://archive.org/stream/abrahamlincolnsx00linc/abrahamlincolnsx00linc_ djvu.txt, (Accessed April 17, 2016).

Herndon wrote:

Mr. Lincoln was a peculiar, mysterious man [with] a double consciousness, a double life. The two states, never in the normal man, co-exist in equal and vigorous activities though they succeed each other quickly.

One state predominates and while it so rules, the other state is somewhat quiescent, shadowy, yet living, a real thing. This is the sole reason why L. [Lincoln] so quickly passes from one state of consciousness to another and a different state.

In one moment he was in a state of abstraction and then quickly in another state when he was a social, talkative, and a communicative fellow.[52]

Lamon described his friend as...morbid, moody, meditative, thinking much of himself, and the things pertaining to himself, regarding other men as instruments furnished to hand for the accomplishment of views which he knew were important to the public. Mr. Lincoln was a man apart from the rest of his kind...He seemed to make boon companions of the coarsest men on the list of his acquaintances—low, vulgar, unfortunate creatures...It is said that he had no heart—that is, no personal attachments warm and strong enough to govern his passions. It was seldom that he praised anybody, and when he did, it was not a rival or an equal in the struggle for popularity and power...No one knew better how to damn with faint praise, or to divide the glory of another by being the first and frankest to acknowledge it.[53]

---

[52] Garrison, 18.

[53] Hon. George L. Christian, *The Life and Character of Abraham Lincoln—Monster or Messiah?* Second Printing (Birmingham, Alabama: Society for Biblical and Southern Studies, 1999), 12-13. [An address

Lamon later wrote:

(Lincoln) did nothing out of mere gratitude, and forgot the devotion of his warmest partisans as soon as the occasion for their services passed...Notwithstanding his overweening ambition, and the breathless eagerness with which he pursued the objects of it, he had no particle of sympathy with the great mass of his fellow citizens who were engaged in similar struggles for place.[54]

Major General J.C. Fremont characterized Lincoln as possessing an:

...incapacity and selfishness, with disregard of personal rights, with violation of personal liberty and liberty of the press, with feebleness and want of principle...The ordinary rights under the Constitution and laws of the country have been violated, and he further accuses Lincoln of 'managing the war for personal ends.'[55]

There were no real or perceived physical or mental limitations that could derail Lincoln's great ambition and personal drive to reach his political goals.

---

delivered before Robert E. Lee Camp No. 1 by Christian on October 29, 1909.] Original source: Ward Hill Lamon, *Life of Lincoln*, 480-481.

[54] Ibid., 13. Original source: Lamon, 482.

[55] Charles L.C. Minor, *The Real Lincoln* (Harrisonburg, Virginia: Sprinkle Publications, 1992), 36-37. Originally published by Everett Waddey Company in 1904 and by Atkins-Rankin Company in 1928. Original source: J.G. Holland, *Abraham Lincoln*, 259, 469, 471.

Chapter Five
Mr. Lincoln's Political Ambition

"Mr. Lincoln coveted honor and was eager for power. He was impatient of any interference that delayed or obstructed his progress...To be popular was to Lincoln the greatest good in life."[56]

William H. Herndon

Before he turned twenty-one years of age, Lincoln proclaimed his desire to be President of the United States; this was the central goal that motivated him throughout his life. He lacked physical attractiveness, was awkward and slovenly, and from his own mouth, was rife with ambiguities about his family lineage. Despite his peculiarities, he possessed a remarkable sense of humor, and his love of vulgar jokes and tales was legendary. Realizing the need to be more attractive and marketable, Lincoln became known for his "fearless disposition, with an inexhaustible store of anecdote and illustration, he became a good speaker, and was in every way fitted to be a successful leader of his party."[57] Despite his often-gregarious nature, Lincoln was difficult to get close to, and those who knew him best were cognizant of his true motivation: "he possessed a primordial combination of cynicism and cunning. His ambition an engine that never rested. Lincoln had one interest—power."[58]

---

[56] George Edmonds, *Facts and Falsehoods* (Wiggins, Mississippi: Crown Rights Book Company Liberty Reprint Series, 1997), 42. Originally published by Spencer Hall Lamb, 1904. Original source: William H. Herndon's *Life of Lincoln*.

[57] Susan Pendleton Lee, *Lee's New School History of the United States 1907 Edition* (Boise, Idaho: Grapevine Publications, Boise, 1995), 252. Original Copyright 1899 and 1900, Susan Pendleton Lee.

[58] Charles T. Pace, *War Between The States—Why?* (Published by Charles T. Pace), 23.

Early in his political career, Lincoln's aggressive self-confidence was apparent in the Illinois Legislature, which he helped lead into insolvency (detailed in the next chapter). While consciously working to make himself socially attractive, he refrained from being too candid with anyone. He possessed remarkable political savvy. On December 6, 1847, he began his term as U.S. Representative from Illinois, an important step in his journey to the presidency.

Prior to entering Congress, Lincoln was not particularly outspoken about his opposition to the Mexican War, but when it became politically expedient he strongly opposed it. Northern Whigs feared annexation of part of Mexico would mean additional States (mainly Slave States) and likely more Democrats.[59] This fear of diluted political power mirrored earlier opposition to the Louisiana Purchase, when Massachusetts threatened to secede in 1803, when the New England States pondered secession (Hartford Convention) in 1814 over the War of 1812, and again in 1845 in opposition to the annexation of Texas, and their hostility to the Kansas-Nebraska Act, which allowed popular sovereignty to the citizens of new States.

Lincoln repeatedly criticized President Polk and his support of war with Mexico. In a December 22, 1847, speech, he introduced what is "referred to as Lincoln's Spot Resolution to 'establish whether the particular spot of soil which the blood of our citizens was so shed was, or was not, our own soil.'"[60] He asked about the spot where something happened to necessitate war while claiming the war was unnecessary, and he asserted Polk had no authority to initiate war, although Congress had declared war as the Constitution mandates. Polk paid no heed to these criticisms. Lincoln backed off once the war began; however, his futile protests

---

[59] John C. Calhoun also opposed the Mexican War, claiming it was unnecessary and that Polk was overstepping his presidential powers.

[60] "Spotty Lincoln," Today's Document, *National Archives*, http://todaysdocument.tumblr.com/post/14622684113/spotty-lincoln-congressman-abraham-lincoln, (Accessed April 29, 2016).

gained him the nickname *Spotty,* and the Whigs refused to re-nominate him.

Lincoln took constitutionally solid positions in Congress that deserve analysis. On one hand, he asserted that a President does not have the right to declare war. The Constitution gives that power to Congress. He stated this fact in a February 15, 1848, letter to William Herndon, who had shown some sympathy with Polk's position. Just a month prior (January 1848), Lincoln had said that any people have the right to throw off an existing oppressive government, a sentiment echoed by numerous politicians, in both North and South, from ratification of the Constitution until 1860.

After leaving Congress, Lincoln returned to his corporate law practice. Throughout the country, the slavery issue was rising to the political forefront. To break Democratic domination, the Whigs moderately jumped on the anti-slavery bandwagon with less than honorable motives. (Radical Republicans later jumped deeper into the fray.) The Whigs were aware of the desire of citizens of the North to keep Blacks confined to the South and Border States, and they capitalized on it. Indeed, a key reason for aversion to slavery expansion in the North and West was the fact they did not want Blacks in their midst. "These selfish politicians put their interest before that of their countrymen, used every method they could find to agitate, to inflame the country, to set citizen against citizen."[61] Many Northern States were so determined to keep Blacks from living within their borders that they passed legislation to enforce this bias. Indiana, Illinois, Ohio, and Oregon all enacted State laws to that effect.

When the Whig Party split in the mid-1850s, most protectionist Northerners became Republicans, reflecting their opposition to the extension of slavery and support of government policies that benefitted them. Most former Southern Whigs became Democrats.

---

[61] Pace, 25.

Lincoln used the issue of slavery to assist in his re-entry into politics. Although generally opposed to the institution, he talked in both directions on the subject. On one hand, he admitted slavery was constitutional and insisted the Fugitive Slave Law should be enforced, and, on the other, he denounced the instances of brutality within the practice. Despite his general denouncement of the institution, he defended slave owners, such as his 1847 defense of Kentuckian Robert Matson. Lincoln never advocated equal rights for Blacks, but instead favored colonization. The free soil policy of the Republican Party was designed to keep slavery out of the territories, reserving settlement strictly for Whites. Lincoln knew the political side of the issue that would benefit him the most, and as a Clay Whig turned Republican, he remained consistent in his opposition to slavery being spread to the North and West.

Lincoln characterized the Democrats and Stephen Douglas as the party of slavery and won favor with many of the politicians who formed the Republican Party. The Republican philosophy was consistently anti-slavery and/or slavery expansion as well as supportive of a strong central government, protective tariffs, corporate welfare, and a national bank. They typically supported whatever benefitted the corporations they were associated with, such as the railroads, iron and steel manufacturers, etc.

Lincoln was transformed into something of an anti-slavery crusader; however, his general opposition to slavery did not necessarily translate into humanitarian concern for the welfare of Blacks. His often-repeated solution to the racial issue was colonization, as his own words reflect:

> Such separation, if ever effected at all, must be effected by colonization; and no political party, as such, is now doing anything directly for colonization. Party operations at present only favor or retard colonization incidentally. The enterprise is a difficult one, but 'when there is a will there is a way:' and what colonization needs most is a hearty will. Will springs from the two elements of moral sense and self-interest. Let us be

brought to believe it is morally right, and, at the same time, favorable to, or, at least, not against, our interest, to transfer the African to his native clime, and we shall find a way to do it, however great the task may be. The children of Israel, to such numbers as to include four hundred thousand fighting men, went out of Egyptian bondage in a body.[62]

Although they did not always see eye-to-eye, Radical Republicans such as Thaddeus Stevens, Charles Sumner, Edwin Stanton, and Benjamin Wade, generally supported and enabled Lincoln. This support came in spite of their generally low regard for him. For example, Stanton spoke of his earliest contact: "I met Lincoln at the bar and found him a low, cunning clown."[63] He also referred to him as "that gorilla at the White House or that ourang outang at the other end of the avenue." [64] There were many influential individuals among the doubters. "Sumner, Trumbull, Chandler, Wade, Winter Davis, and the men to whom the nation then turned as the great representative men of the new political power, did not conceal their distrust of Lincoln, and he had little support from them at any time during his administration."[65] These individuals were known to be Hamiltonian, anti-Southern, staunch centralizers, and protectionists. The *coup de grace*—the destruction of the South—was precisely what they sought. Within the Republican

---

[62] Douglas Harper, "American Colonization Society," *Slavery in the North*, http://slavenorth.com/colonize.htm, (Accessed April 17, 2016).

[63] Edmonds, 19. Original source: Norman Hapgood, *Abraham Lincoln*, 164.

[64] Ibid., 18. Original source: General George McClellan, *Life and Campaigns of George B. McClellan*.

[65] Charles L.C. Minor, *The Real Lincoln* (Harrisonburg, Virginia: Sprinkle Publications, 1992), 37-38. Original source: A.K. McLure, *Lincoln and the Men of the War Time*, 54.

Party was a group of radicals who were "politically shrewd, economically powerful, morally unscrupulous men."[66]

Lincoln was the point man to promote and protect Republican interests. (Discussed in detail in later chapters.) Southern leaders recognized his election "would mean the end of Southern political freedom and economic independence, and the beginning of Southern subordination to Northern industrial interests, the hard core of which had adopted Lincoln as its 'front man.'"[67]

In December 1860, Lincoln wrote Salmon P. Chase, "I'll make a cemetery of the South."[68] Determined that he and his party's agenda would succeed, he broke off all negotiations with the Southern States, killed the Crittenden Compromise, which divided slave and non-slave regions, and created a scenario that would build his party and possibly destroy the country in the process. Lincoln and the Radical Republicans did not share the Founders' view of States Rights as a bulwark to keep the central government in check.

Noted in a somewhat cynical manner, retired University of South Carolina Professor Clyde Wilson, points to the nature of the Republican Party, aka Lincoln's Party:

> In fact, the party is and always has been the party of state capitalism. That, along with the powers and perks it provides its leaders, is the whole reason for its creation and continued existence. By state capitalism I mean a regime of highly concentrated private ownership, subsidized and protected by government.
> The Republican party has never, ever opposed any government interference in the free market or any government expenditure except those that might favor labor unions or threaten Big Business. Consider that for a long time it was the party of high tariffs—when high

---

[66] Francis W. Springer, *War For What?* (Nashville, Tennessee: Bill Coats, Ltd., 1990), 72.

[67] Ibid., 71.

[68] Pace, 28.

tariffs benefited Northern big capital and oppressed the South and most of the population. Now it is the party of so-called free trade—because that is the policy that benefits Northern big capital, whatever it might cost the rest of us.

In succession, Republicans presented opposite policies idealistically as good for America, while carefully avoiding discussion of exactly who it was good for.[69]

The Republicans could have combed the entire earth and likely never found a more ideal and ambitious representative than Lincoln to push their corporate agenda.

---

[69] Clyde Wilson, "The Republican Charade: Lincoln and His Party," Clyde Wilson Library, *Abbeville Institute*, November 19, 2014, http://www.abbevilleinstitute.org/clyde-wilson-library/the-republican-charade-lincoln-and-his-party/, (Accessed April 17, 2016).

Chapter Six
Lincoln: Law, Politics, and Railroads

"The Illinois Central may well be proud of Abraham Lincoln—not because he became President of the United States, but because as an attorney he served his client superlatively well."[70]

Paul M. Angle, Historian and Lincoln Biographer

Much of Lincoln's life was connected to transportation in general and railroads in particular. In 1828 he and his friend, Allen Gentry, traveled via flatboat down the Mississippi River to New Orleans. En route, they encountered problems, fighting "off a robbery attack by seven Black men."[71] Upon reaching New Orleans they witnessed life in a racially and culturally diverse major city, including exposure to slavery.

Lincoln made a second trip to New Orleans in 1831 before returning to New Salem, Illinois, where he worked as a storekeeper. He boarded at Rutledge's Tavern and first met the owner's daughter, Ann.

Early in his life, Lincoln was a transportation advocate who voiced support for cleaning up the Sangamon River near his home to make water travel more efficient. At the time, he preferred water transportation; it was commonly known that railroad construction costs were prohibitive.

In 1832 Lincoln ran unsuccessfully for the Illinois State Legislature. He pushed the program of internal improvements and

---

[70] Carlton J. Corliss, *Abraham Lincoln and the Illinois Central Railroad: Main Line of Mid-America* (Champaign, Illinois: University of Illinois Library, Compliments of the Illinois Central, 1901), 1, https://archive.org/details/abrahamlincolnil00corl, (Accessed April 18, 2016).

[71] "A. Lincoln," *The History Place*, 1996, http://www.historyplace.com/lincoln/, (Accessed April 18, 2016).

began to shift his preference toward railroads over water transportation, emphasizing their superior utility. His support included advocacy of building a railroad through Sangamon County, Illinois. That same year, Lincoln enlisted to fight in the Black Hawk War where he served for three months but never saw combat duty. Another 1832 venture was a store partnership with William Berry. The store was licensed to sell alcoholic beverages. The store venture failed the next year, leaving Lincoln in debt. Attempting to rebound financially, he gained appointment as Postmaster of New Salem and later became Deputy County Surveyor.

In 1834, continuing to pursue a political career, Lincoln won a seat in the Illinois General Assembly as a Whig. Encouraged by John Todd Stuart, Kentucky lawyer and first cousin of Mary Todd Lincoln, he decided to study law. In 1835 a fever took the life of Ann Rutledge, for whom Lincoln had allegedly developed a strong affection.

Lincoln knew much of the money and power in America resided in the Whig Party. From his political infancy, he followed their basic tenets, stating: "My policies are short and sweet, like the old woman's dance. I am in favor of a national bank . . . in favor of the internal improvements system and a high protective tariff."[72]

In March 1836, Lincoln worked toward his attorney's license, and on September 9, he received his license to practice law in Illinois. He was re-elected the same year and admitted to the bar in 1837, settling in Springfield and working for Stuart. From a burgeoning career to ultimate success as a lawyer, Lincoln handled virtually any case that came his way, including representing slaveholders and opposing the railroads; however, he was well aware of the financial benefits of representing the railroads.

---

[72] "Lincoln's New Salem 1830-1837," National Park Service, *Lincoln Home National Historic Site*, http://www.nps.gov/liho/learn/historyculture/newsalem.htm, (Accessed April 18, 2016).

After his first two years of political life, Lincoln became increasingly confident in his abilities. In 1837, he attended the First Session of the Tenth General Assembly that convened at the State Capitol in Vandalia, Illinois. A proposed Michigan and Illinois canal had been discussed for over fifteen years; it was to "connect the Illinois River with the Great Lakes and Chicago."[73] At the time, many Northern States (including Illinois) were enamored with internal improvement policies, which often led to overspending and even bankruptcy.

Construction itself would be difficult, but financing the project presented even more of a challenge. In 1831 the Illinois Commission switched the original plan from construction of a canal to building a railroad. James M. Bucklin, a respected engineer, concurred, citing the greater benefit and flexibility of a railroad. Financing remained a problem. Still unsettled in 1835, the Illinois State Government authorized the governor to secure a loan no greater than $500,000.00.

There were two Senators and nine members of the house from Sangamon County; they were dubbed the "Long Nine"[74] because all members were over six feet tall. As the leader, Lincoln advocated distributing money from the sale of public lands to dig canals and build railroads. Also, as a member of the Committee on Finance, he sought finance and transportation legislation, and, along with his Sangamon contingent, lobbied for the State capitol to be moved to Springfield. Their quest for funding led them to engage in "log rolling"[75], which was simply *quid pro quo*, whereby they voted for myriad internal improvements to get what they wanted. Lincoln's powers of persuasion were on display during this process. After numerous rounds, twice on the brink of defeat, in February

---

[73] John W. Starr, Jr., *Lincoln & the Railroads* (New York, New York: Dodd, Mead & Company, 1927), 18, https://babel.hathitrust.org/cgi/pt?id=uc1.$b68226;view=1up;seq=1, (Accessed May 1, 2016).

[74] Ibid., 19.

[75] Ibid., 20.

1837, twelve million dollars was authorized for internal improvements for canals and railroads. Fellow Long Nine member Robert L. Wilson marveled at the way Lincoln led the fight and noted that politics seemed to be natural to him. "The sum of $3,500,000 was to be expended on the Illinois Central Railroad, which received the largest single appropriation."[76]

Witnessing Lincoln's fight for internal improvements was a legislature laden with influential people, including his future presidential opponent, Stephen Douglas. Another notable was Irish-born James Shields, who served as an "officer in the Mexican and Civil Wars, senator from three States, and the only personage with whom Abraham Lincoln was engaged to fight a duel."[77]

Other accomplished individuals witnessing Lincoln's efforts included:

> John A. McClernand, member of Congress and officer of high command during the Civil War, Orville H. Browning, United States Senator and Cabinet member; William A. Richardson, representative in Congress and candidate for Speaker of the House, and United States Senator; Augustus C. French, twice governor of Illinois; James Semple, foreign Minister and United States Senator...[78]

The legislation called for multiple railroads connecting various cities in Illinois and Indiana; the road designed to run from Galena to Cairo was to be dubbed the Illinois Central. One of the selling points was a predicted escalation in land values, which would attract investors. The end result was a large increase in debt that greatly stymied the economic progress of Illinois. Henry C. Whitney, a law associate of Lincoln, said the plan would have been good if the State could have afforded it. Illinois Governor Thomas

---

[76] Ibid., 25.

[77] Ibid., 24.

[78] Ibid., 24-25.

Ford, a limited-government Democrat and opponent of internal improvements, noted Lincoln's role, "He was a Whig, and as such in favor of internal improvements in general and a liberal construction of constitutional law in such matters."[79] After spearheading the internal improvements project, Lincoln made the long walk from Vandalia to his New Salem home. Despite his ill-advised efforts, Lincoln's relentlessness and determination made a lasting impression on fellow Whigs.

The Northern Cross Railroad, the first railroad line in the State of Illinois, grew out of the internal improvements package. Lincoln rode on this railroad in the 1840s, likely providing his first taste of rail travel, but clearly not his last, as he maintained a close connection with the industry for the duration of his career.

Lincoln's railroad connections were integral to his law practice, which spanned three partnerships—Stuart from 1837-1841; Stephen T. Logan from 1841-1843; and finally, William Herndon, beginning in December 1844. As Herndon's partner, Lincoln had a flourishing appellate practice and appeared before the Illinois Supreme Court in 300 or more cases. They maintained a solid relationship as evidenced by Lincoln's intention to rejoin Herndon at the end of his presidency. Their partnership—put on hold for four years—technically lasted until Lincoln's death in 1865. Research shows Lincoln and his triumvirate of law partners handled over 5,000 cases. In fact, "The Papers of Abraham Lincoln project maintains a database of Lincoln's law practice that currently contains 5,173 cases involving Lincoln and his partners."[80]

Sidney Breese was a politician, Chief Justice of the Illinois Supreme Court, and Speaker of the Illinois House of Representatives. He tried for years to get the government interested in putting a railroad through central Illinois. The 1847 election of

---

[79] Ibid., 27.

[80] Roger J. Norton, "A Very Brief View of the Legal Career of Abraham Lincoln," *Abraham Lincoln Research Site*, December 29, 1996, http://rogerjnorton.com/Lincoln91.html, (Accessed April 18, 2016).

Stephen Douglas, another strong railroad advocate, made these prospects brighter. Interestingly, both Breese and Douglas were often referred to as the "Father of the Illinois Central."[81]

Lincoln was involved in the charter for the Illinois Central through his association with Robert Rantoul, Jr., a lawyer and politician from Massachusetts, and a member of the First Board of Directors of the Illinois Central Railroad Company. According to author John Starr, local capitalists backed Lincoln, and thus opposed Rantoul's proposal to use outside money. They feared Eastern contributors would own the road and minimize local control.

During the 1840s growth of the railroads, Lincoln made numerous trips from Springfield to the East. The first of these was in October 1847 when he left for Washington, D.C., to assume his seat as Representative from Illinois. He traveled mainly via stage with the exception that he likely traveled by rail from Winchester, Virginia, to D.C., via the Winchester and Potomac and the Baltimore and Ohio railroads.

In June 1848, Lincoln attended the Whig Convention, again using the Baltimore and Ohio Railroad to travel from Washington to Philadelphia. There he met Pennsylvanian Thaddeus Stevens, with whom he later corresponded in an attempt to gauge how Stevens' home State would vote in the presidential election.

As a supporter of Zachary Taylor, Lincoln spoke in September 1848, in Worcester, Massachusetts, and later in Boston, Lowell, Dorcester, Dedham, and Cambridge, traveling via a combination of rail and steamship. On Friday, September 22, "he and William H. Seward of New York were the rival attractions at an immense Whig rally held at Tremont Temple in Boston."[82] As Lincoln left Boston the next day, he stopped to speak with Taylor

---

[81] Bill Nunes, "The longest and shortest railroads in the world," *Suburban Journals of Greater St. Louis, St. Louis Dispatch*, October 10, 2007, http://www.stltoday.com/suburban-journals/the-longest-and-shortest-railroads-in-the-world/article_6a5885f2-ae9d-5ed0-b77d-59207fce9acf.html, (Accessed April 18, 2016).

[82] Starr, 51.

supporter, Thurlow Weed, a powerful influence in New York politics. He traveled by rail to Niagara Falls, then on to Detroit and eventually Chicago before returning to Springfield. The combination of travel via stage, steamship, ferry, and rail allowed Lincoln the opportunity to evaluate the quality and conditions of transportation. Partially as a result of his travels, "On February 3, 1849, on his return to Congress we observe our 'Lone Star' addressing the House 'On the Bill Granting Lands to the State to Make Railroads and Canals.' He favored the bill and sought earnestly to meet and combat the objections of those who opposed it."[83]

Railroad construction expanded in Illinois in the 1850s and with it came new legal questions. Lincoln's first major railroad case was *Barret v. Alton and Sangamon* in December 1851. Appearing before the Illinois Supreme Court, Lincoln represented the Alton and Sangamon Railroad against James A. Barret, a defaulting stock subscriber. Barret refused to pay the balance of a stock purchase after the railroad changed the original route. Lincoln sued for damages and won. The victory benefitted the corporate management of Illinois railroads and short-circuited the possibility of other investors withdrawing their monetary pledges and depriving the company of funding. The verdict set a precedent that a contract could only be voided if profound changes were made in railroad charters.[84] Author David Herbert Donald noted the victory "established Lincoln as one of the most prominent and successful Illinois practitioners of railroad law."[85] Besides Alton & Sangamon,

---

[83] Ibid., 53.

[84] Lincoln's partner, Herndon, later handled the Dalby Case that eventually led to employer liabilty for an employee's willful intent to injure. He also represented the same railroad in an eminent domain case based on a question of just compensation; when dealing with the railroads, it limited the compensation to landowners in eminent domain cases.

[85] James W. Ely, Jr., "Abraham Lincoln as a Railroad Attorney," *Indiana History.org*, 4, http://www.indianahistory.org/our-services/books-publications/railroad-symposia-essays-1/Abe%20Lincoln%20as%20a%20Railroad%20Attorney.pdf, (Accessed

Lincoln represented the Ohio and Mississippi Railroad and Rock Island Railroad corporations.

The Illinois Central was chartered through a federal land grant in 1851 and made to construct a line from Northern Illinois to Southern Illinois. Mr. J.G. Drennan, a legal representative of the Illinois Central, claimed Lincoln was not a regular employee but rather someone on call, for which he received an annual pass. Author James W. Weik echoed this view. However, railroad attorney James F. Foy, who became chief counsel for the Illinois Central in 1852, said they "retained Abraham Lincoln as local attorney at Springfield."[86]

In October 1853, Lincoln was put on retainer for the Illinois Central, handling over fifty cases for them until his 1860 election. For services rendered, he not only received fees but also had the benefit of free transportation in private cars. Attorney John T. Richards referenced Lincoln's value as legal counsel, explaining his status "as a lawyer of no ordinary learning and ability."[87] Richards described the Illinois Central Railroad as "the greatest corporation in the state, and one which doubtless had its choice of legal talent."[88]

One of the more significant cases handled by Lincoln was *Illinois Central Railroad v. County of McLean and George Parke*. In the 1857 McLean case, Lincoln represented the Illinois Central with Foy.

> The case, says Mr. Drennan, involves an interpretation of the charter of the company. The charter provides that the company, in lieu of all other taxes, shall pay into the state treasury annually an amount equal, at least, to seven per cent of the gross revenue derived from its charter lines in Illinois...if the company had lost, every county, city and school district in Illinois through which

---

April 18, 2016). [Ely is a Milton R. Underwood professor of law and professor of history, Vanderbilt University.]
[86] Starr, 58.
[87] Ibid., 67.
[88] Ibid.

the road ran or which contained property of the
company would have had the right to assess and collect
local taxes, adding to the considerable burden imposed
upon the revenues of the company by the seven per cent
contract.[89]

Tax exempt for the first six years of operation, the Illinois
Central had to pay a charter tax of up to seven percent of its gross
receipts. Lincoln's argument before the Illinois Supreme Court was
"that the legislature had the constitutional authority to grant tax
exemptions or to commute the tax rate for a fixed sum."[90] He used
examples from other States to back up the argument. "The supreme
court in 1856 adopted Lincoln's analysis, holding that the legislature
had broad power over taxation and could grant tax concessions for
the public benefit."[91] Though the Illinois Central saved millions, in
retrospect, it may have been cheaper in the long run if the charter
tax arrangement had been ruled unconstitutional.

For this case, after receiving a $250.00 retainer, Lincoln
submitted a bill for $5000.00, the highest fee at the time. The Illinois
Central refused to pay; however, this equated to a friendly lawsuit
since representatives for the railroad failed to appear at the June 18,
1857, trial and the company paid the difference in the original
retainer and the $5000.00 fee. Despite the supposed discord, the
company clearly recognized Lincoln's legal skills.

The railroad's willingness to pay the high fee indicated they
wanted Lincoln on their team. As a prime example of his value,
Lincoln represented the railroad in a case involving a dispute with
the state tax auditor, who claimed the Illinois Central owed
$94,000.00 in 1857 taxes plus the seven percent charter tax. Part of
his defense included convincing the State auditor to delay collection
of 1857 and 1858 taxes. Through appeals to the Illinois Supreme
Court, Lincoln succeeded in having the Illinois Central pay lower

---

[89] Ibid., 63.
[90] Ely, Jr., 7.
[91] Ibid, 7-8.

taxes that the railroad itself determined. In 1859, the case came to a close with the court ruling the railroad did not owe any back taxes and that they were only liable for taxes based on current value.

Another impactful Lincoln case was the Effie Afton trial known as *Hurd v. Rock Island Bridge Company*. On May 6, 1856, the Effie Afton, a side-wheel steamboat ran into a bridge built by the Rock Island Railroad. The bridge spanned between Rock Island, Illinois, and Davenport, Iowa, and was the first such railroad bridge to span the Mississippi River. Due to the animosity between steamboat and rail interests, suspicion arose that the accident was intentional. Jacob Hurd, co-owner and steamboat captain, sued the Railroad Bridge Company, claiming the bridge was an illegal obstruction and impediment to travel on the Mississippi River. Hurd and his fellow owners sought to collect damages for "the value of the boat, her cargo, and such other damages as they may be entitled by law and the evidence to recover."[92]

Henry Farnam and Thomas Clark Durant had a vested interest in the railroad, and they sought out Lincoln to represent the Rock Island Bridge Company. A North versus South dimension was also a factor. "A victory for the steamboat interests would mean that the corn and wheat, the pork and timber—all the abundance of the burgeoning Midwest—would continue to move southward along the rivers. St. Louis, Memphis, and New Orleans would become the national centers of trade."[93] Conversely, "a victory for the railroads would mean that commerce could move east and west in a steadily growing volume and thereby assure the destinies of Chicago and New York."[94] Relying on information about river currents gathered from Ben Brayton, son of bridge engineer B.B. Brayton, Lincoln successfully represented the railroad with the 1857 victory. The

---

[92] "Court Documents of Hurd v. Rock Island Railroad Company," *castle.elu.edu*, http://castle.eiu.edu/~wow/classes/sp07/lawdocument.pdf, (Accessed April 18, 2016).

[93] Dee Brown, *Hear That Lonesome Whistle Blow* (New York, New York: Holt, Rinehart and Winston, 1977), 10-11.

[94] Ibid., 11.

victory was a blow to commerce moving south and set a precedent for land routes to bridge waterways, effectively reducing the cost of westward expansion. While representing the Rock Island Bridge Company, Lincoln received information relative to the favored route of the railroad.

Lincoln also successfully handled *Illinois Central Railroad v. Morrison* (1857)—this limited railroad liability for damage to cattle caused by delay in transit. The court ruled the railroad had a right to contractually limit its common carrier liability.

Another important case involved Lincoln and Herndon's representation of Joseph Dalby in a ticket price dispute. On April 4, 1857, Dalby and his wife sought to purchase railroad tickets for a trip from Elkhart to Lincoln, Illinois. Tickets were cheaper when purchased from station agent William Rankin. When Rankin ran out of tickets, he wrote a note to the conductor to let the Dalbys ride at the cheaper price. While en route, upon validation of tickets, the conductor was given Rankin's note but refused to honor it and demanded the higher rate. After a brief exchange, a fight ensued and Dalby was severely beaten, despite the fact Dalby relented and said he would pay the higher price. Represented by Lincoln and Herndon in his personal injury suit, Dalby won the initial case. The railroad appealed and said it was not responsible for the actions of its employees; it led to legislation where non-paying customers could be removed at any point as long as excess force was not used and employers could be held liable when their employees intentionally cause injury.

In August 1859, Lincoln, accompanied by Secretary of State Ozias M. Hatch, left Springfield for a three-day visit to Iowa. They arrived in Council Bluffs, Iowa, on the 12th and registered at the Pacific House. "He was there to inquire about realty holdings that he had taken as security for a debt and also a homestead allotment due him for militia service in the Black Hawk War."[95]

---

[95] Ibid., 41.

Norman B. Judd, Chicago attorney and Lincoln associate, was connected to the M. & M. Railroad. Biographer J.R. Perkins wrote that Judd: "believed that this land would become of great value when the Mississippi and Missouri River Railroad reached Council Bluffs, and as a direct consequence, linked up with the proposed Pacific railroad. So he bought seventeen lots—for which he paid three thousand five hundred dollars—that were but a stone's throw from where the M. & M. had decided to make its terminus."[96]

As a result of financial problems, Judd sought a $3000.00 loan from Lincoln and offered the land as security. Not only did Lincoln want to inspect the land relative to the loan, he also wanted to learn more about the potential railroad situation in western Iowa and eastern Nebraska. Economic historian Olivier Fraysse explained Lincoln's goal was "to evaluate the possibilities of speculating on the passage through that locality of the Pacific Railroad, a proposal that the Republicans had included in the affair...."[97] At the behest of Hatch, Lincoln agreed "to renew and increase a loan of $2,500 made to Judd in 1857 to finance this speculation and took a mortgage for $3,000 on seventeen Iowa plots in Council Bluffs and on ten acres along the route of the Mississippi and Missouri Railroad."[98]

They visited the town and viewed the surrounding area. W.H. Pusey, Lincoln's host and former Springfield resident, suggested Grenville Dodge as a good source of railroad information. Dodge was surveying the forty-second parallel for Farnam of the Rock Island and Mississippi and Missouri Railroads. He had purchased a sizable amount of property in Council Bluffs, some of

---

[96] "Abraham Lincoln and Iowa," *Abraham Lincoln's Classroom*, The Lehrman Institute, http://abrahamlincolnsclassroom.org/abraham-lincoln-state-by-state/abraham-lincoln-and-iowa/, Original source: J.R. Perkins, *Trails, Rails and War: The Life of General G.M. Dodge*, 45, (Accessed April 18, 2016).

[97] Ibid. Original source: Olivier Fraysee, *Lincoln, Land & Labor, 1809-60*, 147-148.

[98] Ibid.

which he had sold. Lincoln met Dodge at the Pacific House. Dodge described Lincoln's curiosity: "he proceeded to find out all about the country we had been through, and all about railroad surveys...he extracted from me the information I had gathered for my employers, and virtually shelled my woods most thoroughly."[99] Dodge later reflected on this meeting and recalled sketching out a western railroad route, suggesting the railroad could follow the Platte River. They talked about the benefits of a transcontinental railroad. Also, Pusey remembered Lincoln saying, "Not one, but many railroads will center here."[100]

In June 1861, Lincoln began work on the Pacific Railroad Act. The President was given the option of choosing the transcontinental railroad's eastern terminus. Despite the clear possibility of being accused of bias, Lincoln chose "Council Bluffs, Iowa—where he had invested in land in 1857."[101]

On July 1, 1862, Lincoln signed the Pacific Railroad Enabling Act into law, the same day as the Battle of Malvern Hill.[102]

> President Lincoln signed the act, creating the Union
> Pacific Railroad Company. Thus was assured the
> fortunes of a dynasty of American families, many of

---

[99] Brown, 41.

[100] "Abraham Lincoln and Iowa," *Abraham Lincoln's Classroom*, Original source: Perkins, *Trails, Rails and War: The Life of General G.M. Dodge*, 50.

[101] "Abraham Lincoln: Another Look—The Republican Party," *House of Paine*, http://www.houseofpaine.org/Abraham_Lincoln/Abraham%20Lincoln%20 main.htm, Original source: John W. Starr, *Lincoln and the Railroads*, 152, (Accessed April 18, 2016).

[102] According to John Starr, Jr., on page 70 of *Lincoln & the Railroads*, the Illinois Central moved troops to the South and returned dead Union soldiers to the North and received payment for these services. There was opposition, in "that the original Land Grant specifically provided that all supplies and troops of the United States should be carried over the road without charge." This led to a reduction in transportation rates in 1863.

whose names appear in the document as 'commissioners,' 158 of them-Brewsters, Bushnells, Olcotts, Harkers, Harrisons, Trowbridges, Langworthys, Reids, Ogdens, Bradfords, Noyeses, Brooks, Cornells, and dozens of others, including Huntington and Judah and a handful of swaggering frontier buccaneers such as Ben Holladay, the stagecoach king of the West.[103]

Later, in 1863, Dodge, serving as an Army engineer overseeing railroad construction and reconstruction in the Mississippi region, claimed he was ordered to Washington to speak with Lincoln. [104] During the meeting, Lincoln sought Dodge's opinion about the best location for the Union Pacific Railroad's starting point on the Missouri River. According to author J.R. Perkins, Dodge recommended that it be "in a township in which Council Bluffs is situated, and near a tract of land to which he held a quitclaim deed." [105] During their conversation, Dodge urged construction of the railroad. Although the law had been passed, a question of funding remained; i.e., there had been no money raised although the U.S. had "the first lien on the property while the company's bonds were only second mortgage bonds.... no one in the United States...had enough confidence in the future of the Union Pacific Railroad to buy second mortgage bonds at any price." [106] Dodge suggested the U.S. Government build the road, claiming it was too costly for private funding. Lamenting the existing issues

---

103 Brown, 49.

104 In *Hear that Lonesome Whistle Blow*, on page 41, Dee Brown wrote: "The record shows...Dodge was nowhere near Washington in the spring of 1863 and that Lincoln made his decision several months later..."

105 "Abraham Lincoln and Iowa," *Abraham Lincoln's Classroom*, Original source: Perkins, *Trails, Rails and War: The Life of General G. M. Dodge*, 47.

106 Ibid. Original source: Grenville M. Dodge, *Personal Recollections of President Abraham Lincoln, General Ulysses S. Grant and General William T. Sherman*, 15-16.

and their costs, but anxious to get the ball rolling, Lincoln "intimated that he was perfectly willing to have the law changed so that the Government should take the second mortgage and the promoters of the road should take the first."[107]

> After the meeting, Dodge traveled to New York to visit his friends who had organized the Union Pacific road, Mr. John A. Dix, Mr. Henry Farnam, Thomas Clark Durant, Francis Train, and others, and I told them in a board meeting what President Lincoln had said and they were greatly encouraged, and made up their minds to take the matter up, and they went before Congress and in 1864 they passed the law which placed the mortgage bonds of the company ahead of the mortgage bonds of the Government, and with the Government's and other mortgage bonds they were enabled to start the road, and by 1865 they had built the road as far west as Fremont.[108]

Despite the ongoing war and its costs, in December 1863, construction of the Union Pacific began at Council Bluffs, Iowa. Dodge was wounded in the war and released from Union service. "In 1866, Dodge became chief engineer for the transcontinental railroad."[109]

This act also created per mile government subsidies for the Union Pacific and Central Pacific Railroads. Lincoln and the railroads benefited; this illustrates a major reason the railroad industry was so supportive of Lincoln's election.[110] Many in the

---

[107] Ibid.

[108] Ibid.

[109] Ibid.

[110] This subject is covered in the AMC show *Hell on Wheels*, where Durant maps out a circuitous railroad route to maximize federal subsidies. Also, the infamous Credit Mobilier scandal grew out of the underhanded activities related to the support of the Union Pacific Railroad.

South, including Jefferson Davis, realized the significance of building a transcontinental railroad, but they differed in the preferred route and the way it should be financed. In 1854, serving as U.S. Secretary of War, Davis reviewed the railroad surveys and advocated a Southern route. Largley due to sectional animosity, Davis' recommendation met strong Northern resistance and never went forward.

Chapter Seven
Activist Support for Lincoln and the Republicans

"To try to hold fifteen States to the Union is preposterous."[111]
Edward Everett, Pastor, educator, and Whig from Massachusetts

Lincoln received support from virtually all constituents of the sectional Republican Party, driven by the North's corporate and/or protectionist interests, devout unionists, the abolitionists in varying degrees, and Northern citizens enraged that anyone would dare "fire on the flag." These and other groups exhibited near blanket support for the party and its candidate. Their support wasn't monolithic but was instead a mixed bag of agendas. The following will provide examples of a few of these groups and their reasons for support.

The Wide Awakes

As early as 1856, numerous military clubs were organized by or in support of the Republican Party. Examples included the Rocky Mountain Clubs, Freedom Clubs and Bear Clubs, with the most notorious being the Wide Awakes, who became a force in 1860. This group differed from the original group of New Yorkers who wore the Wide Awake moniker. The originals were an offshoot of the Know Nothing Party (or The American Party), which existed in the late 1840s and early 1850s.[112] One thing they had in common was support for the Republican Party.

---

[111] Mildred Lewis Rutherford, *Truths of History* (Harrisonburg, Virginia: Old South Institute Press, 2009), 19.

[112] Middle class, blue-collar White Protestants dominated the Know Nothing party. Leery of immigrants taking their jobs and strongly anti-Catholic, they ran Millard Fillmore for president in the 1856 election.

Northern Democrats countered with the Douglas Invincibles, Young Hickories, Earthquakes, and Chloroformers, a clear reference to the goal of anesthetizing the Wide Awakes. Similar groups in the South were known as the Minute Men.

As the 1860 election approached, the Northern militaristic, political, and Unionist organizations became more structured. Most members were young White Protestant males in their teens, twenties, or thirties who were motivated to act by the escalation of sectional friction in the 1850s. The aforementioned Wide Awakes were organized in Hartford, Connecticut, in March 1860. A catalyst for their organization was the political "response to Connecticut's spring election between Republican Governor William A. Buckingham and his challenger, Democrat Thomas Seymour."[113] They strongly supported Buckingham, a longtime Norwich, Connecticut, politician, and mercantilist who helped start the Hayward Rubber Company. Seymour was a lawyer, politician, and Democrat who had served in the Mexican War.

Numerous Wide Awake clubs sprang up throughout the North. Their presence was also felt in the Upper South in such locations as Baltimore and St. Louis. The groups were structured like the military, complete with defined ranks and duties as well as specific attire. A common form of dress consisted of capes or robes and black glazed hats. They often carried bright torches approximately six feet in length. Many also carried an insignia that featured crossed flags—the U.S. Flag and the Tricolor Flag of Revolutionary France. The center of the flags featured the all-seeing

---

Remaining anti-immigrant, anti-Catholic and neutral on slavery, the Know Nothings declined and many former members became Republicans.

[113] "Hartford Wide-Awakes," Today in History: July 26, *ConnecticutHistory.org*, http://connecticuthistory.org/hartford-wide-awakes-today-in-history/; See more at: http://connecticuthistory.org/hartford-wide-awakes-today-in-history/#sthash.M1sdDybs.dpuf, (Accessed April 18, 2016).

"Eye of Providence"[114] —similar to the eye found on a one-dollar bill and often traced back to the Egyptian "Eye of Horus."[115]

The agenda was similar from group to group as reflected in the following example from the Chicago Chapter:

> 1. To act as a political police.
> 2. To do escort duty to all prominent Republican speakers who visit our place to address our citizens.
> 3. To attend all public meetings in a body and see that order is kept and that the speaker and meeting are not disturbed.
> 4. To attend the polls and see that justice is done to every legal voter.
> 5. To conduct themselves in such a manner as to induce all Republicans to join them.
> 6. To be a body joined together in large numbers to work for the good of the Republican Ticket.[116]

Regardless of their geographical location, they never wavered from their uncompromising support of the Republican Party. Though some estimates range as high as 400,000 total members, it is realistic to say there were at least 100,000 members.

Violence often followed the Wide Awakes. For example, bloodshed was common on the East Coast, and bricks, rocks, and torches were often the weapons in play. "In many cases rowdies ambushed Wide Awake parades, hurling bricks and screaming, 'Kill

---

[114] "All-Seeing Eye," *Crystalinks.com*, http://www.crystalinks.com/allseeingeye.html, (Accessed April 18, 2016).

[115] Ibid.

[116] "Absolutely shocking facts about the GOP," from Deny Ignorance, Above Top Secret, *The Above Network*, January 15, 2012, http://www.abovetopsecret.com/forum/thread797646/pg1, (Accessed April 18, 2016).

the damn Wide Awakes.'" [117] There was violence in Manhattan involving an attack on a fire company. "The New York Wide Awakes, when asked about their frequent brawls, complained that their torches were made of soft pine and splintered after just a few blows to the head." [118] Conflicts were also commonplace in the Midwest, such as an Ohio incident involving a clash with a group of Democrats. "The Democratic candidate for coroner in an Indiana town shot a club member in the shoulder, and an Illinois Wide Awake stabbed the 'ring leader of a mob' seven times during a late night brawl."[119] Another incident, known as the Stone's Prairie Riot, occurred in Payson, Illinois, when the Wide Awakes clashed with Stephen Douglas supporters.

The militaristic agenda of the Wide Awakes stoked Southerners' fear of federal coercion. These political clubs were viewed as *de facto* military groups intent on creating unrest and disrupting the structure of the South. Not only were they denounced by Southern secessionists William Lowndes Yancey and Henry A. Wise, Texas Senator Louis Wigfall accused Seward of being an instigator of their nefarious activities. Whether or not Seward was guilty of this charge, he showed support for them as evidenced in a speech delivered in La Crosse, Wisconsin:

> He expressed his gratification at the strength of this Wide-Awake Organization, and said it was possible their services might not cease with the election. They had heard for two months of the last session of Congress an incessant boasting as to what the South would do in case of a Republican triumph in the Presidential election. That contingency was now a

---

[117] John Grinspan, "Young Men for War: The Wide Awakes and Lincoln's 1860 Presidential Campaign," *The Journal of American History*, 96 (September 2009), 357–78, http://archive.oah.org/special-issues/lincoln/contents/grinspan.html, (Accessed April 18, 2016).

[118] Ibid.

[119] Ibid.

certainty; and though he did not apprehend there
would be any effort made to carry out these threats, yet
if any effort should be made, this Wide-Awake
organization would be found mighty convenient in
stifling and crushing out any attempt to overthrow the
Government.[120]

Illinois Congressman Owen Lovejoy strove to heighten
Southern fear by encouraging the Wide Awakes to invade Virginia
and capture Wise. As the war arrived, many of the Wide Awakes
joined the Union Army and got to satisfy their lusty cravings for
actual combat.

The Free Soilers

The Free Soil Party was created in Buffalo, New York, in
August 1848. Anti-slavery, New Hampshire-born politicians Salmon
P. Chase and John P. Hale were leaders in the party's creation.
Philosophically, the party arose from the ashes of the Whig Party,
the Liberty Party, and former members of the Democratic Party,
mainly the disgruntled New York faction known as
"Barnburners,"[121] who opposed the more conservative New Yorkers
known as "Hunkers."[122] The Whigs disintegrated partially as a result
of their failure to take a strong stand on the issue of the expansion of
slavery. Viable and relatively successful since 1834, the Whig Party

---

[120] *"THE WIDE-AWAKES; Fear of the Wide-Awakes at the South Idle Apprehensions," New York Times, September 29, 1860,* excerpted from the *Columbia (S.C.) Guardian,* http://www.nytimes.com/1860/09/29/news/the-wide-awakes-fear-of-the-wide-awakes-at-the-south-idle-apprehensions.html, (Accessed April 18, 2016).

[121] Robert McNamara, "Barnburners and Hunkers," *About Education,* November 26, 2014, http://history1800s.about.com/od/1800sglossary/g/Barnburners-And-Hunkers.htm, (Accessed April 18, 2016).

[122] Ibid.

claimed four presidents—William Henry Harrison, John Tyler, Zachary Taylor, and Millard Fillmore. Whigs were leery of aggressive expansion (Texas in particular) and generally favored protectionism. The Liberty Party was formed in 1840 as a result of dissatisfaction with William Lloyd Garrison's leadership of the Anti-Slavery Society. They ran Kentucky-born James Birney for president in 1840 and 1844 and New York-born Gerrit Smith in 1848 and 1852. Neither candidate made a dent in the elections, but they were a factor in the defeat of pro-slavery Whig presidential aspirant Henry Clay in 1844 and the eventual election of Democrat James K. Polk.

A basic tenet of the Free Soil Party was opposition to the expansion of slavery. Article Two of their 1848 Platform stated, "That slavery in the several states of this Union which recognize its existence depends upon state law...We therefore propose no interference by Congress with slavery within the limits of any state."[123] As new western territory was acquired, this issue became more intense. Article Seven of their platform stated: "That...the only safe means of preventing the extension of slavery into territory now free is to prohibit its extension in all such territory by an act of Congress."[124] Despite their opposition to the extension of slavery, their platform made it clear they had no intentions of interfering with States whose citizens approved of the institution.

Anti-slavery forces were concerned that Texas could be subdivided into as many as six slave States. The Wilmot Proviso, proposed by Pennsylvania politician David Wilmot, sought to outlaw slavery in the territory acquired from Mexico, of which Texas was a major part. The Democratic Party of New York opposed the Wilmot Proviso; this resulted in several members changing parties.

The Free Soilers supported internal improvements; however, their support was for revenue tariffs, not protectionism. They also

---

[123] "1848 Free Soil Party Platform," *Angelfire*, http://www.angelfire.com/indie/ourcampaigns/1848.html, (Accessed April 18, 2016).
[124] Ibid.

supported government enactment of a homestead law, and "the party supported cheap postage, free lands for actual settlers, the abolition of unnecessary offices and salaries, and improvements for rivers and harbors."[125]

During the 1848 Free Soil Party convention in Buffalo, Martin Van Buren was nominated as their presidential candidate and Charles Francis Adams was selected as his running mate. Their slogan was "free soil, free speech, free labor and free men."[126] They gathered over 291,000 votes, and the party had nine members elected to the House of Representatives. In 1852, Hale was the party's presidential nominee with Indiana lawyer and politician, George W. Julian, selected as his running mate. With slavery perceived to be less of an issue as a result of the Compromise of 1850, there was a corresponding decline in support of the Free Soil Party. Free Soilers viewed the Kansas-Nebraska Act of 1854, with its advocacy of popular sovereignty, as a step in the wrong direction and many gravitated to the newly formed Republican Party.

The Forty-Eighters and the Marxists

The history of Europe has been filled with conflict and power struggles. The mid-nineteenth century saw a major political upheaval that eventually crossed the oceans to America. The aftermath of the Napoleonic wars left many countries in disarray, especially the Austrian Empire and the German Confederation. "The rulers, forgetful that the people had saved their thrones, denied [the people constitutional government], and opened instead a long period of reaction which manifested its triumph in dark acts of oppression and tyranny." [127] Economic volatility and disastrous

---

[125] "Free-Soil Party," *United States History*, http://www.u-s-history.com/pages/h139.html, (Accessed April 18, 2016).

[126] Ibid.

[127] "German Revolution of 1848," Quote from Rudolph Cronau, *The Activists*, http://comminfo.rutgers.edu/~dalbello/FLVA/activists/48rev.html, (Accessed April 18, 2016).

harvests fueled the uneasiness and provided the impetus for men with radical ideas, such as socialism, to gain support. In 1848 France, "Louis Blanc and other socialists overthrew King Louis Phillipe and established the Second Republic."[128] The revolutionary fervor spread to neighboring Germany, and resistance, often from students, challenged the army of Prussian Kaiser Frederick Wilhelm IV. The challengers sought a national constitution, centralized power, and a guarantee of basic rights. They fought for democracy in Europe. In America the Founders defined democracy as "nothing more than mob rule, where 51% of the people take away the rights of the other 49%."[129] America's founders insisted a constitutional republic was the most viable and stable form of government.

The Forty-Eighters—especially the Germans—were more ideological than their predecessors. The original German immigrants were largely farmers, tradesmen, etc.; however, the Forty-Eighters included many with an activist political agenda, based largely on social idealism. They possessed similarities with modern leftists. Many of these European advocates of Socialism were adherents to the teachings of Karl Marx. For example, Union Colonel Fritz Anneke had a personal relationship with Marx and was "a member of the 'Deutscher Kommunism, Marx/Engels circle."[130] When the European revolutions failed, many migrated to America.

During the War Between the States, thousands of European immigrants became Union soldiers either voluntarily, via conscription, or as recruits from the streets or various prisons in

---

[128] Ibid.

[129] Thomas Jefferson, "Democracy is nothing more than mob rule...," Thomas Jefferson Foundation, *The Jefferson Monticello*, https://www.monticello.org/site/jefferson/democracy-nothing-more-mob-rule, (Accessed April 18, 2016).

[130] Joan Hough, "The 48'ers, Part 1 of a Critique of Hochbruck's 'Actundvierziger,'" *The Confederate Society of America*, October 22, 2013, http://www.deovindice.org/1/post/2013/10/the-48ers.html, (Accessed April 18, 2016).

Europe. Besides the approximately 180,000 Germans, there were "tens of thousands of Austrians, Poles, Hungarians, and Czechs...up to an estimated five thousand had previously served in the revolutionary armies and insurrections in Baden, the Palatinate, in Hungary, the Rhineland, Transylvania, Poland, Bohemia, Berlin or Saxony."[131] There were Germans, such as Johann Heinrich Heros von Borcke and Baron Maximillian von Meulnier, who fought for the South. However, their number was minimal compared to those who fought for the Union and socialist ideology was not compatible with the primarily Christian, agrarian South. While the South was blockaded and generally insulated from the world, the U.S. government actively recruited in Europe. This recruitment, in combination with the Forty-Eighters with their collectivist ideology, accounted for their large representation in Union armies.

European Forty-Eighters generally favored organized labor and the abolition of slavery. Though the vast majority settled in the North, a portion of them settled in Texas. One German immigrant— Adolph Douai—had been associated with Marx. Settling in West Texas in 1852, "In San Antonio Douai published an Abolitionist paper, until he was finally compelled to leave in peril of his life."[132] Another Marxist named Hermann Meyer settled in Alabama until forced to leave. American Marxists were also vigorous supporters of John Brown.

Marxist leader, Joseph Weydemeyer, noted the political upheaval in America and saw the anti-slavery movement as a key component of their efforts. "He strove to involve the trade unions in the great struggle."[133] Weydermeyer felt a solution to working class issues could not be solved unless slavery was eliminated. They were incensed at the 1854 Kansas-Nebraska Act. There was a natural

---

[131] Ibid.

[132] William Z. Foster, *History of the Communist Party of the United States, Chapter Three: Marxists in the Struggle Against Slavery,* http://williamzfoster.blogspot.com/2013/01/chapter-three-marxists-in-struggle.html, (Accessed April 18, 2016).

[133] Ibid.

attachment to the Republican Party, created in March 1854 in Ripon, Wisconsin, by anti-slavery and pro-protectionist Whigs, anti-Democrat reformers, liberals, and labor leaders. The general response to the new party by northern industrialists was very favorable; they saw it as a way to dilute the political power of slave holders "and to advance their own program: protective tariffs, subsidies to railroads, absorption of the national resources, national banking system, etc." [134] Industrial and banking interests with connections to the South opposed the new party.

During the 1856 election, Marxists worked diligently in their support of the Republican Party. The new party trumpeted themselves as advocates of free labor. Lincoln was popular with the working classes—he was seen as anti-slavery expansion and as a supporter of a Homestead bill. Also, his opposition to the Know Nothings made him popular with the immigrant population. Though the Republicans failed in 1856, these same groups were major supporters in the party's 1860 victory.

During the war itself, support for the Republicans and the Union cause did not wane. Weydemeyer had previous military experience, having served as a German artillery officer. While serving in the Union Army, he "was assigned by Lincoln as commander of the highly strategic area of St. Louis. August Willich, who became a brigadier general, Robert Rosa, a major, and Fritz Jacobi, a lieutenant who was killed at Fredericksburg, were all members of the New York Communist Club."[135]

As the fighting raged, Marx routinely wrote in support of the Union cause in the *New York Daily Tribune* and other newspapers. He saw there "was a conflict between 'two opposing social systems', which must be fought out to 'the victory of one or the other system.'" [136] Marx advocated the advancement of democracy, the very thing the Founding Fathers had discredited. Later, Vladimir

---

[134] Ibid.
[135] Ibid.
[136] Ibid.

Lenin echoed Marx and his support of the Union cause. In the 1930s there were numerous Lincoln-Lenin parades held in New York City. The Communist Party, both in America and abroad, has always held Lincoln in high regard.

The Abolitionists

Although Lincoln opposed slavery most of his life, he was never an abolitionist in the strictest sense of the word. He understood that all parties in the process were guilty to some degree—the African slave sellers, the Arab then European then American slave traders, the corporations that tried to meet an almost insatiable demand for cotton, tobacco, etc., and the Southern and Border State slave owners who tried to fill those needs. Though he felt they should receive basic rights, Lincoln never advocated that Blacks should have equal political and social rights with Whites.

Lincoln readily admitted the North was as guilty as the South for the institution of slavery, and the people of the North had minimal compassion for Blacks. "In early 1862, Lincoln believed that most people in the North cared 'comparatively little about the Negro, and [were] anxious only for military successes.'"[137] Further gauging Northern sentiment relative to slavery, Lincoln "reminded a visiting abolitionist toward the end of January: 'We didn't go into the war to put down slavery. To act differently at this moment would, I have no doubt, not only weaken our cause but smack of bad faith. ... The first thing you'd see would be a mutiny in the army.'"[138]

The aforementioned Free Soilers were primarily concerned with confining slavery to the South and Border States. Many of the

---

[137] David von Drehle, "Lincoln's Reluctant War: How Abolitionists Leaned on the President," *The Atlantic*, October 26, 2012, http://www.theatlantic.com/national/archive/2012/10/lincolns-reluctant-war-how-abolitionists-leaned-on-the-president/264125/, (Accessed April 18, 2016).

[138] Ibid.

abolitionists had the same goal, but some wanted to take it a step further through immediate emancipation, in opposition to gradual, compensated emancipation as had been successfully accomplished in Europe, South America, and other parts of the world. In fact, Garrison's mantra was "immediate, unconditional, uncompensated emancipation."[139]

From a political standpoint, most abolitionists opposed the Democratic Party, which generally sympathized with slaveholders. As a small minority that was despised as much or more in the North than in the South, the abolitionists failed to create a viable party of their own. However, with the Republicans pushing an anti-slavery and anti-slavery expansion agenda, most abolitionists supported them. There were high profile exceptions such as the Massachusetts libertarian abolitionist Lysander Spooner, who supported the South and asserted the North's goal was merely an attempt to consolidate power and enslave all Americans to the corporations and the banks.

Due to their sometimes-extreme beliefs, the abolitionists were not welcome by the majority of Northerners. However, with its wealthy core of ex-Whig protectionists, the Republican Party possessed the financial wherewithal and became the logical vehicle for most abolitionist support. Despite their differences, the Republicans saw the abolitionists as useful and were willing to accept them.

---

[139] "Web Field Trip," *U.S. History—Abolitionism*, http://tdl.org/txlor-dspace/bitstream/handle/2249.3/617/04_abolitionism.htm, (Accessed April 18, 2016).

Chapter Eight
Lincoln wins the 1860 Republican Nomination

"Mr. Lincoln did not possess a single quality for his office as President."[140]
Ward Hill Lamon

The 1856 presidential election marked the first time the fledgling Republican Party entered a candidate. The nominee, John C. Fremont, was an anti-slavery California politician, military officer, and explorer; "Lincoln...in the Republican convention which nominated Fremont for president, rose to 110 votes for the nomination for vice-president." [141] The election also included Democrat James Buchanan and Know Nothing Millard Fillmore, with Buchanan ultimately winning with over forty-five percent of the vote. Fremont carried most of the North and garnered about thirty-three percent of the vote. The Republican Party nominee did not appear on the ballot in the Southern States.

Four years later, from May 16-18, 1860, the Republican Party held their convention in Chicago, an industrial and financial city that had aggressively sought to host the event. New York lawyer, senator, and former Governor William Seward, was a heavy favorite to win the 1860 nomination. Based on the practice of the day, Seward did not attend the convention, but instead sent Thurlow Weed, his political manager. Chicago was bubbling with excitement in anticipation of the second Republican convention, held at the

---

[140] Mildred Lewis Rutherford, *A True Estimate of Abraham Lincoln & Vindication of the South* (Wiggins, Mississippi: Crown Rights Book Company, 1997), 59. (Rutherford's original book appeared in March 1923 under the title, *The South Must Have Her Rightful Place in History*.) Original source: *Life of Salmon P. Chase*, 630.

[141] Edgar Lee Masters, *Lincoln: The Man* (Columbia, South Carolina: The Foundation for American Education, 1997), 136.

Wigwam, a new convention center specifically built as part of the agreement to host the event.

Seward and Weed were rightfully confident of victory. It required 233 votes to win, and New York alone represented almost a third of that total. Others vying for the Republican nomination were Ohio's Salmon P. Chase, Missouri's Edward Bates, and Pennsylvania's Simon Cameron. The dark horse in the contest was Lincoln, accompanied by his campaign manager, Illinois Judge David Davis. On May 8, just over a week before the convention, in Decatur, Lincoln was selected by his home State Republicans.

Although Lincoln was less well known than his main opponent, he had made a powerful impact during his Cooper Union Speech in New York City on February 27, 1860. This speech addressed the Republicans' aversion to the expansion of slavery and their opposition to secession. The effectiveness of the speech was still fresh in the minds of many Republicans.

Seward and Weed anticipated Lincoln would receive all twenty-two Illinois votes. "Since Illinois was considered a doubtful state for candidate Seward should he be the Republican candidate, Weed was prepared to acquire Illinois votes by offering Lincoln the vice-presidential spot."[142] They predicted this deal would put them over the top.

Lincoln did his due diligence in preparing for the convention. Along with Davis, Norman Judd, the New York-born U.S. Representative from Illinois, provided assistance. Judd had also played a key role in convincing the Republicans to meet in Chicago. The Lincoln team correctly predicted Seward would fail to win outright on the first ballot and that they would finish second. They immediately worked to strengthen their position on the second

---

[142] Gordon Leidner, "Lincoln Outfoxed Seward for the Nomination," How Lincoln Won the 1860 Republican Nomination, *Great American History,* September 3, 2015, http://www.greatamericanhistory.net/nomination.htm, (Accessed April 18, 2016).

ballot. This included making sure Seward's New York followers would be separated from others with whom they might collaborate. "They printed hundreds of counterfeit tickets and distributed them to Lincoln supporters with instructions to show up early—in order to displace Seward's supporters."[143] Two strong-voiced individuals assigned to the task, led cheers for the already vocal Lincoln supporters.

May 16 and 17 consisted mainly of administrative and platform procedures and the evenings were filled with Weed wining and dining delegates and promising "oceans of money"[144] for future projects. Davis and Judd worked tirelessly to deal with States that did not support Seward, e.g., Indiana, New Hampshire, Maine, Vermont, etc.

On May 18, about a thousand of Seward's supporters marched with great fanfare behind a brass band toward the Wigwam. Upon their arrival they were unable to enter the venue because Lincoln supporters with counterfeit tickets had taken their seats. Despite this unexpected obstacle, Seward maintained strong support. Each candidate's name was called with the ensuing parade of loud hurrahs. As expected, Seward won the first ballot with 173 votes and Lincoln followed with 102 votes; Cameron, Chase, Bates, and the others received fifty votes or less, meaning the contest now boiled down to Seward and Lincoln. The wheeling and dealing of Lincoln's team now came into play and on the second ballot Seward received 184 votes versus 181 votes for Lincoln. As the third vote commenced, it was clear the momentum had shifted strongly toward the underdog. The third and final ballot resulted in 231 votes for Lincoln, making his stunning victory complete.

Lamon cast doubt on the tactics used to secure Lincoln's eventual nomination as the Republican candidate: "He was also nominated by means of a corrupt bargain entered into by Simon Cameron, of Pennsylvania and Caleb Smith, of Indiana, provided

---

[143] Ibid.
[144] Ibid.

Lincoln would pledge them cabinet positions. These pledges Lincoln fulfilled and thus made them a party to corrupt bargains."[145] These men were handsomely rewarded: Chase was named Secretary of the Treasury and Bates was named Attorney General. Also, runner-up Seward was named Secretary of State.

Entering the 1860 election, the Republican Party had the backing of powerful factions, such as Northern railroad and industrialist interests. The railroads stood to benefit tremendously from federal subsidies. One of Lincoln's supporters at the Chicago Convention was Grenville Dodge, the railroad expert Lincoln had consulted during his Iowa trip in 1859.

J.R. Perkins, author of *Trails, Rails and War; the Life of General G.M. Dodge*, explained how Lincoln's nomination was vital to railroad interests in Iowa:

> At Chicago Dodge joined himself to a group of railroad men who considered the candidacy of Abraham Lincoln vital to their plans of building a Pacific railroad from the Mississippi River, or perhaps from the Missouri, somewhere along the forty-second parallel. They were John A. Dix, president of the Rock Island; Thomas C. Durant, later the moving spirit in the Union Pacific; Sheffield and Farnam, builders of the Rock Island; John I. Blair, then promoting the Cedar Rapids and Missouri Railroad across Iowa; and Norman B. Judd, attorney for the Rock Island and a leader in Lincoln's political affairs.[146]

---

[145] Rutherford, *A True Estimate of Abraham Lincoln*, 59-60.

[146] "Abraham Lincoln and Iowa," *Abraham Lincoln's Classroom*, The Lehrman Institute, http://abrahamlincolnsclassroom.org/abraham-lincoln-state-by-state/abraham-lincoln-and-iowa/, Original source: J.R. Perkins, *Trails, Rails and War: The Life of General G. M. Dodge*, 57, (Accessed April 18, 2016).

Slavery expansion was a point of contention, but the tariff was the real prize for Republican corporate interests. Lincoln staunchly supported his party's platform. "One of the major planks in their platform was a high protective tariff. When it was introduced, the delegates yelled uproariously and threw their canes and hats in the air so suddenly it was 'as if a herd of Buffalo had stampeded through the convention hall.'" [147] The Republicans' feeling of exultation could not be contained.

The results of the election spread quickly to the South. Many Southerners feared "that a Republican administration would result in another 'Tariff of Abomination.'" [148] Though most Republicans were willing to negotiate on slavery, there was no compromise on the tariffs. The election sent a message to the Southern States that they could leave the Union or become the *milch cow* of Northern economic interests.

---

[147] Charles Adams, *Those Dirty Rotten Taxes: The Tax Revolts That Built America* (New York, New York: The Free Press, 1998), 95.
[148] Ibid.

Chapter Nine
The Election of 1860

"The National parties and their presidential candidates, with the Eastern Establishment assiduously fostering the process behind the scenes, moved closer together and nearly met in the center with almost identical candidates and platforms, although the process was concealed as much as possible, by the revival of obsolescent or meaningless war cries and slogans (often going back to the Civil War)...."[149]

Georgetown Professor Carroll Quigley, author of "The Secret Government" and *Tragedy and Hope: A History of the World in Our Time*, 1247-1248.

If Quigley's words are to be taken seriously, the modern left-right paradigm is merely a specious debate on real issues and adds credence to the George Wallace quote that there is not "a dime's worth of difference" [150] in the two major parties. Whatever one believes about the modern political world, the Election of 1860 was

---

[149] You Thought we Had a Two Party System?, *Posted by Savant Noir on May 15, 2010, at: http://recyclewashington.wordpress.com/2010/05/15/1-2/ Quigley went on to say: "The argument that the two parties should represent opposed ideals and policies, one, perhaps, of the Right and the other of the Left, is a foolish idea acceptable only to the doctrinaire and academic thinkers. Instead, the two parties should be almost identical, so that the American people can "throw the rascals out" at any election without leading to any profound or extreme shifts in policy. ... Either party in office becomes in time corrupt, tired, unenterprising, and vigorless. Then it should be possible to replace it, every four years if necessary, by the other party, which will be none of these things but will still pursue, with new vigor, approximately the same basic policies."* (Accessed April 18, 2016).

[150] Richard Pearson, "Former Ala. Gov. George C. Wallace Dies," *Washington Post*, Monday, September 14, 1998; Page A1, http://www.washingtonpost.com/wp-srv/politics/daily/sept98/wallace.htm, (Accessed April 18, 2016).

pivotal in determining the direction of the country. Centralization and consolidation of power simply made Quigley's goals much more attainable by greatly increasing the convergence of business and government.

There were four candidates vying for President in the 1860 election. The candidates included Abraham Lincoln, Stephen Douglas, John Breckinridge, and John Bell.

Lincoln's political background and corporate connections to the Northeast and Upper Midwest have been duly noted. This linkage was reflected in the November 6, 1860, election where his name did not appear on the ballot in Alabama, Arkansas, Florida, Georgia, Louisiana, Mississippi, North Carolina, South Carolina, Tennessee, and Texas. Lincoln was only listed on the ballot in twenty-three of the thirty-three States in the Union at the time of the election (Kansas became a State in January 1861). Although he only received 1,364 votes in Kentucky and 1,887 votes in Virginia, Lincoln carried the New England States, the Upper Midwest, California, and Oregon. He was elected with 1,866,452 votes, 180 electoral votes, and 39.8% of the total.

<u>Stephen A. Douglas</u> – Born April 23, 1813, Douglas hailed from Illinois. Nicknamed the *Little Giant* due to his 5′ 4″ stature, Douglas was unquestionably a political giant. His tactical skill and influence often translated into the passage of key legislation. He became politically successful while also becoming wealthy as a land speculator. Echoing the efforts of his Republican opponent, Douglas lobbied for and represented the interests of the Illinois Central Railroad. He supported the Missouri Compromise and then sponsored the Kansas-Nebraska Act of 1854, whose popular sovereignty provision virtually negated the Missouri Compromise. Also, "the Freeport Doctrine was Stephen Douglas' doctrine that, in spite of the Dred Scott decision, slavery could be excluded from territories of the United States by local legislation."[151] Douglas was

---

[151] Paul M. Angle, "Freeport Doctrine," *Encylopedia.com*— Dictionary of American History, The Gale Group, 2003,

initially the presidential favorite; however, the landscape began to change during the 1858 Lincoln-Douglas debates where they competed in the election for U.S. Senator from Illinois. The debates began Lincoln's elevation from moderate renown; he used his vast political skills to seize the momentum provided by this opening.

Southern Democrats did not support Douglas. He disagreed with the Dred Scott decision, which ruled the federal government could not constitutionally interfere with slavery. Douglas also opposed the Lecompton Constitution, which protected slavery in Kansas. President Buchanan, as well as Southern Democrats, supported it. Douglas' base support was Northern Democrats, who opposed expansion of slavery into the western territories. Echoing the Republican position, Douglas believed westward expansion should be only for White settlers. Richard Taylor, son of Whig President Zachary Taylor and eventually a Confederate General, lamented that the schism in the ranks of Southern Democrats helped get Lincoln elected. This rift resulted in the walkout of the so-called fire-eaters at the May 3, 1860, Democratic Convention in Charleston, South Carolina, followed by a similar walkout when the Democrats reconvened in Baltimore, Maryland on June 18, 1860.

Douglas became the 1860 presidential candidate representing the Northern Democratic Party. He had already defeated Lincoln two years earlier in a post-debate Senate race. Due to the heavy concentration of Electoral College votes for the Republican Party in New England and the Upper Midwest, Lincoln may have won the election regardless of the actions of the Democrats. Douglas and Vice Presidential candidate Herschel Johnson received 1,380,202 votes, which equated to twenty-nine and a half percent of the grand total. However, he only received twelve percent of the electoral votes and he carried only Missouri. Even if Douglas had been elected president, his term would have been very brief—he passed away on June 3, 1861.

---

http://www.encyclopedia.com/doc/1G2-3401801612.html, (Accessed April 18, 2016).

John Cabell Breckinridge – Born on January 16, 1821, near Lexington, Kentucky, Breckinridge studied law at Transylvania University and began practicing after his graduation in 1841. In 1851 he was elected to the House of Representatives and later (1857-61) became Vice-President of the United States. At thirty-six years of age, serving under Buchanan, Breckinridge remains the youngest Vice-President in U.S. history. At that young age he had already witnessed a great deal of sectional turmoil. Breckinridge was a Democrat from an area that was a former Whig stronghold. He was soft on the secession issue, preferring the Union remain intact. Representing the viewpoint of Southern Democrats, he understood that according to the constitution, slavery could not be excluded from the territories. Part of his platform stated:

> all citizens of the United States have an equal right to settle with their property in the Territory, without their rights, either of person or property, being destroyed by Congressional or Territorial legislation...it is the duty of the Federal Government, in all its departments, to protect when necessary, the rights of persons and property in the Territories, and wherever else its constitutional authority extends.[152]

This stance put him on the opposite side of the Republican Party Platform, which advocated confinement of slavery to where it already existed.

In the 1860 election, Breckinridge, with Vice President Joseph Lane, carried the States of the Deep South along with Texas, Delaware, and Maryland. He received 848,019 votes, seventy-two electoral votes, just over eighteen percent of the total vote.

---

[152] Donald R. McClarey and Paul Zummo, "Breckinridge Platform 1860," *Almost Chosen People, A blog about American History, and the development of a great Nation,* October 6, 2010, http://almostchosenpeople.wordpress.com/2010/10/06/breckinridge-platform-1860/, (Accessed April 18, 2016).

John Bell – Bell was born on February 15, 1797, in Mill Creek, Tennessee. He graduated in 1814 from Cumberland College in Nashville, Tennessee, and began practicing law in 1816. As a Democrat, he served seven consecutive terms in the U.S. House of Representatives (1827-1841). Bell fell out with Andrew Jackson over his refusal to renew the charter of the Bank of the United States. In the late 1830s, Bell became a member of the Whig Party. Through appointment by President William H. Harrison, he became Secretary of War in 1841. This position was short-lived. Harrison died and Bell resigned due to new President John Tyler's support of States' Rights Democrats. Initially opposed to secession, Bell reversed his stance after Fort Sumter and Lincoln's request for troops to invade the seceded States.

The disintegration of the Whig Party scattered its former members in several directions. "A remnant of the defunct Whig party organized as the Constitutional Union party and held a national convention in Baltimore in May 1860. Delegates nominated Bell for president and Edward Everett of Massachusetts for vice president."[153] The party took a neutral stance on the slavery issue. Also, in consideration of the four-party race, the Constitutional Party sought to win enough electoral votes to throw the election into the House of Representatives. Bell, a political moderate, carried Tennessee, Virginia, and Kentucky, receiving 590,901 votes, thirty-nine electoral votes, and 12.6% of the total vote.

With powerful players supporting him, Lincoln won the election with less than forty-percent of the vote. In an unprecedented manner, the Republicans now had what they had long sought. Their industrial and banking interests had their man in charge and they took full advantage. For example, Ohio-born banker Jay Cooke, a close friend of U.S. Secretary of the Treasury Chase, ran the banking house of Jay Cooke & Company in Philadelphia,

---

[153] "1860 Lincoln v. Douglas v. Breckinridge v. Bell," John Bell, *HarpWeek Explore History*, http://elections.harpweek.com/1860/bio-1860-Full.asp?UniqueID=1, (Accessed April 18, 2016).

Pennsylvania. Chase granted Cooke's firm monopoly status relative
to the sale of U.S. government bonds. Cooke made over $240,000.00
in commissions selling war bonds. Not only did Cooke support
Lincoln at the 1860 Republican Convention in Chicago, his brother
H.D. Cooke, was one of the founders of the party. Political
connections were used to profit from the financing of a
transcontinental railroad. Even Union General George B.
McClellan—a Democrat—served in leadership positions of two
Midwestern railroads.

Vermont Congressman Justin Morrill was a staunch
protectionist, a steel manufacturer, and one of the founders of the
Republican Party. Morrill and Henry Charles Carey, Pennsylvania
economist, publicist, steel industry lobbyist, Lincoln adviser, and
enemy of free trade, wrote the Morrill Tariff. The House of
Representatives passed the tariff in May 1860, "raising the average
tariff from 15% to 37% with increases to 47% within three years."[154]
These rates were detrimental to the South and similar to the levels
that led to the 1832 nullification crises. "The U.S. House of
Representatives passed the bill 105 to 64. Out of 40 Southern
Congressmen only one Tennessee Congressman voted for it."[155] The
legislation moved to the Senate where the South was outnumbered.

Another powerful proponent of the Morrill Tariff was
Pennsylvania Representative Thaddeus Stevens, a Radical
Republican tied to iron manufacturing as the owner of Caledonia
Iron Works (near Gettysburg, Pennsylvania). Stevens stood to
greatly increase his profits with the new import duties in place.
Besides his support for higher tariffs, Stevens was adamant that
slavery be contained in the South and the Border States. He was also
known to loathe White Southerners.

---

[154] Mike Scruggs, "Understanding the Causes of the Civil War: A
Brief Explanation of the Impact of the Morrill Tariff," *The Tribune Papers,*
June 4, 2005, http://ashevilletribune.com/archives/censored-
truths/Morrill%20Tariff.html, (Accessed April 18, 2016).
[155] Ibid.

Two of the infamous Secret Six (Northerners who financed the exploits of John Brown) stood to reap the rewards of higher tariffs. Gerrit Smith, of Peterboro, New York, owned the Great Wharves at the harbor in Oswego, New York. Smith sought and received federal money for assistance with river and harbor dredging and harbor improvements to minimize damage caused by severe weather. He also benefited from the Federal government's free land policy in the West due to increased port activity.

George Luther Stearns, another Brown financier, was from Medford, Massachusetts. In his youth, Stearns was involved in ship chandlery, i.e., retailing supplies and equipment for ships. This involved items such as rosin, turpentine, tallow, lard, twine, rope, tools, leather, and a long list of other supplies used on a ship. Later in his career, Stearns was involved in the manufacture of sheet and pipe-lead. Regardless of any benevolent intentions, both Smith and Stearns benefitted from protectionism.

Though his election made war more likely, Lincoln did not singularly push for war. He was encouraged by Radical Republicans, such as newspaper editor (and eventual Chicago Mayor in 1871) Joseph Medill, Michigan Senator and Detroit Mayor Zachariah Chandler, Ohio Senator Ben Wade, and others. The North would not allow a free trade Confederacy and they were willing to go to great lengths to put an end to these economic threats once and for all, even if it took a war to accomplish it. The 1860 candidates of all other parties were anti-war; the election of any other candidate would have meant a negotiated peace was at least a possibility.

Where many modern elections feature mostly cosmetic differences among the candidates, with little variation regarding monetary policy, trade deals, etc., the 1860 Election represented real choices as to the direction of the Republic. The Election of 1860 changed the very nature of the country.

Chapter Ten
Southern Peace Efforts

"You, Medill, called for war. I have given you war. What you asked for you have. You demanded war. I have given you what you demanded, and you, Medill, are largely responsible for all of the blood that has flowed."[156]

Abraham Lincoln

The South and concerned individuals in the Border States instigated several peace efforts to avoid a war with the North. On December 3, 1860, John J. Crittenden, Whig Senator from Kentucky, proposed his Crittenden Compromise. Presented during the lame-duck period between Lincoln's election and inauguration, the key component of the Crittenden Compromise was an effort "to revive the Missouri Compromise line by extending the southern boundary of Missouri (36 degrees, 30 minutes) west to the Pacific Ocean...."[157] The central objective was to allow slavery in both present and future territories that lay south of the line while prohibiting slavery north of the line. At least short term, the arrangement was intended to diffuse animosities between the competing factions.

Virginia initiated another attempt at peace on January 19, 1861. The Virginia legislature called for a meeting of delegates from all States. Virginia was still considered by many as the Archetype American State. This meeting was to be held at the Willard Hotel in Washington City on February 4, 1861. The conference consciously modeled itself after the 1787 Constitutional Convention. Twenty-one States sent representatives; however, the Deep South and a few

---

[156] George Edmonds, *Facts and Falsehoods Concerning the War on the South 1861-1865* (Wiggins, Mississippi: Crown Rights Book Company Liberty Reprint Series, 1997), 162. [Also noted by author Lloyd Wendt.]

[157] Richard B. Latner, "Compromise Efforts," *Tulane University,* http://www.tulane.edu/~latner/Background/BackgroundCompromise.html, (Accessed April 18, 2106).

Northern States refused to send any delegates. The meeting was presided over by the seventy-one year old Virginian John Tyler, former U.S. President and strong peace advocate.

There was a struggle to reach common ground, and near the end of February, the Peace Conference presented a plan similar to the Crittenden Compromise. The peace offer was sent to Congress just before it adjourned, but produced no tangible results. Part of the North's incentive for compromise was removed on March 2 when the Morrill Tariff was passed and signed (the next day) by President Buchanan. Though Buchanan was a Democrat, he remained loyal to the protectionist interests of his home State of Pennsylvania.

As the fledgling Confederate States of America endeavored to establish a structured government, its leadership was wary of the possible actions of the Lincoln Administration. To set up a viable government, the selection of a skilled and competent leader was imperative.

Jefferson Davis had a career of service and accomplishment. He fought in the Black Hawk War, the Mexican War (where he introduced the wedge movement that led to victory at Buena Vista); enlarged the U.S. Army by four regiments; was the first to suggest the purchase of the Panama Canal Zone and Cuba; and he supported the linking of both ends of the country with a transcontinental railroad. In the pre-war years, he served under President Franklin Pierce as Secretary of War. In a unique twist of fate, Davis' role in improvements to the U.S. military in the 1850s created a more formidable foe for the South to face in the 1860s.

Davis resigned the office in 1857 to become a senator from Mississippi. As senator, he constantly expounded on the subject of States' Rights. Originally an opponent of secession, Davis emerged as a compromise leader and became the favorite to become President of the Confederate States of America.

The election of Lincoln signaled to Davis war was likely on the horizon. When Mississippi seceded, Davis resigned from the

Senate. He was appointed major general of State troops in Mississippi, before becoming the compromise candidate to serve as the President of the Confederacy. "He was in his garden at Briarfield, supervising rose-cutting when notified."[158] Davis initially presided over the provisional government of the Confederacy before his February 22, 1862, inauguration in Richmond where he became president of the permanent Confederate government. The inauguration date was extremely important in the South; George Washington was born February 22, 1732.

Davis and others in the Confederate inner circle wished for peaceful co-existence with the North. In February 1861, a resolution was passed by the Confederate Congress expressing a desire for commissioners to be appointed and sent to speak with representatives of the U.S. Government. Their charge was to negotiate peaceful relations between the two governments "and for the settlement of all questions of disagreement between the two governments upon principles of right, justice, equity, and good faith."[159]

Fully aware of the Republican Party platform, the Confederate government was eager to compromise. On February 25, Davis appointed commissioners to represent the South's peace efforts. He chose A.B. Roman of Louisiana, Martin J. Crawford of Georgia, and John Forsyth of Alabama. The Montgomery *Weekly Advertiser* evaluated its personnel:

> Mr. Roman has been governor of Louisiana, and was formerly of Opposition politics, having been a supporter of Mr. Bell in the recent contest for President of the United States, and subsequently a Cooperationist.
> Mr. Crawford is familiar to the public as a representative from the neighboring state of Georgia to

---

[158] Clayton Rand, *Sons of the South* (New York, New York: Holt, Rinehart and Winston, 1961), 99.

[159] E.A. Pollard, *The Lost Cause,* A Facsimile of the Original 1886 Edition (Avenel, New Jersey: Gramercy Books, 1994), 105.

the Congress of the United States. His politics have been States Rights. Mr. Forsyth was a secessionist in 1851— was Minister to Mexico under Mr. Buchanan's administration of the old government—and was a leading advocate of Douglas through his paper, the Mobile Register, in the later race for President of the United States. These appointments represent all shades of political and partisan opinion, and the gentlemen being well qualified for the duties of their mission, we doubt not the selection is a good one.[160]

The three-man commission was reputable, politically balanced, and possessed a strong desire to avoid conflict by all honorable means.

On February 27, 1861, the Confederate government informed Buchanan that Crawford would serve as a special peace commissioner. The wording of the Confederate message expressed a strong interest in reaching a compromise. It is believed Buchanan agreed to either meet Crawford or possibly refer him to Congress; however, Buchanan did neither.

Shortly after Lincoln took office, Crawford arrived in Washington City. Realizing the political pressure on the new U.S. President, Crawford decided to wait until the arrival of Forsyth before attempting to contact the new administration. Through communications with Sam Ward, New York lobbyist, Senator Gwin of California, and Senator Hunter of Virginia, the commissioners sought an interview with Secretary of State Seward, who was thought to be a peace advocate. On March 12, the commissioners sent a formal introduction of themselves to Seward, along with their stated goal of peaceful resolution. After being contacted, Seward asked for a twenty-day delay ostensibly to confer with Lincoln before granting an official interview. Concurrent with this requested delay, there was a general understanding on both sides that there

---

[160] John Shipley Tilley, *Lincoln Takes Command* (Nashville, Tennessee: Bill Coats, Ltd., 1991), 273.

would be no changes in the status of Fort Pickens or Fort Sumter. The Confederate commissioners were under the impression Fort Sumter would soon be evacuated.

The appearance of credible Confederate representatives on a mission of peace sparked the interest of two Supreme Court justices—Samuel Nelson from New York and John Archibald Campbell from Alabama. Campbell had strongly opposed the secession efforts in his home region (Georgia and Alabama). Nelson, a personal friend of Seward, did not feel the chief executive had a legitimate constitutional right to coerce the seceded States back into the Union. Based on his study of the respective war powers of the president and Congress, he saw coercion as overstepping constitutionally granted authority.

Both men realized that denying distinguished visitors an opportunity to state their case would be an epic blunder. To quell animosities and encourage useful dialogue, the justices urged Seward to respond in the spirit of peaceful negotiation as reflected in the wording of the communication from the commissioners.

> With a view to the speedy adjustment of all questions growing out of this political separation, upon such terms of amity and good-will as the respective interests, geographical contiguity, and future welfare of the two nations may render necessary, the undersigned are instructed to make to the Government of the United States overtures for the opening of negotiations, assuring the Government of the United States, that the President, Congress, and people of the Confederate States earnestly desire a peaceful solution of these great questions; that it is neither their interest nor their wish to make any demand which is not founded in strictest justice, or to do any act to injure their late confederate.[161]

---

[161] Ibid., 275.

On March 15, Seward told Campbell that Davis would be notified of the withdrawal of Union troops from Fort Sumter. However, on March 20 the Confederate commissioners learned that Commander Robert Anderson was still working on the fortification of Sumter. Campbell and Nelson quizzed Seward and he told them the delay was simply accidental and the troops would indeed evacuate the fort. Following up on March 20, the three commissioners sent a letter to Confederate Secretary of State Robert Toombs, stating: "You have not heard from us because there is no change. If there is faith in man we may rely on the assurances we have as to the status. Time is essential to a peaceful issue of this mission. In the present posture of affairs precipitation is war. We are all agreed."[162]

Seward never offered official recognition to the commissioners, but agreed to communicate with them, with Campbell acting as intermediary. Through Campbell, the commissioners received constant assurance that the U.S. government had peaceful intentions and planned to evacuate Fort Sumter "...and further that no measures, changing the existing *status*, prejudicially to the Confederate States, especially at Fort Pickens, were in contemplation; but that, in the event of any change of intention on the subject, notice would be given to the commissioners."[163]

Through intermediaries, Seward engaged Crawford and Forsyth. Seward carefully guarded his words, never assuming responsibility for the negotiations. He knew concessions on the Union side would have to originate with Lincoln, just as Crawford and Forsyth knew concessions on the Confederate side would have to originate with Davis. As late as April 1, Seward told Judge

---

[162] Robert Hawes, "Fort Sumter, the Untold Story: Failed Negotiations," *The Jeffersonian*, January 5, 2012, http://jeffersonian73.blogspot.com/2012/01/fort-sumter-untold-story.html, (Accessed April 18, 2016).

[163] Pollard, 106.

Campbell, "The president may desire to supply Fort Sumter but will not do so...There is no design to reinforce Fort Sumter."[164]

Finally, on April 8, the commissioners received Seward's response to the March 12 letter. "In this letter, Seward informed the commissioners that he could not recognize the 'so-called Confederate States' as an entity with which 'diplomatic relations ought to be established...'"[165] thus officially declining recognition or any communication relative to diplomacy. He wrote that he had conferred with Lincoln and they were in agreement with this position. Seward misled Crawford and sent this correspondence; with near certain awareness Lincoln had already approved reinforcement of Fort Sumter and Fort Pickens on March 29. Ward Lamon, appointed U.S. Marshall, met with Anderson, the Commander at Fort Sumter, and with South Carolina Governor Francis Pickens in March. Lamon had also led the Southern commissioners to believe Fort Sumter would be evacuated; Seward simply stated that Lamon had acted without authority.

With such overwhelming advantages in the North, the Lincoln Administration had little incentive to compromise. Indeed, there appeared to be an effort to simply dismiss the Southern representatives and their allies. Lincoln did not want to speak with representatives who he claimed did not belong to an internationally recognized foreign government.[166] Such recognition would have been counterproductive to his contention that secession was rebellion instead of a democratically decided departure from the Union by the citizens of sovereign States. Also, the evacuation of Forts Pickens and Sumter would be *de facto* admission that the Confederate States constituted a viable government. The fact Seward

---

[164] H.W. Johnstone, *Truth of the War Conspiracy of 1861* (Wake Forest, North Carolina: The Scuppernong Press, 2012), 19.

[165] Hawes, "Fort Sumter, the Untold Story: Failed Negotiations." (Accessed April 18, 2016).

[166] While not generally considered "official" recognition, the Vatican acknowledged the Confederacy as a separate entity and the five "civilized" Southeastern Indian tribes signed treaties as official allies.

misled the Southern commissioners and Lincoln refused to personally deal with them sent an ominous message. Even the intervention of the two justices produced nothing positive, prompting Seward to say, "had Jefferson Davis known the state of affairs in Washington, he would not have sent the commission."[167]

Another attempt to cease hostilities was made in February 1865. Francis P. Blair, originally from Virginia and known by many Confederates, arranged a meeting with representatives on both sides. The meeting was held on the Union transport *River Queen*, which was anchored off Hampton Roads, Virginia. Representing the Confederacy were Robert M.T. Hunter, John A. Campbell, and Confederate Vice-President Alexander Stephens. Lincoln and U.S. Secretary of State Seward represented the North. Each side presented its case—the South demanding recognition as an independent country, and the North wanting the Confederacy disbanded and returned to the United States. The four-hour meeting ended with no agreement.

---

[167] Tilley, *Lincoln Takes Command*, 278.

Chapter Eleven
The Northern Pro-Slavery Amendment

Reminding his fellow Republicans of their repudiation of interfering with slavery in the South, he was "willing that the principle shall be engraved upon the Mountain rocks, to endure for all time."[168]
Representative David Kilgore of Indiana, arguing for the adoption of the Corwin Amendment

From the mid-1900s to modern times most history books claim the South fought a war to protect slavery. That accusation was refuted by many men in the South, such as Jefferson Davis, Robert E. Lee, Richard Taylor, Edward Porter Alexander, Raphael Semmes, and in the North by men such as George Lunt, Simon Cameron, Edward Channing, and for at least the first half of the war, U.S. Grant and Abraham Lincoln. Slavery in America had never been more secure than on the eve of the war. Congress' July 23, 1861, resolution stated the war's purpose was to maintain the Union.[169] There was no mention of slavery.

The Corwin Amendment was written and proposed by Northerners ostensibly to pacify Southern and Border State slaveholders who feared large financial losses with immediate uncompensated emancipation.

---

[168] Paul C. Graham, "How The War Was About Slavery," *The Abbeville Institute Blog*, January 26, 2015, http://www.abbevilleinstitute.org/blog/how-the-war-was-about-slavery/, (Accessed April 19, 2016).

[169] Raphael Semmes stated: *"So loth was the South to abandon the Union, that she made strenuous efforts to remain in it, even after Mr. Lincoln had been elected President, in 1860. In this election, that dreaded sectional line against which President Washington had warned his countrymen, in his Farewell Address, had at last been drawn…"* From *Memoirs of Service Afloat*, 68.

The wording of the Corwin Amendment is as follows:

[No. 13]

Joint Resolution to Amend the Constitution of the United States.

Resolved by the Senate and House of Representatives of the United States of America in Congress assembled, That the following article be proposed to the several States as an amendment to the Constitution of the United States, which, when ratified by three-fourths of said Legislatures, shall be valid, to all intents and purposes, as part of the said Constitution, vis.:

Article Thirteen

No amendment shall be made to the Constitution which will authorize or give to Congress the power to abolish or interfere, within any State, with the domestic institutions thereof, including that of persons held to labor or service by the laws of said State.

Approved, March 2, 1861[170]

On March 2, 1861, the amendment was passed by a two-thirds vote of the U.S. House and Senate. By the time of its passage, several Southern States had already left the Union, meaning it was approved by a majority of representatives from non-Southern States. Viewed by many as a last ditch attempt to keep the Southern States in the Union, the Corwin Amendment was sent to the States for ratification.

The amendment was framed as protecting slavery where it already existed, and Representative Thomas Corwin of Ohio is generally credited as its author. Though it bears Corwin's name, he

---

[170] *United States at Large, Volume 12*, ed. George P. Sanger, Counsellor at Law, Little, Brown and Company, Boston, Massachusetts, 1863, 251. Reprinted by Dennis & Co., Buffalo, New York, August 1961, https://www.loc.gov/law/help/statutes-at-large/36th-congress/c36.pdf, (Accessed April 19, 2016).

was not the original amendment sponsor; he served as the Republican chairman of the ad hoc Committee of Thirty Three from whence it was introduced and thus his name appeared on the proposal. The original sponsor, Charles Francis Adams, received the text from Seward, prior to his selection as U.S. Secretary of State. Adams, the son of President John Quincy Adams, was an editor, politician, and diplomat. Going deeper into the amendment's chronology, after meeting with Republican politician and newspaper publisher Thurlow Weed, Seward introduced it to the Senate. Weed met with Lincoln in Springfield, Illinois, on December 20, 1860, to discuss the fugitive slave law and other compromise options. Not only was Weed in the loop, on December 21, Lincoln "notified Illinois Senator Lyman Trumball to expect 'three short resolutions which I drew up, and which, on the substance of which, I think would do much good.'"[171]

After back and forth communications, Seward wrote a letter to Lincoln on December 26, 1860, referencing "Weed's verbal conveyance as a resolution stating 'That the constitution should never be altered so as to authorize Congress to abolish or interfere with slavery in the states'—a clear description of the Corwin Amendment, which he presented the same day to the Republican members of the Senate's compromise 'Committee of Thirteen.'"[172] Whether Lincoln originated the Corwin Amendment or not, he was aware of its existence over three months prior to his inauguration.

The proposed amendment simply re-stated existing constitutional rights, and Lincoln even admitted he had no legal authority to interfere with State matters regarding slave labor. The South could have construed it as simply a reiteration of Lincoln's known position regarding the protection of slavery where it existed (and opposition to expansion) or as an attempt to bribe the seceded

---

[171] Phillip W. Magness, "Abraham Lincoln and the Corwin Amendment," Phillip W. Magness-Historian, *philmagness.com*, http://philmagness.com/?page_id=398, (Accessed April 19, 2016).
[172] Ibid.

States into returning to the Union. Lincoln's acknowledgement that he had no legal jurisdiction to interfere with slavery where it existed indicates there was insufficient reason for the destruction of slavery to be the *casus belli.*

There had been much discussion of the slavery issue leading up to the Corwin Amendment. The push for a resolution was paramount to Stephen Douglas and other peace seekers. Contra the Republican position, Douglas, the Illinois Democrat and architect of the Kansas-Nebraska Act, vehemently opposed sectional conflict and was willing to compromise with the South. Douglas' desire to diffuse sectional issues and diminish the potential for conflict was exhibited through his compromise efforts; he was credited as being the driving force for passage of the Corwin Amendment in the Senate.[173]

In addition to Douglas' endeavors, Democratic President Buchanan sought to remove slavery from the list of the South's grievances and signed the Corwin Amendment on March 3, 1861, his last day in office. Under the Constitution, proposed amendments do not require presidential approval. As mentioned previously, Buchanan was from pro-protectionist Pennsylvania, whose financial interests were served by keeping the Southern States in the Union.

The opening of hostilities minimized debate on this matter; the Corwin Amendment "was ratified by only two states—Ohio on May 13, 1861, and by Maryland on January 10, 1862—and therefore fell far short of the necessary three-quarters majority of states in order to become part of the U.S. Constitution."[174] Furthermore, in

---

[173] "Corwin Amendment," Slavery and the Secession Crisis, *Harp Week,* 2001-2008, http://13thamendment.harpweek.com/HubPages/CommentaryPage.asp?Co mmentary=02CorwinAmend, [The March 16,1861 issue of *Harpers Weekly* ran a featured article entitled 'Two Nights in the Senate' that gave Senator Douglas of Illinois credit for securing passage of the Corwin Amendment in that chamber.], (Accessed April 19, 2016).

[174] Ibid.

Lincoln's home State, the Illinois Constitutional Convention endorsed the Corwin Amendment in 1862.

The ratification of the Corwin Amendment by three quarters of the States would have become the law of the land, i.e., the original thirteenth amendment to the U.S. Constitution. Although the amendment would not have solved the issue of transporting slaves to non-slave States, it would have removed one grievance from the plate. Why would the slaveholding States not agree to this reaffirmation if protection of slavery were the primary goal?

Lincoln delivered his First Inaugural Address on March 4, 1861. He made several interesting comments regarding slavery: "I have no purpose, directly or indirectly, to interfere with the institution of slavery in the States where it exists. I believe I have no lawful right to do so, and I have no inclination to do so."[175]

He then quoted from the 1860 Republican Party Platform, which decried aggression: "[W]e denounce the lawless invasion by armed force of the soil of any State or Territory, no matter what pretext, as among the gravest of crimes."[176]

Within his address, Lincoln also discussed the amendment:

> I understand a proposed amendment to the Constitution—which amendment, however, I have not seen—has passed Congress, to the effect that the Federal Government shall never interfere with the domestic institutions of the States, including that of persons held to service. To avoid misconstruction of what I have said, I depart from my purpose not to speak of particular

---

[175] "Abraham Lincoln, First Inaugural Address," Monday, March 4, 1861, *Bartleby.com,* http://www.bartleby.com/124/pres31.html, (Accessed April 19, 2016).

[176] Thomas J. DiLorenzo, "Abraham Delano Messiah Obama?," *FourWinds10.com,* January 19, 2009, http://www.fourwinds10.net/siterun_data/history/american/news.php?q=1 232403799, (Accessed April 28, 2016).

amendments so far as to say that, holding such a provision to now be implied constitutional law, I have no objection to its being made express and irrevocable.[177]

Relative to timing, the amendment was ratified over a month before the events at Fort Sumter. Echoing Lincoln's support for the amendment, "Henry Adams noted that the 24-12 victory for the amendment in the senate was due largely to the lobbying of president-elect Abraham Lincoln." [178] The son of Francis Adams, Henry was a member of one of Massachusetts' first and most influential families.

Lincoln was adept at steering discussions of slavery in the direction that best suited his political agenda. His statement to free some, all, or none of the slaves is indicative of his flexibility. Another part of Lincoln's strategy was his instructions to Seward "to work on federal legislation that would outlaw the various personal liberty laws that existed in some of the Northern states. These laws were used to attempt to nullify the federal Fugitive Slave Act."[179] Lincoln had two angles to play. The Corwin Amendment, restating the constitutional protection of slavery, was designed to pacify the already seceded States. Lincoln's support of the enforcement of the Fugitive Slave Act would ostensibly calm the fears of the slaveholding Border States (Maryland, Missouri, Kentucky, Delaware, and later West Virginia) who were concerned their runaway slaves would not be returned. It was critical that the

---

[177] Ibid.

[178] Samuel Ashwood, "The Corwin Amendment—The Forgotten Amendment," *dixieoutfitters.com*, October 1, 2008, http://dixieoutfitters.com/pages/blog/corwin-amendment/, (Accessed April 28, 2016).

[179] Thomas J. DiLorenzo, "The Lincoln Cult's Latest Cover-Up," *Information Liberation*, July 24, 2006, http://www.informationliberation.com/?id=13613, (Accessed April 19, 2016).

Border States remain pro-Union; their secession would have made forced reunification more difficult.

The mystery that routinely shrouded Lincoln is seen here—he supported an amendment to remove federal interference from slavery in perpetuity while simultaneously undermining the Northern States' efforts to nullify the Fugitive Slave Act, yet some characterize him as a champion of liberty. As a master of sophistry, Lincoln's later two-part Emancipation Proclamation exemplified his uncanny ability to play both sides against the middle.

✳ ✳ ✳

This entire exercise would have been avoided if the U.S. Constitution had been followed. Under the constitutional scenario, the States would have been allowed to emancipate slaves on their own. Although slavery was legal, many Southern leaders felt the institution was detrimental to the region. Not only did it skew the available work, it also discouraged more Whites from settling in the South. Many countries in Europe and South America had successfully ended slavery via gradual emancipation and compensation of slave owners. If other countries were able to free their slaves without violence, there is no logical reason the American States could not have done the same. Since both the North and South shared guilt for slavery, mutual cooperation was required to resolve the matter.

Sizable anti-slavery sentiment existed in the South. Slavery often took work away from the average White man, who had more personal freedom, but was frequently as bad or worse off economically than the average slave. An individual was at a competitive disadvantage when pitted against the larger slave-owners who typically had greater resources to purchase prime property and equipment. This buying power often raised the price of land, creating an even higher barrier for the common man to climb. History is filled with the little man being crowded out by larger enterprises and being deprived of equitable employment opportunities. During the 1850s, many White Southerners simply left the business and became employees as tenant farmers, essentially competing with Black slave labor, many of whom possessed skills comparable to their own.

The Confederate Constitution with its low average import duty would have leveled the playing field for the average worker. Its free market underpinnings would have essentially set up a Free Trade Zone in the South. Slavery would have been vulnerable under this system; free trade breeds innovation and reduces costs, which would encourage the elimination of the fixed costs and inefficiencies of the slave system. "When treated as chattel, man renders a smaller yield per unit of cost expended for current sustenance and guarding than domestic animals."[180]

Many Southern men, such as Robert E. Lee, sought a humane way to ease slaves into freedom where they could utilize their ample God-given talents by becoming self-sufficient and avoiding relegation into a perpetual underclass. The transition from slavery to self-sufficiency is rarely an overnight accomplishment.

During the latter stages of the war, Lee contended it was more sensible to utilize the manpower and services of Blacks in support of the South than have the enemy use them for their benefit. Lee believed they could smoothly transition into military service, stating, "I believe that with proper regulations they can be made efficient soldiers. They possess the physical qualifications in an eminent degree."[181] Lee did not stop there; he believed all Blacks who served the Confederacy should be rewarded with "immediate freedom to all who enlist, and freedom at the end of the war to the families of those who discharge their duties faithfully (whether they

---

[180] Mark Thornton, "The Quotable Mises," *mises.org,* http://mises.org/quotes.aspx?action=subject&subject=Slavery, Quoted from *Human Action,* 626; 630-31, (Accessed April 19, 2016).

[181] "Lee Supports Slave Soldiers, Gradual Emancipation," *Civil War Daily Gazette,* January 11, 1865 (Wednesday), http://civilwardailygazette.com/2015/01/11/lee-supports-slave-soldiers-gradual-emancipation/, (Accessed April 19, 2016).

survive or not), together with the privilege of residing at the South. To this might be added a bounty for faithful service."[182]

Austrian economist Ludwig von Mises, a proponent of free markets and free labor, noted: "At no time and at no place was it possible for enterprises employing servile labor to compete on the market with enterprises employing free labor."[183] If the South had been left alone, slavery would have likely died due to the basic laws of economics brought about by such laborsaving inventions as McCormick's Virginia Reaper.

The Corwin Amendment poses two distinct questions. First, if the North's goal were to abolish slavery, such an amendment would have never been considered in the first place, much less passed. Second, if the South were fighting to protect slavery, it would have made sense for the Southern States to remain and/or rejoin the Union and ratify this amendment. The Corwin Amendment would be the Thirteenth Amendment today if the South had been willing to accept it. If the South simply wanted to protect slavery, all she had to do was remain in the Union. By leaving the Union, those guarantees were abandoned.

★★★

By taking essentially a hands-off position regarding slavery where it existed, the Corwin Amendment did not touch any alleged moral considerations since the slaves' status remained unchanged. This amendment was essentially a Union war measure. Seven Southern States were not even represented due to their respective State's secession.

Had the North let the South go, there would have been economic competition. The laws of economics and common sense indicate the North's import duties, almost five times greater than the South's, would have been uncompetitive and led to economic

---

[182] Ibid.

[183] Thornton, "The Quotable Mises," from *Human Action*, 626; 630.

calamity. "A successful mugger doesn't let the victim get away."[184] Furthermore, if the people of the South were backward drains as some alleged, why would the supposedly moral upright citizens of the North want to remain in a Union with them?

Perhaps as simply an effort to convince slave owners in the South and Border States that slavery was a negotiable issue, Lincoln expressed his support for the enforcement of the Fugitive Slave Law:

> There is much controversy about the delivering up of fugitives from service or labor. The clause I now read is as plainly written in the Constitution as any other of its provisions: No person held to service or labor in one State, under the laws thereof, escaping into another, shall, in consequence of any law or regulation therein, be discharged from such labor or service, but shall be delivered up on claim of the party to whom such service or labor may be due.
>
> It is scarcely questioned that this provision was intended by those who made it, for the reclaiming of what we call fugitive slaves; and the intention of the law-giver is the law. All members of Congress swear their support to the whole Constitution to this provision as much as to any other. To the proposition, then, that slaves whose cases come within the terms of this clause, shall be delivered up, their oaths are unanimous. Now, if they make the effort in good temper, could they not, with near equal unanimity, frame and pass a law, by means of which to keep good that unanimous oath?[185]

---

[184] Excerpted from a July 2015 private conversation with Auburn University Economics Instructor, John P. Sophocleus, in Beauregard, Alabama.

[185] Patrick J. Buchanan, "Mr. Lincoln's War: An Irrepressible Conflict?," *Patrick J. Buchanan—Official Website*, February 13, 2009, http://buchanan.org/blog/pjb-mr-lincolns-war-an-irrepressible-conflict-1440, (Accessed April 19, 2016).

Slavery was an area of significant controversy; however, there were deeper issues embodied in trade policies and differing regional views as to the nature of the Union itself. Patrick Henry expressed his distrust for New England corporate and religious interests as part of his concern for adoption of the U.S. Constitution: "I am sure that the dangers of this system are real, when those who have no similar interests with the people of this country are to legislate for us—when our dearest interests are to be left in the hands of those whose advantage it will be to infringe them."[186]

Leading up to the war, Confederate President Davis echoed similar sentiments, lamenting, "I worked night and day for twelve years to prevent war, but I could not. The North was mad and blind, would not let us govern ourselves, and so the war came."[187]

---

[186] Admiral Raphael Semmes, CSN Captain of the Alabama, *Memoirs of Service Afloat* (Secaucus, New Jersey: The Blue & Grey Press, 1987), 18.

[187] "Jefferson Davis Quotes," *Brainy Quote*, http://www.brainyquote.com/quotes/authors/j/jefferson_davis.html, (Accessed April 19, 2016). [Roger Broxton of Flags Across Alabama has written numerous articles explaining the tax reasons for the war.]

Chapter Twelve
The Confederate Constitution

"The use of tariffs to shelter domestic industries from foreign competition had been an important issue since tariffs were first adopted in 1816. Southern states had borne heavy costs since tariffs protected northern manufacturing at the expense of Southern imports."[188]

The Confederate Constitution has been overlooked or ignored by most historians. While closely resembling the U.S. Constitution, many of its features were improvements on the original Constitution relative to unambiguously defining the role of the central government and placing limits on its powers. The Confederate Constitution specified that it was a voluntary league of sovereign States. It addressed the grievances accumulated since the early days of the republic, i.e., the safeguards included in this constitution were designed to remedy issues that had evolved from the South's seventy-five years of struggle against incessant efforts in part of the North to control Southern life, both politically and economically.

The U.S. Constitution was originally intended to define and limit the powers of the central government with primary functions of defense and regulating interstate commerce. Other rights were reserved to the States. As President John Adams expressed, if adhered to by moral and religious men, the Constitution will successfully sustain a republican form of government.

The Confederate Constitution was written March 11, 1861, and was established on February 22, 1862. Howell Cobb served as President of the Confederate Congress.

---

[188] Randall G. Holcombe, "The Confederate Constitution," Volume 10, Number 6, *The Free Market*, Mises Institute, June 1992, https://mises.org/library/confederate-constitution, (Accessed April 20, 2016).

Representatives from seven Southern States signed the document:

"South Carolina: Robert Barnwell Rhett, C. G. Memminger, William Porcher Miles, James Chestnut, Jr., R. W. Barnwell, William W. Boyce, Lawrence M. Keitt, T. J. Withers.

Georgia: Francis S. Bartow, Martin J. Crawford, Benjamin H. Hill, Thomas R. R. Cobb.

Florida: Jackson Morton, J. Patton Anderson, Jas. B. Owens.

Alabama: Richard W. Walker, Robert H. Smith, Colin J. McRae, William P. Chilton, Stephen F. Hale, David P. Lewis, Thomas Fearn, John Gill Shorter, J. L. M. Curry.

Mississippi: Alex. M. Clayton, James T. Harrison, William S. Barry, W. S. Wilson, Walker Brooke, W. P. Harris, J. A. P. Campbell.

Louisiana: Alex. de Clouet, C. M. Conrad, Duncan F. Kenner, Henry Marshall.

Texas: John Hemphill, Thomas N. Waul, John H. Reagan, Williamson S. Oldham, Louis T. Wigfall, John Gregg, William Beck Ochiltree."[189]

Ambiguities in the U.S. Constitution were clarified in the Confederate Constitution, thus removing any doubt as to their meaning. For example, Patrick Henry immediately questioned the term "We, the people"[190] in the U.S. Constitution, saying it should be "We, the States."[191] This terminology would denote the entities that created it and reaffirm State sovereignty. "The term 'We the People' was cited by the centralizers as evidence that the government formed by the 1787 Constitution was a general government of all the

---

[189] "Signers of the Confederate Constitution," Hargrett Rare Book & Manuscript Library, *University of Georgia Libraries*, August 26, 2013, http://www.libs.uga.edu/hargrett/selections/confed/signers.html, (Accessed April 20, 2016).

[190] "Patrick Henry, Virginia Ratifying Convention," *The Founder's Constitution*, Volume 2, Preamble, Document 14, 4 June 1788—Elliot 3:22—23, http://press-pubs.uchicago.edu/founders/documents/preambles14.html, (Accessed April 20, 2016).

[191] Ibid.

people and not a creation of the states." [192] Simply put, the centralizers' preference for *We the people* made it appear the constitution was a creation of the American people as a whole instead of the representatives of the States who actually created it. This terminology appeared in The Federalist Papers, authored by Alexander Hamilton, John Jay, and James Madison, but also received varying degrees of support from John Adams, Benjamin Franklin, and George Washington.

Rebutting the nationalists, Virginia's John Taylor of Caroline County, published *New Views of the Constitution of the United States* in 1823.[193] As a key source, Taylor referenced Robert Yates' book, *Secret Proceedings and Debates of the Constitutional Convention.* Yates attended the Constitutional Convention and took detailed notes of the proceedings. Using critical information documented by Yates, "Taylor shredded the false notions of 'nationalists' like Hamilton (and later, Clay and Lincoln)."[194] The wording of the Confederate Constitution made it clear an all-powerful central government was not being created; there was no way to interpret this constitution as anything other than a creation of the Southern States.

The Confederate Constitution consisted of seven Articles: Article I dealt with legislative powers; Article II dealt with executive powers; Article III dealt with judicial powers; Article IV defined relations of the States to each other and to the national government; Article V provided the process for amending the Constitution; Article VI dealt with legal principle and international law; and Article VII gave the provisions for ratification. The majority of reform amendments were made in Article I.

---

[192] James Ronald Kennedy and Walter Donald Kennedy, *The South Was Right!* (Gretna, Louisiana: Pelican Publishing Company, 1994), 335.

[193] In 2005, The Lawbook Exchange, Ltd. Of Union, New Jersey published a reprint of Taylor's book.

[194] Thomas J. DiLorenzo, "Traitors to the American Revolution," *LewRockwell.com*, September 12, 2006, https://www.lewrockwell.com/2006/09/thomas-dilorenzo/traitors-to-the-american-revolution/, (Accessed April 20, 2016).

The Preamble reflected the South's belief in God, sovereignty, and independence:

> We the people of the Confederate States, each state acting in its sovereign and independent character, in order to form a permanent Federal government, establish justice, insure domestic tranquility, and secure the blessings of liberty to ourselves and our posterity— invoking the favor and guidance of Almighty God—do ordain and establish this Constitution for the Confederate States of America.[195]

Article I, Section 2 of the Confederate Constitution contains an election reform, forbidding non-citizens and foreigners from voting in elections. It states: "No person of foreign birth, not a citizen of the Confederate States, shall be allowed to vote for any office, civil or political, State or Federal."[196]

Article I, Section 2 of the U.S. Constitution gives impeachment power entirely to the U.S. House of Representatives. The Confederate Constitution also granted this power to the House, but added, "that any judicial or other Federal officer resident and acting solely within the limits of any state, may be impeached by a vote of two thirds of both branches of the Legislature thereof."[197] This gave each State legal authority to impeach corrupt Federal officials, including judges.

Article I, Section 3 of the Confederate Constitution stated when a senatorial election would be held. Prior to this, senators were elected by each State's legislature with no time limit for election. This created a sometimes-confusing situation where a new

---

[195] "Constitution of the Confederate States; March 11, 1861," *The Avalon Project*, Yale Law School, Lillian Goldman Law Library, http://avalon.law.yale.edu/19th_century/csa_csa.asp, (Accessed April 20, 2016).

[196] Ibid.

[197] Kennedy and Kennedy, 337-338.

senator could be elected (sometimes as much as two years) before the completion of the sitting senator's term. The party in power often used this to their political advantage.

Article I, Section 7 expanded the role of the Executive Branch by including a presidential line-item veto, where the C.S.A. President could veto parts of a spending bill without vetoing the entire bill. This feature encouraged budget accountability and discouraged over-runs.

From a historical standpoint, the North had a tremendous advantage over the South under the U.S. Constitution, especially in terms of representation and spending. As much as $100 million a year was collected from the South and used for "internal improvements"[198] in the North. In modern American vernacular, these projects typically fall into categories such as pork barrel spending, corporate welfare, or crony capitalism.

The Confederate Constitution prevented Congress from appropriating money "'for any internal improvement intended to facilitate commerce,' except for improvement to facilitate waterway navigation. But 'in all such cases, such duties shall be laid on the navigation facilitated thereby, as may be necessary to pay for the costs and expenses thereof....'"[199] This specifically outlawed a core program pushed by the protectionist Whigs and later, the Republicans. "The Southern Founders sought to prohibit general revenues from being used for the benefit of special interests. Tax revenues were to be spent for programs that benefited everyone, not a specific segment of the population."[200]

---

[198] "American System," *United States History*, http://www.u-s-history.com/pages/h278.html, (Accessed April 20, 2016).

[199] Holcombe, "The Confederate Constitution," Volume 10, Number 6, *The Free Market*, Mises Institute, June 1992, (Accessed April 20, 2016).

[200] Ibid.

Admiral Raphael Semmes wrote in his memoirs:

The exports of the South have been the basis of the Federal revenue...Virginia, the two Carolinas, and Georgia, may be said to defray three-fourths of the annual expense of supporting the Federal Government; and of this great sum, annually furnished by them, nothing, or next to nothing is returned to them, in the shape of Government expenditures. That expenditure flows in an opposite direction—it flows northwardly, in one uniform, uninterrupted, and perennial stream.[201]

Semmes offered a succinct description of what he considered a rigged system, by adding, "this is the reason why wealth disappears from the South and rises up in the North. Federal legislation does all this. It does it by the simple process of eternally taking from the South, and returning nothing to it."[202]

A weakness of the U.S. Constitution was the vague general welfare clause, questioned by Virginians Henry and Mason. This language was eliminated from the Confederate Constitution and reworded to eliminate tax and spend discrimination. According to Article I, Section 8: "Congress shall have power to lay and collect taxes, duties, imposts and excises, for revenue necessary to pay the debts, provide for the common defense, and carry on the Government of the Confederate States..." The U.S. Constitution stated the power to collect taxes, duties, impost and excises was "to promote the general welfare" [203] instead of "carry on the

---

[201] Admiral Raphael Semmes, CSN Captain of the Alabama, *Memoirs of Service Afloat* (Secaucus, New Jersey: The Blue & Grey Press, 1987), 58. [This echoed commentary made in 1828 by Missouri Senator Thomas Hart Benton.]

[202] Ibid.

[203] Martha F. Davis, "To Promote the General Welfare," *ACS Blog, American Constitution Society for Law and Policy*, September 15, 2011. [Davis is Professor of Law, Northeastern University School of Law.]

government."[204] The Confederate States were determined to limit special interests. They saw the general welfare clause as an open invitation for government intervention. By eliminating the ambiguous wording, they sought to remove the temptation.

There is no parallel to the Confederate Constitution's Article I, Section 8 in the U.S. Constitution. Pro-free trade and anti-protectionist, it states: "…no bounties shall be granted from the Treasury; nor shall any duties or taxes on importation from foreign nations be laid to promote or foster any branch of industry. "[205] This effectively outlawed corporate welfare and the use of the federal government to disproportionately aid favored industries.

Like agrarian-based civilizations throughout history, the overwhelming majority of the South opposed protectionism and supported the freest markets possible. One exception was Louisiana's sugar producers who received tariff protection.[206] With limited manufacturing, the South could purchase finished goods from Europe, with duties added, or buy from the North, with inland transportation charges added. Higher import duties benefitted Northern industry by making imported goods more expensive. They harmed the South as the largest exporting region in America; higher import duties increased the likelihood of retaliation from European trading partners and this extra cost affected the amount of goods purchased from the South. "Tariffs on imports create a disincentive

---

http://www.acslaw.org/acsblog/to-promote-the-general-welfare, (Accessed April 20, 2016).

[204] "Constitution of the Confederate States; March 11, 1861," *The Avalon Project*, Yale Law School.

[205] Holcombe, "The Confederate Constitution," Volume 10, Number 6, *The Free Market*, Mises Institute, June 1992, (Accessed April 20, 2016).

[206] The Louisiana exception is often cited as a reason the tariff issue was less emphasized than slavery relative to the areas of concern for the first seven seceding States.

to export by directly raising the domestic price of imports, or equivalently, by reducing the price of exports relative to imports."[207]

Furthermore, "Tariffs on imports discourage all types of exports—not just exports from a single sector—because they tend to cause a country's real exchange rate to appreciate. By raising the prices of imports and non-traded goods relative to the price of exports, a tariff creates an incentive to shift production toward non-tradeables and away from exports."[208]

The South's role as chief exporter and importer meant they paid a higher percentage into the Federal treasury than any other region. Due to numerical under-representation in the government, the South received very little money back while they saw sizable revenue being used for internal improvements in the North; this was a violation of the uniformity clause of the constitution (Article I, Section 8, Clause 1). Dating back to the colonial period, most Southerners felt tariffs should be maintained only at a level to cover the cost of trade.

John C. Calhoun, Raphael Semmes, Charles Dickens, Robert Toombs, and others argued the economic position of the South. Calhoun emphasized the equity of a twenty-percent benchmark rate as well as strict enforcement of the uniformity clause.[209] Also, Frank W. Taussig, the renowned Missouri economist, whose career spanned part of the Nineteenth and Twentieth centuries, explained the relationship of high and low import duties in his 1888 book, *The Tariff History of the United States*. Southerners realized there are legitimate costs inherent in trade and they considered the

---

[207] Steven Tokarick, "How large is the bias against exports from import tariffs?" Research Department, International Monetary Fund, *Dartmouth.edu*,
http://www.dartmouth.edu/~rstaiger/lerner.symmetry.theorem.evidence.pdf, (Accessed April 20, 2016).

[208] Ibid.

[209] According to John Sophocleus, Calhoun's calculation is still accurate today. The Confederate State's ten percent average was viable, even at ten percent below benchmark.

benchmark import rate of twenty-percent to be fair. The South did not threaten nullification or secession when uniform import duties were set near or below the benchmark level. As discussed earlier, many Southerners even agreed to the temporarily high rates of the 1816 Tariff to assist Northern industry and help defray the costs of the War of 1812. However, the South strongly resisted the protectionism of 1828 and 1832. The 1846 Walker Tariff and the 1857 Tariff were generally friendly to the South. It was not until the 1860 election of Lincoln, that true protectionism returned as a key part of the Republican Platform. The South protested the Morrill Tariff of 1860/1861, which passed after several Southern States seceded and may have passed had they remained.

For years, the States of New England and the Upper Midwest sought protection of their own industries. When territories were added, it was in the South's best interest to insist on an equal number of slave states—not specifically to protect slavery, but to maintain a political balance. Slavery was best suited for labor-intensive crops such as cotton (before and after the invention of the cotton gin), tobacco, sugar, and rice. Slave labor was largely impractical in most areas of potential expansion. For example, though tobacco and rice continued to be grown, agriculture in the Upper South and Border States was diversifying into "wheat, corn, rye, and oats for local consumption. Half of the country's corn was grown in the South. These cereal grains were not as labor intensive as cotton or tobacco, and planters in the region were finding themselves with more slaves than they needed." [210] Southern secession provided a way out of an inequitable tax system and many outside the South recognized this fact. The South's low import duties were seen as a nightmare for protection-seeking Northern

---

[210] "Slavery, the Economy, and Society," *Cliffs Notes*, Houghton, Mifflin, Harcourt, 2016, http://www.cliffsnotes.com/study-guides/history/us-history-i/slavery-and-the-south/slavery-the-economy-and-society, (Accessed April 20, 2016).

industry. An editorial in the March 18, 1861, *Boston Transcript*, noted the economic reality of Southern secession:

> It does not require extraordinary sagacity to perceive that trade is perhaps the controlling motive operating to prevent the return of the seceding states to the Union which they have abandoned. Alleged grievances in regard to slavery were originally the causes for the separation of the cotton states; but the mask has been thrown off, and it is apparent that the people of the principal seceding states are now for commercial independence. They dream that the centres of traffic can be changed from Northern to Southern ports. The merchants of New Orleans, Charleston and Savannah are possessed with the idea that New York, Boston, and Philadelphia may be shorn, in the future, of their mercantile greatness, by a revenue system verging on free trade. If the Southern Confederation is allowed to carry out a policy by which only a nominal duty is laid upon imports, no doubt the business of the chief Northern cities will be seriously injured thereby.
>
> The difference is so great between the tariff of the Union and that of the Confederate States that the entire Northwest must find it to their advantage to purchase their imported goods at New Orleans rather than New York. In addition to this, the manufacturing interests of the country will suffer from the increased importation resulting from low duties…The [government] would be false to its obligations if this state of things were not provided against.[211]

---

[211] Charles Adams, *For Good and Evil: The Impact of Taxes on the Course of Civilization* (Lanham, Maryland: Madison Books, 1993), 333-334. Excerpted from Kenneth M. Stampp's 1959 book, *The Causes of the Civil War*, this is just one of many editorials in Northern newspapers identifying this pivotal issue.

Lincoln told Southern peace representatives in three separate interviews that he could not let the South go and compete with their stated 10% average import duty.[212] The industrial interests of the North and Upper Midwest, represented by Lincoln, were not about to allow an independent Confederacy.

Article I, Section 9 of the Confederate Constitution attempted to create an avenue toward resolving the slavery issue.

> The importation of Negroes of the African race, from any foreign country, other than the slaveholding States or Territories of the United States of America, is hereby forbidden, and Congress is required to pass such laws as shall effectually prevent the same.[213]

The Confederate Constitution was the first American government to include a slave trade prohibition in the original text, i.e., it immediately ended the foreign slave trade, whereas the U.S. Constitution pushed the date back twenty years (1808), largely to pacify Northern shipping and slave-importing interests. "The New England shipping was the chief sinner in bringing negroes to the South. And when the constitution was formed in 1787, New England delegates voted a continuance of the slave trade for twenty years. This fixed slavery on the South."[214] John Tyler, Sr., the father of President John Tyler was irate about this development and "he

---

[212] Covered in *Colonel Baldwin meets Lincoln*, the interviews with Lincoln included: John Baldwin on April 4, 1861; William B. Preston, A.H.H. Stuart, and George W. Randolph on April 12, 1861; and Reverend Richard Fuller with representatives from five Christian associations in Baltimore, Maryland on April 22, 1861.

[213] "Constitution of the Confederate States; March 11, 1861," *The Avalon Project*, Yale Law School.

[214] Lyon Gardiner Tyler, *The Gray Book: A Confederate Catechism* (Wiggins, Mississippi: Crown Rights Books—The Liberty Reprint Series, 1997), 15. Originally printed in *Tyler's Quarterly* in Volume 33, October and January issues, 1935.

wanted it handed down to posterity that he opposed that wicked clause permitting the slave trade."[215] The State of Virginia tried for years to stop the slave trade. On October 5, 1778, Virginia, led by Governor Henry, outlawed the slave trade by an act of the General Assembly. Not only did Northern shippers resist, according to James Madison, "The British government constantly checked the attempts of Virginia to put a stop to this infernal traffick."[216]

Northern shipping companies involved in the slave trade reaped substantial profits, with many families building massive fortunes. Perhaps the most well known was the DeWolf family of Rhode Island, a State that dominated the slave trade. Captain James DeWolf of Bristol, Rhode Island, and John Brown of Providence, Rhode Island—one of the brothers who founded Brown University in Providence—"joined forces to protect the trade."[217] Dominance of the slave trade was a financial windfall: "It was one of the foundations of New England's economic structure; it created a wealthy class of slave-trading merchants, while the profits derived from this commerce stimulated cultural development and philanthropy...Even after slavery was outlawed in the North, ships out of New England continued to carry thousands of Africans to the U.S. South."[218]

The legacy of transporting slaves was a lucrative enterprise that the profiteers found difficult to abandon. Slavery existed well before Jesus Christ walked on earth; Arabs and Africans initiated a

---

[215] Ibid.

[216] Kennedy and Kennedy, 73.

[217] Anne Farrow, Joel Lang and Jenifer Frank, "The Myth Of Northern Innocence: Before Emancipation, The North Perpetuated And Profited From Slavery," *Hartford Courant*, September 25, 2005, http://articles.courant.com/2005-09-25/news/0509230479_1_civil-war-slaves-cotton/2, (Accessed April 20, 2016).

[218] "A Southern View of History: The War for Southern Independence, Part III: Servitude, Slavery, Abolitionists," *Sons of Confederate Veterans*, http://www.scv.org/curriculum/part3.htm, (Accessed April 28, 2016).

system in the Seventh Century that Europeans got involved with in the Fifteenth Century. Eventually the British dominated what morphed into the Triangular slave trade. Europeans, Americans, and Africans all benefitted from this transportation of human cargo. Cloth, tobacco, etc. was shipped from Europe to Africa in exchange for slaves. The slaves were transported from Africa to the American Colonies; this was known as Middle Passage and was often incredibly brutal. The last leg of the triangle was the return of ships to Europe with molasses and rum from New England as well as cotton, sugar, and tobacco produced on the plantations.

Many Southern leaders (including Lee, Davis, and Jackson) wanted to end slavery, preferably through gradual compensated emancipation as had been successfully accomplished in Europe, Great Britain, South America, etc.

Article I, Section 9 of the Confederate Constitution reflects a far-sighted maneuver. The writers of the Confederate Constitution sought to eliminate the possibility of entitlements and never-ending commitments by clearly stating, "'All bills appropriating money shall specify...the exact amount of each appropriation, and the purposes for which it is made,' said the document. 'And Congress shall grant no extra compensation to any public contractor, officer, agent, or servant, after such contract shall have been made or such service rendered.'" [219] This provision effectively eliminated cost overruns, a favorite of modern-day government contractors, and placed a premium on accountability and accuracy within the bid process.

Another feature involved the elimination of omnibus spending. All legislation was required to "'relate to but one subject,' which had to be 'expressed in the title.' There would be no 'Christmas-tree' appropriations bills or hidden expenditures." [220]

---

[219] Holcombe, "The Confederate Constitution," Volume 10, Number 6, *The Free Market*, Mises Institute, June 1992, (Accessed April 20, 2016).

[220] Ibid.

This eliminated passing a bill by stealth when it would not pass on its own merit.

Although most of Article II of the Confederate Constitution mirrors the U.S. Constitution, there is one major difference. The Confederate President was elected to one six-year term only, rendering re-election irrelevant. This allowed time to devote presidential energies to policy implementation and removed the modern phenomenon of perpetual campaigning.

Article III contained some minor improvements over the U.S. Constitution. Section 2 eliminated Diversity Jurisdiction, which allowed a Federal judge to intervene when citizens of two different States were at issue over a legal matter. In other words, under the U.S. Constitution, a Federal judge could intervene and decide cases that should be decided by the States.

The last major difference in these two documents appears in Article V, Section 1 of the Confederate Constitution and concerns the amendment process. Under the U.S. Constitution, Congress assumed the lead role, but under the Confederate Constitution, the States initiated the amendment process. When three or more States called for a Constitutional Convention, Congress was required to call a convention. Discussion was confined only to the amendment that led to the convention. This eliminated the possibility of a runaway convention. Also, two thirds of the States had to ratify an amendment for it to become part of the Constitution.

The Confederate Constitution provided a barometer as to how most Southerners felt government should function. On the front end, it emphasized the sanctity and blessings of God and recognized the States as the actual sovereign entities, with the central government as the agent of those States.

Chapter Thirteen
Colonel Baldwin Meets Mr. Lincoln

"I supported President Lincoln. I believed his war policy would be the only way to save the country, but I see my mistake. I visited Washington a few weeks ago, and I saw the corruption of the present administration—and so long as Abraham Lincoln and his Cabinet are in power, so long will war continue. And for what? For the preservation of the Constitution and the Union? No, but for the sake of politicians and government contractors."[221]

J.P. Morgan—American financier and banker, 1864.

The assertion that Lincoln genuinely attempted to avoid war has been preached since General Lee's surrender at Appomattox. The testimony of a Southern peace representative who spoke with Lincoln on April 4, 1861, in an effort to avert war provides keen insight into a side of the issue seldom heard or taught.[222] Some historians dismiss the importance of the meeting between Lincoln and Colonel John Brown Baldwin, but it is beyond dispute the meeting happened and pivotal issues were seriously discussed. On February 10, 1866, Baldwin testified before the Joint Committee on Reconstruction in Washington, D.C. His comments appeared in a pamphlet published in 1866 by the *Staunton Speculator* and he provided his account to a fellow Confederate in 1865 just prior to the end of the war.

---

[221] Mildred Lewis Rutherford, *A True Estimate of Abraham Lincoln & Vindication of the South* (Wiggins, Mississippi: Crown Rights Book Company, 1997.), 58-59. This quote appeared on page 11 of the December 25, 1922, edition of *Barron's*. Original source: *New Haven Register*; copied in *New York World*, September 15, 1864.

[222] Dr. Grady McWhiney, former Professor at the University of Alabama, Texas Christian, etc. said: "What passes as standard American history is really Yankee history written by New Englanders or their puppets to glorify Yankee heroes and ideals." (From *The Unforgiven*, 11).

Reverend Robert L. Dabney, Chief of Staff to Stonewall Jackson, met Baldwin in March of 1865 in Petersburg, Virginia, when the Army of Northern Virginia was under siege. Baldwin told Dabney, that prior to hostilities, he had been selected by the Virginia Secession Convention to surreptitiously meet with Lincoln in April 1861 and negotiate a peaceful settlement. This meeting occurred at the time the Virginia legislature was debating the secession issue.

The citizens of the Southern States were well aware of the disadvantages they faced. The failure of the Peace Congress, rejection of the Crittenden Amendment, and the clandestine arming of the Federal government raised concerns in the South that war may be on the horizon.

There was lingering frustration in the South resulting from the failed compromise effort of A.B. Roman, Martin Crawford, and John Forsyth. As sectional hostility continued to fester, further attempts at peace became critical. Most Virginians were strong Unionists, a fact mirrored in the make up of the anti-secession Virginia Convention. Considering the situation dire, representatives from Virginia decided to make another attempt to diffuse the sectional schism.

William Ballard Preston, an anti-slavery defense lawyer and prominent member of the Virginia Convention, summed up the concerns of Virginians about the direction of the country:

> If our voices and votes are to be exerted farther to hold Virginia in the Union, **we must know** (emphasis author) what the nature of the Union is to be. We have valued Union, but we are also Virginians, and we love the Union only as it is based upon the Constitution. If the power of the United States is to be perverted to invade the rights of States and of the people, we would support the Federal Government no farther. And now that the attitude of that Government was so ominous of

usurpation, we must know whither it is going, or we can go with it no farther.[223]

Preston was disturbed about threats of coercion through federal overreach and the possibility of destroying the voluntary relationship of the compact. His view paralleled that of Robert E. Lee, who refused to participate in the invasion of the seceded States.[224]

Seward sent a messenger, Allen B. Magruder, to consult with members of the Virginia Convention and request that they send a representative to Washington to confer with the U.S. President. Lincoln's preference was G.W. Summers, a pro-Unionist from the western part of Virginia. The Virginia group included Mr. John Janney, Convention President, Mr. John S. Preston, Mr. A.H.H. Stuart, and others. Since this mission was of a discreet nature, the Convention did not send Summers, but instead sent a lesser-known representative named John Brown Baldwin. Though Baldwin lacked the notoriety of other potential candidates, he was imminently qualified and widely respected. Also, as the brother-in-law of Stuart, he had strong inside support from a key convention member. Baldwin's credentials included graduation from Staunton Academy and the University of Virginia combined with a reputation as a capable lawyer and man of integrity. He was also one of Virginia's strongest Unionists. Though somewhat reluctant, Baldwin realized

---

[223] Robert L. Dabney, D.D., *The Origin & Real Cause of the War, A Memoir of a Narrative Received of Colonel John B. Baldwin*, Reprinted from Discussions, Volume IV, 2-3.

[224] Lee referenced his West Point teaching from Rawles' 1825 textbook, *A View of the Constitution of the United States of America*, that the Union is a voluntary coalition and States have a legal right to secede. Lee was duty-bound to fight for Virginia; he understood the meaning of Article III, Section 3. Virginia's Alexander R. Boteler, while serving in the U.S. House of Representatives, warned the Lincoln Administration that Virginia would secede if there was a call to invade the Southern States.

the magnitude of this mission and dutifully accepted the role as Virginia representative.

Dabney summarized Baldwin's instructions:

> Mr. Magruder stated that he was authorized by Mr. Seward to say that Fort Sumter would be evacuated on the Friday of the ensuing week, and that the Pawnee would sail on the following Monday for Charleston, to effect the evacuation. Mr. Seward said that secrecy was all important, and while it was extremely desirable that one of them should see Mr. Lincoln, it was equally important that the public should know nothing of the interview.[225]

Baldwin and Magruder prepared for their trip to Washington, choosing to travel the Acquia Creek Route. On April 4, Baldwin rode with Magruder, in a carriage with raised glasses (for maximum secrecy), to meet Seward. Seward took Baldwin to the White House, arriving slightly after 9:00 A.M. The porter immediately admitted him, and, along with Seward, led Baldwin to "what he (Baldwin) presumed was the President's ordinary business room, where he (Baldwin) found him in evidently anxious consultation with three or four elderly men, who appeared to wear importance in their aspect."[226] Though these gentlemen appeared to be very influential, it does not appear Baldwin knew them, as he did not identify them when he recounted the meeting.

Seward informed Lincoln of his guest's arrival, whereupon, Lincoln immediately excused himself from the meeting, took Baldwin upstairs to a bedroom and formally greeted his visitor: "Well, I suppose this is Colonel Baldwin of Virginia? I have hearn

---

[225] Dabney, 3.
[226] Ibid., 4.

[sic] of you a good deal, and am glad to see you. How d'ye, do sir?"[227]

Baldwin presented his credentials. Lincoln sat on the bed and occasionally spat on the carpet as he read through them. Once satisfied with the introduction, Lincoln conveyed that he was aware of the purpose of the visit.

Lincoln admitted Virginians were good Unionists, but he did not favor their kind of conditional Unionism. However, he was willing to listen to Virginian's proposal for resolution. Baldwin reaffirmed Virginia's belief in the Constitution as it was written and expressed Virginia would not subscribe to a conflict based on the sectional, free-soil question. He told Lincoln that as much as Virginia opposed his platform, she would support him as long as he adhered to the Constitution and the laws of the land. To lessen the acrimony that arose from the election, Baldwin suggested Lincoln issue a simple proclamation asserting that his administration would respect the Constitution, the rule of law, and the rights of the States. This proclamation should include a willingness to clarify the misunderstandings and motives of each side. Baldwin told Lincoln that Virginia would assist and stand by him, even to the point of treating him like her native son, George Washington. Embellishing his point, Baldwin added, "So sure am I, of this, and of the inevitable ruin which will be precipitated by the opposite policy, that I would this day freely consent, if you would let me write those decisive lines, you might cut off my head, were my own life my own, the hour after you signed them."[228]

He also suggested that Lincoln "call a national convention of the people of the United States and urge upon them to come together and settle this thing."[229] Furthermore, Lincoln should make

---

[227] Ibid.

[228] Ibid., 8.

[229] "Interview Between President Lincoln and Col. John B. Baldwin, April 4th, 1861, Statements and Evidence," *Staunton Speculator* (Staunton, Virginia: Spectator Job Office, D.E. Strasburg, Printer, 1866), 12,

it clear that the seceded States would not be militarily forced to return to the Union, but rather a course of compromise and conciliation would be pursued to bring them back in. According to Baldwin, with a simple agreement to this proposition, Virginia would use all possible influence to keep the Border States in the Union and convince the already seceded seven States to rejoin. Baldwin made it clear that Virginia would never support unconstitutional attempts to coerce the seceded States against the will of the people of those States.

The fate and direction of the Constitutional Union sat squarely on Lincoln's shoulders; he had the power to diffuse the situation. Baldwin did everything he could to convince Lincoln the secession movement could be put down, stressing that Virginia was eager and willing to help.

During the conversation, it became obvious to Baldwin that the issue of slavery was not Lincoln's primary concern. Digesting Lincoln's comments, Baldwin began to see the issue as "the attempted overthrow of the Constitution and liberty, by the usurpation of a power to crush states. The question of free-soil had no such importance in the eyes of the people of the border States, nor even of the seceded States, as to become at once a casus belli." [230]

Lincoln did not like what he heard. He painted the South as insincere, as people with hollow words backed by no action, and claimed the resolutions, speeches, and declarations from Southerners "a game of brag"[231] meant to intimidate the Federal administration.

Baldwin told Lincoln repeatedly that Virginia would not fight over the free-soil issue. As a basic point of fact, only about six percent of Southerners were slave owners, affecting perhaps twenty-five to thirty percent of Southern families. Fighting over slavery

---

https://ia800301.us.archive.org/5/items/interviewbetween00bald/interviewbetween00bald.pdf, (Accessed April 21, 2016).

[230] Dabney, 7.

[231] Ibid., 6.

made little sense, especially given the fact slavery was already constitutionally legal. However, Baldwin emphasized that coercion would undoubtedly lead to further separation and likely war.

Baldwin probed for the primary sticking point, leading Lincoln to ask, "Well…what about the revenue? What would I do about the collection of duties."[232] In response, Baldwin asked how much import revenue would be lost per year. Lincoln responded "fifty or sixty millions."[233] Baldwin answered by saying a total of two hundred and fifty million dollars in lost revenue (based on an assumed four-year presidential term) would be trivial compared to the cost of war and Virginia's plan was all that was necessary to solve the issue. Lincoln also briefly mentioned concern about the troops at Fort Sumter being properly fed. Baldwin responded that the people of Charleston were feeding them and would continue to do so as long as a resolution was in sight.

Though Lincoln appeared to be genuinely touched by Baldwin's plea for peace, he was alarmed at the prospect of lost revenue; he did not like the idea of the Southern States remaining out of the Union until a compromise could be reached. His reply underscored this deep concern: "And open Charleston, etc., as ports of entry, with their ten per cent tariff. What, then, would become of my tariff?"[234] Though it was Fort Sumter in Charleston Harbor where things came to a head, lower duties would have applied and attracted trade to all Southern ports, e.g., Richmond, Savannah, Wilmington, New Orleans, Mobile, Galveston, etc.

Lincoln's reply to Baldwin made it clear slavery was not the central issue. He did not mention slavery but voiced alarm at the amount of revenue that would be lost if he allowed the Confederate States to exist as a separate country. Import duties comprised the vast majority of government revenue at that time.

---

[232] "Interview Between President Lincoln and Col. John B. Baldwin, April 4th, 1861, Statements and Evidence," 12-13, (Accessed April 21, 2016).

[233] Ibid., 13.

[234] Dabney, 8.

Baldwin asked Lincoln if he trusted him as an honest representative of the sentiment of Virginia and received an affirmative response. After confirming Lincoln's confidence in him, Baldwin stated, "I tell you, before God and man, that if there is a gun fired at Sumter this thing is gone."[235] He stressed that action should be taken as soon as possible, stating that if the situation festered two more weeks, it would likely be too late.

Lincoln awkwardly paced about in obvious dismay and exclaimed: "I ought to have known this sooner! You are too late, sir, too late! Why did you not come here four days ago, and tell me all this?"[236] Another fact not revealed in the conversation by Lincoln was that he had already authorized reinforcement of Forts Sumter and Pickens on March 29 and the ships were preparing to sail.

Baldwin replied: "Why, Mr. President, you did not ask our advice. Besides, as soon as we received permission to tender it, I came by the first train, as fast as steam could bring me."[237]

Once more, Lincoln responded: "Yes, but you are too late, I tell you, *too* late!"[238] Perhaps this was the point when it sunk in as to how serious the Southern States viewed the situation.

Lincoln claimed secession was unconstitutional, though it had been taught at West Point using Rawles' textbook, that the Union is a voluntary coalition of States and secession was up to the people of the respective States. Conversely, Lincoln saw nothing wrong with coercion, which was historically considered unconstitutional in both North and South. He felt secession automatically signaled war, when it should have signified the opposite. Concerning the Constitution, "if followed, civil war—the fight for control over the government—is impossible."[239]

---

[235] "Interview Between President Lincoln and Col. John B. Baldwin, April 4th, 1861, Statements and Evidence," 13, (Accessed April 21, 2016).

[236] Dabney, 6.

[237] Ibid.

[238] Ibid.

[239] From a May 2013 conversation with John P. Sophocleus, Auburn University Economics Instructor.

Lincoln made no promises and dismissed Baldwin. Later the same day, Baldwin engaged in a lengthy conversation with Seward. From their conversation, Baldwin surmised that Seward preferred and desired to work toward peace but felt conflict was very likely. Baldwin had fulfilled his duty and returned to Virginia with the verdict. Dabney later speculated from Baldwin's testimony that Lincoln had succumbed to the pro-war fanaticism of Stevens and abandoned the more sensible warnings from Seward about the unconstitutionality of coercion.

Stuart confirmed the accuracy of Baldwin's account to Dabney. Indeed, Stuart, along with William B. Preston and George W. Randolph, spoke with Lincoln on April 12, 1861, and received virtually the same message as Baldwin. "I remember," says Mr. Stuart, "that he used this homely expression: 'If I do that, what will become of my revenue? I might as well shut up housekeeping at once.'"[240]

Highlighting Stuart's meeting was Lincoln's insinuation that he was not interested in war; however, the day after their meeting the very train on which they returned to Richmond carried the proclamation calling for 75,000 troops to coerce the seceded States.

Another attempt at compromise was detailed in the April 23, 1861, edition of the *Baltimore Exchange* and reprinted in the May 8, 1861, edition of the *Memphis Daily Avalanche*. This involved a meeting between a group led by Dr. Richard Fuller, a preacher from the Seventh Baptist Church in Baltimore, and Lincoln. Fuller was a South Carolina native and Southern supporter. The article states:

> We learned that a delegation from five of the Young Men's Christian Associations of Baltimore, consisting of six members each, yesterday (April 22, 1861) proceeded to Washington for an interview with the President, the purpose being to intercede with him in behalf a peaceful

---

[240] Dabney, 11.

policy, and to entreat him not to pass troops through Baltimore or Maryland.[241]

Fuller acted as the chairman and conducted the interview. After Fuller's plea for peace and recognition of the rights of the Southern States, Lincoln responded, "But what am I to do?...what shall become of the revenue? I shall have no government? No resources?"[242]

Former U.S. President John Tyler was intimately knowledgeable of the situation, and he worked diligently to avoid war. With the benefit of Tyler's insight, Lyon Gardiner Tyler's account echoes those of the Virginia and Maryland representatives:

> ...the deciding factor with him (Lincoln) was the tariff question. In three separate interviews, he asked what would become of his revenue if he allowed the government at Montgomery to go on with their ten percent tariff... Final action was taken when nine governors of high tariff states waited upon Lincoln and offered him men and supplies.[243]

Lyon Tyler, as President Tyler's son, almost certainly had inside information about the three aforementioned meetings with Lincoln, especially in consideration of his father's tireless attempts to achieve a peaceful resolution.

---

[241] Bruce Gourley, "Baptists and the American Civil War: April 23, 1861," *In Their Own Words,* April 23, 2011, http://www.civilwarbaptists.com/thisdayinhistory/1861-april-23/, (As reprinted in the *Memphis Daily Avalanche,* May 8, 1861, p. 1, col. 4), (Accessed April 21, 2016).

[242] Ibid.

[243] Lyon Gardiner Tyler, *The Gray Book: A Confederate Catechism,* (Wiggins, Mississippi: Crown Rights Book Company—The Liberty Reprint Series, 1997), 5. Originally printed in *Tyler's Quarterly* in Volume 33, October and January issues, 1935.

Dabney summed up the circumstances surrounding the war by identifying Lincoln's reference to the sectional tariff as the tipping point. "His single objection, both to the wise advice of Colonel Baldwin and Mr. Stuart, was: "Then what would become of my tariffs?"[244] Lincoln saw a free trade policy in the South as an economic threat to the North that could not be allowed to stand. Through Colonel Baldwin, Virginia provided a viable option to avoid war and preserve the Union. Referencing Lincoln's course of action, Dabney lamented, "he preferred to destroy the Union and preserve his [redistributive] tariffs. The war was conceived in duplicity, and brought forth in iniquity."[245]

---

[244] Dabney, 14.
[245] Ibid.

Chapter Fourteen
Fort Sumter

Constitutional Violation: Article 1, Section 8, Clauses 11, 12: *War Declared without Consent of Congress, 1861*

"I knew they would do it!"[246]
Abraham Lincoln's reaction upon hearing South Carolinians had fired on Fort Sumter.

Fort Sumter, named after Revolutionary hero, General Thomas Sumter, is generally regarded as the location in which the war began. The fort was one of many built on the Southern coast after the War of 1812. Designated to be a tax collection point upon completion, Fort Sumter possessed a touch of symbolism relative to Lincoln's uncompromising attitude on import duties.

South Carolina seceded from the Union on December 20, 1860. Six days later, U.S. Army Major Robert Anderson abandoned Fort Moultrie and relocated his troops to Fort Sumter. His command consisted of companies E and H of the 1st U.S. Artillery, totaling 127 men, including thirteen musicians. Anderson reasoned the move to a more defensive location would slow down any attack from the South Carolina militia.

Upon hearing about Anderson's move into Sumter, Secretary of War J.B. Floyd, wrote:

> Intelligence has reached here this morning that you have abandoned Fort Moultrie, spiked your guns, burned the carriages, and gone to Fort Sumter. It is not

---

[246] Charles T. Pace, *War Between The States — Why?* (Published by Charles T. Pace), 29.

believed, because there is no order for any such movement. Explain the meaning of this report.[247]

Anderson responded:

> The telegram is correct. I abandoned Fort Moultrie because I was certain that if attacked my men must have been sacrificed, and the command of the harbor lost. I spiked the guns and destroyed the carriages to keep the guns from being used against us.[248]

Over the next several months, there were multiple pleas from the South Carolina government for Union troops to evacuate the fort. Those and later pleas from Confederate Brigadier General Beauregard were ignored.

Prior to Lincoln's election, President Buchanan attempted to reinforce Fort Sumter. In January 1861, the *Star of the West*, a merchant ship, carried troops below the deck as it headed to Fort Sumter. The Confederates intercepted the vessel and fired a cannon volley across its bow. Receiving no support from the fort, the *Star of the West* promptly turned around and headed back north. This effort to resupply and/or reinforce Fort Sumter was derailed and signaled that South Carolina was serious about defending her sovereign rights.

Lack of a decisive response by Lincoln would show him as a weak leader and likely alienate many in the North, especially fellow

---

[247] *The War of the Rebellion: A Compilation of the Official Records of the Union and Confederate Armies: Reports:—No. 1: Maj. Robert Anderson, First U.S. Artillery, of the evacuation of Fort Moultrie,* Prepared under the direction of the Secretary of War, by Bvt. Lieut. Col. Robert N. Scott, Third U.S. Artillery and published pursuant to Act of Congress approved June 16, 1880, (Washington: Government Printing Office, 1883), 2-3, http://www.simmonsgames.com/research/authors/USWarDept/ORA/TOC.html, (Accessed April 23, 2016).

[248] Ibid.

Republicans. However, blatant aggression would almost assuredly diminish support in the Border States and fuel reaction from the anti-war segment of the North. Simply withdrawing from the fort would give legitimacy to the Confederate States, which Lincoln vehemently opposed.[249]

The day after his inauguration,[250] Lincoln received a message from Major Anderson, explaining the fort had less than six weeks of food remaining. Through an agreement with South Carolina Governor Francis W. Pickens, food was routinely sent to the garrison at Fort Sumter. However, the Confederate government was growing tired of Lincoln's refusal to compromise, and it was fast approaching time for the federal troops to leave Southern territory.

Lincoln's refusal to negotiate peace after numerous attempts by the South bought time for him and his cabinet to develop a plan to paint the South as the aggressor. From a strategic and perception perspective, it was in the Lincoln Administration's best interest for the South to fire the first shot. In war, the guilty party is not

---

[249] Fort Sumter was critical to the Lincoln Administration. On March 3, 1861, Lincoln and his cabinet met to discuss the situation. Attendees included: New York Republican William Seward, called "Prime Minister", Salmon P. Chase (treasury), Simon Cameron (war), Montgomery Blair (postmaster general), Edward Bates (attorney general), Gideon Welles (Navy secretary), Caleb Smith (interior) and Lincoln's secretary, John Nicolay. Inaction was seen as potentially embarrassing for the Union and his party; however, nothing was settled at this meeting. To rally support, Lincoln knew he needed a confrontation before Congress returned in July 1861. Actual military action would likely receive rubber-stamp approval from Congress.

[250] A line in the sand was drawn the day after Lincoln and his cabinet met to discuss supplying Fort Sumter. In his Inaugural Address, Lincoln set the stage for invasion and bloodshed; the Southern people understood the threat. Lincoln said he would... "use federal power to hold federal property (the forts) and 'collect the duties and imposts: but beyond what may be necessary for these objects, there will be no invasion, no using of force against or among the people anywhere.'" The forts were directly linked to tariff collection, declared to be the reason for invasion.

necessarily who fires the first shot but rather the party that creates a reason for the first shot to be fired.[251]

Winfield "Old Fuss and Feathers" Scott's military career covered over fifty years and multiple wars. He had also run unsuccessfully for the presidency in 1852 as a Whig. His opinions were valued, and on March 11, 1861, Lincoln read Scott's opinion to the cabinet. Scott leaned toward conciliation and withdrawal of federal troops from Sumter and Pickens. He estimated Anderson could hold out for a short time, but the magnitude of a "relief expedition would have to include 25,000 men and a fleet of warships."[252] However, Postmaster General Montgomery Blair saw things differently. Blair, a Maryland politician, lawyer, and abolitionist from a slave holding family, was less pessimistic about losing the fort. He based this reasoning on his knowledge of a well-conceived plan devised by his brother-in-law, Gustavus V. Fox. An eighteen year navy veteran, Fox developed a strategy to make the South appear as the aggressor while simultaneously saving face for the Union. The plan had been proposed to Buchanan and he rejected it. Fox suggested a naval expedition consisting of a fleet of ships with an announced intention of taking only food and supplies to Anderson and his men. They would sail under the pretense the mission was strictly benevolent, thus there should be no attack on the fort. The ruse was that the ships would also secretly carry armed soldiers and sailors.

Lincoln met with Fox on March 14 and listened to his proposed plan. The next day Lincoln provided a summary of the proposal for his cabinet to consider. He asked each member to

---

[251] Astute observers of the situation, Jefferson Davis and Alexander Stephens both knew Lincoln's goal was to portray the South as the instigator. Lincoln would gain a political edge at home and abroad if it was perceived that the South initiated the conflict.

[252] Webb Garrison, *The Lincoln No One Knows* (Nashville, Tennessee: Rutledge Hill Press, 1993), 81.

provide a written response stating whether or not they thought resupplying Fort Sumter was the right course.[253]

Lamon and S.A. Hurlbut, an Illinois politician and diplomat, were sent by Lincoln to Charleston to monitor Union support, but there was little to be found. Lamon met with Governor Pickens, who explained an attempt to resupply the fort would be considered an act of war that would evoke a military response. Upon their return, Hurlbut and Lamon reported their findings.

Lincoln favored taking action to relieve the fort, and on March 29, interviewed army engineer Montgomery Meigs about the possibility of reinforcing both Fort Sumter and Fort Pickens.[254] Meigs told Lincoln enough volunteers could be found to accomplish reinforcement, but higher-ranking officers (than Meigs) should make the final decision. Navy Secretary Welles agreed with Lincoln and the decision was made to reinforce.

One factor either overlooked or intentionally ignored was the December 6, 1860, armistice between the U.S. government and the State of South Carolina. There was also a January 29, 1861, armistice between the U.S. government and authorities from the State of Florida. Under these armistices, reinforcement of Sumter or Pickens was considered an act of war. These agreements did not go unnoticed in the South. Confederate General Braxton Bragg commented: "They have placed an engineer officer at Fort Pickens to violate, as I consider, our agreement not to reinforce. I do not believe that we are entirely absolved from all agreement of January 29."[255]

---

[253] There was a considerable degree of reluctance resulting in five no votes, one yes vote (Blair) and one maybe (Chase).

[254] Lincoln sent follow-up inquiries to his cabinet and only Attorney General Bates and War Secretary Cameron failed to support reinforcement. Perhaps a re-reading of Lincoln's inaugural address or his clear displeasure about the initial vote caused the rest of the cabinet to reverse their earlier opinions.

[255] Mildred Lewis Rutherford, *Truths of History* (Harrisonburg, Virginia: Old South Institute Press, 2009), 8. Original source: O.R.I., 457.

Regardless of any armistice violations, once the decision was made, the plan was to be executed.

Despite Seward's insistence that Fort Sumter would be abandoned by Federal troops, Lincoln had gotten his way. Under the command of Fox, a fleet of ships departed for Fort Sumter on April 6, 1861. The steamers USS *Pawnee* and USS *Powhatan* transported about 300 sailors. The armed steamer USS *Pocahontas* along with Revenue Cutter USS *Harriet Lane* and the steamer *Baltic* carried additional troops. After rebuffing Confederate peace efforts, the "Lincoln government...announced to Governor Pickens that twelve vessels with an aggregate force of 285 guns and 2,400 men had already sailed for Fort Sumter!"[256] The USS *Harriet Lane* was first to reach South Carolina waters, arriving just prior to midnight on April 11, 1861. Lincoln's alleged reason for reinforcing Fort Sumter was largely based on the possibility that Anderson's men would run out of food by April 15.[257]

Lincoln notified South Carolina Governor Pickens of the expedition. Pickens told Beauregard, who imparted the information to Davis, whereupon Davis instructed Beauregard to handle the situation. On April 11, Beauregard sent Colonel James Chestnut, Jr., Captain Stephen D. Lee, and Lieutenant A.R. Chisolm to meet with Anderson and demand surrender of the fort or face possible military reprisal. Anderson refused to surrender.

---

[256] Michael Andrew Grissom, *Southern By The Grace Of God* (Gretna, Louisiana: Pelican Publishing Company, 1990), 104.

[257] Many on both sides noted the Union aggression: *"But the fact remained that the sailing of this expedition was the second act of hostile aggression. Yet nearly all present historians with a full knowledge of these facts unite in saying the South struck the first blow. But as already stated the onus of beginning it was on the South in the popular mind and all parties at the North were now in support of war. And a similar effect on a smaller scale took place at the South. Virginia and some other states had not yet seceded and would not have seceded at all in all probability, had not the North committed itself to the policy of coercion."* — General E. P. Alexander, *Fighting for the Confederacy* (Chapel Hill, North Carolina: The University of North Carolina Press, 1989), 29-30.

Beauregard consulted with Secretary of War, Leroy Walker, and on April 12 at 1:00 A.M., the aides were sent back to the fort. They told Anderson, that if he would provide a specific time for evacuating the fort, Union troops would be allowed to leave peacefully. After Anderson consulted with his senior officers, he sent word that the fort would be abandoned at noon on April 15 unless he received instructions to the contrary, or additional U.S. government supplies were delivered to him. Based on instructions from Beauregard, Anderson's ambiguous answer was unsatisfactory to Chestnut, and Chestnut told Anderson that Confederate troops would fire on the fort within the hour. Anderson walked back to the boat with the departing Confederate representatives, then shook their hands and commented, "If we do not meet again in this world, I hope we may meet in the better one."[258]

On April 12 at 4:30 A.M., Confederate batteries commenced firing on Fort Sumter, and the firing continued for thirty-four straight hours. Reports vary as to who actually initiated the firing. Edmund Ruffin, a Virginia agronomist and ardent secessionist, made the claim that he fired the first shot. There is also a contention that Lieutenant Henry S. Farley, while commanding two mortars on James Island, fired the first shots. There was return fire from the garrison but it accomplished nothing.

On April 13, Anderson surrendered, and the fort was evacuated. There was much jubilation among the Charleston residents. No Union deaths resulted and one Confederate bled to death after receiving a wound from a cannon misfire. One Union soldier died and another was mortally wounded midway through a 100 shot salute to the federal occupants of Fort Sumter.[259]

The South's firing on Fort Sumter achieved the expected results. After the initial bombardment, Northern newspapers rallied behind Lincoln's call for 75,000 volunteers from each State. Most

---

[258] "Fort Sumter - April 12-14, 1861," *US CivilWar.com*, http://www.us-civilwar.com/sumter.htm, (Accessed April 23, 2016).

[259] The practice was later changed to 50 shot salutes.

Northern States responded quickly but the Southern States of Virginia, Tennessee, North Carolina, and Arkansas refused to take up arms in response to what they felt was an unconstitutional directive.[260] War had become a reality.[261]

As a point of historical fact, an incident at Fort Barrancas predated the hostilities at Fort Sumter. Fort Barrancas was critical regarding protection of Pensacola Bay and the Pensacola Navy Yard. During Buchanan's administration, Union troops committed the first act of aggression against the South. Fort Barrancas was the only fort

---

[260] Confederate spy Rose O'Neal Greenhow frequented Washington's high society. Curious about Fort Sumter, Greenhow asked Oregon Senator and Lincoln adviser Edward D. Baker, about the South Carolina situation. Baker surmised Lincoln felt he had a debt to pay his supporters and needed a cause to unify the North: *"It is true, a great many lives may be lost, and we may not succeed in reinforcing Fort Sumter. But the President was elected by a Northern majority, and they are now becoming dissatisfied; and the President owes it to them to strike some blow by which he will make a unified Northern party."* – From Grissom's *Southern By The Grace Of God* (Gretna, Louisiana: Pelican Publishing Company, 1990), 103.

[261] Alexander Stephens and Jefferson Davis remarked that it was Lincoln who refused to negotiate and sought conflict. Robert Toombs, Georgia attorney and the Confederacy's first Secretary of State, often feuded with Davis; he said firing on the Union fleet would lose most of the South's support in the North but Davis felt a hostile fleet could not be allowed to enter Southern waters without retaliation. The December 1860 armistice-believed to still be in effect by the Confederacy-was seen as an avenue of retaliation; however, Lincoln had used Fox's plan to orchestrate events to make it appear the South initiated hostilities. As Davis said: "The attempt to represent us as the aggressors is as unfounded as the complaint made by the wolf against the lamb in the familiar fable. He who makes the assault is not necessarily he that strikes the blow or fires the first gun." – from *Lincoln Provoked the War*, Reflections (referencing Davis, Stephens, and Ramsdell) at: http://www.tulane.edu/~sumter/Reflections/LinWar.html (Accessed April 23, 2016).

occupied by a sizable force of federal troops. Small groups were stationed at nearby Fort Pickens and Fort McRee and the Advanced Redoubt, a part of Fort Barrancas, had no troops at all.

Lieutenant Adam J. Slemmer moved the Union soldiers occupying Fort Barrancas from their barracks into the main fort. This movement was spurred by rumors the Florida State Militia planned to seize the fort. An earlier report indicated Fort Barrancas was well armed. "The Ordnance Department in Washington had reported on January 3rd that the fort contained forty-four seacoast and garrison cannon and 20,244 pounds of gunpowder."[262] Fears of Southern troops taking the fort put the sentries on edge. On January 8, as unidentified figures walked on the drawbridge, the sentries called out but received no response. They then opened fire in the direction of the unknown men, and the figures rapidly faded from sight. The first hostile shots of the war had been fired.

It was later discovered that the men on the drawbridge dodging Union fire were volunteer soldiers from Alabama, checking out a rumor that Federal troops had evacuated the fort. Slemmer then decided Fort Pickens on Santa Rosa Island would be a more secure location and he proceeded to evacuate Fort Barrancas.

This event, which pre-dated the *Star of the West* incident as well as Fort Sumter, produced no injuries. On January 12, 1861, under the direction of Governor John Milton, Florida troops seized Fort Barrancas, which was strategically located in Pensacola Bay. Buchanan disapproved of the incident but offered no response. In May 1862, Union control of New Orleans led to the South's abandonment of the Pensacola area.

---

[262] Dale Cox, "Fort Barrancas, Florida—First Hostile Shots of the Civil War," *Explore Southern History Blog*, April 20, 2010, http://southernhistory.blogspot.com/2010/04/fort-barrancas-florida-first-hostile.html, (Accessed April 23, 2016).

Chapter Fifteen
Coercion of the Southern States

Constitutional Violation: Coercion. Article IV: *The Citizens of each State shall be entitled to all Privileges and Immunities of Citizens in the several States.*

"Your dispatch is received. In answer, I say emphatically that Kentucky will furnish no troops for the wicked purpose of subduing her sister Southern States."[263]
Kentucky Governor Beriah Magoffin responding to Secretary of War Cameron's request for troops to invade the seceded States.

"Your requisition, in my judgment, is illegal, unconstitutional, and revolutionary in its objects, inhuman and diabolical, and can not be complied with. Not one man will, of the State of Missouri, furnish or carry on such an unholy crusade."[264]
Missouri Governor C. F. Jackson responding to Cameron's request for troops.

The first question to consider is whether or not a forced Union squares with the American founding. In the early 1800s, Thomas Jefferson recognized an ominous trend. On May 26, 1810, he wrote a letter to John Tyler suggesting the country be broken into 100-person self-governing mini-republics. Witnessing the erosion of the liberties gained from the colonies' secession from the British Empire, Jefferson saw the drift toward consolidation, and

---

[263] "Lincoln's Call for Volunteers," Civil War's *Harpers Weekly*, April 27, 1861, *Son of the South*, http://www.sonofthesouth.net/leefoundation/civil-war/1861/april/call-for-volunteers.htm, (Accessed April 23, 2016).
[264] Ibid. [Similar strongly worded responses came from the governors of Tennessee, North Carolina, Arkansas, Virginia, etc.]

envisioned the inevitable path to corruption. In 1816, Jefferson shared his opinion about the perpetuity of the Union through correspondence with William Crawford, then Secretary of War, and eventually Secretary of the Treasury:

> If any State in the Union will declare that it prefers separation with the first alternative, to a continuance in union without it, I have no hesitation in saying let us separate. I would rather the States should withdraw which are for unlimited commerce and war, and confederate with those alone which are for peace and agriculture.[265]

Until the mid-1820s, Jefferson continued to write letters to friends, expressing alarm over the consolidation of power, the loss of liberty, and the growth of political parties (generally referred to as cabals in that era). Even after Jefferson's death, others who supported the States' Rights/limited government philosophy in both the South and the North maintained the Union is voluntary and States could leave it if it was in their best interest to do so.

Within the text of the Constitution, there is no mention of the union of the States being permanent. The omission of such wording by the Founders was likely intentional since States were generally seen as mini-republics within a larger republic. As a condition of ratification of the U.S. Constitution, the States of New York, Rhode Island, and Virginia included language "that they reserved the right to resume the governmental powers granted to the United States."[266]

---

[265] Cajun Huguenot, "Thomas Jefferson and Secession," *As I See It*, Sunday, August 3, 2008,
http://cajunhuguenot1.blogspot.com/2008/08/thomas-jefferson-and-secession-thomas.html, (Accessed April 23, 2016).

[266] Secession Crisis: "U.S. Constitution—The Right to Secede," March 4, 1789, The War for States' Rights, *Civil War Bluegrass*, http://civilwar.bluegrass.net/secessioncrisis/890304.html, (Accessed April 23, 2016).

Reserving the right to withdraw from the compact was understood, as withdrawal from any voluntary contractual agreement would be. George Washington served as a delegate from Virginia and presided over the Constitutional Convention. Having served such a critical role in the secession of the colonies from the British Empire, he understood the voluntary and experimental nature of the agreement, as did political leaders from both North and South.[267]

In *A View of the Constitution*, Rawle wrote that it is up to the people of a given State to decide whether or not to remain in the Union or leave it. For the majority of Southerners who attended West Point, Rawle's words simply mirrored their teaching and beliefs about American government and history.

Lincoln's refusal to negotiate peace with the South set a course toward war. As mentioned in the previous chapter, his authorization to reinforce Fort Sumter violated the December 1860 armistice the Buchanan administration had agreed upon with South Carolina.[268] Such a violation allowed for legitimate reprisal by the Confederate government. Against the wishes of many in his cabinet, Lincoln put the South in a retaliatory position. This initiation of hostilities caused a military response on April 12, 1861, when South Carolina forces fired on Fort Sumter. Once South Carolina retaliated, the Pro-Union press branded the secession of the Southern States as armed rebellion while simultaneously urging Lincoln to suppress it.

Not only did Lincoln call for 75,000 men from each State remaining in the Union to invade the seceded States to force their return, he did it with no input from Congress. It is the constitutional duty of Congress—the legislative branch—to approve war, but Lincoln chose not to immediately call them back into session.

---

[267] Senator Henry Cabot Lodge echoing this sentiment in his book about Daniel Webster, entitled *Life of Webster*, noted that the system was experimental and any State could peacefully withdraw from it.

[268] The "special agreement, armistice, at Pensacola, entered into by the United States and Florida authorities on January 29, 1861" - H.W. Johnstone's, *Truth of the War Conspiracy of 1861*, The Scuppernong Press, Wake Forest, North Carolina, 2012, 9. [Details at Cornell Univ. Library.]

When Lincoln made his initial call for coercion, only seven Southern States had left the Union. After Lincoln's request for troops "four additional states—Virginia, North Carolina, Tennessee, and Arkansas—seceded and joined the Confederacy."[269] Lincoln's call to invade the seceded States was a major reason for the secession of these four States. They questioned the nature and direction of the Union. Their logic was, "If the President of the United States intended to hold the Union together by force, they wanted out."[270] The leadership and citizenry of these four States were horrified at the thought of military coercion. Believing the Union to be a voluntary association, their addition made the Confederate States much more formidable and made the conflict more horrific.

One only has to refer back to Lincoln's January 1848 speech on the floor of the House of Representatives, while a congressman, defending the right of secession. Lincoln was making an argument about the disputed Texas-Mexico border, yet his commentary is framed as a statement of principle—a principle that mirrors the wording of the Declaration of Independence:

> Any people anywhere, being inclined and having the power, have the right to rise up and shake off the existing government, and form a new one that suits them better. This is a most valuable, a most sacred right—a right which we hope and believe is to liberate the world. Nor is this right confined to cases in which the whole people of an existing government may choose to exercise it. Any portion of such people, that can, may

---

[269] Donald W. Miller, Jr., MD, "A Jeffersonian View of the Civil War," *LewRockwell.com,* https://www.lewrockwell.com/2001/09/donald-w-miller-jr-md/a-jeffersonian-view-of-the-civil-war/, (Accessed April 23, 2016).

[270] Ibid.

revolutionize, and make their own of so much of the territory as they inhabit.[271]

Once elected, he initiated his plan of coercion, despite the lack of a force bill from Congress. Had Lincoln been so empowered, he would have had congressional authority to use the military to collect import duties. President Jackson was given a force bill in the 1830s when the nullification crises between the Federal Government and South Carolina nearly came to blows over the tariff.

There was widespread disapproval of Lincoln's coercive tactics even outside the South. Many in the North and West were just as adamant as Southerners about the voluntary nature of the Republic. The level of support for the Southern position varied within the Democratic Party, but there was general disagreement with the way Lincoln and his party handled the situation. Throughout the war, the States of New York, Ohio, and Illinois were rife with Pro-Southern sentiment.

The Republicans were aware of the strong anti-war sentiment in the North. Union Navy Secretary Welles, said, "The Democrats were in sympathy with the rebels... and opposed to the war itself." [272] The Pro-Southern Democrats were adamant about their God-given right to government by consent. The intensity of resistance from the North is reflected in the multitude of statements and actions against Lincoln's plan.

In Indiana, Radical Republican Governor Oliver P. Morton ordered the arrest of Southern sympathizers and used any tactics he

---

[271] "Lincoln on Secession in 48 and 61," This Sacred Right will Liberate the World, Richmond Times Dispatch—July 10, 1861, *Civil War Daily,* http://dlxs.richmond.edu/cgi/t/text/text-idx?c=ddr;cc=ddr;type=simple;rgn=div2;q1=july%2010%2C%201861;view=text;subview=detail;sort=occur;idno=ddr0214.0020.009;node=ddr0214.0020.009%3A6.1, (Accessed April 23, 2016).

[272] Charles L.C. Minor, *The Real Lincoln* (Harrisonburg, Virginia: Sprinkle Publications, 1904), 134. Original source: *Atlantic Monthly, Vol. XVI,* 266.

felt necessary to undermine the anti-war Democrats who controlled the Indiana General Assembly.

Thomas Reynolds, the Democratic ex-Governor of Missouri and Chief Justice of the Illinois Supreme Court, said on December 28, 1860: "I am heart and soul with the South. She is right in principle from the Constitution."[273]

Democrat James S. Thayer of New York made an ominous prediction on January 21, 1861:

> If the incoming Administration shall attempt to carry out a line of policy which has been foreshadowed, we announce that, when the hand of Black Republicanism turns to blood red, and seeks from the fragment of the Constitution to construct a scaffolding for coercion, another name for execution, we will reverse the order of the French Revolution and save the blood of the people by making those who would inaugurate a Reign of Terror the first victim of a national guillotine.[274]

In an April 4, 1861, interview with Mr. Russell, a correspondent with the *London Times*, Secretary of State Seward said forceful subjugation of the South was the antithesis of the way American Government was supposed to work. Seward stated, "It would be contrary to the spirit of American Government to use armed force to subjugate the South. If the people of the South want to stay out of the Union, if they desire independence, let them have it."[275]

---

[273] Mildred Lewis Rutherford, *Truths of History* (Harrisonburg, Virginia: Old South Institute Press, 2009), 21.

[274] Ezra Carman, *The Maryland Campaign of 1862 — Volume I, South Mountain*, Edited and Annotated by Thomas G. Clemens, New York, New York: Savos Beatie LLC, 2010), 63.

[275] George Edmonds, *Facts and Falsehoods Concerning the War on the South 1861-1865* (Wiggins, Mississippi: Crown Rights Book Company Liberty Reprint Series, 1997), 160.

Less than a week later, on April 10, 1861, Seward wrote to Charles Francis Adams, Sr., Minister to England: "Only a despotic and imperial government can coerce seceding States." [276] Seward made these comments with near certain awareness that such a program was being formulated.

The *New York Herald* editorialized:

> The day before Fort Sumter was surrendered two-thirds of the newspapers in the North opposed coercion in any shape or form, and sympathized with the South. Three-fifths of the entire American people sympathized with the South. Over 200,000 voters opposed coercion and believed the South had a right to secede. [277]

Gerald Hallock and David Hale, both staunch opponents of the tactics of the Republican Party, published *The Journal of Commerce*. Their strong stance against coercion was met with the U.S. Post Office's refusal to carry their papers.

President Buchanan expressed to Stanton, who served as his Attorney General and later as Secretary of War under Lincoln and Johnson, that the Constitution did not provide any power to the central government to coerce a seceding State.

In his book, *American Conflict*, Horace Greeley wrote: "There was not a moment when a large portion of the Northern Democracy was not hostile to any form or shade of coercion. Many openly condemned and stigmatized a war on the South as atrocious, unjustifiable, and aggressive." [278]

Charles Beecher Stowe, son of Harriet Beecher Stowe, in an address at Fisk University in Nashville, Tennessee, offered the following commentary:

---

[276] Rutherford, *Truths of History*, 19. [From Seward's April 10, 1861, correspondence with Charles Francis Adams, Sr., Minister in England.]

[277] Ibid. Original source: The *New York Herald*.

[278] Ibid., 20-21. Original source: Horace Greeley, *American Conflict*, 513.

Many patriotic men of the South who cared little or nothing about slavery were stirred with the deepest indignation at the suggestion of the National government subduing a sovereign State by force of arms, and said that a Union that could only be held together by bayonets had better be dissolved; and for the principle of State rights and State sovereignty the Southern men fought with a holy ardor and self-denying patriotism that have covered even defeat with imperishable glory.[279]

Stowe admitted the Southern belief in limited, consensual government was an admirable endeavor despite the tragic results the South endured.

Massachusetts lawyer, editor, and author John T. Morse wrote in his two-volume biography about Lincoln. "History is crowded with tales of despots, but of no despot who thought or decided with the taciturn independence which marked this president of the Free American Republic in regard to coercing seceding States."[280]

There was a sizable group of abolitionists mainly associated with Garrison and Phillips that opposed coercion. They recognized the Southern States had a right to self-determination and that it was best for slaveholding States to secede and form their own country. Under this logic, the four slave States that remained in the Union (five counting West Virginia) should have had the same option.

Even within the Republican Party, there was a lack of universal agreement. The party's platform strongly denounced an

---

[279] Charles Beecher Stowe, "Honest Confession Good for the Country," *Confederate Veteran Magazine* (Publication of the United Confederate Veterans), Volume 19, Number 7, July 1911, 326, http://www.usgennet.org/usa/ga/county/macon/newspapers/CV/cv1911pg 12.htm, (Accessed April 23, 2016).

[280] Rutherford, *Truths of History*, 20. Original source: *American Statesman Series*, Morse in *Vol. II.*, 'Life of Abraham Lincoln.'

armed invasion of any State or territory under any pretext. Stanton biographer George Gorham noted the internal split in the party. Where Lincoln and his supporters demanded an unbroken Union, prominent Republicans such as Greeley and Chase were fine with disunion, feeling "a union of non-slave-holding States would be preferable to any attempt to maintain by force the Union with the slaveholding States."[281]

Indeed, Horace Greeley summed it up succinctly in November 1860, by recognizing the South's right to consider whether or not the Union served its interests. Greeley wrote:

> ...we maintain that they have a perfect right to discuss it; nay, we hold with Jefferson to the inalienable right of communities to alter or abolish forms of government that have become oppressive or injurious, and if the Cotton States decide that they can do better out of the Union than in it, we insist on letting them go in peace. The right to secede may be a revolutionary one, but it exists nevertheless, and we don't see how one party can have a right to do what another has a right to prevent.[282]

Halfway through the war, negative reaction had not abated. In 1863, a myriad of issues remained. The Peace Democrats in the North became emboldened by the anti-war sentiment of Northerners whose constitutional rights were being violated by the Lincoln Administration. In some areas of the North, reaction to draft

---

[281] George C. Gorham, *Life and Public Services of Edwin M. Stanton* (Boston and New York: Houghton, Mifflin and Company, Boston and New York, 1899, Volume I), 193, University of California, http://babel.hathitrust.org/cgi/pt?id=ucl.$b539234;view=1up;seq=231, (Accessed April 23, 2016).

[282] Lyon Gardiner Tyler, *The Gray Book: A Confederate Catechism* (Wiggins, Mississippi: Crown Rights Book Co. — The Liberty Reprint Series, 1997), 33. Originally printed in *Tyler's Quarterly* in Volume 33, October and January issues, 1935.

officers included forced resistance. The severity of anti-war sentiment in the North led Lincoln to suspend the *writ of habeas corpus* throughout the Union. (Detailed in the chapter concerning suspension of the *Writ of Habeas Corpus*.)

Lincoln felt an obligation to promote his party's survival. Failure to subdue the South would have likely destroyed the Republican Party. Union General McClellan noted this element of party rivalry and distrust. McClellan, a Democrat who believed in honorable warfare as he was taught at West Point, opposed the destruction of civilian property and felt the violation of the civil rights of Northerners was wrong. For these and other reasons, he was widely distrusted by the Radical Republicans.

McClellan felt Stanton and Lincoln had betrayed him during the Peninsula Campaign in the spring of 1862 when thousands of his troops were pulled and his recommended troop movements were rejected. W.C. Prime, journalist and historian from Cambridge, New York, echoed this sentiment by arguing the Radical Republicans sabotaged McClellan during this campaign "because they wanted to prolong the war so they could ravage and subjugate the South and consolidate their own political power."[283] The Radical Republicans, in particular, saw the opportunity for both financial and political gain. "If McClellan had taken Richmond, it would have been an end of the Republican party."[284] Also, if (hypothetically) President McClellan had spared the South from Reconstruction, occupation, and martial law, the Republican Party could not have instituted their Hamiltonian ideology. For many Republicans, the party and its corporate interests held more importance than the constitution.

Lincoln scholar David Herbert Donald summarized the rewards expected by coercion of the Southern States, noting the

---

[283] Michael T. Griffith, "The Smearing of General George B. McClellan," 2014, *miketgriffith.com*, http://miketgriffith.com/files/smearingmcclellan.htm, (Accessed April 23, 2016).

[284] Minor, 138. [From a conversation between A.K. McLure and Charles Minor.]

Radicals were anxious to control the government to promote their industrial interests. John Sherman, Republican Senator from Ohio and brother to Union General Sherman, was not bashful in expressing their goals. Sherman's expectations for Lincoln were "to secure to free labor its just right to the Territories of the United States; to protect...by wise revenue laws, the labor of our people; to secure the public lands to actual settlers...; to develop the internal resources of the country by opening new means of communication between the Atlantic and the Pacific."[285] Donald keenly translated the meaning that "the Radicals intended to enact a high protective tariff that mothered monopoly, to pass a homestead law that invited speculators to loot the public domain, and to subsidize a transcontinental railroad that afforded infinite opportunities for jobbery."[286] Charles Sumner complained that key Union victories too soon might not allow the Radicals enough time to completely institute their program of industrial supremacy.

Echoing Donald's observations were those of Southern Conservative scholar, M.E. Bradford, who noted, "A great increase in the tariff and the formation of a national banking network...were the cornerstones of this great alteration in the posture of the Federal government toward the sponsorship of business."[287] Bradford went on to describe Lincoln's cautious manner relative to openly expressing the underlying Republican (largely Radical Republican) agenda. However, "in private he made it clear that the hidden agenda of the Republicans would have its turn, once the stick was in their hand."[288] Lincoln ultimately delivered as "the tariff rose from 18.84 percent to 47.56 percent. And it stayed above 40 percent in all but two years of the period concluded with the election of Woodrow

---

[285] David Herbert Donald, *Lincoln Reconsidered* (New York, New York: Vintage Books, A Division of Random House, Inc., 2001), 106.

[286] Ibid.

[287] M.E. Bradford, *Remembering Who We Are — Observations of a Southern Conservative* (Athens, Georgia: The University of Georgia Press, 1985), 147.

[288] Ibid.

Wilson."[289] Virginia historian Ludwell H. Johnson referenced that such a massive welfare transfer was one of Calhoun's greatest fears. Then, as now, factions within Wall Street held strong influence over government actions.

Another vital part of this agenda lay in passage of the 1862 Legal Tender Act along with the National Banking Acts of 1863 and 1864. This resulted in "$480 million of fiat money that was soon depreciated by two-thirds in relation to specie...all notes but the greenback dollar were taxed out of existence, excepting only United States Treasury bonds that all banks were required to purchase to have a share in the war boom."[290] The bonds were supported by debt, as advocated by Hamilton, and the central bankers controlled the supply of money, credit, lending, etc.

Keeping the South in the Union and eliminating the Plains Indians (impediments to the railroads) were critical for the success of this agenda. Military coercion of the Southern States, rather than legitimate attempts to compromise, was the route chosen. Ultimately, Lincoln delivered to the Radical Republicans what they expected.

---

[289] Ibid.
[290] Ibid., 147-148.

Chapter Sixteen
Blockading Southern Ports

Constitutional Violation: Article 1, Section 8: *Unauthorized declaration of war through Blockading Parts of States that Were Held by the Federal Government to still be in the Union.*[291]

"The Northern States could not claim the rights of belligerents for themselves, and on the other hand deal with other parties not as belligerents, but as rebels."[292]
Earl Derby, in the British House of Lords

General Winfield Scott developed the Anaconda Plan to surround and squeeze the Southern States like a boa constrictor. Scott's goal was to impede trade into and out of the Confederate States by placing a strong barrier around the Southern coast. Part of the logic arose from the dearth of manufacturing and industry as well as the limited number of major ports in the South. This military measure was seen as a way to severely cripple the South's ability to wage war against the North. The blockade was intended to harm every Southern man, woman, and child.[293] Following Scott's advice, on April 19, 1861, Lincoln imposed a blockade on Southern ports

---

[291] Throughout the course of history, blockades have been considered acts of war.

[292] Edgar Lee Masters, *Lincoln The Man* (Columbia, South Carolina: The Foundation for American Education, 1997), 406.

[293] Lyon Gardiner Tyler claimed: "A low tariff would have attracted the trade of the world to the South, and its cities would have become great and important centers of commerce. A fear of this prosperity induced Lincoln to make war upon the South." Source: *The Gray Book—A Confederate Catechism*, 8. Originally printed in *Tyler's Quarterly* in Volume 33, October and January issues, 1935.

"thereby assuming authority to take actions hitherto considered as requiring a declaration of war."[294]

The Union Navy violated the U.S. Constitution by blockading the ports of States Lincoln claimed never actually left the Union.[295] A country cannot blockade its own ports; the blockade was a *de facto* admission that the Confederate States of America was indeed a separate country. Lincoln lacked constitutional authority to start a war via a blockade or any other means. Knowing the deprivation associated with a blockade, even Lincoln's most ardent admirers do not describe his actions as humanitarian.[296] The points of emphasis of Abraham Lincoln's *Proclamation of Blockade* are revealing.

---

[294] Myles Kantor, "Getting Right with Lincoln as a Libertarian," *LewRockwell.com*, Dec. 14, 2000, https://www.lewrockwell.com/2000/12/myles-kantor/getting-right-with-lincoln-as-a-libertarian/, (Accessed April 23, 2016).

[295] April 19 is the same date as First Blood, when the Sixth Massachusetts clashed with Baltimore civilians. By initiating conflict, a Rubicon was crossed; when Congress convened in July 1861 they would have little choice but to sanction Lincoln's actions. By then, the Union army would be ready for action and the press could sway public opinion in the North to defend the flag. Free speech and press could be controlled as needed. As Edgar Lee Masters noted, Lincoln "was master of the lives of men under the laws of piracy for trying to run the blockade. He was thus an emperor with full despotic power and his rightful masters had had no word to say about it."[295] From: Masters, *Lincoln The Man*, 399.

[296] Blockading Southern ports centered on revenue collection, as stated in the first paragraph of the proclamation. During a memorable exchange between English author Charles Dickens and English economist John Stuart Mill, Dickens explained the fiscal nature of the schism: "Union means so many millions a year lost to the South; secession means the loss of the same millions to the North." From: Adams, *Those Dirty Rotten Taxes*, 88.

BY THE PRESIDENT OF THE UNITED STATES OF AMERICA:

A PROCLAMATION:

Whereas an insurrection against the Government of the United States has broken out in the States of South Carolina, Georgia, Alabama, Florida, Mississippi, Louisiana, and Texas, and the laws of the United States for the collection of the revenue cannot be effectually executed therein conformably to that provision of the Constitution which requires duties to be uniform throughout the United States:

And whereas a combination of persons engaged in such insurrection, have threatened to grant pretended letters of marque to authorize the bearers thereof to commit assaults on the lives, vessels, and property of good citizens of the country lawfully engaged in commerce on the high seas, and in waters of the United States: And whereas an Executive Proclamation has been already issued, requiring the persons engaged in these disorderly proceedings to desist therefrom, calling out a militia force for the purpose of repressing the same, and convening Congress in extraordinary session, to deliberate and determine thereon:

Now, therefore, I, Abraham Lincoln, President of the United States, with a view to the same purposes before mentioned, and to the protection of the public peace, and the lives and property of quiet and orderly citizens pursuing their lawful occupations, until Congress shall have assembled and deliberated on the said unlawful proceedings, or until the same shall have ceased, have further deemed it advisable to set on foot a blockade of the ports within the States aforesaid, in pursuance of the laws of the United States, and of the law of Nations, in such case provided. For this purpose a competent force will be posted so as to prevent entrance and exit of vessels from the ports aforesaid. If, therefore, with a view to violate such blockade, a vessel shall approach, or shall attempt to leave either of the said ports, she will be duly warned by the Commander of one of the blockading vessels, who will endorse on her register the fact and date of such warning, and if the same vessel shall again attempt to enter or leave the blockaded port, she will be captured and sent to the nearest convenient port, for such proceedings against her and her cargo as prize, as may be deemed advisable.

And I hereby proclaim and declare that if any person, under the pretended authority of the said States, or under any other pretense, shall molest a vessel of the United States, or the persons or cargo on board of her, such person will be held amenable to the laws of the United States for the prevention and punishment of piracy.

In witness whereof, I have hereunto set my hand, and caused the seal of the United States to be affixed.

Done at the City of Washington, this nineteenth day of April, in the year of our Lord one thousand eight hundred and sixty-one, and of the Independence of the United States the eighty-fifth.

ABRAHAM LINCOLN

By the President:

WILLIAM H. SEWARD, Secretary of State[297]

In the first paragraph, Lincoln mentions *the laws of the United States for the collection of the revenue* but nowhere in the text is there any mention of slavery. The blockade was a war measure with a stated goal of revenue collection from the seceded Southern States and to keep imported goods from coming to the South. In the proclamation, Lincoln referenced violation of the regulatory and nondiscriminatory trade element, noted in the Constitution's Commerce Clause: "No preference shall be given by any regulation of commerce or revenue to the ports of one state over those of

---

[297] "Proclamation of Blockade Against Southern Ports, April 19, 1861," *Angelfire*,
http://www.angelfire.com/my/abrahamlincoln/Blockade.html, (Accessed April 23, 2016).

another."[298] This issue of discriminatory import taxes had raised its head periodically since the creation of the original confederation. Every time the average import rate far exceeded the benchmark, the Southern States protested it.

Despite the wording of the constitution and his insistence that the Southern States weren't really out of the Union, Lincoln asserted the blockade was legal and part of his oath as President of the United States. He claimed the South was not adhering to the nebulous concept he referred to as the *national authority*. This event was a prelude to the post-war policy of supposedly *letting the Southern States back in the Union* when Lincoln repeatedly claimed the States never left it.

To rationalize the blockade, Lincoln used sophistry, by claiming the Southern States weren't *literally* out of the Union but instead they were out of their *practical relationship* with the Union. Conversely, if it is acknowledged that the Southern States legitimately left the Union, the Confederacy was "a foreign nation, and his proclamation was an act of war; and thus he had usurped power, for the war power is vested in Congress, not in the president." [299] Each seceded State held a popular vote or called representatives from their individual counties to their respective capitols and voted whether or not to leave the Union; the criterion of government by consent was fulfilled.

The blockade had several detrimental economic effects on Southern life. For example, "the blockade had an influence on *relative prices* within the Confederacy and, even more important, on relative shortages of goods and services."[300] An almost immediate problem was that "Speculation and hoarding caused prices to rise in advance of the initial currency depreciation by the Confederates in

---

[298] Masters, 404.

[299] Ibid.

[300] Mark Thornton and Robert B. Ekelund, Jr., *Tariffs, Blockades and Inflation: The Economics of the Civil War* (Wilmington, Delaware: A Scholarly Resources Inc. Imprint, 2004), 34.

these markets."[301] Also, military and civilian supplies were routed circuitously (increasing transit times) through the Bahamas and Bermuda to ensure delivery. As often happens during conflict, human ingenuity adapts to the situation; the blockade helped stimulate technological advancements and served as a catalyst for the development of steam-powered vessels versus the generally less efficient sail-powered ships.

Despite the Union's actions, the South was capable of breaking the blockade and managed to harass many of the Union ships. The CSS *Alabama*, built in Liverpool, England, and commanded by Admiral Raphael Semmes was probably the most effective. Indeed, the notoriety and courage of Semmes is legendary. Not only was he an accomplished admiral, the economically astute Semmes knew major damage was done to U.S. shipping through the escalation of insurance costs. "His exploits raised maritime insurance rates in the United States and encouraged merchant vessels to change their national registry. At one point Welles committed more than two dozen ships to the search for the elusive *Alabama*."[302] Concern over insurance was reflected in the reaction from Massachusetts Governor John A. Andrews, in his July 16, 1861, letter to U.S. Navy Secretary Welles: "In view of the exploits of Southern privateers within the last few days off our coast, a feeling of apprehension has come to pervade our mercantile community...[and] there is serious trouble among all our insurance companies."[303]

Semmes and other Confederate raiders were considered to be pirates in much of the North. Semmes, dubbed by Welles as "this

[301] Ibid.

[302] Craig L. Symonds, *The Naval Institute Historical Atlas of the U.S. Navy* (Annapolis, Maryland: Naval Institute Press) January 15, 2013, 102.

[303] Rick Beard (Civil War Historian), "The Pirate Sumter," *The New York Times,* June 29, 2011, http://opinionator.blogs.nytimes.com/2011/06/29/the-pirate-sumter/?_php=true&_type=blogs&_r=0, (Accessed April 23, 2016).

wolf from Liverpool," [304] inflicted upwards of six million dollars of damage on U.S. shipping interests with the affect of "driving insurance rates through the roof, effectively wrecking Union shipping for almost two years and inflicting a wound to American commerce from which it took almost a century to recover." [305] Though Semmes and the *Alabama* set the standard, other active cruisers, such as the *Florida*, captained by John H. Maffett, and the *Shenandoah*, captained by James Waddell, also damaged Northern shipping interests.

As the Confederacy attempted to hold its ground, there were notable successes despite the fact the South's Navy was almost non-existent. For example, through sleight of hand, the Confederates made it appear their troop strength was greater than it actually was and the Federals abandoned Gosport Navy Yard (now the Norfolk Naval Shipyard) in Portsmouth, Virginia on April 20, 1861. Also, though they lacked resources to keep pace with Union shipbuilding, the Confederates were able to salvage and/or capture some Yankee warships and put them in service. One of the captured Union ships was the partially burned *USS Merrimac*, which the Confederacy converted into the *CSS Virginia*. This ship later engaged in the epic ironclad battle with the *USS Monitor*. At the beginning of the war, there was criticism of the Union having a paper blockade, but given the extreme limitations in the South, "the Confederate Navy was just as often hardly more than a paper navy." [306]

The blockade also created a profit incentive for private blockade-runners. There were some Confederate-owned blockade-runners, but most "blockade-running was carried on by private interests and contractors who shipped combined cargoes of private

---

[304] John C. Fazio, "Intrepid Mariners: John Winslow & Raphael Semmes of the CSS Alabama," *The Cleveland Civil War Roundtable*, http://clevelandcivilwarroundtable.com/articles/naval/intrepid_mariners.htm, (Accessed April 23, 2016).

[305] Ibid.

[306] Richard B. Harwell, *The Confederate Reader* (New York, New York: Barnes & Noble Books, 1992), 65.

goods and supplies for the Confederate military." [307] Private blockade running, like any other market activity with a profit incentive, was superior to that provided by government. Defying common sense, the Confederate government's attempts at controlling blockade running only decreased its effectiveness. Just as the self-imposed King Cotton policy,[308] which was initially more effective than the Union blockade, this strategy was self-defeating and void of economic logic.

The initially suspect Union Navy, with advantages in manufacturing and funding, was strengthened throughout the war whereas the Confederate Navy eventually (and predictably) went into decline. When the Union initiated the blockade it had less than fifty vessels, with only a few suitable for such duty. Welles started a massive buildup of ships and had others converted to blockade duty. "By the end of the year, Welles reported to Congress that the navy had purchased 136 ships and had 52 under construction."[309]

Despite all of these efforts, the government's buildup of ships and threats to capture pirates slowed down, but did not stop blockade-runners from getting goods to the South. Through bravery, ingenuity, and the rewards of handsome profits, a high percentage of blockade-runners were successful. "About 300 ships tried to run

---

[307] Thornton and Ekelund, Jr., 29.

[308] Using poor economic judgment, the Confederate Government intentionally withheld cotton from the European market, hoping it would encourage England and France to intervene on the South's behalf. "Advocates of the King Cotton thesis thought that an embargo would cause a shortage of cotton in Europe, devastate the European (as well as Northern) textile industry..." The policy backfired, diminished the South's market, and caused Europeans to seek alternative suppliers in India, Egypt, etc.—Source: Thornton and Ekelund, Jr., *Tariffs, Blockades and Inflation: The Economics of the Civil War*, 31.

[309] Secession Crises: "Ships, Blockades and Raiders," The War for States' Rights, *Civil War Bluegrass*, http://civilwar.bluegrass.net/ShipsBlockadesAndRaiders/theblockade1.html, (Accessed April 23, 2016).

the blockade a total of 1,300 times during the war, succeeding over 1,000 times. Blockading ships captured 136 runners and destroyed 85. The average runner made four trips; the *Syren* was the most successful with 33 trips, while the Denbigh made 26 trips."[310]

The blockade of the South's ports illustrates the no-holds-barred measures instituted by the Lincoln Administration. The rarely mentioned, yet important historical significance of the blockade is found in the Official Records of the U.S. Government. Referencing the United States Supreme Court case, The Protector, 79 U.S. 12 Wall 700 700, from 1870, it is written about the war's beginning and ending:

> Its commencement in certain states will be referred to the first proclamation of blockade embracing them and made on the 19th April, 1861, and as to other states to the second proclamation of blockade embracing them, and made on the 27th April, 1861....and...Its termination as to certain states will be referred to the proclamation of the 2nd April, 1866, declaring that the war had closed in those states, and as to Texas to the proclamation of the 20th August, 1866, declaring it had closed in that state also.[311]

A little known fact is that the Confederate Navy broke the blockade in Charleston, South Carolina, at 5:00 A.M. on January 31, 1863. This prompted the following communication to Europe's consular representatives:

---

[310] Secession Crises: "Ships, Blockades and Raiders, Blockade Running 'Profits Worth the Risk,'" The War for States' Rights, *Civil War Bluegrass*, http://civilwar.bluegrass.net/ShipsBlockadesAndRaiders/blockaderunning-profits.html, (Accessed April 23, 2016).

[311] "The Protector, 70, U.S. 12 Wall 700 700, 1870," Justia, *US Supreme Court*, https://supreme.justia.com/cases/federal/us/79/700/, (Accessed April 23, 2016).

DEPARTMENT OF STATE,
RICHMOND, JANUARY 31, 1863,
Sir:

I am instructed by the President of the Confederate States of America to inform you that his government has received an official dispatch from Flag Officer Ingraham, commanding the naval forces of Confederacy in the coast of South Carolina, stating that the blockade of the harbor of Charleston has been broken by the complete dispersion and disappearance of the blockading squadron, in consequence of a successful attack made on it by the iron-clad steamers commanded by Flag Officer Ingraham. During the attack one or more of the blockading vessels were sunk or burnt.

As you are doubtless aware that, by the law of nations, a blockade when thus broken by superior force ceases to exist, and cannot be subsequently enforced unless established de novo, with adequate forces and after due notice to neutral powers, it has been deemed proper to give you the information herein contained for the guidance of such vessels of your nation as may choose to carry on commerce with the now open port of Charleston.

Respectfully, your obedient servant –
J.P. Benjamin, Secretary of State.[312]

Once the blockade was broken in Charleston, Benjamin immediately announced it to the world and proclaimed the port open for business. However, likely due to a large dose of skepticism, denial, political propaganda (detailed later in a review of the two-part Emancipation Proclamation), and the repositioning of Union ships, the breaking of the blockade went virtually unheeded.

Not only was Lincoln a master of the game of politics, he was quite the realist. He had to have realized the precarious nature of

---

[312] John Thomas Scharf, *History of the Confederate States Navy from its Organization to the Surrender of its Last Vessel* (New York, New York: Crown Publishers, 1977), 682. Originally published in Baltimore, Maryland, by Fairfax Press, 1887.

blockading roughly 3,000 miles of Southern coastline for an indeterminate time period with a Navy that was essentially a work in progress. Lincoln also knew if Britain intervened on behalf of the South, the British Navy would likely put a quick end to the blockade.

By giving the South 100 days to return to the Union and resume business as usual or have its slaves (figuratively) freed by the Emancipation Proclamation, Lincoln and Stanton had a hedge against the blockade being broken. They also had immense influence on much of the Northern media to deny any such occurrence and successfully sell it to the public. A careful study of these events leads one to surmise the Emancipation Proclamation was carefully thought out and timed for maximum benefit.

By creating the perception that the conflict had suddenly changed into a war to free the slaves, it was virtually assured that neither England nor France would formally acknowledge the Confederate States of America. Any edict issued by Lincoln should have been irrelevant, since according to international law, Charleston, South Carolina, should have been open for trade once the blockade was broken.

Chapter Seventeen
Illegal Suspension of the Writ of Habeas Corpus

Article I, Section IX, Clause 2: *The Privilege of the Writ of Habeas Corpus shall not be suspended, unless when in cases of Rebellion or Invasion the public Safety may require it.*

"Habeas corpus, a fundamental tenet of English common law, does not appear anywhere in the Bill of Rights. Its importance was such that it was enshrined in the Constitution itself. And it is of such magnitude that all other rights, including those in the Bill of Rights, are dependent upon it. Without habeas corpus, the significance of all other rights crumbles."[313]

The *Writ of Habeas Corpus* (meaning "to bring in the body") is an American citizen's right to due process under the law and is foundational to human justice. The writ is a judicial order that commands a person or government official to bring a prisoner to a specific place at a specified time to determine if the prisoner is being legally detained or if they should be released. The protection of people's legal right of defense is critical to any society that believes in liberty. The lack of *Habeas Corpus* is typical of a totalitarian government or a police state.[314]

----

[313] John Whitehead, "Habeas Corpus," *The Rutherford Institute— Dedicated to the Defense of Civil Liberties and Human Rights,* https://www.rutherford.org/constitutional_corner/habeas_corpus/, (Accessed April 23, 2016).

[314] Jacob Hornberger, attorney, former professor at the University of Dallas, founder and president of The Future of Freedom Foundation, describes the *Writ of Habeas Corpus* as "The Lynchpin of Freedom" (October 12, 2006), https://www.lewrockwell.com/2006/10/jacob-hornberger/the-linchpin-of-freedom/, (Accessed April 28, 2016).

The *Writ of Habeas Corpus* can be traced to the Magna Charta of 1215, where the rights of Englishmen were first codified under King John. Clause 39 states:

> No free man shall be seized or imprisoned, or stripped of his rights or possessions, or outlawed or exiled, or deprived of his standing in any other way, nor will we proceed with force against him, or send others to do so, except by the lawful judgement of his equals or by the law of the land.[315]

On April 15, 1861, a few days after the bombardment of Fort Sumter, Lincoln issued a call for troops to reinforce and protect Washington, D.C. The initial fear was that troops in nearby Virginia would attack the Union capitol. Virginia was alarmed by the way the federal government handled the Fort Sumter incident, but the call for volunteers to invade the seceded States was the final straw that caused the Virginia Convention to vote to leave the Union on April 17, 1861. Citizens of the State agreed and secession was ratified on May 23, 1861.

On the same day Virginia seceded, the Sixth Massachusetts Regiment boarded a train in Boston, and, along with a regiment from Pennsylvania, reached Baltimore on April 19, 1861.[316] When the civilians of Baltimore attempted to halt the federal troops near Camden Station, a riot broke out, ending in the deaths of four soldiers and twelve civilians. The tragic incident known as the Pratt

---

[315] "Magna Carta, #39," Historic Documents, *ushistory.org*, http://www.ushistory.org/documents/magnacarta.htm, (Accessed April 23, 2016).

[316] The Twenty-fifth Pennsylvania marched through Baltimore the previous day. Colonel Edward F. Jones of the Sixth Massachusetts was warned that Southern sympathizers objected to their presence; however, the regiment opted to travel via the shortest route to Washington. The Pro-Southern Eastern part of Maryland was rife with anti-Lincoln feelings. Like Virginia, they were incensed at Lincoln's call for 75,000 volunteers.

Street Riot or First Blood served as a catalyst for Baltimore's Mayor George William Brown and Maryland Governor Thomas Holliday Hicks to strongly request that future movement of troops should not come through Maryland.

After the clash, the Lincoln Administration severely restricted the rights of their opposition. On April 27, 1861, orders were sent from Lincoln to General Scott "to arrest anyone between Washington and Philadelphia suspected of subversive acts or speech, and his order specifically authorized suspension of the *writ of habeas corpus.*"[317]

Scott took Lincoln's orders and sent them down the line of command whereupon several Pro-Southern Marylanders were arrested. The arrests included George P. Kane, Baltimore Police Marshal, and George W. Brown, Mayor of Baltimore.[318] As the Maryland legislature prepared to meet, Lincoln suspected they would actively work to impede the movement of federal troops through their State.

One of the men arrested was the outspoken secessionist John Merryman, a prominent citizen of Baltimore who had served as the Maryland State Agricultural Society President. Merryman was arrested May 25, 1861, at his home in Cockeysville, Maryland, and taken to Fort McHenry. His lawyer responded the same day by filing a petition in circuit court. In that era, Supreme Court justices presided over circuit courts when the Supreme Court was not in session. Chief Justice Roger B. Taney handled the Merryman case. Based on normal legal procedure, Taney had Merryman brought before him on a *writ of habeas corpus.* He then "commanded the

---

[317] "Habeas Corpus," The American Civil War, *Online Etymology*, http://www.etymonline.com/cw/habeas.htm, (Accessed April 23, 2016).

[318] Maryland proved difficult to cross early in the war when the Lincoln administration sought additional troops to defend the U.S. Capital. There were strong secessionist leanings and many of its citizens resented the unwanted presence of the Union army on sovereign Maryland soil.

military officer in charge of Merryman to show 'the cause, if any, for his arrest and detention.'"[319]

The *writ of habeas corpus* issued by Taney was to be carried out by the arresting officer, General George Cadwalader, the Commander of Fort McHenry, where Merryman was being held. Under Lincoln's orders, Cadwalader disobeyed the writ issued by Taney, leading Taney to cite Cadwalader for contempt. In *Ex Parte Merryman*, Taney based his opinion on the Judiciary Act of 1789, Thomas Jefferson's acknowledgement that the suspension of habeas corpus is not a presidential power, and on the wording of the U.S. Constitution, which states in Article I, Section 9, that this power belongs to the legislative branch.

Though Taney had sworn Lincoln in as U.S. President, they had divergent political views. Taney, a pro-Union, States' Rights Democrat, who had freed his slaves, questioned Lincoln's seizure of powers not granted to the Executive Branch in the Constitution. One of their greatest points of contention involved presidential war powers or lack thereof.[320]

Regarding Merryman, Taney wrote a highly critical opinion of Lincoln's actions, relative to overstepping the powers granted, "holding that the arrest was unlawful and violated the Constitution and that only Congress can suspend the *writ of habeas corpus*."[321]

Taney speculated, if Lincoln's actions were allowed to stand, the people would no longer have a government of laws, but rather their right to life, liberty, and property would lie in the hands of the army officer presiding over the military district in which they reside. Highlighting the breach of constitutional law, Taney wrote, if the

---

[319] "Habeas Corpus," The American Civil War, *Online Etymology,* (Accessed April 23, 2016).

[320] Some researchers claim Seward signed the executive orders suspending habeas corpus. As with Lincoln, Taney distrusted Seward and stated he would not administer the oath of office if he became president.

[321] Charles Adams, *When in the Course of Human Events-Arguing the Case for Southern Secession* (Lanham, Maryland: Rowman & Littlefield Publishers Inc., 2000), 46.

president was allowed to suspend the *writ of habeas corpus,* then "the constitution of the United States has conferred upon him more regal and absolute power over the liberty of the citizen."[322] Concerning constitutional law, the views of Taney and Lincoln were on the opposite end of the spectrum.[323] Lincoln never attempted to appeal the ruling. He simply ignored the Supreme Court's orders.[324]

Although some skeptics allege there was no warrant to arrest Taney, multiple sources indicate otherwise. The account of Lincoln's order to arrest Taney is referenced in Lamon's private papers. Lamon, the U.S. Marshall given the warrant, also claimed Lincoln gave him discretion whether or not to issue the order. Frederick S. Calhoun, contemporary historian for the Marshall's Service, examined the records of federal marshals over a two hundred year span in *The Lawman: United States Marshall and their Deputies, 1789-1989.* This research led to Lamon's personal papers, including the time he served as Federal Marshall for the District of Colombia. The reference to the Taney arrest order was found "in a subchapter, 'Arrest of Traitors and Suspension of Habeas Corpus.'"[325] Another

---

[322] Andrew P. Napolitano, *The Constitution in Exile* (Nashville, Tennessee: Thomas Nelson, Inc. 2006), 71.

[323] As a historical reference, Taney cited William Blackstone's *Commentaries on the Laws of England* (1765-1769). Blackstone was an 18th Century English judge, jurist, author, and lecturer whose work served as a foundation on common law. To the framers, Blackstone was second only to Baron de Montesquieu's *The Spirit of Laws.* Montesquieu, a French Enlightenment era social commentator and political thinker, was an advocate of the separation of powers, which prominently found its way into the U.S. Constitution.

[324] Lincoln likely resented Taney's repudiation of his actions and signed a warrant to have Taney arrested. They disagreed about the wording of the constitution, separation of powers, protection of civil liberties, and the manner in which government should be run.

[325] Charles Adams, "The Warrant to Arrest Chief Justice Roger B. Taney: 'A Great Crime, a fabrication or Seward's Folly?'" *LewRockwell.com,* March 18, 2002, https://www.lewrockwell.com/2002/03/charles-adams/the-

reference to the order appears in the book, *Baltimore and the Nineteenth of April, 1861: A Study of War*, by Baltimore Mayor George W. Brown. Taney told Brown he was aware that his arrest had been contemplated within the Lincoln Administration. U.S. Supreme Court Justice Benjamin Robbins Curtis also referenced the order in his memoirs. Finally, author Phillip Magness referenced an account of it through the writings of Judge W.M. Merrick, Assistant Judge of the Circuit Court of the District of Colombia. There are various explanations as to why the warrant was not served.

As an example of the dangers inherent in suspension of citizen's rights, an examination of the District of Columbia Provost Marshall's records over the five-year span of June 1861 through January 1, 1866, reveals 38,000 citizens were arrested, imprisoned, and denied their habeas corpus rights. In conversation with England's Lord Lyons, Seward boasted, "that he 'could ring a bell on his desk and arrest a citizen anywhere in the United States. Could even the Queen of England do as much?'"[326]

Lincoln took the position that it was within his power to suspend the writ without approval of the Congress. He claimed, since Congress was not in session, he had the right to suspend *habeas corpus* if, in his opinion, the public safety required it. Lincoln appeared to disagree with Taney's ruling, based on his belief, "It was perfectly all right to disobey one law in order to save the nation and protect the Constitution."[327]

At the outset, many on both sides predicted a short war. In the early stages of the conflict, the various requests for Union volunteers were met through a system that essentially left recruiting up to the individual States. As early as December 1861, Union War Secretary Cameron told Northern governors not to send troops unless they were called for, even going to the extreme of closing

---

warrant-to-arrest-chief-justice-roger-b-taney-a-great-crime-a-fabrication-or-sewards-real-folly/, (Accessed April 23, 2016).

[326] Ibid.

[327] Adams, *When in the Course of Human Events*, 211.

recruiting offices. Stanton's feelings echoed those of Cameron, believing troop levels were satisfactory. Recruiting was halted on April 3, 1862, and in the spring of 1862 over 600,000 men were in uniform for the Union. There was a tenor of anticipation that victory was eminent. A mere three months later, through attrition, desertion, military losses, and deflated enthusiasm, the demand for Union manpower became a problem. On June 6, 1862, recruiting efforts were restarted.

One of the arguments of the Lincoln Administration was its insistence that resistance to the war adversely affected enlistments. It became apparent the war would last much longer than most had anticipated. Anti-draft riots broke out in Indiana and Wisconsin. Governors of several Northern States bemoaned the fact that new enlistments were becoming increasingly difficult.[328] The incidents of arbitrary arrests continued, and, in 1862, the Lincoln Administration expanded the suspension of habeas corpus "to include anyone who 'discouraged voluntary enlistments' in the army or who participated in any 'disloyal practice'..." [329] Into late summer, the Lincoln Administration intensified efforts to add additional troops.[330]

On August 9, 1862, Lincoln ordered a draft calling for 300,000 men for nine-months of service. Anyone subject to the draft was forbidden to go to a foreign country or leave his State before the actual enactment of the draft. Furthermore, anyone in violation of

---

[328] Northern States included: New Hampshire, Pennsylvania, Maine, Massachusetts, New York, Minnesota, etc.

[329] Thomas J. DiLorenzo, *The Real Lincoln — A New Look at Abraham Lincoln, His Agenda, and an Unnecessary War* (Roseville, California: Prima Publishing, 2002), 137.

[330] On July 1, 1862, Lincoln instructed the States' governors to enlist 300,000 more men, but the effort only yielded about 87,000 volunteers. On July 17, 1862, the Second Confiscation Act was signed into law stating if those in 'rebellion' did not capitulate to the U.S. Government within sixty days, their property, including slaves, would be seized. Lincoln signed the Militia Act of 1862; it included the enlistment of Blacks, who would receive just over half the pay of White enlistees. The 37th Congress had a busy July.

the draft was subject to arrest and fine. The order stated that anyone who circumvented the edict would forfeit their *habeas corpus* rights and be arrested and detained for disloyalty. "Made public on August 8, the stern edict was supplemented by an order giving military commissions authority to try civilian offenders."[331] As the war progressed, efforts to attract volunteers intensified, and anyone resisting the draft was faced with suspension of their *habeas corpus* rights.

On September 25, 1862, through General Order No. 141, Lincoln issued the Proclamation Suspending the *Writ of Habeas Corpus*, this time covering the entire North.[332] "The new directive specifically cited the resistance to the draft. It had been urged privately well before that, by several governors...."[333] Anyone who protested would not only lose their habeas corpus rights but would also be subject to martial law.[334]

Lincoln's suspension of *habeas corpus* violated the rights of his fellow Northerners and those in the Border States if they disagreed with his war and war policies. Maryland was the most obvious case, but violations occurred in Kentucky, Illinois, Indiana, Ohio, Delaware, and other States.

The combination of the suspension of *habeas corpus* with the preliminary issuance of an Emancipation Proclamation created an avalanche of criticism of Lincoln's actions in the Northern press. The *Harrisonburg Union* described his actions as "an outrage upon the

---

[331] Webb Garrison, *The Lincoln No One Knows* (Nashville, Tennessee: Rutledge Hill Press, 1993), 151.

[332] In early Autumn of 1862, Lincoln was faced with military failings in the east, a bleak view of near-term elections, an unpopular view of conscription, and doubt about how the public would react to his September 22, 1862, preliminary Emancipation Proclamation.

[333] "Habeas Corpus," The American Civil War, *Online Etymology*. (Accessed April 23, 2016).

[334] Lincoln's contention was that he was putting down disloyal persons in what he referred to as a rebellion. Through this series of steps, he eventually signed the first conscription act on March 3, 1863.

humanity and good sense of the country, to say nothing of its gross unconstitutionality."[335] Editors of the *New York World* commented, "President Lincoln has swung loose from the constitutional moorings of his inaugural address."[336] The *New York Times'* Henry J. Raymond felt the Union would be destroyed if abolition were given prominence in the struggle. "According to the New York *Journal of Commerce*, the preliminary proclamation could be described in a single word: disastrous."[337] Even modern advocates of civil rights have commented on Lincoln's actions.[338]

In November 1862, what amounted to *ex post facto* legislation was introduced in Congress to ostensibly cover Lincoln's actions regarding suspension of *habeas corpus*, i.e., this move served the purpose of making his actions *legal* and negating Taney's ruling that only Congress can suspend *habeas corpus* according to the wording of the U.S. Constitution. The legislation passed on December 8, 1862, and, after some debate, Lincoln signed it on March 3, 1863. It is

---

[335] Garrison, 170.

[336] Ibid.

[337] Ibid.

[338] "Of all his constitutionally dubious activities, Lincoln's determination to suspend habeas corpus was the most egregious and controversial. He issued a proclamation on September 24[25], 1862, that implemented martial law and suspended habeas corpus....The right is guaranteed in the Constitution unless suspended by the Congress in time of rebellion." - Author and Judge Andrew P. Napolitano, *The Constitution in Exile*, 70.

"The writ of habeas corpus is probably the most important provision of the Bill of Rights. It can be traced to the Magna Charta, and even today, in many countries without this protection—this most fundamental principle of English liberty—people are arrested and confined in prison indefinitely, with no trial and no means of ever being freed or even tried if the government should so decide. If Lincoln and his generals could get away with this kind of imprisonment, the liberties of all Americans would be at the whim of the general."- From the late author & tax attorney Charles Adams, *When in the Course of Human Events—Arguing the Case for Southern Secession*, 46.

known as the Habeas Corpus Act and became effective on precisely the same day as the first Union Conscription Act, which made Northern males ages 20-45 who were already citizens or had applied for citizenship, subject to the draft.[339] Lincoln exercised powers not granted by the constitution.

---

[339] Jacob Hornberger, founder of the Future of Freedom Foundation commented, that although the Military Commissions Act of 2006 was only applicable to foreigners, history indicates time as the only variable before it is made applicable to American citizens.

Chapter Eighteen
Suppression of the Press, Speech, and War Resistance

Constitutional Violation: Amendment One: *Congress shall make no law respecting an establishment of religion, or prohibiting the free exercise thereof; or abridging the freedom of speech, or of the press; or the right of the people peaceably to assemble, and to petition the Government for a redress of grievances.*

"Freedom of speech and freedom of the press, precious relics of former history, must not be construed too largely."[340]
General William T. Sherman

In the original American model, freedom of speech, press, and religion were literally God-given cornerstones of liberty. Lincoln sought to squelch or eliminate freedom of speech and freedom of the press for any Northern citizen who criticized the war through speech or print or objected to the draft. Numerous States felt the full force of this policy.

Kentucky—Lincoln held a general paranoia about losing the State, exclaiming, "I hope to have God on my side, but I must have Kentucky."[341] Wishing to remain neutral, the Kentucky legislature passed a resolution claiming their neutrality and disallowing troops from either side to belligerently pass through or occupy her soil. The pro-Union political element in Kentucky led her citizens into thinking they would get their wish. "The Federal Government had

---

[340] James Ronald Kennedy and Walter Donald Kennedy, *The South Was Right!* (Gretna, Louisiana: Pelican Publishing Company, 1994), 311.

[341] William E. Gienapp, "Abraham Lincoln and the Border States," *Journal of the Abraham Lincoln Association*, Volume 13, Issue 1, 1992, http://quod.lib.umich.edu/j/jala/2629860.0013.104/--abraham-lincoln-and-the-border-states?rgn=main;view=fulltext, (Accessed April 23, 2016).

disregarded the neutrality of Kentucky, and Mr. Lincoln had hooted it..."[342]

Legislators were elected in August, and as the results were known "it soon became evident that the Federals intended to occupy Kentucky, and to use her roads and mountains for marching invading columns upon the Confederate States."[343] In September 1861, Confederate General Leonidas Polk moved into Columbus, Kentucky, despite orders from Jefferson Davis to stay out. Davis wanted to respect Kentucky's desire to remain neutral and refrain from putting political or military pressure on the State to join the Confederacy. Polk's miscalculation led to Kentucky's request for Union assistance. This allowed Grant an opportunity to take Paducah, and establish a Union presence in the State. In response to Kentucky Governor Beriah Magoffin's request for all troops to leave his State, Polk agreed to withdraw if Federal forces withdrew simultaneously.

There was no intention of forcing the State to side with the Confederacy; strategically, a neutral Kentucky was geographically positioned to serve as a buffer zone advantageous to the South. Despite Union promises to the contrary, "it was well understood that the people of that State had been deceived into a mistaken security, were unarmed, and in danger of being subjugated by the Federal forces,...."[344] The general sentiment was that most Kentuckians identified themselves culturally as Southern, and, given the right to choose, most would likely side with the Confederacy. Magoffin had also refused Lincoln's request to furnish troops to coerce the seceded States. Lincoln was determined to do whatever was necessary to keep Kentucky from joining the Confederacy.

There was divided sentiment in Kentucky regarding the slavery issue and Lincoln sent mixed signals himself. Norman

---

[342] E.A. Pollard, *The Lost Cause,* A Facsimile of the Original 1886 Edition (Avenel, New Jersey: Gramercy Books, 1994), 179.

[343] Ibid.

[344] Ibid., 180.

Hapgood, Illinois-born writer, editor, and journalist quoted Lincoln from a September 22, 1862, confidential letter sent to Illinois Republican Senator Orville H. Browning referencing one reason he denied the enactment of Fremont's proclamation. "The Kentucky Legislature would not budge—would be turned against us. I think to lose Kentucky is nearly the same as to lose the whole game. Kentucky gone, we cannot hold Missouri, nor, I think, Maryland."[345] The letter referenced Lincoln's veto of Union Major General John Fremont's August 30, 1861, order to free the slaves in Missouri. Also, on May 9, 1862, Union Major General David Hunter issued an emancipation order, declaring, "'slavery and martial law in a free country are altogether incompatible' and all former slaves in his command, the Department of the South, 'are therefore declared forever free.'"[346] As with Fremont's declaration, Lincoln quickly vetoed it.

George D. Prentice, a pro-Union, anti-abolitionist, edited the pro-Republican *Louisville Journal*. While Prentice had no reason to fear suppression or closure, the *Louisville Courier* did. The *Courier's* editor, Walter N. Haldeman, was a strong supporter of the Confederacy. When Kentucky's neutrality ended, the *Courier* was suppressed and later published in Bowling Green as long as a Confederate presence remained. "Less outspoken than Haldeman, John H. Harney, editor of the *Louisville Democrat*, became the voice of the Peace Democrats; he grew increasingly critical of Lincoln and his policies...; the *Kentucky Yeoman*, which had supported secession, modified its views sufficiently that it avoided suppression. A

---

[345] Charles L.C. Minor, *The Real Lincoln* (Harrisonburg, Virginia: Sprinkle Publications, 1992), 156. Original source: Norman Hapgood, *Abraham Lincoln*, 245.

[346] Robert Gould Shaw, *Blue-Eyed Child of Fortune: The Civil War Letters of Colonel Robert Gould Shaw*, Ed. Russell Duncan (Athens, Georgia: The University of Georgia Press, 1992), 19.

number of small newspapers were victims of wartime shortages and high prices or were suppressed by the army."[347]

With abundant pro-South and anti-war sentiment in the State, Union forces in Kentucky were leery of incidents such as John Hunt Morgan's raids early in the war. Kentucky-born Brigadier General J.T. Boyle referenced this fear in a July 19, 1862, letter to Secretary Stanton. Boyle feared Morgan's meager force of perhaps 3500 men would overrun the State. In another correspondence from Boyle to Stanton, he stated that Morgan's forces had a maximum of 1200 men and "There are bands of guerillas in Henderson, Davis, and Webster counties." [348] Alluding to Anti-war/Pro-Southern sentiment within Indiana, Illinois and other Northern States, Ohio Governor John Brough wrote Secretary Stanton on June 9, 1864, expressing his belief that Kentucky would have to be treated like Maryland to keep them in line. On July 5, 1864, referencing his September 15, 1863, proclamation, Lincoln declared martial law and suspended the *writ of habeas corpus* in Kentucky.

A footnote of history involving Kentucky was General Order No. 11, issued by U.S. Grant on December 17, 1862. This order called for all Jews to be expelled from his district, i.e., Kentucky, Tennessee, and Mississippi. This blatantly bigoted order, based on the allegation that Jews spearheaded an unprincipled black market trade was short-lived and has been generally ignored by historians. Years later, as a candidate for president, Grant said he did not read the order before he signed it and placed the blame on a subordinate.

Indiana—Indiana was subject to shutdowns of the press. Having few large newspapers in the State, the closures were of smaller, more local Democratic papers. The high point of this activity was in the spring of 1863. Union Brigadier General Milo Hascall, a native New Yorker, had lived in Goshen, Indiana since 1847. On April 25, 1863, Hascall issued Order No. 9, as his version of

---

[347] Lowell Harrison, *The Civil War in Kentucky* (Lexington, Kentucky: The University of Kentucky Press, 1975), 104.

[348] Minor, 158.

Burnside's Order No. 38. Both orders were spurred by the intense anti-war sentiment in the North. Hascall claimed, "The country will have to be saved or lost during the time this administration remains in power, and therefore he who is factiously and actively opposed to the war policy of the Administration, is as much opposed to his Government."[349] Hascall echoed the familiar mantra often associated with centralizers that you are either with us or against us, leaving no room for middle ground. "The first editor arrested was Daniel E. Van Valkenburgh of the *Plymouth Weekly Democrat*." [350] VanValkenburgh had ridiculed Order No. 9 as well as its author and was arrested on May 4, 1863.

There were other arrests of Democratic newspaper editors. "Rufus Magee, editor of the *Pulaski Democrat* in Winamac, was arrested and his newspaper suspended for two weeks...The *Columbia City News* was shut down and its editor, Englebert Zimmerman, was ordered to Indianapolis to answer for his offense."[351] Given the option of retracting its condemnation of Order No. 9 or closing its publication, W.H. and Ariel Draper, editors of the Democratic *South Bend Forum*, decided to shut it down. Other Democratic publications that were threatened by Hascall "included the *Starke County Press*, the *Bluffton Banner*, the *Blackford Democrat*, the *Warsaw Union*, and the *Franklin Weekly Democratic Herald*."[352]

General sentiment in Indiana was unfavorable toward the abolitionists, realizing that radical elements existed within the movement. Apparently, many Indianans wanted to distance themselves from the slavery issue altogether. A new constitution had been submitted to the people of Indiana in 1851. This

---

[349] Stephen E. Towne, *Killing the Serpent Speedily: Governor Morton, General Hascall, and the Suppression of the Democratic Press in Indiana, 1863*, 50, scholarworks.iupui.edu, https://scholarworks.iupui.edu/bitstream/handle/1805/696/Killing%20the%20Serpent%20Speedily.pdf?sequence=1, (Accessed April 23, 2016).

[350] Ibid., 51.

[351] Ibid., 52.

[352] Ibid.

constitution forbade Blacks from coming to the State and it levied punishment on anyone who employed them. A popular majority of almost 90,000 ratified it. Indiana Governor Oliver P. Morton, a Radical Republican, and a steady opponent of the abolitionists, supported this new State constitution. Harrison H. Dodd provided another perspective. Dodd, born in New York, later moved to Ohio and finally Indiana, where he served as the Grand Commander of the Sons of Liberty. He commented that "'the real cause of the war was the breach of faith by the North in not adhering to the original compact of the States...that 'in twenty-three States we had governments assisting the tyrants at Washington to carry on a *military despotism.*'"[353]

From the Lincoln Administration's standpoint, Indiana had too many army desertions and too many of its citizens favoring peace with the South. There was armed resistance in Rush County, and the Union Army "sent one hundred infantry by special train to arrest deserters and ringleaders. Southern Indiana is ripe for revolution."[354] Meetings were held on the local and county level in many parts of the State; the results of some of these meetings "...declared the war cruel and unnecessary, denounced President Lincoln as a tyrant and usurper..."[355]

Ohio—Clement Vallandigham was not the only Ohioan who disagreed with the war. Lincoln's supporters flexed their military and political muscle, as they felt necessary to silence resistance. Burnside's district consisted of Ohio, Indiana, and Illinois and within his region the *New York Herald* was excluded and the *Chicago Times* suppressed. This was an area absent of war, but anti-war and anti-draft sentiment was often openly expressed. Ohio's Governor

---

[353] Minor, 160. Original source: William Dudley Fowlke, *Life of Morton, Vol. I,* 35.

[354] Ibid., 165-166. Original source: Correspondence between Colonel Carrington, 18th U.S. Infantry to General Thomas, Adjutant-General of the U.S. Army, *The War of the Rebellion: Official Records of Union and Confederate Armies,* Serial No. 124, 75.

[355] Ibid., 167-168. Original source: *Life and Services of O.P. Morton,* 43.

Brough wrote to Stanton on August 9, 1864, lamenting the slow recruitment of new soldiers. He predicted the necessity of a heavy draft and encouraged the use of strong force against those who resisted. Brough, a strong Lincoln supporter, had already meddled in the affairs of Kentucky.

Three Muskingham River Valley Democratic-leaning newspapers were targeted—"the McConnelsville *Enquirer,* Zanesville *Citizens' Press,* and Marietta *Republican*...operatives in the Republican Party circulated a document that states the *Enquirer* had discouraged enlistments...and In March 1863, a mob ransacked the office of the Marietta Republican."[356] The Democrats of Washington County met and proclaimed that a free press and a free conscience should be allowed in wartime just as in times of peace. Samuel Chapman, editor of the *Citizens' Press,* was threatened by Burnside, and then arrested for his own protection against a mob, so he shut down the paper. Continuing the aggression against Democratic, anti-war papers, "in March 1863, Company M of the Second Ohio Volunteer Cavalry attacked the *Columbus Crises,* a relatively new Democratic newspaper owned by Samuel Medary." [357] Another publication that faced suppression was the *Ohio Democrat,* based out of Starke County.

Illinois—The citizens of Illinois had a strong aversion to emancipation and enacted a law similar to Indiana, disallowing Blacks from living in their State. In his *Life of Oliver P. Morton,* William Dudley Foulke shows that, in January 1863, the Illinois General assembly offered several resolutions; some that passed were against emancipation and conscription. Like Indiana, there was severe resistance to the war within the general population. Illinois Governor Yates wrote to Stanton expressing the fear his State would face strong resistance to the draft.

---

[356] David W. Bulla & Gregory A. Borchard, *Journalism in the Civil War Era* (New York, New York: Peter Lang Publishing, Inc., 2010), 170.
[357] Ibid.

Several newspapers were temporarily suppressed. One was the *Jonesborogh Gazette* (now Jonesboro) in Southern Illinois. The more high-profile *Chicago Times* perhaps initiated a rebuke from the Lincoln Administration by wondering in print how a Christian nation could engage in the slaughter of thousands of its own people without a valid motive. "To assume a different ground, would be to confess ourselves barbarians or demons. We then repeat the question as to what adequate motive we have for inaugurating a civil war?"[358]

Burnside was behind the suppression of the *Chicago Times*. Wilbur F. Storey, an accomplished editor, took over the *Times* in June 1861. Though he was not initially anti-war, after the Emancipation Proclamation was issued, Storey denounced the folly of trying to change the goal of the war to emancipation. "On June 1, 1863, Burnside issued General Order No. 84, the suppression order for Storey's newspaper."[359] Shortly thereafter a military officer shut down the *Times* and its presses. Questioning why the country should get involved in what many considered an unnecessary war drew a strong and sudden response from the Lincoln Administration.

Pennsylvania—There were pockets of resistance in the State of Pennsylvania. Reverend A.V.G. Allen, an Episcopal clergyman from Cambridge, Massachusetts, published several biographical works of fellow Massachusetts Episcopalian clergyman Phillips Brooks (who wrote the lyrics for 'O Little Town of Bethlehem). In *Life, &c., of Phillips Brooks*, Allen states that in Philadelphia there was "avowed hostility towards the Government in its prosecution of the war. That such sentiments towards Lincoln and his Administration did exist in Philadelphia is evident, but it should also be said that the same apathy or hostility might be found in the Northern cities, in

---

[358] Charles Adams, *When in the Course of Human Events—Arguing the Case for Southern Secession* (Lanham, Maryland: Rowman & Littlefield Publishers, 2000), 43.

[359] Bulla & Borchard, 173.

New York and in Boston."[360] The State of Pennsylvania contained strong support for the Democratic Party. In Philadelphia, Democrats were dominant, and despite the ongoing war, there remained anti-war and pro-South sentiment. Two Philadelphia papers—the *Christian Observer* and the *Evening Journal*—were suppressed for their criticism of the war. The Lincoln administration accused these papers of providing "aid and comfort"[361] to the South. Other Pennsylvania newspapers that faced suppression included the *Sentinel* in Easton and the *Jeffersonian* in West Chester.

There were other forms of war resistance in Pennsylvania. For example, Captain Richard I. Dodge, acting Provost Marshall General, wrote to General Fry, Provost Marshall General, on August 10, 1864: "In several counties of the Western Division of Pennsylvania, particularly in Columbia and Cambria, I am credibly informed that there are large bands of deserters and delinquent drafted men banded together, armed and organized for resistance to the United States authorities."[362]

New York—In New York, Governor Horatio Seymour was one of the most prominent Northerners to come to the defense of the seceded States, acknowledging the legitimacy of their grievances and protesting Lincoln's program of coercion. The anti-war and anti-draft sentiment of New York City was witnessed by Union General John Dix, who wrote to Secretary Stanton that State and city authorities could not be relied on to enforce the draft "and, while I impute no such designs to them, they are men in constant communication with them who, I am satisfied, desire nothing so

---

[360] Minor, 176. Original source: Alexander V.G. Allen, *Life and Letters of Phillips Brooks*, Vol. I, 448.

[361] "Freedom of the Press? The Suppression of the Christian Observer and the Evening Journal," *Historical Society of Pennsylvania*, https://hsp.org/education/unit-plans/civil-liberties-and-the-civil-war-in-pennsylvania-0/freedom-of-the-press-the-suppression-of-the-christian-observer-and-the-evening-journal, (Accessed April 23, 2016).

[362] Minor, 178.

much as a collision between the State and General Governments and an insurrection in the North in aid of the Southern rebellion."[363]

New York was America's news center in the 1860s, and it was there that suppression of the print media began. Horace Greeley, originally a proponent of peace, eventually became a supporter of Lincoln and the war and his paper, the *New York Tribune*, reflected it. However, the *Journal of Commerce* and the *New York Daily News* were in opposition. Simply put, if the paper supported the Republicans and their war, it was safe from government interference whereas anti-war, pro-Democratic newspapers were open targets. "In May 1861 the *Journal of Commerce* published a list of more than a hundred Northern newspapers that had editorialized against going to war. The Lincoln Administration responded by ordering the Postmaster General to deny these papers mail delivery."[364] The *New York Herald*, the city's largest newspaper, supported the legality of secession and opposed coercion, "But a mob compelled the publisher to change his tune, and editorials stopped expressing hostility to Lincoln's war." [365] This same technique "was used by the Lincoln administration against the *New York Daily News, The Daybrook, Brooklyn Eagle, Freeman's Journal*, and several other smaller New York newspapers."[366]

Iowa—In a seemingly unlikely place like Iowa, there was Pro-Southern sentiment. There was a legal case involving William H. Hill, an Iowan and Southern sympathizer, accused of discouraging enlistments and aiding the Confederate cause. U.S. Marshall Hoxie and Iowa Governor Kirkwood reported to Secretary Seward their belief that Hill was guilty, but both men felt he would be cleared because the jury is "in sympathy with the rebels."[367] In

---

[363] Ibid., 181.

[364] Thomas J. DiLorenzo, *The Real Lincoln* (Roseville, California: Prima Publishing, 2002), 145.

[365] Adams, *When in the Course of Human Events—Arguing the Case for Southern Secession*, 43.

[366] DiLorenzo, *The Real Lincoln*, 146.

[367] Minor, 185.

Hoxie's December 1861 letter to Seward he stated there was little doubt as to Hill's guilt but he would be found not guilty because "There is a large secession element in the jury selected to try him."[368] Like so many of the States in the Midwest, many Iowans had an aversion to war and recognized that the South had a valid constitutional position. In July 28, 1862, correspondence to Secretary Stanton, James F. Wilson reported from Fairfield, Iowa: "Men in this and surrounding counties are daily in the habit of denouncing the Government, the war, and all engaged in it, and are doing all they can to prevent enlistments;....'"[369]

Iowa Catholics were leery of the strong antipathy toward their religion within the Republican Party, especially from former Know Nothings. The *Dubuque Herald* was anti-war and concerned about Lincoln's armies being plunderers with a corresponding loss of civility. The *Herald* and the *Iowa City Press* were severe critics of the war. The *Keokuk Constitution* felt the wrath of their anti-Lincoln stance when a group of Union soldiers in a convalescent hospital took the law in their own hands. They literally destroyed the newspaper's office. "The types were thrown into the street and the presses broken up and part of them thrown into the river."[370]

Wisconsin — Wisconsin Governor James T. Lewis sent a letter in August 1864, claiming there had been rampant fleeing from the draft in Wisconsin and Minnesota. According to Lewis, in Wisconsin, "Out of 17,000 drafted in this State during the last year, I

---

[368] Ibid., 186. Original source: Correspondence from H.M. Hoxie, U.S. Marshall of the District of Iowa, to Secretary Seward in December 1861. From *War of the Rebellion, Series II, Vol. II*, 1322.

[369] Ibid.

[370] "*A Rebel Newspaper in Iowa Suppressed; The Keokuk Constitution Destroyed*," Chicago, Friday, February 20, Published February 21, 1863, The *New York Times*, 2014, http://www.nytimes.com/1863/02/21/news/a-rebel-newspaper-in-iowa-suppressed-the-keokuk-constitution-destroyed.html, (Accessed April 23, 2016).

am informed that but about 3,000 are in the service."[371] This was part of the sentiment throughout the Midwest that showed both strong resistance to war and belief in the voluntary nature of the U.S. Constitution.

When he described Lincoln as a butcher, bigot, fanatic, and a tyrant, Marcus "Brick" Pomeroy made quick enemies with the Lincoln Administration and supporters of the war. Considered a Copperhead during the war, "Pomeroy, editor of the *La Crosse Democrat*, had a turkey pushed into his face." [372] He was also threatened by a mob and questioned by a sheriff after his 1864 suggestion that Lincoln should be assassinated if reelected.

The *Prairie Du Chien Courier* was another anti-war, pro-Democratic Wisconsin newspaper. Though it was not subject to suppression, "William D. Merrell's newspaper covered the murder of a Democratic politician by a mob of Union soldiers in New Lisbon, Wisconsin."[373]

Connecticut—Pro-Southern sympathy existed in the heart of the Northeast. In January 1862, Connecticut's Deputy Collector, Fred H. Thompson, wrote to Union Secretary Seward about events in Bridgeport, claiming the city had pockets of strong sympathy for the Confederacy and that a Knights of the Golden Circle lodge was located there.

There was also suppression of Democratic newspapers in Connecticut; the *Bridgeport Advertiser & Farmer* ran afoul of both local Republicans and the Federal government due to its anti-Lincoln and anti-war stance. "The *Farmer* was indeed anti-Lincoln, calling him a 'despot' and accusing him of assuming more power than the Constitution allowed a President." [374] In Stepney, a

---

[371] Minor, 187. Original source: A letter from the Governor of Wisconsin to Secretary Stanton, asking for federal help with draft resistance, *War of the Rebellion*, 1010.

[372] Bulla & Borchard, 171.

[373] Ibid.

[374] "Another Newspaper Suppressed; Missouri in Doubt; Kentucky in Turmoil," Saturday, August 24, 1861, *Civil War Daily Gazette*,

scheduled Democratic Peace Meeting was interrupted by pro-Unionists, led by none other than P.T. Barnum. After threats of violence by both sides, the pro-Unionists marched south to Bridgeport and proceeded to attack the *Farmer's* office where they destroyed the presses along with the books, paper, etc., and put the paper out of business. No arrests were made for the mob's destruction of private property.

There were many other newspapers that felt the wrath of Lincoln and his supporters. A partial list of those censored or suppressed include the *"Dayton Empire, Louisville Courier, Maryland News Sheet, Baltimore Gazette, Daily Baltimore Republican, Baltimore Bulletin, Philadelphia Evening Journal, New Orleans Advocate, New Orleans Courier, Baltimore Transcript, Thibodaux* (Louisiana) *Sentinel, Cambridge Democrat* (Maryland), *Wheeling Register, Memphis News, Baltimore Loyalist, and Louisville True Presbyterian."*[375]

Other acts of oppression were directed at opposition opinions. "The editor of the *Essex County Democrat* in Haverhill, Massachusetts, was tarred and feathered by a mob of Unionists who destroyed the paper's printing equipment."[376] Lincoln's followers even harassed and suppressed non-American sources. A foreign newspaper operating in New York, "the French *Courier des Etats Unis*, was ordered to print the news of the day only, no commentaries, and its editor, M.E. Masseras, was ordered to resign."[377]

Additional States showed their disagreement with the war, draft efforts, and the disregard for the U.S. Constitution and the rule of law. In their book *Abraham Lincoln*, Nicholay and Hay referenced "'deep seated disaffection' in New Jersey, shown by legislation and

---

http://civilwardailygazette.com/2011/08/24/another-newspaper-suppressed-missouri-in-doubt-kentucky-in-turmoil/, (Accessed April 23, 2016).

[375] DiLorenzo, *The Real Lincoln*, 147.

[376] Ibid., 148.

[377] Adams, *When in the Course of Human Events*, 43-44.

elsewise."[378] They also referenced the use of soldiers to enforce the draft in Detroit, Michigan, and put down draft resistance in Rutland, Vermont. There was constant contact between the States and members of the Lincoln Administration. "Governor Gilmore, of New Hampshire, wrote Secretary Stanton January 13th, 1864, of a clamor against the Government and that 'Copperheads are jubilant.'"[379] Their jubilation centered on the continued resistance to the draft.

John Codman Ropes, the Massachusetts lawyer, writer, and eulogizer of Lincoln, recognized the underlying support for the South. He noted that Maryland, Kentucky, and Missouri were still Union States, "yet the feeling of a considerable part of the people in those States in favor of the new movement was so strong...that the Southern cause received substantial aid from each of them."[380]

With multiple pockets of resistance in the North and the Border States, Lincoln set about suppressing his opposition. Union General Fremont, a staunch Republican, lamented, "The administration has managed the war for personal ends, and with incapacity and selfish disregard of Constitutional rights, with violation of personal liberty of the press."[381]

Just a few weeks into the war, on April 27, 1861, Lincoln suspended the *writ of habeas corpus,* depriving his opposition of their most basic rights. This was soon followed by the program of shutting down newspapers and, finally, the call for more troops to

---

[378] Minor, 188. Original source: Nicholay and Hay, *Abraham Lincoln,* Vol. VI, p. 217; Major Hill, 2nd Artillery, Acting Provost Marshal, asks from the Provost Marshal General at Washington, in August, 1863, for soldiers to execute the draft in Detroit, Michigan. Captain Conner of 17th United States Infantry reports using soldiers to put down resistance to the draft at Rutland, Vermont, August 3rd, 1863.

[379] Ibid., 188-189.

[380] Ibid., 189.

[381] Mildred Lewis Rutherford, *Truths of History* (Harrisonburg, Virginia: Old South Institute Press, 2009), 52.

invade the seceded States. No stone was left unturned as the Union war machine readied to coerce the seceded States.

Suppression of newspapers generally worked hand-in-hand with draft resistance. As the war progressed, and it became clear the Union would subdue the seceded States, there was a corresponding decline in dissent. Ever the politician, Lincoln and his minions silenced critics, as they felt necessary to advance their agenda.

Chapter Nineteen
An Act of Tyranny

Constitutional Violation: Amendment One. *Freedom of Speech Denied. Vallandigham Imprisoned in Ohio.*

"From the beginning to the end of these proceedings law and justice were set at naught;...the President should have rescinded the sentence and released Vallandigham:...a large portion of the Republican press of the east condemned Vallandigham's arrest and the tribunal before which he was arraigned."[382]

James Ford Rhodes, historian and industrialist from Ohio

Clement L. Vallandigham was born July 29, 1820, in New Lisbon, Ohio. He was Scots-Irish on his mother's side (Laird) and Flemish Huguenot on his father's side (Van Landegham). Vallandigham was educated at New Lisbon Academy and Jefferson College in Canonsburg, Pennsylvania. He built a respected law practice and became a popular political speaker. His qualifications helped open the door for his election in 1845 as the Ohio State legislature's youngest member. Vallandigham admired Southern character and honor; there was a personal aspect as well because the South (Stafford, Virginia) was part of his family lineage. He opposed a strong central government and slavery, but felt the Federal government should not interfere where it existed.

Vallandigham was a Jeffersonian States' Rights Democrat who believed in interpreting the Constitution as it was written. He publicly denounced the Radical Republicans and opposed the 1857 Tariff. In a February 24, 1859, address to the House of Representatives he stated his belief that the legislation "was

---

[382] Charles L.C. Minor, *The Real Lincoln* (Harrisonburg, Virginia: Sprinkle Publications, 1992), 171. Original source: James Ford Rhodes, *History of the United States, Vol. IV*, 248.

peculiarly a manufacturer's tariff and a highly protective tariff too...He then referred to the manner in which the interests of his constituents and the farmers, especially the wool-growers of Ohio, had been disregarded in the Act of 1857."[383] Somewhat ironically, the 1857 agreement gave some degree of relief to the South and ruffled the feathers of Northern industrialists who almost immediately lobbied for an increase in tariff rates.[384]

Comments by Vallandigham during the early stages of the war likely put him on the wrong side of the Lincoln Administration. In a February 3, 1862, speech delivered on the floor of the House of Representatives, Vallandigham criticized the Lincoln Administration's Legal Tender Act. From an economic and historical standpoint, he saw the creation of a fiat money system, i.e., greenbacks backed by nothing, as a risky maneuver relative to helping finance the war on the South. Vallandigham accurately predicted this Act would result in "... high prices, extravagant speculation, enormous sudden fortunes, immense fictitious wealth, general insanity. These belong to all inordinate and excessive paper issues."[385]

---

[383] Rev. James Laird Vallandigham, *A Life of Clement L. Vallandigham* (Baltimore: Turnbull Brothers, 8 North Charles Street, 1872), 107, *The Library of Congress Internet Archive*, https://archive.org/stream/lifeofclementlva00vall#page/106/mode/2up, (Accessed April 24, 2016).

[384] In autumn of 1859, Vallandigham questioned John Brown at Harper's Ferry, after his arrest. From the conversation, Vallandigham deduced Brown was a pawn in a large-scale conspiracy. Brown's activities, eventually ruled as treason against the Commonwealth of Virginia, were financed primarily by the Secret Six—New Englanders that included Gerrit Smith, Thomas Wentworth Higginson, Theodore Parker, Samuel Gridley Howe, Franklin Benjamin Sanborn, and George Luther Stearns.

[385] Thomas J. DiLorenzo, "The Real Reason Why Lincoln Imprisoned and Deported a Democratic Congressman," *LewRockwell.com*, http://www.lewrockwell.com/lrc-blog/the-real-reason-why-lincoln-imprisoned-and-deported-a-democratic-congressman/, (Accessed April 24, 2016).

During the war, Vallandigham served as U.S. Representative from Ohio, which was part of a military district that included Indiana and Illinois. The district was under the command of Ambrose Burnside, a Union general with a record of mediocrity as a field commander. Vallandigham was labeled as a Peace Democrat and a Copperhead as he espoused the importance of individual liberty, constitutional government, and the dangers of increased centralization. His vocal criticism of the war against the South made many enemies.

Vallandigham was troubled by the Lincoln Administration's claim of changing the goal of the war from preservation of the Union to suddenly being a quest to end slavery. He voiced his concerns to Congress on January 14, 1863:

> The war for the Union is in our hands, a most bloody and costly failure. The President confessed it on the September 22…War for the Union was abandoned; war for the Negro openly began…I trust I am not "discouraging enlistments." If I am, then arrest Lincoln and Stanton and Halleck… But can you draft again? …Ask Massachusetts… Ask not Ohio, nor the Northwest. She thought you were in earnest and gave you all, all-more than you demanded… But ought this war to continue? I answer, No, not a day, not an hour. What then? Shall we separate? Again I answer no, No, no, no! What then? …Stop fighting. Make an armistice. Accept at once the friendly foreign mediation and begin the work of reunion, we shall yet escape.[386]

Vallandigham recognized military failure as a catalyst for this diversionary political tactic, arising on the heels of several Northern military defeats and increasing apprehension that a foreign power (beyond the Vatican's vague affirmation) might officially recognize the Confederacy. According to Illinois politician

---

[386] Minor, 169.

and U.S. soldier John A. Logan (aka *Black Jack* Logan), there was a gathering at Springfield, Illinois, (Lincoln's home) of almost 100,000 Vallandigham, Anti-War, Peace Democrats voicing their opposition to the invasion of the South and calling for an end to the war.

On April 13, 1863, Burnside issued General Order Number 38, which stated that free speech would not be tolerated if that speech were in defense of the South. Burnside felt Lincoln's September 24, 1862, suspension of habeas corpus gave him the authority to issue his order.

During a May 1, 1863, speech, Vallandigham described the Union war as "wicked, cruel, and unnecessary."[387] He went on to say this "was a 'war for the purpose of crushing out liberty and erecting a despotism'"[388] and he called for Lincoln's removal from office. Unknown to Vallandigham, Burnside had sent two captains, dressed in civilian clothing, to Mount Vernon, Ohio, to listen to this speech where he ridiculed the unconstitutional activities of "King Lincoln"[389] and publicly denounced Burnside's order. In retaliation for his comments, officers surrounded, and then broke into Vallandigham's house at 2:00 A.M. on May 5th. He was arrested and sent to face trial before a military commission. Vallandigham was charged with violation of Burnside's General Order Number 38, by expressing disloyal opinions that weakened government efforts to suppress a rebellion. He was also accused of illegally discouraging military enlistments. Though military commissions are not designed to handle civilians and the regular civilian courts were in operation at the time, Vallandigham was placed before a military tribunal (based on Lincoln's suspension of habeas corpus). Trying a civilian

---

[387] "Civil War Tested Lincoln's Tolerance for Free Speech," *First Amendment Center*, February 11, 2009, http://www.firstamendmentcenter.org/civil-war-tested-lincolns-tolerance-for-free-speech-press, (Accessed April 24, 2016).

[388] Ibid.

[389] "Clement L. Vallandigham," *National Park Service Quick Facts*, http://www.nps.gov/resources/person.htm?id=111, (Accessed April 28, 2016).

in a military court typically indicates the verdict has been predetermined or as Daniel Webster, an opponent of such activities, stated, "military courts are organized to convict."[390] Lincoln favored the use of military courts for civilians in such circumstances.

In response to the arrest, on May 6, 1863, a crowd of 500-600 gathered at the newspaper office of the pro-Republican *Dayton Journal*; Vallandigham had lived in Dayton since 1847. They took over the building and burned it to the ground. The fire spread "and all the property from the south end of the Phillips House to the middle of the square was destroyed. All the telegraph lines in the city were cut down and destroyed."[391] It was also reported that the Xenia Road Bridge had been destroyed.

The *New York Herald* demanded a release of Vallandigham in its May 24, 1863, edition. Burnside disallowed circulation of the *Herald* and also ordered suppression of the anti-Republican *Chicago Times* on June 3, 1863. Under Burnside, not only did infringements of liberty increase, the death penalty was prescribed for certain offenses. Although violations of individual civil and constitutional rights were common, Vallandigham's case was the highest profile as he was considered the quintessential Copperhead.

During his confinement, a letter in Vallandigham's handwriting emerged from his prison cell with the comment: "I am here in a military bastille for no other offense than my political opinions...I am a Democrat-for the Constitution, for law, for Union, for liberty—this is my only crime."[392] Vallandigham was tried in

---

[390] George Edmonds, *Facts and Falsehoods Concerning the War on the South 1861-1865* (Wiggins, Mississippi: Crown Rights Book Company Liberty Reprint Series, 1997), 211.

[391] "The Arrest of Vallandigham," *Montgomery County, Ohio Genealogy and History, Genealogy Trails,* http://genealogytrails.com/ohio/montgomery/news_crime.html, (Accessed April 24, 2016).

[392] Edgar J. McManus and Tara Helfman, *Liberty and Union: A Constitutional History of the United States, Concise Edition* (New York, New York: Routlegde, an Imprint of the Taylor & Francis Group, 2014), 207.

Cincinnati and initially *convicted* of being disloyal to the U.S. and
sympathetic to the Confederacy. He was sentenced to two years at
the military prison in Fort Warren, located at the entrance of Boston
Harbor. George Pugh, Vallandigham's attorney, appealed the
verdict to Federal Judge Humphrey Leavitt based on the lack of
jurisdiction of a military tribunal combined with the fact his client's
free speech and habeas corpus rights had been violated. Leavitt
would not budge and the verdict was left intact.

Vallandigham was sentenced to close confinement for the
duration of the war; however, there was such a public outcry in both
North and South "that Lincoln commuted the sentence to
banishment—a penalty not before known to the country, and 'not
for deeds alone, but for words spoken,' to use the language in which
it was denounced by John Sherman, and these were words that had
been spoken in public debate and received with wild applause by
thousands of his constituents."[393]

Lincoln had sought to minimize political damage from
Burnside's illegal arrest and it was Burnside himself who suggested
Vallandigham be sent to General William S. Rosecrans, commanding
the Army of the Cumberland, at Murfreesboro, Tennessee. From
there, Vallandigham was sent into Confederate territory, with the
warning that he would be imprisoned if he returned to Union soil.

In early June of 1863, Vallandigham was banished to the
South although Lincoln refused to admit the Confederate States
existed as a separate country. Lincoln had initially supported
Burnside's arrest of Vallandigham; however, it is unclear if he knew
ahead of time that it would take place. Lincoln was very aware of
the often vocal, pesky, Ohio Copperhead whom he referred to as
this "Wily agitator"[394] and his initial support of Burnside's actions

---

[393] Minor, 170-171. Original source: Rhodes, *History of the United
States, Vol. IV*, 247.

[394] Frank J. Williams, "When Albany Challenged the President,"
New York State Archives, Winter 2009,
http://nysa32.nysed.gov/apt/magazine/archivesmag_winter09_Williams.pdf,
(Accessed April 24, 2016).

exacerbated the situation. This arrest and banishment was not entirely unprecedented in American history; it echoed the 1798 Alien and Sedition Acts, under President Adams, where verbal criticism of specific individuals in government was prohibited and punished, sometimes severely.

Though the arrest and harsh treatment of Vallandigham was endorsed in many Republican circles, there were others who were alarmed, including some who opposed his peace efforts. Denying Vallandigham his First Amendment and *habeas corpus* rights ignited a firestorm of opposition and indignant reactions. The *Detroit Free Press* responded:

> We have never been champions of Mr. Vallandigham. In many particulars we have disagreed with him in opinion; but we have seen nothing in his course which he was not permitted by the [C]onstitution and laws to do; but even if he is guilty of any offense, he is entitled to a trial by a jury of his country and by the law of the land. If, in his case, a military court—the most offensive of tribunals to a free people—is allowed to usurp the office and functions of these, we will be justified in asserting that the worst apprehensions of the designs of the administration are fulfilled, and that American liberty is so dead, that even its forms are no longer observed.[395]

Even a portion of the Republican press of the East condemned the whole affair. For example, the anti-slavery, pro-Republican, *New York Evening Post* referenced Burnsides' subversion of democratic government by stating:

---

[395] Michael Kent Curtis, "Lincoln, Vallandigham and Anti-war Speech in the Civil War," *William and Mary Bill of Rights Journal*, Volume 7, Issue 1, Article 3, 1998, 138, http://scholarship.law.wm.edu/cgi/viewcontent.cgi?article=1428&context=wmborj, (Accessed April 24, 2016).

[N]o governments and no authorities are to be held above criticism, or even denunciation. We know of no other way of correcting their faults, spurring on their sluggishness, or restraining their tyrannies, than by open and bold discussion. How can a popular Government, most of all, know the popular will, and guide its course in the interests of the community, unless it be told from time to time what the popular convictions and wishes are?[396]

The *New York Daily Tribune*, another anti-slavery Republican newspaper, simultaneously criticized the beliefs of Vallandigham (though they misstated some of his views) and the tactics of the Lincoln Administration:

Vallandigham [was] a Pro-Slavery Democrat of an exceedingly coppery hue...[I]f there were penalties for holding irrational, unpatriotic and inhuman views with regard to political questions, he would be one of the most flagrant offenders. But our Federal and State Constitutions do not recognize perverse opinions, nor unpatriotic speeches, as grounds of infliction.[397]

The list of prominent individuals protesting Vallandigham's arrest included Wilbur Storey, Editor of the *Chicago Times*; Gideon Welles, Union Secretary of the Navy; Erastus Corning, New York businessman; and Horatio Seymour, Governor of New York. "The *Allentown Democrat* in its edition of June 10, 1863, decried Vallandigham's treatment calling it unconstitutional. There were rallies in Buffalo, Newark, N.J., New York City and Philadelphia,

---

[396] Ibid., 145.
[397] Ibid., 146.

according to the newspaper, defending Vallandigham's right of free speech."[398]

There were also protests in Vallandigham's home State of Ohio. At the Democratic State Convention on June 11, 1863, prominent party members wrote a lengthy plea for Lincoln to revoke the banishment. Vallandigham was nominated for governor of Ohio at the convention. Many Ohioans voiced their displeasure with Lincoln, calling him a *usurper* and a *despot*. George Pugh, running for Lieutenant Governor in Ohio, delivered a scathing and cynical address on August 15, 1863, commenting:

> Beyond the limits and powers confided to him by the Constitution, he is a mere County court lawyer, not entitled to any obedience or respect, so help me God [Cheers and cries of 'Good.'] And when he attempts to compel disobedience beyond the limits of the Constitution by bayonets and by swords, I say that he is a base and despotic usurper, whom it is your duty to restrict by every possible means if necessary, by force of arms. [Cheers and cries 'That's the talk.'] If I must have a despot, if I must be subject to the will of any one man, for God's sake let him be a man who possesses some great civil or military virtues. Give me a man eminent in council, or eminent in the field, but for God's sake don't give me the miserable mountebank who at present exercises the office of President of the United States.[399]

---

[398] J.D. Malone, "June 10, 1863: Arrest of Copperhead angers The Allentown Democrat," *Lehigh Valley's Newspaper The Morning Call*, June 6, 2013, http://articles.mcall.com/2013-06-06/news/mc-pa-153rd-pennsylvania-volunteers-gettysburg-150-20130606_1_allentown-democrat-copperheads-war-effort, (Accessed April 24, 2016).

[399] Frank J. Williams, "Abraham Lincoln, Civil Liberties and the Corning Letter," Rhode Island Superior Court, *Roger Williams University Law Review*, Volume 5, Issue 2, Article 1, Spring 2000, 336, http://docs.rwu.edu/cgi/viewcontent.cgi?article=1132&context=rwu_LR, (Accessed April 24, 2016).

Though he felt the Confederacy should be recognized as a legitimate entity, Vallandigham did not support Southern Independence. He favored returning the Southern States to the Union through peaceful negotiation instead of military coercion. This placed Vallandigham and his Confederate hosts in an awkward position. Remaining in the South for only a few weeks, Vallandigham was allowed to leave and work his way back home. He ran the blockade to Bermuda and moved on to Halifax before finally settling in Windsor, Ontario, Canada, where he ran unsuccessfully for governor.

Vallandigham consistently represented the principles of Ohio's Peace Democrats; mobs rioted in his support, and constant efforts were made to have him returned to Ohio. Seemingly from out of nowhere, on June 15, 1864, Vallandigham appeared at Hamilton and Dayton, Ohio, denouncing Lincoln and his actions and spitting upon General Order Number 38.

This time, the Lincoln Administration made no attempts to have him arrested. Vallandigham, along with his friend and supporter, Dr. John McElwee, the editor of the *Hamilton True Telegraph,* insisted the 1864 Democratic Party Platform include a declaration that the war was a failure and that there should be an immediate end to hostilities. Their incessant advocacy of peace possibly backfired during the latter stages of the war. Significant Northern victories shifted popular sentiment away from the Democrats, and the North, with a reenergized morale, could see victory within their grasp, given the depleted manpower and resources of the Confederacy. Vallandigham's last-ditch effort at peace was an unsuccessful appeal to Horace Greeley to help end the war.

Lincoln's death brought great sadness to Vallandigham; he feared the Radical Republicans would respond with even greater retribution on the Southern people. Also, after the war, Vallandigham's political success waned. Initially, he stood against Black voting rights and equality. After losing a couple of post-war elections based on his anti-reconstruction platform, Vallandigham returned to his law practice. Realizing the situation of the country under Republican control, he moderated his views and advocated a policy called New Departure, a program of burying the issues of the war and moving on. Vallandigham accepted that reconstruction was a *fait accompli* and the logical course was to work for the benefit of all citizens. He directed his efforts toward joining Democrats and disgruntled Republicans into what became the Liberal Republican Party in 1872.

Clement L. Vallandigham died in 1871 of an accidental self-inflicted gunshot wound. While defending his client in a murder case, he attempted to show the victim had actually killed himself but the demonstration went awry and he accidentally shot himself, suffering a tragic demise before his well-intentioned political efforts came to fruition. James W. Wall, a former New Jersey senator who had also been imprisoned by Union authorities during the war, performed his eulogy.

Vallandigham's legacy factored into the short story, *The Man Without a Country*, which appeared in the *Atlantic Monthly* in August 1863. Written by Unitarian Minister Edward Everett Hale, the story was based on the life of Philip Nolan. Hale was disturbed by Vallandigham's actions and referenced the legacy of Nolan, who had been tried and convicted of treason in 1807. Nolan was placed on a boat and banished to the sea, with any news of events in America withheld from his sight. As time passed, Nolan decided he loved his country despite its government's flaws.

Chapter Twenty
Maryland! Oh Maryland!

Constitutional Violations: Habeas Corpus, Freedom of Speech, Freedom of the Press, and Treason *(based on its definition in the U.S. Constitution and on the premise that the Union is a voluntary coalition of Sovereign States).*

"It was as perfect an act of despotism as can be conceived. It was a coup d'état in every essential feature."[400]
> Commentary about the arrest of Maryland legislators,
> from the *Saturday Review of London*

The States of Maryland and Delaware had a common link with Virginia. The original Cavaliers who migrated to Virginia were primarily from Southern and Western England. Large numbers settled in the Southern regions of Maryland and Delaware, as evidenced by the English county names still prevalent in these areas. Common bloodlines tend to produce like-minded people, regardless of where they settle in the world. [401] There were also similar commercial interests shared by the individual regions within the Chesapeake area. A large portion of the population of Maryland felt a strong sympathy with the South. Also, all three were slave States.

Lincoln felt he had to derail any possibility of Maryland siding with the South.[402] Had the battle line been drawn from the

---

[400] Edgar Lee Masters, *Lincoln: The Man* (Columbia, South Carolina: The Foundation for American Education, 1997), 422.

[401] David Hackett Fischer's *Albion's Seed* details the settlement of immigrants from Great Britain and the surrounding isles.

[402] Lyon Gardiner contended, "Washington based the Union upon the Democratic principle of free consent. Lincoln ridiculed the idea and asserted that force was the only sound principle of government." Source: *The Gray Book—A Confederate Catechism*, 45. Originally printed in *Tyler's Quarterly* in Volume 33, October and January issues, 1935.

Susquehanna rather than the Potomac, Washington, D.C., would have faced quite a conundrum. Though the Confederacy showed no signs of aggression, Maryland's alignment with the South would have placed the U.S. Capitol in the middle of the Confederate States, making coercion exponentially more difficult. Lincoln had already let it be known the only peace he would accept was complete capitulation by the seceded States.

In the neighboring State of Delaware, Governor Dr. William Burton, a Democrat of the Episcopalian faith, was sympathetic with the South as was "Secretary of State Edward Ridgeley, Senators James Bayard and William Saulsbury and Congressman William Whitely." [403] Democrats were viewed much more favorably than Republicans in the State. In the 1860 election, Breckinridge received almost twice as many votes as Lincoln, who finished third, just behind Bell, and in front of last place Douglas.

The sentiment among Delaware's Pro-South politicians was that they would not seriously consider secession unless Virginia chose that route. In January 1861, Delaware "adopted a resolution by a decisive vote (unanimous in the lower house, 5 to 3 in the state senate) disapproving of secession as a remedy for grievances." [404] Virginia initially desired to remain in the Union until Fort Sumter and the call for coercion led her to reverse course. In April 1861, Virginia voted to secede and ratified the ordinance in May 1861. Delaware's decision to forego secession came four full months before Virginia voted to leave the Union.

Maryland, like Delaware, was not a strong Republican State. In his book, *Abraham Lincoln*, author J.G. Holland wrote: "Out of 92,000 votes cast (in Maryland) at the presidential election of 1860, only a little more than 2,000 had been cast for Mr. Lincoln...The

---

[403] John A. Munroe, *History of Delaware* (Cranbury, New Jersey: Associated University Presses, 2006), 132-133.

[404] Ibid., 132.

sympathies of four persons in every five were with the rebellion."[405]
Baltimore was a culturally Southern town; Lincoln received about
1100 votes of the 30,000 cast in the city. After the election, many
Marylanders lampooned and ridiculed Lincoln for his cowardice,
when, supposedly fearing assassination, he traveled surreptitiously
through Baltimore to Washington, D.C., in the middle of the night in
February 1861. Also, many Marylanders were incensed by the
events at Fort Sumter and the call for troops to invade the South.

Lincoln asked for additional troops to protect Washington,
D.C., and the shortest route was through Baltimore. Baltimore
Mayor George W. Brown was aware of the animosity in his city
toward Lincoln and the Republicans. Troops from Pennsylvania
marched through the city on April 18 and received taunts and
harassment for their unwanted presence. Sensing further trouble
with the movement of more troops from other States through his
city, Brown sent a warning letter to Lincoln on the same day.

> The people are exasperated to the highest degree by the
> passage of troops, and the citizens are universally
> decided in the opinion that no more should be ordered
> to come. The authorities...did their best to day [sic] to
> protect both strangers and citizens and to prevent a
> collision, but [in] vain...it is my solemn duty to inform
> you that it is not possible for more soldiers to pass
> through Baltimore unless they fight their way at every
> step.[406]

Ignoring Brown's plea, federal troops were ordered to march
directly through Baltimore, hoping to reach Washington, D.C., as

---

[405] Charles L.C. Minor, *The Real Lincoln* (Harrisonburg, Virginia:
Sprinkle Publications, 1992), 145.

[406] Michael G. Williams, "Baltimore Riot of 1861," *Weider History*,
History.net, August 8, 2011, Originally published by *Civil War Times*,
http://www.historynet.com/baltimore-riot-of-1861.htm, (Accessed April 24,
2016).

quickly as possible. Though they received cheers over most of the 300 miles from Massachusetts, their commander, Colonel Edward F. Jones was aware of the animosity that awaited them in Baltimore and warned the soldiers to be prepared for a violent reception. He urged them to show restraint.

On April 19, 1861, soldiers of the Sixth Massachusetts entered Baltimore. City law prohibited locomotives from passing through the thoroughfares so the troops had to get off the B&O Lines train and have teams of horses pull the rail cars through the middle of town down Pratt Street to Camden Station where the cars would be recoupled to a B&O engine. After getting off the train, the Massachusetts troops marched in formation through an openly hostile crowd. The situation reached a boiling point, ultimately leading to an exchange of gunfire. This resulted in as many as twelve Baltimore civilians being killed by federal troops and four soldiers being killed by civilians before the Massachusetts troops were able to escape the city. Their escape was aided by the intervention of Police Marshal George Proctor Kane and fifty of his men. This episode is generally referred to as the Pratt Street Riot or First Blood. The ill-advised actions of the Sixth Massachusetts and later misdeeds, such as federal occupation and post-war martial law in the South, helped lead to the June 18, 1878, *Posse Comitatus Act*, prohibiting soldiers from being involved in domestic law enforcement.

On April 27, 1861, Lincoln issued his order to suspend the *writ of habeas corpus* in Maryland, which led to the Merryman case. Much of the fear in Washington, D.C., centered on the possibility of Pro-Confederate forces surrounding the city. General Butler envisioned forces forming in South Carolina, and then combining with troops from Maryland and Virginia to overwhelm the U.S. Capitol. Based on orders from Lincoln, Butler, Winfield Scott, George Cadwalader, and Nathaniel P. Banks were told to suspend *habeas corpus* where resistance was met. Scott said, "In vain did

Justice Taney record his protest against such suspension." ⁴⁰
Cadwalader and Banks carried out Washington's suspension orders
On April 29, the Maryland legislature voted fifty-three to thirteen
against secession; this was no surprise, given the circumstances and
the fact there was strong sentiment to simply remain neutral.

At no point was the federal government invited into the State
of Maryland as prescribed in Article IV, Section 4 of the U.S
Constitution. After suffering through the various federal invasions
and suspensions of rights, on May 10, 1861, the frustrated Maryland
Legislature passed the following resolution:

> Whereas, The war against the Confederate States is
> unconstitutional and repugnant to civilization, and will
> result in a bloody and shameful overthrow of our
> institution; and while recognizing the obligations of
> Maryland to the Union, we sympathize with the South
> in the struggle for their rights—for the sake of
> humanity, we are for peace and reconciliation, and
> solemnly protest against this war, and will take no part
> in it;
>
> Resolved, That Maryland implores the President, in the
> name of God, to cease this unholy war, at least until
> Congress assembles; that Maryland desires and
> consents to the recognition of the independence of the
> Confederate States. The military occupation of
> Maryland is unconstitutional, and she protests against
> it, though the violent interference with the transit of
> Federal troops is discountenanced; that the vindication
> of her rights be left to time and reason, and that a
> convention, under the existing circumstances is
> inexpedient.[408]

---

[407] Minor, 146. Original source: James Schouler, *History of the United States, Vol. IV*, 47.

[408] Alfred H. Guernsey and Henry M. Alden, *Harper's Pictorial History of the Civil War* (McLean, Virginia: The Fairfax Press, 1987), 101.

On May 13, Butler and his troops entered Baltimore with instructions to arrest anyone suspected of disloyalty, deemed to be resistance to federal authority. "Civilians who had demonstrated secessionist sympathies were arrested and taken to Fort McHenry, where they were held without charge." [409] Fort McHenry's Commander, Major Morris, "suspended the Habeas Corpus privileges of those prisoners. Baltimore fell under military rule."[410] Butler's troops built earthworks and placed about fifty cannons on Federal Hill, overlooking Baltimore. Urged on by Lincoln, Butler threatened to bomb the city's civilians if Southern sympathizers offered too much resistance to federal authority.

Exemplifying the degree of force used, "as many as nine companies of Massachusetts soldiers were sent to arrest William H. Gatchell, and seven companies of the same to arrest Messrs. John W. Davis and Charles D. Hinks."[411] In late June 1861, a large force arrested Baltimore Police Marshall Kane in his bed at 3:00 A.M. This was the same Marshal Kane that helped the Massachusetts troops escape from Baltimore.

Despite the directives from the federal government, resistance remained within Maryland. Though the State rejected secession in April, the Lincoln Administration was determined Maryland would not be allowed to change its mind at their September 17 meeting of the General Assembly. On September 11, 1861, Union Secretary of War Cameron sent instructions to Banks,

---

From Florida International University Libraries, http://dpanther.fiu.edu/dpService/dpPurlService/purl/FI11081206/#dvFileP anel,   (Accessed July 24, 2016). [This book includes primary source correspondence illustrating the frustration in Maryland concerning their uninvited visitors. This is also within the time frame the federal occupiers hoisted the U.S. Flag above the Baltimore Customs House.]

[409] "The Pratt Street Riot," *National Park Service,* http://www.nps.gov/fomc/historyculture/the-pratt-street-riot.htm, (Accessed April 24, 2016).

[410] Ibid.

[411] Minor, 152.

who was with his troops near Darnestown, Maryland. Cameron explained "Passage of any act of secession by the legislature of Maryland must be prevented. If necessary, all or any part of the members must be arrested."[412] Identifying those suspected of being pro-secession and/or sympathetic to the Confederate cause, Federal agents arrested several members of the Maryland legislature as well as several prominent citizens between September 12 and 17, 1861.

On September 13, 1861, Union Major John A. Dix, sent an update on the situation in Baltimore to General Wool, stationed at Fort Monroe:

> The following...have been taken in custody by order of the government: George William Brown, mayor of...Baltimore; members-elect of the legislature, S. Teakle Wallis, Henry M. Warfield, Charles H. Pitts, T. Parkin Scott, Lawrence Sangston, Ross Winans, John Hanson Thomas, William G. Harrison, Leonard G. Quinlan, and Robert M. Denison; Henry May, member of Congress; F. Key Howard, Andrew A. Lynch, and Thomas W. Hall, citizens of Baltimore.[413]

Dix added that Cameron's instructions were to guard the detainees closely and allow no one on the outside to communicate with them. A week later Banks sent a message to the commander of the Army of the Potomac, Major General McClellan. The message referenced members of the Maryland legislature that had assembled in Frederick City on September 17, 1861; these were members known or suspected of being disloyal to the federal government.

> General Banks added,...the names of the parties thus arrested...were...B.H.   Salmon,   Frederick;   R.C.

---

[412] Thomas Bland Keys, *The Uncivil War: Union Army and Navy Excesses in the Official Records* (Biloxi, Mississippi: The Beauvoir Press, 1991), 8.

[413] Ibid., 8-9.

McCubbin, Annapolis; William R. Miller, Cecil county; Thomas Claggett, Frederick; Josiah H. Gordon, Alleghany County; Clark J. Durant, Saint Mary's county; J. Lawrence Jones, Talbot County; Andrew Kessler, Jr., Frederick; Bernard Mills, Carroll County; J.W. Brecolt, chief clerk of the senate.[414]

The War Department sent an unusual proclamation to Marylanders, claiming it was necessary to arrest the sizable number of prominent citizens and elected officials "and expressing regret that 'public policy' did not permit the charges on which they were arrested to be revealed to themselves or their friends, with assurances that no private grudges have been allowed to have influence in the arrests."[415] Author and Lincoln supporter, James Ford Rhodes, described these actions as unconstitutional.

New Hampshire-born Charles Dana was a supporter of Lincoln and served as his Assistant Secretary of War. Dana was a journalist, managing editor of the *New York Tribune*, and manager and writer for the *Harbinger*, the publication of the utopian, socialist commune Brook Farm, located in West Roxbury, Massachusetts. He recorded that ninety-seven prominent citizens of Baltimore were arrested and most put in solitary confinement.

In October 1861, General John A. Dix predicted that Maryland would be a Union State by November. Given that Federal intervention had essentially purged or arrested every prominent citizen of Maryland even remotely suspected of being pro-Confederate, Dix was essentially stating the obvious. Noting the dubious actions required to silence the anti-Lincoln forces, Union General Banks said: "While I confidently assure the Government that their detention is yet necessary, I do not think that a trial for any

---

[414] Ibid., 9. Recorded in the Official Records of *The War of the Rebellion*.

[415] Minor, 150.

positive crime can result in their conviction."[416] Charles D. Hinks, a police commissioner arrested by Union forces was said to be dying according to Dr. John Buckler, his physician. "Dr. Smith, physician at the city infirmary, and Dr. Martin, of the Massachusetts Rifles, concur in the opinion of Doctor Buckler and represent Mr. Hinks as in the last stages of consumption."[417] Fearing an unpopular public reaction, Banks ordered Hinks' release, stating: "His death in prison would make an unpleasant public impression."[418]

Up to the point of the State election, Dix and Seward debated who should or should not be released. This was essentially a moot point since the Federal government's invasion, occupation, and arrest of any Marylander suspected of favoring the South had virtually assured a pro-Union majority. Maryland's pro-secession spirit was essentially destroyed as a result of these coercive efforts. In November 1861, the newly chosen legislature was composed of members loyal to the Lincoln Administration.

Francis Key Howard, grandson of Francis Scott Key, the author of *The Star Spangled Banner*, was one of the prominent citizens arrested in Baltimore. Howard was the editor of the Baltimore *Exchange*, a newspaper sympathetic to the South. He was arrested September 13, 1861, by orders of General Banks and then transported to Fort McHenry. Lamenting the activities of which he was intimately involved, he wrote:

> When I looked out in the morning, I could not help being struck by an odd and not pleasant coincidence. On that day forty-seven years before my grandfather, Mr. F.S. Key, then prisoner on a British ship, had witnessed the bombardment of Fort McHenry. When on the following morning the hostile fleet drew off,

---

[416] Ibid., 151. Original source: *War of the Rebellion*, Series II, Vol. I, 586.

[417] Charles W. Mitchell, *Maryland Voices of the Civil War* (Baltimore, Maryland: The Johns Hopkins University Press, 2007), 264.

[418] Ibid.

defeated, he wrote the song so long popular throughout the country, the Star-Spangled Banner. As I stood upon the very scene of that conflict, I could not but contrast my position with his, forty-seven years before. The flag which he had then so proudly hailed, I saw waving at the same place over the victims of as vulgar and brutal a despotism as modern times have witnessed.[419]

In Lincoln's First Inaugural Address, he insisted the Union was formed by the 1774 Articles of Association and was unbreakable. It is improbable he would have ever admitted the invasion and occupation of Maryland was treasonous. Although circumstances were different, there was precedent involving a State, when, in 1859, John Brown led an invasion of Virginia. After his capture, Brown was tried, convicted, and hanged for *treason against the Commonwealth of Virginia*. Article III, Section 3 of the U.S. Constitution refers to levying war against *them*, a plural form referencing a State or States (the sovereigns), not a reference to the federal government. Many in the North opposed Brown's actions; even the Republican Party voiced opposition and felt he should be executed—one Republican who favored Brown's execution, citing his treasonous activity, was Abraham Lincoln.

This episode highlights a difference in interpretation of the nature of American government. One view held the States as sovereign entities who voluntarily entered into compacts or leagues—the Articles of Confederation and the U.S. Constitution— and never relinquished their sovereignty (as plainly stated in the Treaty of Paris of 1783). Conversely, there were those who believed the States were mere appendages of the central government, which they considered the master. Robert E. Lee famously remarked that his loyalty was with Virginia, quite the antithesis of Lincoln's contention States were part of an arrangement they could not leave on their own volition.

---

[419] Minor, 148-149. Original source: Francis Key Howard, *Fourteen Months in American Bastille*, 9.

Many Marylanders who opposed federal occupation were arrested and imprisoned. The bulk of the arrests were carried out by troops from Vermont, Pennsylvania, and Massachusetts. Secession from the Union became virtually impossible. With the upheaval in their State, approximately 25,000 Marylanders went south and fought for the Confederate States of America.

The State Song of Maryland captures the sentiment of Marylanders who believed Lincoln's actions were despotic. Often offensive to Lincoln admirers and advocates of political correctness (Cultural Marxism), numerous efforts have been made to alter or completely do away with the song. In the lyrics, it is relatively easy to discern references to the 1861 Baltimore Riots, victims of the federal invasion, and the despot accused of authoring all of it. Written by James Ryder Randall, a Pro-Southern native of Maryland, the meter was taken from *Karamanian Exile*, by the Irish poet, James Clarence Magnan. The song is found under the titles of *My Maryland* and *Maryland, My Maryland*:

My Maryland
James Ryder Randall, 1839-1908

The despot's heel is on thy shore,
Maryland!
His torch is at thy temple door,
Maryland!
Avenge the patriotic gore
That flecked the streets of Baltimore,
And be the battle queen of yore.
Maryland! My Maryland!

Hark to an exiled son's appeal,
Maryland!
My mother State, to thee I kneel,
Maryland!
For life or death, for woe and seal,
Thy peerless chivalry reveal,
And gird thy beauteous limbs with steel,

Maryland! My Maryland!
Thou wilt not cower in the dust,
Maryland!
They beaming sword shall never rust,
Maryland!
Remember Carroll's sacred trust,
Remember Howard's warlike thrust,
And all thy slumberers with the just,
Maryland! My Maryland!

Come! 'tis the red dawn of the day,
Maryland!
Come with thy panoplied array,
Maryland!
With Ringgold's spirit of the fray,
With Watson's blood at Monterey,
With fearless Lowe and dashing May,
Maryland! My Maryland!

Come! For they shield is bright and strong,
Maryland!
Come! For thy dalliance does thee wrong,
Maryland!
Come to thine own heroic throng,
That stalks with Liberty along,
And ring dauntless slogan-song,
Maryland! My Maryland!

Dear mother! Burst the tyrant's chain,
Maryland!
Virginia should not call in vain,
Maryland!
She meets her sisters on the plain –
"Sic Semper," 'tis the proud refrain
That baffles minions back amain,
Maryland!
Arise in majesty again,
Maryland! My Maryland!

I see the blush upon thy cheek,
Maryland!
For thou wast ever bravely meek,
Maryland!
But lo! There surges forth a shriek
From hill to hill, from creek to creek –
Potomac calls to Chesapeake,
Maryland! My Maryland!

Thou wilt not yield the Vandal toll,
Maryland!
Thou wilt not crook to his control,
Maryland!
Better the fire upon thee roll,
Better the shot, the blade, the bowl,
Than crucifixion of the soul,
Maryland! My Maryland!

I hear the distant thunder hum,
Maryland!
The old-time bugle, fife, and drum,
Maryland!
She is not dead, nor deaf, nor dumb –
Huzzah! She spurns the Northern scum!
She breathes – she burns! She'll come! She'll come!
Maryland! My Maryland![420]

*Verses 1,5,6, and 9 are the most commonly sung.

---

[420] Colonel Henry King Burgwyn, *Confederate War Poems* (Nashville, Tennessee: Bill Coats, Ltd., 1990), 50-52.

Chapter Twenty-One
Violation of the Fugitive Slave Law

Constitutional Violation: Article IV, Section II, Clause 3: *No Person held to Service or Labour in one State, under the Laws thereof, escaping into another, shall, in Consequence of any Law or Regulation therein, be discharged from such Service or Labour, but shall be delivered up on Claim of the Party to whom such Service or Labour may be due.*

"The slaveholder has a legal and moral right to his slaves."[421]
Abraham Lincoln, from an October 16, 1854, speech in Peoria, Illinois

Slavery was one of the most contentious subjects in the 18th and 19th centuries. By the mid-1800s, emotions had intensified on both sides of the issue. There were several compromises, such as the Kansas-Nebraska Act, the Missouri Compromise, etc., but there was always a degree of animosity simmering below the surface.[422]

On September 18, 1850, the Fugitive Slave Act was passed by the U.S. Congress as part of the Compromise of 1850, to pacify slaveholders in the Southern and Border States and Free Soilers in the North. As with previous legislation, this law was laden with controversy highlighted by fears from some Northerners of a so-called slavocracy in the South. This, despite the fact only about six percent of White Southerners owned slaves, translating into perhaps

---

[421] Mildred Lewis Rutherford, *Truths of History* (Harrisonburg, Virginia: Old South Institute Press, 2009), 45.

[422] Confederate Admiral Raphael Semmes stated, "Great pains have been taken, by the North, to make it appear to the world that the war was a sort of moral and religious crusade against slavery. Such was not the fact. The people of the North were, indeed, opposed to slavery but merely because they thought it stood in the way in their struggle for empire." Source: *Memoirs of Service Afloat*, 62.

thirty percent of Southern families having a connection to the institution. Of this group, about half had less than five slaves and often worked with them in the fields. The ostensible fear in the North was that this relatively small number of slave owners would gain too much political control. Another fact seldom acknowledged is that there were over 3500 Blacks and/or Mulattos and an indeterminate number of American Indians who were slave owners.

The Compromise of 1850 consisted of five bills with the five distinct provisions intended to strike a sectional balance. First, California would enter the Union as a free State. Second, New Mexico and Utah would be allowed to use popular sovereignty (Douglas' position) relative to slavery. Third, the Republic of Texas would receive ten million dollars to pay its debt to Mexico while giving up its claim on the land that eventually became the State of New Mexico. Fourth, the slave trade would be abolished in Washington, D.C. Fifth, a provision in the Fugitive Slave Act established a fine against any federal official that failed to arrest a runaway slave. This created the greatest controversy "and caused many abolitionists to increase their efforts against slavery."[423]

There were underlying economic ramifications of a possible schism between North and South. As stated by Lincoln on numerous occasions, preservation of the Union was his goal, not the abolition of slavery. Maintaining a single union "was foremost in the minds of influential Republican bankers, manufacturers and heads of corporations..."[424] The Compromise of 1850 was generally seen as a palatable compromise effort.

Clay, the Kentucky lawyer, pushed his mercantilist Hamiltonian-inspired American System. As a slave owner and

---

[423] Martin Kelly, "Compromise of 1850," *About Education,*
http://americanhistory.about.com/od/beforethewar/g/compromise1850.htm,
(Accessed April 28, 2016).

[424] Derek Sheriff, "The Untold History of Nullification: Resisting Slavery," *Tenth Amendment Center,*
http://www.tenthamendmentcenter.com/2010/02/10/the-untold-history-of-nullification/, (Accessed April 24, 2016).

founding member of the American Colonization Society, Clay sought to deport Blacks (if freed) to a country or countries more suited to them. Lincoln also supported this program. A master negotiator with a vested interest in this controversy, Clay authored the key points of the compromise, part of which included putting legal force into the Fugitive Slave Clause. This directive "compelled citizens of all states to assist federal marshals and their deputies with the apprehension of suspected runaway slaves and brought all trials involving alleged fugitive slaves under federal jurisdiction."[425] Fines were to be levied against anyone who assisted in the escape of a slave. Merely providing slaves with food and shelter was a violation. "The act also suspended habeas corpus and the right to a trial by jury for suspected slaves, and made their testimony inadmissible in court. The written testimony of the alleged slave's master, on the other hand, which could be presented to the court by slave hunters, was given preferential treatment."[426] The draconian elements in this legislation further enraged many of the abolitionists and even raised the ire of previously uninterested parties.

Northern opposition to the Fugitive Slave Clause in the U.S. Constitution (Article IV, Section 2, Clause 3) had grown through the nineteenth century. Vermont and Massachusetts passed legislation in 1843 to nullify the 1793 federal Fugitive Slave Act. The 1850 Act brought a similar legislative reaction from both States. The Wisconsin Supreme Court responded in re Booth and Rycraft, 3 Wis. 157 (1854). This case involved Missouri slave owner Benjamin Garland and his fugitive slave Joshua Glover. Glover was located in Racine, Wisconsin; a warrant was issued for his arrest and he was captured. Sherman M. Booth, an abolitionist editor and John Rycraft, a settler and former slave owner, successfully led efforts to break Glover out of jail; Glover was not recaptured.

The Wisconsin Supreme Court declared the Fugitive Slave Law unconstitutional. "The same political interests that had

---

[425] Ibid.
[426] Ibid.

opposed South Carolina's nullification of an arguably unconstitutional protective tariff now supported nullification of the Fugitive Slave Clause of the Constitution itself."[427] This was a classic case of the selective use of nullification based on political and financial benefits. "The events that lead up to this monumental decision, which is a milestone in the history of the states' rights tradition, is one of the best stories most Americans have never heard."[428] The Wisconsin legislature laid out their decision:

> Resolved, That the government formed by the Constitution of the United States was not the exclusive or final judge of the extent of the powers delegated to itself; but that, as in all other cases of compact among parties having no common judge, each party has an equal right to judge for itself, as well of infractions as of the mode and measure of redress.
>
> Resolved, that the principle and construction contended for by the party which now rules in the councils of the nation, that the general government is the exclusive judge of the extent of the powers delegated to it, stop nothing short of despotism, since the discretion of those who administer the government, and not the Constitution, would be the measure of their powers; that the several states which formed that instrument, being sovereign and independent, have the unquestionable right to judge of its infractions; and that a positive defiance of those sovereignties, of all unauthorized acts done or attempted to be done under color of that instrument, is the rightful remedy.[429]

---

[427] Kevin R.C. Gutzman, *The Politically Incorrect Guide to the Constitution* (Washington, DC: Regnery Publishing, Inc., 2007), 116.

[428] Derek Sheriff, "The Untold History of Nullification: Resisting Slavery," *Tenth Amendment Center.* (Accessed April 24, 2016).

[429] Thomas E. Woods, Jr., *The Politically Incorrect Guide to American History* (Washington, DC: Regnery Publishing, Inc.), 2007, 39-40.

Using the States' Rights doctrine of nullification, Northern States were able to express their disagreement with the Fugitive Slave Act. There was strong resistance in the North, specifically toward the requirement of capturing and returning runaway slaves to their owners. "It was natural for them to think of states' rights as a tool to be used for the liberation of runaway slaves." [430] The Fugitive Slave Act created a great deal of chaos in the North. In a practical sense, this Act "brought the abolitionists into open conflict with the law. Their defense was, essentially, religious. Their creed was that slavery was a sin, and that unbounded opposition was a sacred duty."[431] Massachusetts abolitionist William Lloyd Garrison went so far as to encourage several preachers to proclaim the Bible described slavery as a sin. This was not based on anything written in the Bible, but rather on the opinion of Garrison.

The South's (and Border States') argument, based on the U.S. Constitution, was that slaves were their property and they had purchased them from their previous owners in the North. The Compromise of 1850 simply reaffirmed that constitutional guarantee, a key component being the return of runaway slaves.

The Dred Scott Case, issued by Chief Justice Roger B. Taney, reflected the same understanding. This case stated that a slave was not freed by being taken into a free State but instead freedom came at the slave-owner's discretion. Again reflecting this subject as a State issue, the House of Representatives resolved: "That Congress has no authority to interfere in the emancipation of slaves or in the treatment of them within any of the States; it remaining with the several States alone to provide any regulations there which humanity and true policy may require.'"[432]

---

[430] Thomas J. DiLorenzo, *Lincoln Unmasked—What You're Not Supposed to Know About Dishonest Abe* (New York, New York: Crown Forum, 2006), 68.

[431] Paul Gottfried, *Through European Eyes, So Good A Cause: A Decade of Southern Partisan* (Columbia, South Carolina: The Foundation for American Education, 1993), 66.

[432] Rutherford, *Truths of History*, 46.

Going back to earlier American history, efforts to free the slaves were undertaken by Benjamin Franklin (who dabbled with slavery himself) and the Quakers. Based on the U.S. Constitution, it was ruled that Congress had no legal right to interfere with slavery or slaveholders. Illinois Representative Judd said Lincoln claimed the Fugitive Slave Law to be ungodly, "But it is the law of the land,' he pointed out, 'and we must obey it as we find it."[433] Lincoln showed considerable favor to Gideon Welles, who became his Secretary of the Navy. He was also aware of Welles' skepticism about enforcing the Fugitive Slave Law; therefore, before Welles was allowed to join Lincoln's inner circle, "the new president exacted from him a pledge to support the law—even in Massachusetts."[434]

One of Lincoln's efforts to diffuse the slavery issue was centered on the introduction of the previously mentioned Corwin Amendment (the Original 13th Amendment). After his election, but before he was inaugurated, Lincoln directed William Seward to introduce this amendment in the Senate Committee of Thirteen but to be discreet about its Springfield origins. Using Seward as his point man, Lincoln wished to enact this constitutional amendment with the message, "'the Constitution should never be altered so as to authorize Congress to abolish or interfere with slavery in the states.' Lincoln also instructed Seward to get through Congress a law making illegal various 'personal liberty laws' that existed in some Northern States. (Such State laws nullified the federal Fugitive Slave Act, which required Northerners to apprehend runaway slaves)."[435] Most States in the North passed some form of Personal Liberty Law, primarily to prevent enforcement of the Fugitive Slave Law in the respective States, i.e., to nullify a federal law.

In summary, we have the Corwin Amendment (rejected by the South), which would have forever removed slavery from all

---

[433] Webb Garrison, *The Lincoln No One Knows* (Nashville, Tennessee: Rutledge Hill Press, 1993), 243.

[434] Ibid.

[435] DiLorenzo, *Lincoln Unmasked*, 54.

federal jurisdiction and theoretically allowed slavery in perpetuity where it existed, combined with Lincoln's efforts to destroy the Northern States' Personal Liberty laws, which equated to nullification of the Fugitive Slave Law.

Southerners knew history and the Constitution and they recognized hypocrisy. They knew much of the infrastructure of the North had been built off slave trade profits, and now many Northerners feigned innocence and denied active participation. "The interference on the part of the Northern politicians with the institution of slavery and the rights of the slaveholder to take his slaves where he pleased was illegal and unconstitutional."[436]

Referencing another bit of hypocrisy from the Northern side, the following facts were duly noted: the North American slave trade began in the North in 1636. The first slave ship, *Desire*, was built and launched in Massachusetts, which was also the first colony to legalize slavery in 1641 (followed by Connecticut in 1650). Massachusetts even linked slavery to the Bible and "established for slaves the set of rules 'which the law of God, established in Israel concerning such people, doth morally require.'"[437] Additionally, in 1643 "The New England Confederation of Plymouth, Massachusetts, Connecticut, and New Haven"[438] adopted a fugitive law, fourteen years before Virginia duplicated their effort. In light of the history of New England's role in American slavery, many Southerners were indignant when Northerners asserted returning slaves to their masters was an immoral act that should not be forced upon them.

There was concern in the Southern States about the motives of Lincoln and the Republicans. Aside from the party's call for higher import duties, many in the South had a legitimate fear that the Republicans would try to stir up servile insurrection through the

---

[436] Rutherford, *Truths of History*, 45.

[437] Douglas Harper, "Slavery in Massachusetts," *Slavery in the North*, http://slavenorth.com/massachusetts.htm, (Accessed April 28, 2016).

[438] Sharon Draper, "Timeline of Slavery in America 1501-1865," *SharonDraper.com*, https://sharondraper.com/timeline.pdf, (Accessed April 2016).

circulation of anti-slavery literature. *The Impending Crisis of the South*, the 1857 book written by Hinton Rowan Helper of North Carolina, attacked slavery, not from a moral standpoint, but rather as an economic detriment to White Southerners. Helper, who had no love for Blacks, asserted slavery was inefficient and retarded the development of industry in the South. Helper made an economically sound argument relative to slavery harming White non-slave owning Southerners, yet he made the dubious claim abolitionists and Free Soilers were friends of the South.

There was a strong negative reaction to Helper's book, probably second only to Harriet Beecher Stowe's *Uncle Tom's Cabin*, written in reaction to the Fugitive Slave Law and laden with stereotypes. Stowe, a Connecticut-born author and abolitionist, only had cursory real life experience with the institution of slavery but she succeeded in fanning racial flames in the North and South. Slave owners in the South and Border States were also concerned the Fugitive Slave Law would not be enforced and that slaves would not be allowed in the territories. A fear in the South was the Republicans would do everything they could to unsettle the region. The concern of the Republican Party was the economic interests of the Northeast and Upper Midwest. "Not a single southern state had voted for Lincoln, and between his election in 1860 and his inauguration in 1861, the seven Deep South states seceded from the union."[439]

Lincoln assured the property rights of secessionists would be respected; this included property in slaves. His position had always been that slavery should not spread outside of the States where it already existed. According to Union Secretary of State Seward, part of the reasoning "against the extension of slavery had always really been concern for the welfare of the white man, and not an unnatural sympathy for the Negro."[440] Horace Greeley, editor of the *New York*

---

[439] Gutzman, 121.

[440] Thomas J. DiLorenzo, "The Economics of Slavery," *LewRockwell.com,* http://www.lewrockwell.com/2002/09/thomas-dilorenzo/the-economics-of-slavery/, (Accessed April 24, 2016).

Tribune, echoed this sentiment by saying "All the unoccupied territory...shall be preserved for the benefit of the White Caucasian race—a thing which cannot be except by the exclusion of slavery."[441]

Lincoln asserted the Fugitive Slave Law would be enforced as a means of guaranteeing these rights. After a few months, the U.S. Congress adopted the new status of contraband, replacing the runaway slave designation. This bit of semantics provided a technicality around the Fugitive Slave Law and the Union Army used many of these contrabands as a newly found source of manual labor. "On New Year's Day 1863, this usage became obsolete; persons in Confederate-held regions were suddenly declared to have lost all property rights in slaves."[442]

Though it sounds strange in the modern era, slavery was constitutionally protected in nineteenth century America. Abolitionist Garrison and Confederate Vice President Stephens both stated slavery was more secure in the Union than out of it. Lincoln repeatedly promised to protect the institution and enforce the Fugitive Slave Law. Although he generally enforced it, he often looked the other way as others in his administration worked to undermine it.

---

[441] Ibid.
[442] Garrison, 233-235.

Chapter Twenty-Two
West Virginia

Constitutional Violation: Article IV, Section III, Clause 1. *New States may be admitted by the Congress into this Union; but no new State shall be formed or erected within the Jurisdiction of any other State; nor any State be formed by the Junction of two or more States, or Parts of States, without the Consent of the Legislatures of the States concerned as well as of the Congress.*

"The division of a State is a dreaded precedent. But a measure made expedient by a war, is no precedent for times of peace...I believe the admission of West Virginia into the Union is expedient."[443]
Abraham Lincoln, December 31, 1862

The original home of Jamestown, the first permanent English settlement in America, Virginia occupies a position of historical importance among all States. Virginia was pivotal during the war from both a military and symbolic standpoint, representing the epitome of the American South.

Lincoln's contention that the Union was indivisible did not mesh with the Jeffersonian philosophy strongly held in the South. He outlined his beliefs and intentions in his First Inaugural Address by claiming "'No state upon its own mere motion can lawfully get out of the Union.' This meant that 'resolves and ordinances to that effect are legally void...In view of the Constitution and the laws, the

---

[443] "A State of Convenience: The Creation of West Virginia," Opinion of Abraham Lincoln on the Admission of West Virginia from the Lincoln Papers, Library of Congress, *West Virginia Division of Culture and History*, http://www.wvculture.org/history/statehood/lincolnopinion.html, (Accessed April 24, 2016).

Union is unbroken…'"[444] Insisting the Southern States never actually left the Union, Lincoln framed his military responses as being designed "to suppress an insurrection existing within the United States."[445] Many in the North shared the South's view that the Republic is a voluntary confederation of States. An interesting observation about Lincoln's First Address appeared in the March 5, 1861, New York *Journal of Commerce*: "he commits the practical error of setting up the theory of *an unbroken Union*, against the stubborn fact of a divided and dissevered one."[446]

Virginia was divided into two distinct regions separated by mountains; this limited their interaction. The Eastern part was more Anglican (Episcopalian), the Western part more non-Anglican Protestant. There was minimal trade between the two sections and there were differences in their trading partners. The Eastern region was more agricultural and the Western part was more industrial, possessing a geographical and economic connection to the contiguous States of Ohio and Pennsylvania. Also, the Baltimore and Ohio Railroad that ran through the area was critical to the Union as a connection between Washington D.C. and the Midwest. Furthermore, many in the western part of the State felt their taxes were disproportionately spent in the eastern part of the State.

Most of the State's anti-secession sentiment was around the Wheeling area. The 1860 election mirrored their varying economic interests. Lincoln only received votes in fourteen of Virginia's 160 counties with both Fauquier and Marion counties supplying only one vote each. There were 167,223 total votes cast from Virginia; 1929 votes were cast for Lincoln, and 1402 of those were from the area that became West Virginia.[447]

---

[444] Webb Garrison, *The Lincoln No One Knows* (Nashville, Tennessee: Rutledge Hill Press, 1993), 193.

[445] Ibid.

[446] Ibid., 194.

[447] "The 1860 Presidential Vote in Virginia," Extracted from *The Tribune Almanac and Political Register for 1861* (New York: The Tribune Association), *West Virginia Division of Culture and History*,

Virginia adopted an Ordinance of Secession on April 17, 1861, and the ordinance was put to a vote of the people in the form of a referendum on May 23, 1861. In response to the initial adoption of the Ordinance of Secession, representatives from the western part of the State held the First Wheeling Convention May 13-15, 1861. This meeting included delegates from twenty-seven counties in western Virginia and was specifically called to discuss what steps to take if the majority of Virginians approved secession.[448] Connecticut-born Chester D. Hubbard, banker, manufacturer, and Virginia transplant, suggested if the State voted to secede the western representatives should reconvene on June 11 and elect delegates for a new State. This was the First Session of the Second Wheeling Convention "and the Committee on Permanent Organization selected Arthur I. Boreman to serve as president of the convention."[449] Pennsylvania-born Virginia transplant Boreman was a lawyer, politician, and advocate of internal improvements in his area. Francis H. Pierpont also advocated reorganization of the government; he was a lawyer, who "served as counsel for the Baltimore and Ohio Railroad until 1856...and was involved in various business ventures that included mining and shipping coal

---

http://www.wvculture.org/history/statehood/1860presidentialvote.html, (Accessed April 24, 2016).

[448] Prominent members from western Virginia included George Latham (lawyer and politician), William Zinn (politician, owner of an 1100 acre farm and one of the largest slave owners in Preston County), General John Jay Jackson (attorney, politician and soldier in the Seminole War under Andrew Jackson), John S. Carlile (lawyer, politician and slave owner), Waitman Willey (lawyer, politician and one time slave owner) and Chester D. Hubbard (banker who was also involved in the manufacture of iron and lumber).

[449] "Chapter Seven, First Session of the Second Wheeling Convention, June 11-25, 1861," *West Virginia Division of Culture and History*, http://www.wvculture.org/history/statehood/statehood07.html, (Accessed April 24, 2016).

by rail."[450] Many of the advocates of secession from Virginia were connected to manufacturing and stood to benefit from Northern economic policies.

A key player in the Second Wheeling Convention was Archibald Campbell, son of Dr. Archibald W. Campbell. The junior Campbell was born in Steubenville, Ohio, in 1833. With family roots in Virginia, he returned to the Wheeling area, and become the editor of the *Wheeling Intelligencer*. A supporter of Lincoln, Campbell opposed slavery and Virginia's secession from the Union; however, he supported the secession of the western counties of Virginia. Largely through Campbell's efforts, "the rump body reassembled on June 11 and disavowed all allegiance to the C.S.A. Six days later, fifty-six persons from about two-thirds of the counties involved signed a 'declaration of independence' from the old government of Virginia."[451] They formed a provisional government, including a legislature, and they elected Pierpont as their governor. Pierpont was born in Monongalia County, Virginia, and educated at Allegheny College in Pennsylvania. Although he campaigned for Bell in 1860, Pierpont eventually became a Lincoln supporter.

As another act of defiance, around the midpoint of the First Session of the Second Wheeling Convention, Campbell wrote in the June 18, 1861, *Daily Intelligencer*: "The people of western Virginia will never and ought never to be satisfied with anything short of division of the state; and that division should be put in train at once by this convention, so that it may be secured at the earliest possible moment."[452]

---

[450] Craig Moore, "A Guide to the Francis H. Pierpont Restored Government Executive Papers, 1861-1865," A Collection in the Library of Virginia, Accession Number 36928, *Library of Virginia*, 2002, http://ead.lib.virginia.edu/vivaxtf/view?docId=lva/vi00167.xml, (Accessed April 28, 2016).

[451] Garrison, 194.

[452] "Archibald Campbell: A Champion for West Virginia, http://wvweb.com/page/content.detail/id/500125/Archibald-Campbell--A-Champion-for-West-Virginia.html?nav=5032, (Accessed April 24, 2016).

Those present at the First Session of the Second Wheeling Convention decided that western Virginia should reorganize the government of the entire State of Virginia. The next step unfolded the following month. On July 1, there was a meeting held in Wheeling. John S. Carlile and Waitman T. Willy were selected as senators. "They, together with the representatives, William G. Brown, Jacob B. Blair, K. V. Whaley, as Congressmen, were admitted to seats in the Senate and House of Representatives from the State of Virginia."[453] Delegates reassembled on August 6, 1861, at the Second Session of the Second Wheeling Convention and they passed "an ordinance that nullified the proceedings of the Richmond Convention and declared all actions of the convention 'illegal, inoperative, null, void, and without force or effect.'"[454] Also, during the August meeting they passed an ordinance establishing the name of their new State as Kanawha, an Indian moniker already referencing a tributary of the Ohio River. Three months later, the name was dropped and West Virginia was chosen as its replacement. By then, the Union Army controlled western Virginia.

Article IV, Section III, Clause 1 of the constitution specifies that the legislature of an existing State and Congress must approve the creation of a State. Pro-Union factions, with approval from the Lincoln Administration, went through the motions for West Virginia to secede from Virginia. Lincoln, who insisted Virginia was still in the Union, was aware of the constitutional requirement regarding the creation of a State and he was aware slavery existed in the area in question. Although the effort to secede from Virginia appears to have been initiated by the aforementioned citizens of West Virginia,

---

[453] "First Wheeling Convention," The Bar, *West Virginia Division of Culture and History,*
http://www.wvculture.org/history///statehood/sayre.html, (Accessed April 24, 2016).

[454] "Chapter Nine, Second Session of the Second Wheeling Convention, August 6-21, 1861," *West Virginia Division of Culture and History,* http://www.wvculture.org/history/statehood/statehood09.html, (Accessed April 24, 2016).

Lincoln recognized the political expediency of adding another State to the Union cause and thus gave his approval.

Adding West Virginia to the Union provided multiple strategic advantages: it was an ideal buffer zone to protect Pennsylvania and Ohio from Confederate incursions; a substantial section of the Baltimore and Ohio Railroad lay in the Western part of Virginia, providing a linkage from Washington D.C. to St. Louis, Missouri; and many agreed with Republican economic policies.

On December 31, 1862, Lincoln announced West Virginia had been added as a *Slave State* with the proviso that slavery would be gradually ended; the effective date of Statehood was to be six months out—on June 20, 1863. The next day the Emancipation Proclamation was issued, which symbolically ended slavery in the States out of Union control.

As essentially a trial run of reconstruction, many of the citizens of West Virginia quickly soured on the idea of their new State; this group included John S. Carlile, lawyer, politician, and slaveholder and early advocate for the secession of the Western counties. The doubters were divided over slavery, internal improvements, and the belligerence of the Union Army. Many resented the force of the Republican Party in its displacement of officials in an area that had supported Bell and was not unfriendly to Democrats. Ironically, the people of western Virginia had long complained that internal improvements favored eastern Virginia. Valid arguments can be made that Virginia and West Virginia should be separate States, but the division should have been accomplished via the prescribed constitutional procedure.

Another touch of irony lies within the Virginia schism. Although the leaders for West Virginia's creation were unionist, the constituency of the area was split. Within the counties of western Virginia "eighteen West Virginia counties voted in favor of secession. Twenty voted against secession, and one resulted in a tie. Vote records for the remaining nine counties were lost during the war."[455] Despite West Virginia's admission as a Union Slave State in June 1863, allegiance to the Federal Government was mixed.

The case involving West Virginia illustrates Lincoln's ability to successfully manipulate matters politically and remain relatively unscathed. If secession was to his political benefit, Lincoln was approving. Not only did he *conditionally* approve the creation of a new State, Lincoln helped concoct the West Virginia puppet government in Alexandria, Virginia near Washington, D.C. "His own attorney, Edward Bates, believed that this act was unconstitutional, arguing the obvious-that a state must first exist before being accepted into the Union." [456] There is no legally constitutional way to create a new State without the consent of the citizens of the original State. Again, Lincoln recognized the political benefit of adding West Virginia; it would boost his Electoral College votes in the 1864 election and make it more difficult to reverse his favored legislation.

As a traditional Whig stronghold, East Tennessee and Western North Carolina also contained numerous opponents of Southern secession. Like West Virginia, the area was anti-secession but not particularly anti-slavery. Had efforts in East Tennessee reached the level of Virginia, it is likely Lincoln would have *approved* the area as a new State as well.

Individual States and the Federal Government exist under a system of dual sovereignty or federalism, whereas counties are simply sub-divisions of a State (the counties did not create the States). The process and requirements for creating a new State is spelled out clearly in the constitution. Approval by the legislature of the State or States to be divided is given the utmost priority and approval by the Congress supports the will of the State or States to

---

[455] "West Virginia," *Hometown USA*, http://www.hometownusa.com/wv/index.html, (Accessed April 28, 2016).

[456] Thomas DiLorenzo, *The Real Lincoln* (Roseville, California: Prima Publishing, 2002), 148-149.

be divided. All parties must consent to the division for constitutional legitimacy.

The Founding Fathers opposed mass democracy, referring to it as mob rule. They limited the legitimate functions of the central government to the enumerated powers in Article I, Section 8 of the U.S. Constitution. The system of checks and balances was designed to keep one branch of government from dominating another one. Lincoln violated this system and exercised ungranted powers to force his will on the South. One of the ironies is "the legislation establishing West Virginia allowed for the people of the new state to vote on a gradual emancipation policy."[457] This position mirrors Douglas' popular sovereignty stance during his debates with Lincoln, who opposed the concept of allowing the territories to decide for themselves whether or not to allow slavery.[458]

The situation with West Virginia required circumvention of the U. S. Constitution. As noted tax attorney, the late Charles Adams, stated: "In one of the strangest acts of contempt of the Constitution, he (Lincoln) created the state of West Virginia, in contravention of Article IV, Section 3, which required the approval of Virginia. No such approval was obtained. Lincoln excused this because it was 'expedient.'"[459] The crux of the violation lies within the language "but no new State shall be formed or erected within the Jurisdiction of any other State...without the consent of the

---

[457] Ibid., 149.

[458] After the war, Virginia attempted to regain its lost counties, filing suit in 1867 and 1871 to regain "her lost provinces, but the Reconstruction Congress, and later the Supreme Court, gave sanction to the farcical plebiscite of '63." From: DiLorenzo, *The Real Lincoln*, 149. The Reconstruction Congress (1860s-1870s) controlled the South and created pseudo governments that disenfranchised ex-Confederate soldiers. Using and manipulating freedmen, they stole vast amounts of money from the Southern States' treasuries.

[459] Charles Adams, *When in the Course of Human Events — Arguing the Case for Southern Secession* (Lanham, Maryland: Rowman & Littlefield Publishers Inc., 2000), 58.

Legislatures concerned as well as of the Congress."[460] None of the required criteria were met. The representatives of Virginia voted to leave the Union and the legitimate government did not consent to giving up approximately one-fourth of its territory. A faction in the western counties that opposed Virginia's secession declared itself to be the legitimate State government and the Lincoln Administration recognized the reformed government as valid. Military force cemented it.

A somewhat bittersweet legacy of the West Virginia story is reflected from those who were born as Virginians:

> It is one thing to have gone down fighting off an invader; something else to have been kidnapped and taken alive. It is proud memory for a community to boast itself an unreconstructed rebel, flaunting its Stars and Bars; but it is ironic and mournful for a constituency to have supplied these same Stars and Bars with more troops than any section in the South, and yet have its mail postmarked West Virginia. But just that happened here.[461]

---

[460] Legal Information Institute, Article IV, U.S. Constitution, from *Cornell University Law School*, https://www.law.cornell.edu/constitution/articleiv, (Accessed April 24, 2016).

[461] Holmes Alexander, "Virginia's 'Lost Counties,'" in *So Good A Cause: A Decade Of Southern Partisan*, ed. Oran P. Smith, 90-95. (Columbia, South Carolina: The Foundation for American Education, 1993), 91.

Chapter Twenty-Three
The Trent Affair

Constitutional Violation: Laws of Neutrality. Article VI, Clause 2:
This Constitution, and the Laws of the United States which shall be made in Pursuance thereof; and all Treaties made, or which shall be made, under the Authority of the United States, shall be the supreme Law of the Land; and the Judges in every State shall be bound thereby, any Thing in the Constitution or Laws of any State to the Contrary notwithstanding.

"Either you must surrender those prisoners or you will have war with England, and war with England means we cannot keep the South in the Union."[462]

Union General George B. McClellan

On October 12, 1861, almost six months into the war, the Confederate government dispatched two commissioners: James Mason, commissioner to Great Britain and France, and New York-born John Slidell, commissioner to France. These gentlemen were charged with securing recognition for the Confederate States of America. Already representing the Confederacy was the Liverpool based James Dunwoody Bullock, Theodore Roosevelt's uncle on his mother's side. Bullock's strength was buying weapons—not diplomacy. Mason and Slidell were charged with finding military supplies and negotiating trade agreements to support their fledgling country.

Mason and Slidell, along with their secretaries, George Eustis and J.E. McFarland, boarded the CSS *Theodora* in Charleston, South Carolina. The *Theodora* navigated the Union blockade and arrived at Nassau, Bahamas. From there, the men sailed to Havana, Cuba. The

---

[462] Mildred Lewis Rutherford, *A True Estimate of Abraham Lincoln & Vindication of the South* (Wiggins, Mississippi: Crown Rights Book Company, 1997), 49-50.

governor of Cuba entertained them for a few weeks before they were finally booked on the *Trent*, a British royal mail steamship.

The *Trent* departed Cuba on November 8, 1861. Mason and Slidell made no effort to conceal their trip since they were confident their mission would be fully protected under international law, which guaranteed the sovereignty of shipping vessels of all countries. Furthermore, Britain and France had unambiguously maintained their neutrality in the American conflict.

At Cienfuegos, on the southern coast of Cuba, news of their trip reached Charles Wilkes, captain of the USS *San Jacinto*. Wilkes weighed the political and international ramifications of intervening with the *Trent* and decided to intercept the vessel. On November 8, 1861, Wilkes located the *Trent* 240 miles east of Havana and fired a shell across the ship's bow. The *San Jacinto* pulled up beside the *Trent* and Wilkes boarded the ship. Captain James Moir denied Wilkes' request to search his vessel and refused to provide papers or a passenger list. Wilkes said he had information that Mason, Slidell, Eustis, and McFarland were on board. Upon hearing the conversation, each of the Southern passengers joined the discussion. After meeting a degree of resistance, Wilkes called four or five armed officers to help force the Southern representatives off the *Trent*. Commander Richard Williams, Royal Mail Agent, witnessed the actions of Wilkes and vehemently protested:

> In this ship, I am the representative of Her Majesty's government, and I call upon the officers of the ship and passengers generally, to mark my words, when in the name of the British government, and in distinct language, I denounce this as an illegal act, an act in violation of international law; and act indeed of wanton piracy, which, had we the means of defence, you would not dare to attempt.[463]

---

[463] E.A. Pollard, *The Lost Cause*, A Facsimile of the Original 1886 Edition (Avenel, New Jersey: Gramercy Books, 1994), 195. [Union Navy

Williams' words were ignored; Mason and Slidell were taken off the ship and placed on the *San Jacinto*. Wilkes set out for Hampton Roads, Virginia, while the *Trent* headed to St. Thomas. Wilkes communicated via dispatch with Navy Secretary Welles and Secretary of State Seward. Seward ordered Wilkes to take the prisoners to Fort Warren in Boston Harbor. The *San Jacinto* was passionately greeted upon arrival in Boston on November 23, 1861.

Many in the North celebrated the seizure of commissioners traveling on an unarmed ship as a victory over both the South and Great Britain. Though Wilkes faced no personal danger during the event, he became an instant hero and received gratitude from the public and official thanks from Congress. Wilkes also received media support in the Northeast and personal praise from Welles. Adulation of Wilkes' actions resulted in his characterization as a man of "intelligence, ability, decision, and firmness."[464]

The *New York Times* wrote: "There is no drawback to our jubilation. The universal Yankee nation is getting decidedly awake. As for Captain Wilkes, let the handsome thing be done.'"[465] Much of the Northern press encouraged the government to hold Mason and Slidell. The sentiment of many supporters was that the Union was only giving Great Britain a taste of its own medicine meted out over previous years. Wilkes received a Congressional medal for his actions.

The seizure of Mason and Slidell added fuel to an already smoldering situation. In his book, *American Statesman*, New Hampshire lawyer and author Thornton Lothrop wrote: "...that Seward could not conceal his gratification and approval of the act."[466] However, General McClellan (as reflected in the opening

---

Lieutenant D. M. Fairfax, ironically a Virginian by birth, boarded the ship with a party of marines to carry out the deed.]

[464] Ibid.

[465] Ibid., 196.

[466] Rutherford, *A True Estimate of Abraham Lincoln*, 49.

quote) saw this move as a possible disaster in the North's attempt to keep the Southern States in the Union.

Unlikely as it would have been, Seward speculated that a British threat might actually motivate the South to rejoin the Union to repel a common foe. Lincoln did not agree with this hypothesis. However, the very real possibility of military reprisal from Great Britain, so astutely noted by McClellan, caused Seward to back off his hardline stance, and ultimately throw all of the blame on Wilkes.

Lincoln, who lacked expertise in international law, feared the incident could possibly cause Britain to sympathize and align with the Confederacy, thus creating two military opponents. There was already a measure of concern about the French and Spanish possibly causing problems for the United States through Mexico. This prompted Lincoln to caution Seward: "One war at a time."[467]

Lincoln was aware the United States had violated Great Britain's rights as a neutral nation under international law. "I am not getting much sleep out of that exploit of Wilkes, and I suppose we must look up the law of the case. I am not much of a prize lawyer, but it seems to me pretty clear that if Wilkes saw fit to make that capture on the high seas, he had no right to turn his quarterdeck into a prize court."[468] A prize court is a municipal court that determines the legality of captured goods and vessels during war. From the standpoint of international law, this determination must be adjudicated by the captor state's prize court. This did not happen.

There was outrage in the South over the seizure. The *Richmond Enquirer* and the *Atlanta Southern Confederacy* condemned the act. Confederate Secretary of War Benjamin echoed the

---

[467]"Foreign Influences: Trent Affair," One War at a Time, November 8, 1861, The War for States' Rights, *Civil War Bluegrass,* http://civilwar.bluegrass.net/ForeignInfluences/trentaffair-onewar.html, (Accessed April 24, 2016).

[468] Richard "Shotgun" Weeks, "The Trent Affair," excerpted from The Confederate Military History, Volume I, Chapter XV, *Shotgun's Home of the American Civil War,* http://civilwarhome.com/trent.htm, (Accessed April 24, 2016).

sentiment of these newspapers. The South saw Britain's disapproval of the incident as a potential silver lining that might motivate them to officially support the Confederacy.

Great Britain and the United States had a long history of both hostility and cooperation. After the Revolution, there had been disputes over the boundaries in Maine, Oregon, and Canada; disputes over the acquisition of Texas and California; and the British recruitment of American mercenaries to fight in the Crimean War. Furthermore, Seward felt antagonistic toward the British concerning its possible recognition of the Confederate States. Despite Great Britain's known sympathy for the South, on May 13, 1861, the British government proclaimed its neutrality in the American dispute.

On November 27, word of the seizure reached London. The British were outraged and insulted by the incident and considerable discussion arose within the government. During an emergency meeting of the British Cabinet, Prime Minister Lord Palmerston exclaimed, "I don't know whether you are going to stand for this, but I'll be damned if I do."[469] Echoing Palmerston's response, the general sentiment in England was against arbitration, and the severity and threat of the *Trent Affair* led to the creation of a War Committee in the British cabinet. The Law Officers of the Crown, which included the Queen's advocate, the Attorney General and the Solicitor General, declared the commander of the *San Jacinto* had violated international law.

> *If the Government of Washington holds that the Confederates are belligerents, then it is bound by the laws of war, which treat only military and naval persons traveling for belligerent purposes as contraband, and even*

---

[469] "The Trent Affair," *U.S. Department of State,* http://future.state.gov/when/timeline/1861_timeline/trent_affair.html, (Accessed April 24, 2016).

in that case direct that the contraband character shall be duly established in a Prize Court. If, on the other hand, it declares that Messrs. MASON and SLIDELL were seized as rebels by virtue of its Municipal Law, then the right of asylum has been clearly violated. Indeed, on the latter plea the Federal Government might station a sloop in the Channel to board the Dover and Folkestone steamers daily, and carry off every Southerner who might be found. The principle on which our Government rests its demand is, that a British ship must—until her violation of neutral rights is fully proved—be held to be British ground, as much as if she were an actual piece of British soil, and the right to protection of all persons on board is as valid as if they were on British territory. Now, no such violation has been proved, or has been sought to be proved, against the Trent, and consequently the seizure of the four persons who were forcibly dragged from her decks was entirely illegal.[470]

Her Majesty's minister to the United States, Richard B. Pemell Lyons (Lord Lyons), advocated action against the Union; he did not advocate an alliance with the Confederacy but he felt their representatives should be welcomed. There was general distrust of Seward amongst the British. In a February 11, 1852, Senate speech, Seward sympathized with the Irish and made other comments advocating that the United States should be the only power on the North American continent. Lyons did not think Seward wanted a war with Britain, but he was concerned Seward might manipulate matters to gain an advantage both politically and in worldwide perception.

---

[470] "The Trent Affair; Opinion of the Law Officers of the Crown," the *London Globe* (Reprint), December 19, 1861, *The New York Times*, http://www.nytimes.com/1861/12/19/news/the-trent-affair-opinion-of-the-law-officers-of-the-crown.html?pagewanted=2, (Accessed April 24, 2016).

On November 30, 1861, Lord John Russell (1ˢᵗ Earl Russell), English Whig and two-time British Prime Minister, sent Queen Victoria the draft of the dispatches Lyons was to deliver to Seward. As the British formulated their revised response, other communications also took place. Lincoln had appointed Charles Francis Adams as minister to Britain. Adams, an editor, politician and diplomat, was descended from the prominent Massachusetts family that included two presidents. He was charged with trying to convince the British that the war was an internal insurrection and that the Confederacy should not be recognized as having rights under international law. Queen Victoria asked for input from her husband and consort, Prince Albert. While in his sick bed, Albert softened the wording to help diffuse a potentially volatile situation.

This intervention provided an avenue for the American Government to disavow Wilkes' actions, and lessen the chance of conflict. On December 17, Adams received the dispatch from Seward stating Wilkes acted on his own, whereupon Adams immediately shared the dispatch with Russell. Lyons met with Seward on December 19, but, per instructions given by Lord Russell, he only described the contents of the ultimatum to Seward. Upon Seward's request, Lyons gave him an unofficial copy of the ultimatum, and both men agreed the official ultimatum would be delivered on December 23. Seward shared the unofficial ultimatum with Lincoln; it stated the American government had seven days to respond. If no decision was rendered within the prescribed time period, "Lord Lyons was ordered to close the legation, remove the archives, notify the British Atlantic fleet, and return home."[471]

After waiting the seven days as demanded, Lyons contacted Seward again. Seward informed Lyons that the response would be delayed, claiming he could not give an answer until after Christmas. Lyons was greatly displeased with the response.

The issue was hotly debated in the public and in Congress. There were many things to consider and much Northern sentiment

---

[471] Rutherford, *A True Estimate of Abraham Lincoln*, 50.

favored an unyielding stance against the British. The position of France had to be factored in as well. Although neutral in the war, France had maintained generally good relationships with the South since the American Revolution, especially during the presidency of Jefferson, a known admirer of the French.

In response to the Federal government's actions that precipitated the *Trent Affair*, Antoine Edouard Thouvenel, France's Minister of Foreign Affairs, condemned the Lincoln Administration's violation of international law. Feelings were so intense the French announced they would align with the British if a conflict with the United States developed. The cordial relationships Slidell had developed with Louis Napoleon and his ministers certainly did not hurt the Southern cause.

In consideration of the potential volatility of the situation and despite the possibility of alienating the citizens of the North, Seward and Lincoln reversed course. Though the Russians had let it be known they would support the United States, a possible British invasion through Canada, alienation of the French, and the ongoing war with the South would have placed the North in a difficult position. The Cabinet quickly moved from a feeling of euphoria to one of humility. "Seward shut himself in his room, barred the door against interruption, and began his apology."[472]

On December 27, Seward announced that the Confederate representatives would be freed. As a means of claiming a partial victory in the affair, he also insisted "that Britain had finally adopted the American conception of neutral rights over which the two nations had fought a war in 1812."[473]

One important thing this violation signaled to Britain was the necessity of clearly defining its own sovereignty, including its vast possessions around the world. Indeed, the *Trent Affair* reverberated throughout British North America and Canada as

---

[472] Ibid.

[473] "The Trent Affair," *U.S. Department of State*, (Accessed April 24, 2016).

"they realized they could become a battlefield in a potential Anglo-Northern war."[474] In preparation for defense of one of its colonies, London called out 14,000 officers and men of the Canadian militia prior to the Union's capitulation.

During this entire episode, the British were suspicious about the Lincoln Administration's motives, especially the claim that Wilkes acted on his own. As reflected in the earlier commentary from The *London Globe*, the British claimed that if the Confederate representatives were considered to be belligerents, the laws of war "treat only military and naval persons traveling for belligerent purposes as contraband...duly established in a Prize Court."[475] The other option was, that if the Southern representatives were seized as rebels by Union forces, there was a violation of the right of asylum.[476]

The *London Times, London Herald,* and *London Evening Star* all reported on the questionable validity of the blame falling entirely on Wilkes. Prior to the actual event involving the *Trent,* the British were informed that according to information gathered from General Scott after his arrival in Paris, the Cabinet in Washington had discussed seizure of the Confederate agents for quite some time.

---

[474] "Towards Confederation—Influence of the American Civil War: The Trent Affair," *Library and Archives Canada,* https://www.collectionscanada.gc.ca/confederation/023001-2400.03-e.html, (Accessed April 24, 2016).

[475] "The Trent Affair; Opinion of the Law Officers of the Crown," from the *London Times,* December 19, 1861, *New York Times Reprints,* http://www.nytimes.com/1861/12/19/news/the-trent-affair-opinion-of-the-law-officers-of-the-crown.html, (Accessed April 24, 2016).

[476] Another factor was British awareness of the activities of the USS *James Adger,* originally owned by James Adger II of Charleston, but confiscated in New York and converted into a Union Steamer. Thinking Mason and Slidell were on board the CSS *Nashville,* the *James Adger* searched for the *Nashville* until the ship entered British waters.

It was reported-the captain of the San Jacinto acted entirely in pursuance of orders given months ago by Mr. Seward, after the mature deliberation of the President's Cabinet...,we have been informed that the determination of the United States government to arrest the Southern commissioners, wherever and whenever their capture could be effected, was formally known some time back to our own government, and that a certain man-of-war is now well on its way to the Bahamas to protect the Trent from the anticipated outrage. This does not look as if the president would disavow the act of Captain Wilkes; nor is it, indeed, in the nature of things that any officer would have been guilty of such an outrage on the British flag, unless he had received special instruction, unless the insult had been premeditated and the intent hostile.[477]

Despite suspicion of the U.S. government's action, the British did not retaliate. One probable reason was Russia's threat of intervention on the side of the North if Britain and France aligned with the Confederacy. As recorded by Thurlow Weed, Russia's Tsar Alexander II let it be known his country would provide military support for the North, ostensibly to maintain a worldwide balance of power. Also, Great Britain and France had attacked Russia and its Baltic fleet, which meant there was existing hostility.

Weed, the New York Whig/Republican publisher and envoy to Great Britain, wrote about the likelihood of Russian intervention, noting the Russians stationed a fleet off the coast of San Francisco for several months early in the war. At the time, Union Admiral David Farragut resided at the Astor House and a frequent visitor was a Russian Admiral he befriended during his youth when both

---

[477] "The Trent Affair; Opinion of the Law Officers of the Crown," from the *London Herald*, December 19, 1861, *New York Times Reprints*, http://www.nytimes.com/1861/12/19/news/the-trent-affair-opinion-of-the-law-officers-of-the-crown.html, (Accessed April 24, 2016).

men spent time in the Mediterranean. During one of their visits, Farragut asked the Russian the reason for his presence in San Francisco:

> Why are you spending the winter here in idleness? 'I am here,' replied the Russian Admiral, under sealed orders, to be broken only in a contingency that has not yet occurred.' He added that other Russian war vessels were lying off San Francisco with similar orders. During the conversation the Russian Admiral admitted that he had received orders to break the seals, if during the Rebellion we became involved in a war with foreign nations. Strict confidence was then enjoined. When in Washington a few days later, Secretary Seward informed me that he had asked the Russian Minister why his government kept their ships of war so long in our harbors, who, while in answering he disclaimed any knowledge of the nature of their visit, felt at liberty to say that it had no unfriendly purpose.[478]

Louis Napoleon of France asked Russia and England to join them and break the Union blockade. The Russian Ambassador in London told his country's government that England was readying for war with the U.S. because of the *Trent Affair*. "Hence two fleets were immediately sent across the Atlantic under sealed orders, so that if their services were not needed, the intentions of the Emperor would remain, as they have to this day, secret."[479]

Weed went on to add that Russia would be a powerful ally of the United States if England and France decided to officially assist

---

[478] "Tsar Alexander II Pledges support for the Union," Excerpted from his autobiography, *Memoir of Thurlow Weed, Vol. II*, Boston, Massachusetts: Houghton-Mifflin Co., 1884, 346-347. *Reformation.org*, http://www.reformation.org/czar-alexander.html, (Accessed April 24, 2016).

[479] Ibid.

the Confederate States. This information was validated by Russian Prince Gortchakoff, who possessed an order written by Tsar Alexander directing the Russian admiral to report to Lincoln for orders if Great Britain and France sided with the Confederacy.

Mason and Slidell were released on January 1, 1862, and made their way back to the Confederate States of America. Seward's agreement to release the representatives and apologize for accosting the British mail ship dashed Southern hopes for recognition. The South's delight in seeing the North humiliated provided little compensation for the failure of England and France to come to the aid of the Confederacy and virtually assure its goal of independence.

The *Trent Affair* presented the most volatile diplomatic crises the U.S. government faced during the war. Eventually, a resolution was reached that satisfied the United States and Great Britain, but the affair left myriad questions that lingered for years. Many issues came to the forefront as a result of the actions of the Americans, e.g., search and seizure, rights of neutrality, contraband issues, transport of military personnel, diplomatic privilege, and immunity.

Ultimately, the Lincoln Administration's actions caused only minimal damage. They avoided the nightmare of having to face the British Navy, with more than enough power to end the naval blockade of the South. Lincoln and the U.S Government actually received some benefit in the end. Although the majority of British sentiment was with the Confederacy, Lincoln's and Seward's capitulation and eventual settlement of the issue created a greater bond between Great Britain and the United States. The American-British cooperation in resolving the *Trent Affair* and Seward's political savvy helped deter England's intervention on behalf of the Confederate States of America. In April 1862, the Lyons-Seward Treaty clamped down on the movement of slaves over the Atlantic.

Chapter Twenty-Four
The Emancipation Proclamation: A Worthless Piece of Paper or Ingenious War Measure?
(Part 1)

Constitutional Violation: Article IV, Section III, Clause 2: *The Congress shall have Power to dispose of and make all needful Rules and Regulations respecting the Territory or other Property belonging to the United States; and nothing in this Constitution shall be so construed as to Prejudice any Claims of the United States, or of any particular State.*

"Lincoln well knew that the North was not fighting to free slaves, nor was the South fighting to preserve slavery. In that awful conflict slavery went to pieces."[480]

Union General Don Piatt

One of the myths surrounding the Emancipation Proclamation is the assertion that it was a humanitarian gesture.[481] Lincoln did not consider Blacks equal to Whites and his often-repeated ideal scenario was to have all of them shipped out of the United States. On this issue he remained consistent virtually until his death.

---

[480] George Edmonds, *Facts and Falsehoods Concerning the War on the South 1861-1865* (Wiggins, Mississippi: Crown Rights Book Company, 1997), 218.

[481] Since its issuance, questions have arisen about the Emancipation Proclamation. Referencing the proclamation as "a worthless piece of paper" is attributed to Dr. Leonard Haynes, a Black Professor at Southern University in Baton Rouge, Louisiana. Haynes trumpeted Black loyalty to the South.

On September 18, 1858, in a debate with Stephen Douglas in Charleston, Illinois, Lincoln said:

> I will say, then, that I am not, nor ever have been, in favor of bringing about in anyway the social and political equality of the white and black races—that I am not, nor ever have been, in favor of making voters or jurors of negroes, nor of qualifying them to hold office, nor to intermarry with white people; and I will say in addition to this that there is a physical difference between the white and black races...I, as much as any other man, am in favor of having the superior position assigned to the white race.[482]

In the same debate Lincoln said this about the geographical separation of Blacks and Whites:

> Such separation if effected at all, must be effected by colonization: what colonization most needs is a hearty will...Let us be brought to believe that it is morally right, and at the same time favorable to, or at least not against, our interests to transfer the African to his native clime, and we shall find a way to do it, however great the task may be.[483]

Four years later, Lincoln's view remained unaltered. On August 14, 1862, during a conference at the White House with a group of free Blacks, Lincoln told them:

> You and we are different races. We have between us a broader difference that exists between almost any other two races. Whether it is right or wrong, I need not

---

[482] James Ronald Kennedy and Walter Donald Kennedy, *The South Was Right!* (Gretna, Louisiana: Pelican Publishing Company, 1994), 27.
[483] Ibid., 28.

discuss; but this physical difference is a great disadvantage to us both, as I think. Your race suffers very greatly, many of them, by living among us, while ours suffers from your presence. In a way, we suffer on each side... If this is admitted, it affords a reason, at least, why we should be separated... You are freemen, I suppose. Perhaps you have long been free, or all your lives. Your race is suffering, in my judgment, the greatest wrong inflicted on any people...

But, even when you cease to be slaves, you are yet far removed from being placed on an equality with the white race. The aspiration of young men is to enjoy equality with the best when free, but on this broad continent not a single man of your race is made the equal of a single man of ours.[484]

Reiterating his deportation goals, Lincoln later added: "The practical thing I want to ascertain is whether I can get a number of able-bodied men, with their wives and children, who are willing to go to Central America."[485] Lincoln's views remained steadfast that Blacks would be better off in another country. Modern research has discovered Lincoln actively continued to work on ways to deport them into the early part of 1865.[486] He worked every conceivable angle of the slavery question to his political benefit.[487]

---

[484] John S. Tilley, *Facts The Historians Leave Out,* Twenty-Second Printing (Nashville, Tennessee: Bill Coats, Ltd., 1991), 21-22.

[485] Webb Garrison, *The Lincoln No One Knows* (Nashville, Tennessee: Rutledge Hill Press, 1991), 172.

[486] In the book, *Colonization After Emancipation: Lincoln and the Movement for Black Resettlement*, economic historians Phillip W. Magness and Sebastian N. Page researched British archives and found that Lincoln continued to work on his deportation plans until shortly before his death in April 1865.

[487] Lincoln's own words consistently point out he was motivated neither by compassion nor humanitarianism regarding Blacks. In November 1775, Lord Dunmore promised freedom to slaves and

So what was actually behind the issuance of the Emancipation Proclamation? A key fact is that in late 1862, Union forces had suffered several military setbacks. Lincoln was ever cognizant of political sentiments and the growing restlessness in the North. He knew most able-bodied White Southerners were engaged in the war effort and slave labor was especially critical in support roles, i.e., slaves helped keep many plantations going, they helped supply food for the Confederate armies, built fortifications, dug trenches, and performed many other duties for the Confederacy. The Lincoln Administration reasoned that incitement of a slave revolt would destabilize the South, impede military efforts, and cause a collapse on the home front. However, Blacks in the South did not stage a bloody revolt as some had anticipated.

Lincoln tried to appease all elements of support, e.g., corporate and banking interests, Radical Republicans, and extremists in the abolitionist movement. If the South refused to capitulate, many of the Radicals wanted the region destroyed. The extreme abolitionists advocated immediate emancipation and arming the slaves, with no regard to the consequences of such actions. There was precedent for this program. David Walker, a slave from North Carolina, advocated armed rebellion in the 1820s and 1830s. In 1831 Nat Turner led a slave uprising in Virginia, resulting in the murder of over fifty-five White men, women and children as well as the deaths of around 200 slaves. This uprising led to the execution of fifty-six slaves involved in the rebellion. These incidents greatly hampered Southern abolitionist efforts and helped lead to suppression of legally teaching slaves how to read and write, although some clandestine teaching continued. Abolitionists such as Garrison and Douglas pushed for immediate emancipation and John Brown tried to initiate an all out slave rebellion. "The more radical

---

indentured servants who joined the British Army. The British proclamation applied only to slaves held by *American rebels* but none held by loyalists. The intent was to disrupt, terrorize, and punish the *rebels* while adding troops and laborers to their army.

abolitionists had always been hoping for more Nat Turners and more wholesale murders of white women and children. The sudden deification of John Brown in the North was especially revealing."[488] Much of the Northern press sympathized with Brown's cause and they worked to foment racial trouble; however, their efforts did not produce wholesale violence.

Lincoln had to word the proclamation carefully to satisfy Union supporters and discourage outside forces from entering the fray. One exception to Lincoln's agenda was the Massachusetts abolitionist Lysander Spooner, who sympathized with slaves who used violence to free themselves, but supported the South's right to secede and govern itself. He did not view the war as an attempt to end slavery but rather as a means to centralize power and benefit politically connected corporations and banks. Spooner saw that when the wealth transfer agenda failed politically, Lincoln was willing to accomplish it militarily.

Lincoln saw the Emancipation Proclamation as a possible way to reinvigorate waning support of the general public in the North. However, this effort failed to produce the anticipated results as large numbers of Northerners were offended by the proclamation, causing Union desertion rates to soar. Most Northerners had no desire to associate with Blacks or compete with them in the job market and they had no intention of fighting on their behalf. The war itself was so unpopular in the North that the Union actively recruited mercenaries in England, Ireland, Germany, and other European countries to fill the ranks of the Federal armies.

Lincoln also feared the British or the French might decide to officially align with the Confederacy. Official assistance from one or both countries would not only create insurmountable opposition but official recognition of the Confederate States would be politically disastrous. Lincoln had gone out of his way to portray the Confederacy as a non-entity, and he could not allow trade between

---

[488] Francis W. Springer, *War for What?* (Nashville, Tennessee: Bill Coats, Ltd., 1990), 110.

the Confederate States and Europe. Intervention on the side of the Confederacy by England or France would have likely destroyed the Union cause and Lincoln's political career with it.

With all of these issues on his plate, Lincoln set out to politically capitalize on British aversion to slavery, control the fanatics in the abolition camp, pacify the Border States still in the Union, and convince the slaves they had been or would be freed. Noting the sleight of hand, Secretary of State Seward said: "We show our sympathy with slavery by emancipating slaves where we cannot reach them and holding them in bondage where we can set them free."[489] Despite the clever wording of the proclamation, President Woodrow Wilson observed that Lincoln simply had to make it appear the South was not on a moral footing.[490] Though the moral crusade was mainly a veneer, it was successful.[491]

On September 22, 1861, Lincoln wrote a letter to his friend Orville H. Browning, who had reacted negatively to his earlier revocation of John C. Fremont's order to free the slaves in Missouri.

---

[489] Kirkpatrick Sale, *Emancipation Hell* (Mt. Pleasant, South Carolina: Kirkpatrick Sale, 2012), 6.

[490] Though descended from Confederates, Wilson admired Lincoln and took his big government, big bank, centralization, spreading democracy mentality to a "world government" level with his support of the League of Nations. Lincoln supported central banking and initiated the first fiat currency with greenbacks; Wilson supported the Federal Reserve System that allowed bankers to create a central bank for their own benefit. Wilson recognized Lincoln's political strategy, stating: "*It was necessary to put the South at a moral disadvantage by transforming the contest from a war waged against states fighting for their independence into a war waged against states fighting for the maintenance and extension of slavery, by making some move for the emancipation as the real motive of the struggle.*" - Kirkpatrick Sale, *Emancipation Hell*, 56.

[491] Many fanatical abolitionists tended to be Unitarians, humanists, agnostics, etc., who did not relate to the average person, North or South.

Lincoln explained:

Liberation of slaves is purely political and not within the range of military law or necessity... Can there be a pretense that the Constitution and laws govern... when a general, or a president, may make permanent rules of property by proclamation? I, as a president, shall expressly or impliedly seize and exercise the permanent legislative functions of the government.[492]

Referencing the Proclamation, New England historian Edward Channing remarked: "Of course, it did not abolish slavery as an institution anywhere."[493] However, a political illusion was all that was needed. In light of military failings, Lincoln had to reassure his supporters in the North and block every possible avenue of outside assistance for the South.

Lincoln realized a bold move was needed, despite possible civilian and military backlash. Viewing the proclamation's issuance as the last straw and feeling it necessary to change the perception of why the war was being fought, Lincoln related: "Things had gone from bad to worse, until I felt we had reached the end of our rope on the plan we were pursuing; that we had about played our last card, and must change our tactics or lose the game. I now determined upon the adoption of the emancipation proclamation."[494]

Relative to the timing of the proclamation, perhaps through intuition or simply the logistical improbability of indefinitely blockading such a wide expanse of Southern coastline, Lincoln seemed to sense it was only a matter of time before the South broke the blockade (discussed in *Blockading Southern Ports*). By international law, once a blockade is broken, trade cannot legally be

---

[492] Garrison, 163.

[493] John S. Tilley, *The Coming of the Glory* (Nashville, Tennessee: Bill Coats, Ltd., 1991), 56.

[494] Charles Adams, *For Good and Evil — The Impact of Taxes in the Course of Civilization* (Lanham, Maryland: Madison Books, 1993), 324.

impeded. As seen with the *Trent Affair*, Lincoln was able to live and survive on the edges of the law. Another factor in Lincoln's favor was that Europeans in general and the British in particular, developed a no compromise philosophy to slave trading. Therefore, it was in the Lincoln Administration's best interest to cast as much doubt as possible toward the intentions of the Confederate States.

John Stuart Mill, English economist, political theorist, and influential nineteenth century philosopher, was a virtual mouthpiece for the Union, claiming slavery was the only reason for hostility, whereas English writer Charles Dickens—known for his social consciousness and compassion toward the most unfortunate in life—vehemently insisted the struggle was over tariffs.

> *The Emancipation Proclamation was imposed specifically to evoke rhetoric (aided and abetted by pro-government economists like Mill)...which would discourage trade with a pro-trade coalition of States. Those nations signed onto the Treaty of 1842, which would put teeth into dealing with illegal slave traders would be much less likely to re-engage in commerce with Southern ports if misled to believe the CSA was going to engage in international slave trade upon ending their embargo and breaking the blockade.*[495]

The Webster-Ashburton Treaty of 1842, signed by Daniel Webster of the U.S. and British Foreign Minister, Alexander Baring, settled border disputes between British colonies in North America and the United States. It called for the final end of slave trading over the seas and stated that the misuse of ensigns to engage in illegal slave trading was tantamount to piracy. Under this agreement, the U.S. consented to station ships off the coast of Africa to monitor possible treaty violations. Britain strongly supported this treaty, devoting considerable blood and treasure toward its enforcement.

---

[495] John P. Sophocleus, "Emancipation Proclamation Sesquicentennial (Slavery? Bah, Humbug!)," *The Alabama Gazette*, January 2013.

Lincoln recognized this agreement would be critical in casting doubt on the Confederacy's intentions. Assistance from individuals such as Mill helped to deter British involvement on the side of the South.

Perhaps the British were unaware the Confederate States' Constitution immediately outlawed the international slave trade (in the main text), unlike the U.S. Constitution that gradually phased it out largely to appease Northern business. This issue dated back to the very origins of the Republic. "To get Northern shipping interests to agree to secede from the Articles of Confederation and Perpetual Union in 1789 and join the more perfect Union under the Constitution, importation of slaves could not be abolished until 1808 or later."[496]

Another reason Great Britain and France did not officially recognize the Confederate States could have simply been perception. Who could oppose something as humanitarian and benevolent sounding as the Emancipation Proclamation? Lincoln's political cunning achieved the goal he sought; the proclamation was simply a cleverly worded war measure that did not legally free any slaves.[497]

Political expediency was a key reason Lincoln reversed his well-known declaration about slavery during his March 1861 inaugural address: "I have no purpose directly or indirectly to interfere with the institution of slavery in the States where it exists. I believe I have no lawful right to do so, and I have no inclination to do so." [498] Also, the simple economics of free trade versus protectionism would have dramatically shifted the flow of commerce, and Lincoln knew it; therefore, he played his next card with the issuance of the Emancipation Proclamation.

---

[496] Ibid.

[497] In a modern context, the Patriot Act was passed several years ago. Although the legislation undermines the Fourth Amendment, in terms of perception, who could vote against legislation with such a name, especially in the aftermath of a crisis? Perception is often reality.

[498] Garrison, 165.

The Emancipation Proclamation

Whereas, on the twenty-second day of September, in the year of our Lord one thousand eight hundred and sixty-two, a proclamation was issued by the President of the United States, containing, among other things, the following, to wit:

That on the first day of January, in the year of our Lord one thousand eight hundred and sixty-three, all persons held as slaves within any State, or designated part of a State, the people whereof shall then be in rebellion against the United States, shall be then, thenceforward, and forever free; and the Executive Government of the United States, including the military and naval authority, will recognize and maintain the freedom of such persons, or will do no act or acts to repress such persons, or any of them, in any efforts they may make for their actual freedom.

That the Executive will, on the first day of January aforesaid, by proclamation, designate the states and parts of States, if any, in which the people thereof respectively shall then be in rebellion against the United States; and the fact that any State, or the people thereof, shall on that day be in good faith represented in the Congress of the United States by members chosen thereto at elections wherein a majority of the qualified voters of such State shall have participated, shall in the absence of strong countervailing testimony be deemed conclusive evidence that such State and the people thereof are not then in rebellion against the United States.

Now, therefore, I, Abraham Lincoln, President of the United States, by virtue of the power in me vested as Commander-in-Chief of the Army and Navy of the United States, in time of actual armed rebellion against the authority and government of the United States, and as a fit and necessary war measure for suppressing said rebellion, do on this first day of January, in the year of our Lord one thousand eight hundred and sixty-three, and in accordance with my purpose so to do, publicly proclaimed for the full period of 100 days from the day first above mentioned, order and designate as the States and parts of States wherein the people thereof, respectively, are this day in rebellion against the United States, the following, to wit:

Arkansas, Texas, Louisiana (except the parishes of St. Bernard, Plaquemines, Jefferson, St. John, St. Charles, St. James, Ascension, Assumption, Terre Bonne, Lafourche, St. Mary, St. Martin, and Orleans, including the city of New Orleans), Mississippi, Alabama, Florida, Georgia, South Carolina, North Carolina, and Virginia (except the forty-eight counties designated as West Virginia, and also the counties of Berkely, Accomac, Northampton, Elizabeth City, York, Princess Anne, and Norfolk, including the cities of Norfolk and Portsmouth), and which excepted parts are for the present left precisely as if this proclamation were not issued.

And by virtue of the power and for the purpose aforesaid, I do order and declare that all persons held as slaves within said designated States and parts of States are, and henceforward shall be, free; and that the Executive Government of the United States, including the military and naval authorities thereof, shall recognize and maintain the freedom of said persons.

And I hereby enjoin upon the people so declared to be free to abstain from violence, unless in necessary self-defense; and I recommend to them that, in all cases where allowed, they labor faithfully for reasonable wages.

And I further declare and make known that such persons of suitable condition will be received into the armed service of the United States to garrison forts, positions, stations, and other places, and to man vessels of all sorts in said service.

And upon this act, sincerely believed to be an act of justice, warranted by the Constitution upon military necessity, I invoke the considerate judgement of mankind and the gracious favor of Almighty God.

In witness thereof, I have hereunto set by hand and caused the seal of the United States to be affixed.

Done at the city of Washington, the first day of January, in the year of our Lord one thousand eight hundred and sixty-three, and of the independence of the United States of America the eighty-seventh.

By the President Abraham Lincoln

William H. Seward, Secretary of State[499]

---

[499] "The Emancipation Proclamation," U.S. History Online Textbook, 2016, *ushistory.org*, http://www.ushistory.org/us/34a.asp, (Accessed Sunday, April 24, 2016).

Chapter Twenty-Five
The Emancipation Proclamation: A Worthless Piece of Paper or Ingenious War Measure? An Analysis (Part 2)

"Neither President, nor Congress, nor Courts possess any power not given by the Constitution."[500]

Chief Justice Salmon P. Chase

The first proclamation was issued on September 22, 1862, seventeen months after the beginning of the war, to be effective January 1, 1863, just over twenty months after the beginning of the war. In the first paragraph of the proclamation Lincoln wrote that slaves residing in specifically defined areas would be freed on January 1, 1863, and the U.S. Government would maintain their freedom if the described States and parts of States remain in *rebellion against the United States*. This delay shows the proclamation was an afterthought and not a primary motivation for conflict.

The September announcement frames the proclamation as an ultimatum. Lincoln is saying "that he would allow one hundred days in which to return into the Union; and that, at the expiration of the named period, he would free the slaves in any state, or part of a state, then remaining recalcitrant."[501] The South was given two distinct options: 1. They could return to the Union by the required deadline and keep their slaves. 2. They could continue to fight and have their slaves freed by force and without compensation if the States did not return prior to the deadline. This exemplifies how Lincoln's primary concern was not ending slavery but keeping the

---

[500] Mildred Lewis Rutherford, *Truths of History* (Harrisonburg, Virginia: Old South Institute Press, 2009), 47.

[501] John S. Tilley, *The Coming of the Glory* (Nashville, Tennessee: Bill Coats, Ltd., 1995), 49.

Union together. Although he lacked the constitutional authority to issue either option, many people in the South knew Lincoln and the Radical Republicans were serious about forcing the return of the Southern States by whatever means they felt necessary.[502]

In the second paragraph, Lincoln said he would name the States and parts of States in rebellion and make allowances for any State, or part of a State that met his requirements for being part of the Union. By exercising non-existent constitutional powers, Lincoln espoused the antithesis of his own pro self-government, States' Rights words uttered on the floor of Congress in January 1848.

In the third paragraph, Lincoln claims he is putting down a rebellion and has the power to do so. He gives the South one hundred-days to return to the Union. Relative to this assumed war power, Northern historian, James Ford Rhodes wrote: "There was, as every one knows, no authority for the proclamation in the letter of the Constitution, nor was there any statute that warranted it."[503]

The fourth paragraph names the specific places where the slaves will supposedly be freed and regions specifically excluded from the proclamation. The document states: "...and which excepted parts are for the present left precisely as if this Proclamation were not issued."[504] All of the areas excluded from the proclamation were

---

[502] The January 1 deadline also reveals Lincoln's recognition that the South was likely to break the Union blockade.

[503] Hon. George L. Christian, *The Life and Character of Abraham Lincoln* (Birmingham, Alabama: Society for Biblical and Southern Studies, 1996), 22. Original source: William Ford Rhodes, *History of the United States, Vol. 4*, 213. Also, from G.L. Christian, the U.S. Supreme Court, in *Ex parte Milligan, 4 Wallace 120* stated: "The Constitution of the United States is a law for rulers and people equally in war and in peace, and covers with the shield of its protection all classes of men at all times and under all circumstances. No doctrine involving more pernicious consequences was ever invented by the wit of man than that any of its provisions could be suspended during any of the great exigencies of government. Such a doctrine leads directly to anarchy or despotism."

[504] Tilley, *The Coming of the Glory*, 50.

under Union control and all areas included were under Confederate control. Lincoln's political strategy was simple; he desired to soothe the sensitivities of the people of the Union slaveholding States of Kentucky, Maryland, Delaware, and Missouri as well as the June 1863 addition of West Virginia. Therefore, the careful wording specifically excluded the slaveholding Border States. His intent was not to benefit the slaves but rather to keep from angering crucial areas of support. Whether intentional or not, Lincoln mirrored Lord Dunmore's tactics during the American Revolution when he offered freedom only to the slaves of *American rebels* who promised to join the British Army during the Revolutionary War.

The proclamation's contradictions and deceptions did not escape the attention of the English, such as Lord Palmerston, renowned statesman and two-time Prime Minister. "Palmerston arose tauntingly to remark that Lincoln undertook to abolish slavery where he was without power to do so, while protecting it where he had the power to destroy it."[505] Similarly, British journalist Goldwyn Smith saw the ruse as well. Noting the obvious omission of Kentucky, Maryland, and Missouri "the English historian was at a loss to grasp whither Lincoln was heading, inasmuch as the reader was left no option other than to conclude that the Proclamation simply left the slaves of those states in slavery."[506] England's Earl Russell, liberal politician and twice Prime Minister of Great Britain, mused how a proclamation could make something both legal and illegal at the same time. The *London Times* moved beyond the clever wording and openly pondered the possibility of servile insurrection.

In the fifth paragraph, Lincoln refers back to his self-created presidential power to free slaves outside of his control and reinforces his commitment to use the military to accomplish it, i.e., he re-states what the Executive Government and the Union military will do if the Southern States do not return.

---

[505] Tilley, *Facts The Historians Leave Out,* Twenty-Second Printing (Nashville, Tennessee: Bill Coats, Ltd., 1991), 18.

[506] Tilley, *The Coming of the Glory,* 50.

In the sixth paragraph, Lincoln calls for these freed persons to refrain from violence and work for reasonable wages. Though framed as benign, there were fears expressed within the British government as well as President Davis, Virginia Governor John Letcher, and others in the Confederacy that it was actually a veiled attempt to incite servile insurrection. Although apprehension was genuine, slave violence in the South was isolated and rare; social upheaval would have destroyed the South's ability to fight a war.[507]

Concerning Lincoln's reference to reasonable wages, the Union paid Blacks about half what Whites made, while the Confederacy paid everybody the same. For example, "General Order Number 38, issued by Confederate General Braxton Bragg at Tullahoma, Tennessee, in January 1863, stated, 'All employees of this army, black as well as white, shall receive the same rations, quarters, and medical treatment. The Confederate government authorized equal pay for musicians, many of whom were black...Free black musicians, cooks, soldiers and teamsters earned the same pay as white Confederate privates.'"[508]

In the seventh paragraph, Lincoln appeals to these freed persons to support the Union. He saw the potential for more soldiers and support personnel. Lincoln was deeply involved in the execution of the war and was aware of considerable racial prejudice within the Union ranks. This was reflected in the correspondence of

---

[507] In *Emancipation Hell*, Kirkpatrick Sale discussed Lincoln's December 1, 1862, proposal for gradual emancipation to be completed before 1900, compensation for slaveowners since the Federal government had been an enabler of the institution from its outset, and for Congress to appropriate money to colonize the freed Blacks outside the United States. The Radical Republicans and the abolitionists opposed it and none of these provisions made it into the final version of the proclamation.

[508] Vernon R. Padgett, Ph. D., Division Adjutant, California Division, Sons of Confederate Veterans "Did Blacks Serve in the Confederate Army as Soldiers?" *CaliforniaSCV.org*, http://californiascv.org/Did%20Blacks%20Serve%20in%20the%20Confedera te%20Army%20as%20Soldiers%20PDF.pdf, (Accessed April 24, 2016).

Union officers. On September 20, 1862, while in Hilton Head, South Carolina, Union General O.M. Mitchel communicated with Secretary Stanton "I find a feeling prevailing among the officers and soldiers of prejudice against blacks;..."[509] Mitchell went on to say the such prejudices were unlikely to abate. General Joseph Hooker, Commander of the Army of the Potomac, revealed shortly after the proclamation's issuance: "The Emancipation Proclamation had been published a short time before, and a large element of the army had taken sides antagonistic to it, declaring they would never have embarked in the war had they anticipated the action of the Government."[510] In March 1863, Mitchell informed General Henry Halleck: "I was saddled with pro-slavery generals in whom I had not the least confidence."[511]

In the eighth paragraph, Lincoln contends the Constitution gives him the power to issue the proclamation through military necessity and he calls on the judgment of mankind and God. Again, this is a reference to the proclamation as a war measure.

Under the U.S. Constitution, the president was intentionally not granted dictatorial powers. After issuing the proclamation, Lincoln admitted its lack of legality in written correspondence with U.S. Treasury Secretary Chase: "The original proclamation has no constitutional or legal justification, except as a military measure."[512]

---

[509] Charles L.C. Minor, *The Real Lincoln* (Harrisonburg, Virginia: Sprinkle Publications, 1992), 95-96. Original source: Robert B. Warden, *An Account of the Private Life and Public Services of Salmon Portland Chase.*

[510] Ibid., 94. [Stephen Sears' book, *Chancellorsville*, and Jonathan W. White's book, *Emancipation, the Union Army, and the Reelection of Abraham Lincoln,* contain letters and commentary of Union deserters who left due to the Proclamation and Lincoln's attempt to change the reason for war.]

[511] Ibid., 96.

[512] Webb Garrison, *The Lincoln No One Knows* (Nashville, Tennessee: Rutledge Hill Press, 1993), 179.

On August 22, 1862, Lincoln wrote to Horace Greeley:

My paramount object in this struggle is to save the Union, and is not either to save or destroy slavery. If I could save the Union without freeing any slave I would do it, and if I could save it by freeing all the slaves I would do it; and if I could save it by freeing some and leaving others alone I would also do that...What I do about slavery, and the colored race, I do because I believe it helps to save the Union....[513]

If the proclamation had actually abolished slavery, Lincoln's own family could have felt repercussions since his father-in-law held slaves, meaning a portion of Mary Todd Lincoln's share of her father's estate came from the institution of slavery.

The ninth and tenth paragraphs attempt to frame the document as official, including the date and place of its origins.

John Sophocleus offers a summary of the Proclamation:

The Proclamation did not compensate owners in blatant disregard for the 5th Amendment, nor did it outlaw slavery, nor make emancipated slaves citizens. These were not Mr. Lincoln's objectives as the September/January proclamations are timed in response to mounting CSA victories and more importantly Charleston's forecasted success in breaking the blockade. This would allow the Confederate pro-trade zone to invite international commerce which would find the Union bloc's 47% tax rate difficult to bear compared to a 10% CSA rate.[514]

---

[513] Matthew Pinsker, *"Letter to Horace Greeley* (August 22, 1862)," Dickinson College, Carlisle, Pennsylvania, *House Divided Project*, http://housedivided.dickinson.edu/sites/lincoln/letter-to-horace-greeley-august-22-1862/, (Accessed April 24, 2016).

[514] John P. Sophocleus, "Emancipation Proclamation Sesquicentennial (Slavery? Bah, Humbug!)," *The Alabama Gazette*, January 2013.

The Emancipation Proclamation sent ripples throughout the world. Relative to the attempt to turn the war into a crusade against slavery, Rhodes quoted William E. Gladstone, Liberal politician and four time Prime Minister of Great Britain: "In England I think nearly all consider war against slavery unjustifiable...We have no faith in the propagation of free institutions at the point of the sword."[515] Despite this and other skepticism, the proclamation appears to have had some influence on the English, who adamantly supported the previously discussed Webster-Ashburton Treaty of 1842.

When weighing the ramifications of intervening on the South's behalf, Great Britain and France had a litany of things to consider, most of which worked against official recognition of the Confederacy. Considerations included the fact war-weary Great Britain was not anxious to fight the Union. Also, the North was a British trading partner, as a large supplier of wheat. After the South's King Cotton miscalculation, Britain and France established a cotton trade with India and Egypt, thus minimizing the significance of Southern cotton. Furthermore, there was a large amount of chaos in the Southern States, relative to a shortage of manpower, manufacturing, etc. This made the South's chance of success less certain, even with outside assistance.

Despite its lack of constitutionality, the proclamation succeeded in skewing the perception of the Confederacy. Although general sentiment in Great Britain and France was Pro-Southern, aiding a country using slave labor would have created a degree of negativity internationally. The fact that there were *five Union Slave States* did not seem to factor into the discussion. Although neither country gave official diplomatic recognition, both did help the South in other ways, e.g., ships, weapons, ammunition, etc. Also, in Britain's case, official recognition of the Confederate States would have made it more difficult to keep Ireland and India in the British Empire without appearing hypocritical.

---

[515] Minor, 113. Original source: William Ford Rhodes, *History of the United States, Vol. IV*, 392.

Another previously mentioned factor is, during the 1861 *Trent Affair*, the Russians, under Tsar Alexander II, threatened to assist the North if Great Britain and France sided with the Confederacy. This threat still had potential to become a reality.

It is difficult to calculate whether or not the proclamation had any appreciable psychological affect on Southern Blacks as a whole. As Ervin L. Jordan, Jr. described in his book, *Black Confederates and Afro-Yankees in Civil War Virginia*, reactions were wide ranging. Some slaves rejoiced and believed the proclamation was real; some remained loyal to the South; some were in the process of manumission (paying their way out of slavery); and some weren't even aware of the proclamation's existence until the war ended and the Thirteenth Amendment legally freed them in December 1865.

The immediate effect in the North was one of angry protests, denunciations, and desertions. Even from part of the Abolitionist camp, there came criticism. In his book, *Abraham Lincoln*, Charles Godfrey Leland wrote: "The ultra abolition adherents of General Fremont were willing to see a pro-slavery president—McClellan—elected rather than Mr. Lincoln, so great was their hatred for him and emancipation." [516] In the January 1899 issue of *McClure's Magazine*, Ida Tarbell wrote:

> Many and many a man deserted in the winter of 1862/1863 because of the Emancipation Proclamation. He did not believe the President had the right to issue it, and he refused to fight. Lincoln knew, too, that the Copperhead agitation had reached the army, and that hundreds of them were being urged by parents and friends hostile to the Administration to desert.[517]

---

[516] Ibid., 136.
[517] Ibid., 100-101.

A.K. McClure, Pennsylvania writer, editor, Republican politician, and strong supporter of Lincoln, wrote: "The Emancipation Proclamation had been issued that caused a cold chill throughout the Republican ranks, and there was little prospect of filling up the broken ranks of our army."[518] A.B. Hart, author of *Life of Salmon Chase*, wrote: "But one of the effects...of the first Proclamation of Emancipation was an increase of the Democratic vote in Ohio and in Indiana, and the consequent election of many Democratic members of Congress."[519]

Northern author, Charles Eugene Hamlin, stated: "The generally accepted explanation of the Republican reverses in the election of 1862 is that they were primarily due to the Emancipation Proclamation, which was issued in September."[520]

Relative to deeper, long-term effects of the proclamation and other unconstitutional moves by the Lincoln Administration, a telling observation in the November 7, 1861, *London Times*, noted that the general opinion in England was "The contest is really for empire on the side of the North and for independence on that of the South,...."[521]

Edwin Lawrence Godkin, Irish-born founder of *The Nation* and later Editor-in-chief of *The New York Evening Post*, noted another long-term effect of the Proclamation. In Volume 68, No. 1750, January 12, 1899, edition of *The Nation*, he wrote: "The first real breach in the Constitution was made by the invention of the 'war power'...it made it possible for any President practically to suspend the Constitution by getting up a war anywhere."[522]

Lincoln assumed ungranted constitutional authority and set a precedent for what is known as the *imperial presidency*. In addition, precedent was established for further usurpations, expansion of

---

[518] Ibid., 97.

[519] Ibid., 98.

[520] Ibid., 98-99.

[521] Ibid., 112.

[522] Garrison, 181.

power by the Executive Branch, and reduction in the liberties of every citizen.

Was The Emancipation Proclamation a worthless piece of paper or an ingenious war measure? Though Northern backlash was strong, the importation of foreign mercenaries into Union service and the passing of time probably neutralized much of the dissension. Former slaves, often used by the national politicians, were given an empty promise of forty acres and a mule. In many instances, the newly freed slaves of the post-war were worse off economically than they were under slavery. During the February 3, 1865, Hampton Roads Conference, Southern representative R.M.T. Hunter asked Lincoln about the plight of very old and very young Negroes when so many of the able-bodied were encouraged to run away. Lincoln's response was to "'let 'em root!' ...Mr. Stephens said he supposed that was the original of 'Root Hog or Die,' and a fair indication of the future of the negroes."[523] Lincoln was essentially saying it was entirely up to Blacks to figure out how to survive on their own. (Alexander Stephens, R.M.T. Hunter, and John A. Campbell verified this conversation.)

The Emancipation Proclamation had no constitutional basis and could not do what it claimed. It did not legally free anyone; an amendment is required to change the Constitution. Nonetheless, the proclamation served its purpose as a political strategy to discourage foreign entities from assisting the fledgling Confederate States of America. The myth that Lincoln freed the slaves still lives. It was not until the Thirteenth Amendment was adopted on December 6, 1865, eight months after Lincoln's death, that slavery was actually abolished.

---

[523] "The Fortress Monroe Conference," An Inside History-What was done and What was Said-The Terms Offered the South-Mr. Lincoln's Suggestions, *New York Times*, June 26, 1865, *Marshall University.edu*, http://www.marshall.edu/special-collections/hampton_roads/pdf/NYT-article.pdf, (Accessed April 24, 2016).

Chapter Twenty-Six
The Election of 1864 and the War's Conclusion

"The Republican party is in no sense a National party; it is a party pledged to work for the downfall of Democracy, the downfall of the Union, and the destruction of the United States Constitution. The religious creed of the party was hate of Democracy, hate of the Union, hate of the Constitution and hate of the Southern people."[524]
Wendell Phillips – Abolitionist from Boston, Massachusetts

Despite the devastating 1863 losses at Vicksburg and Gettysburg, Confederate forces exhibited great resilience throughout much of 1864. "During three months in the summer of 1864, over 65,000 Union soldiers were killed, wounded, or missing-in-action. In comparison, there had been 108,000 Union casualties in the first three years."[525] One incident that sent shock waves through the North was Jubal Early's 1864 movement into Maryland where his approximately 10,000 Confederate troops routed Lew Wallace's Union forces on July 9. Reaching the suburbs of D.C., Early never completed the attack on the U.S. Capitol as forces more than double the size of his own rushed to defend the city. This unfulfilled action marked one of the last opportunities for the Confederacy to force a peaceful resolution. As 1864 wore on, lack of manpower and resources further reduced the possibility of negotiated peace and Southern independence.

---

[524] Mildred Lewis Rutherford, *Truths of History* (Harrisonburg, Virginia: Old South Institute Press, 2009), 27.
[525] "The Election of 1864," U.S. History Online Textbook, 2016, *ushistory.org*, http://www.ushistory.org/us/34e.asp, (Accessed Sunday, April 24, 2016).

The North was not immune to in-fighting and military concerns. Different political factions sniped at Lincoln as the war dragged on, with some of the most intense criticism coming from within his own party. Combined with frustration over a seemingly endless war, there was also discontent in the North over the Lincoln Administration's violations of constitutional and civil rights, which further fueled Northern anti-war resistance.

With numerous factors working against him, Lincoln was very skeptical of his chances for re-election. He was so uncertain of his political future that he took a peculiar approach in response. In late August of 1864, Lincoln lamented, "it seems exceedingly probable that the Administration will not be re-elected."[526] Included in his prediction of impending defeat was an offer to assist with the transition period of a newly elected U.S. President. Lincoln showed concern about the expediency of keeping the Union pinned together and felt it necessary "to save the Union between the election and the inauguration; as he (the next president) will have secured his election on such ground that he can not possibly save it afterwards."[527] According to biographer John Hay, Lincoln secured the signatures of his cabinet secretaries, without revealing the contents, so they would agree to assist with the anticipated transition to a new president.

New parties rose up, as did derivations of the Republican and Democratic parties. The National Union Party consisted of pro-war Democrats and Republicans. With the support of Benjamin Wade and Horace Greeley, Salmon P. Chase became its short-lived presidential candidate. He contended Lincoln was not electable and should not be re-nominated. However, in March 1864, as more

---

[526] David Herbert Donald, *Lincoln Reconsidered* (New York, New York: Vintage Books, A Division of Random House, Inc., 2001), 157.

[527] Richard "Shotgun" Weeks, "Election of 1864," Excerpted from "The Civil War and Reconstruction" by J.G. Randall and David Herbert Donald, *Shotgun's Home of the American Civil War*, http://civilwarhome.com/elections1864.htm, (Accessed April 24, 2016).

Republicans gravitated to the Lincoln camp, Chase withdrew from the race.

Due to discord within the Republican Party, a small contingent of disgruntled abolitionists, led by Massachusetts' senators Charles Sumner, Henry Wilson, and other Radicals, gathered in Cleveland, Ohio, on May 31, 1864. Calling themselves the Radical Democracy Party, they nominated John C. Fremont for president. Fremont had been the 1856 Republican presidential nominee. They wanted a prohibition of slavery via a Constitutional amendment and a legal guarantee of racial equality. After a brief run, Fremont abandoned his presidential efforts on September 22, 1864. Part of his reason for withdrawal was Lincoln's agreement to remove Postmaster General Montgomery Blair from office. Blair was moderate on racial issues and a known enemy of the Radical Republicans, especially Stanton and Chase.

Republicans loyal to Lincoln held a National Union Convention on June 7-8, 1864, in Baltimore, Maryland. They attempted to attract pro-war Democrats and draw a distinction between themselves and the Copperheads. Hannibal Hamlin was dropped as the Vice President and Tennessee Democrat Andrew Johnson was added.

There was an effort by some Republicans to remove Lincoln and replace him with either a committed peace advocate or someone extremely aggressive militarily. This led to the call for a Convention of disgruntled Republicans to meet in Cincinnati, Ohio, on September 28, 1864. This convention never happened.

With all of the political jockeying during 1864, there were other pleas for peace. Early in the year, Charles Francis Adams communicated informally with Tennessee's Thomas Yeatman, who felt the South would re-enter the Union if a system of gradual emancipation were agreed upon. However, Seward doubted this contention and squashed negotiations with Yeatman, leaving Adams bitterly disappointed.

Union supporters such as Greeley and Henry Winter Davis were vocal in their belief that Lincoln could not be re-elected. In a July 7, 1864, letter to Lincoln, Greeley acknowledged the South's willingness to achieve peace, and he encouraged the U.S. President to welcome such overtures. Voicing frustration, Greeley wrote: "And thereupon I venture to remind you that our bleeding, bankrupt, almost dying country also longs for peace–shudders at the prospect of fresh conscriptions, of further wholesale devastations, and of new rivers of human blood."[528]

Lincoln's July 9 response proffered that he would be willing to meet with any Southerner who could validate Jefferson Davis' agreement to return the States of the South to the Union. Lincoln again wrote to Greeley on July 15 claiming his willingness to receive Southern peace commissioners sent by Davis. This involved Lincoln extending "to C. C. Clay, Jacob Thompson, J. P. Holcombe, and G. N. Sanders, the Southern commissioners in question, a formal letter of safe conduct to Washington. It has been maintained that the purpose of these Confederate agents in Canada was to harass the Lincoln government, promote the Confederate cause in certain Northern districts, and stir up peace sentiment among the Northern people."[529] It was determined these commissioners lacked official authority. To Greeley's dismay, nothing tangible came from these discussions.

James Jaquess, a Methodist preacher and soldier from Illinois, and J.R. Gilmore, a New York businessman, instigated another attempt at a peaceful resolution. These men visited Richmond in July 1864, with no success. Lincoln said Davis "declared to Jaquess and Gilmore that he had no terms of peace but

---

[528] "Letter to Abraham Lincoln, Horace Greeley, July 07, 1864," *TeachingAmericanHistroy.org*, http://teachingamericanhistory.org/library/document/letter-to-abraham-lincoln/, (Accessed April 24, 2016).

[529] Richard "Shotgun" Weeks, "Election of 1864," excerpted from "The Civil War and Reconstruction" by J.G. Randall and David Herbert Donald, *Shotgun's Home of the American Civil War*, http://civilwarhome.com/elections1864.htm, (Accessed July 20, 2016).

the independence of the South—the dissolution of the Union...."[530] The July 22, 1864, *Boston Evening Transcript* quoted Davis from the Jaquess-Gilmore meeting, "This war must go on till the last of the generation falls in his tracks...unless you acknowledge our right to self-government."[531]

The Democratic Party held their convention in Chicago on August 29. Ohioan Clement L. Vallandigham and Illinois politician James W. Singleton were leaders of the anti-war faction and they greatly influenced the peace plank in the party's platform. The peace-seeking Democrats, many from the Western regions, were willing to end the war at virtually any cost. There was also a pro-war faction within the Democratic ranks. The party nominated George B. McClellan for President and George H. Pendleton, Democrat U.S. Senator from Ohio, as his running mate. McClellan was a War Democrat who was willing to achieve peace only under the condition of re-unification; to add balance to the ticket, Pendleton was considered a Peace Democrat. McClellan, with railroad, political, and military experience was intensely pro-Union. He was far from being a dynamic candidate; he was the virtual antithesis of the aggressive Lincoln.

Likely due to his aversion for playing the political game, McClellan "left the direction of the campaign to August Belmont, Samuel Barlow, and newspaper editors Manton Marble and William Prime. He made just two public appearances, at rallies in Newark and in New York; as he told a supporter on October 3, 'I have made up my mind on reflection that it would be better for me not to

---

[530] "The Preachers: James Jaquess," *Mr. Lincoln & Friends*, http://www.mrlincolnandfriends.org/inside.asp?pageID=100&subjectID=10, (Accessed April 24, 2016).

[531] Richard "Shotgun" Weeks, "Election of 1864," excerpted from *The Civil War and Reconstruction*, by J.G. Randall and David Herbert Donald, *Shotgun's Home of the American Civil War*, http://civilwarhome.com/elections1864.htm, (Accessed April 24, 2016).

participate in person in the canvass.'"[532] Another sign that politics was not McClellan's natural realm is the fact that "midway through the campaign he secluded himself and his wife for a week at the country home of his friend Joseph W. Alsop, in Connecticut."[533]

Southerners were aware of the level of discontent in the North. They also knew if the Southern armies could hold their own and avoid any major military catastrophes, a peaceful resolution was much more likely. However, a combination of factors changed the landscape in the North's favor. Sherman's capture of Atlanta on September 6, 1864, gave the Union a major military victory. This was followed up in October 1864 when Sheridan's troops plundered Virginia's Shenandoah Valley and removed virtually all threats from the ill-equipped and malnourished Confederate Army. The morale of Southern civilians steadily declined as well. Mere survival became increasingly difficult. The North saw victory clearly within its reach.

As the November election approached, Lincoln and his supporters worked diligently to insure victory. The emotional shift in public opinion resulting from military victories and a crumbling Confederacy sparked momentum. In their back pocket, the Republicans had traditional supporters, i.e., pro-Unionists, industrial workers, etc., along with anti-slavery factions. However, there was also lingering resistance to the war and resentment of Republican tactics regarding constitutional rights and civil liberties. One pivotal segment to capitalize on was the Union soldier vote. Although McClellan was once very popular among Union troops, most supported Lincoln whom they knew was determined to keep the war going until the South surrendered. With that, the

---

[532] "Abraham Lincoln and the Election of 1864," Referencing Jennifer Weber's book *The Rise and Fall of Lincoln's Opponents in the North*, Oxford Press, *Abraham Lincoln's Classroom*, The Lehrman Institute, Sourced from Stephen W. Sears, editor, *Civil War Papers of George B. McClellan*, 588-589, http://abrahamlincolnsclassroom.org/abraham-lincoln-in-depth/abraham-lincoln-and-the-election-of-1864/, (Accessed April 24, 2016).

[533] Ibid.

Republicans made sure as many soldiers as possible were allowed to vote. Simultaneously they tried to link McClellan with the Peace Democrats at every opportunity. Grant played a key role and encouraged Secretary of War Stanton to buy into these efforts.

It is debatable whether or not the Union soldier vote was going to be the deciding factor to swing the election, but the Republicans were nonetheless determined to capitalize on this voting segment. As long as there was no apparent disruption in military operations, Lincoln supported the use of furloughs and shifting troops wherever possible to get them to the voting booth. "Federal officials like Assistant Secretary of War Charles Dana and state officials like New York Secretary of State Chauncey M. Depew worked hard to maximize the number of soldier votes."[534] Lack of support for McClellan from Union soldiers was a clear indicator of the effectiveness of the Republican Party's tactics.

The Election of 1864 was held on November 8. As the Republican candidate, Lincoln represented his party with his running mate, War Democrat Johnson. Votes were cast in the twenty-five Union States, plus Louisiana and Tennessee, two Southern States occupied by Union forces. The remaining Confederate States were not involved in these elections.

When the results were tabulated, the Lincoln-Johnson ticket won in a landslide with 212 Electoral votes and about fifty-five percent of the popular vote compared to twenty-one electoral votes and about forty-five percent of the popular vote for McClellan. Lincoln carried twenty-two States while McClellan carried only three States—Kentucky, Delaware, and his home State of New Jersey. Lincoln received approximately 400,000 more votes than McClellan, including overwhelming support from the Union Army. "From Sherman's Army in Georgia, results were 86% for Lincoln while McClellan's old Army of the Potomac, now under Ulysses S.

---

[534] Ibid.

Grant and George Meade went 78% for Lincoln."[535] The Army of the Potomac alone represented 100,000 or more votes, and it is probable that most of the friends and relatives shared the beliefs of these Union soldiers.

Although the 1864 election involved only the States remaining in the Union at that time, much of Louisiana and Tennessee was under Union occupation. However, the votes in those States were not counted. Also, in 1864, Nevada was added as a new State. This addition dated back to the spring of 1864 when enabling acts were pushed through as part of reconstruction measures and to assist the Republican Party. On October 31, 1864, a mere eight days before the election, Lincoln recognized the addition of this new State.

Lincoln and McClellan were more similar than dissimilar. Both parties wanted to restore the Union—there were few in the North willing to allow the South to establish a separate republic. As E. A. Pollard surmised:

> This struggle [of 1864] did not turn upon a sufficiently tangible issue to give it importance. As a Union party, the great body of the opposition [i.e., Democratic] party was committed to the war as the only practicable means of preserving and restoring the Union...It would have been vain to expect success upon the principles of the very few Democrats...who believed...that the war had been unrighteous...in its leading object...The great body of the opposition concurred with Gen. McClellan in the opinion that secession was unwarrantable...and that it ought to be resisted by all the power of the Union.[536]

---

[535] "Election of 1864," Georgia's Blue and Gray Trail presents America's Civil War, November 8, 2006, *blueandgraytrail.com*, http://blueandgraytrail.com/event/Election_of_1864, (Accessed April 24, 2016).

[536] Weeks, "Election of 1864," *Shotgun's Home of the American Civil War*, (Accessed April 24, 2016).

Even with the Democrats, the pivotal issue concerning peace was reunification, and the anti-war Democrats had little choice but to support their candidate. Lincoln's victory assured the war would continue.

Chapter Twenty-Seven
Was That Really The Way To Save The Union?

"There is a class of people [in the South] men, women, and children, who must be killed or banished before you can hope for peace and order."[537]
William Tecumseh Sherman

The North entered the conflict with a massive advantage in manpower, an edge that ballooned to well over three-to-one, when you include the foreign troops (some were mercenaries) and the Blacks who either volunteered or were conscripted. By some estimates the total number of foreigners and Blacks in the Union Army exceeded the total number in the entire Confederate Army.[538] It was common for Confederate troops to fight Union soldiers who couldn't speak English as noted by Confederate General Richard Taylor. The North actively recruited and offered money and citizenship to foreigners who agreed to fight for the Union.

For some of the foreigners, America was attractive enough to escape the dreadful conditions in their native countries. Like mercenaries throughout history, many of the foreign recruits were of questionable character and background, but even a divided America was an upgrade from whence they came. The South's insular existence and blockaded ports made it virtually impossible for

---

[537] James Bovard, "Ethnic Cleansing, American-Style," Explore Freedom, October 1, 1999, *The Future of Freedom Foundation*, http://fff.org/explore-freedom/article/ethnic-cleansing-americanstyle/ [This comment was in a June 21, 1864 letter to the Secretary of War.], (Accessed April 24, 2016).
[538] Robert C. Wood, *Confederate Hand-Book* (Falls Church, Virginia: Sterling Press, 1982), 27. [Wood breaks down the numbers as follows: "Germans 176,800; Irish 144,200; British-Americans 53,500; English 45,500; Others 74,900. This makes a total of 494,900."]

foreigners to join the Confederacy, although a few did. The South did receive outside support from Great Britain and France, mainly in the form of ships, weapons, etc. and was portrayed favorably by much of the foreign media.

The combination of 494,900 foreigners and 186,017 Blacks in the Union Army totals 680,917 men. One of the most common estimates puts the number of Confederate soldiers at 600,000 men.[539] Many dispute this relatively low number, but the high-end projection of about a million Confederates is even less likely. The most realistic estimate of Confederates falls somewhere in the middle of these two numbers, more in the range of 800,000 men.[540] Some Southerners fought for their homeland without ever being included in the official troop estimations, serving as Reserves, Militia, State Cadets, Home Guards, etc.; record keeping was an inexact science. The numbers would include boys and men from age twelve to probably eighty, far beyond the traditional military population of eighteen to forty-five. Estimates of the number of Union soldiers typically run over 2,400,000 men.

★ ★ ★

Along with the overwhelming disparity in the actual number of soldiers there was also a sizable difference in the potential for new recruits, given the North's foreign recruitment and the South's isolated status. The South possessed a few advantages in that many Southerners were descended from English Cavaliers, French Huguenots, Germans, and especially the Scots-Irish, whose fighting prowess was second to none. Added to this is the simple fact people of the South were literally fighting to defend their homes

---

[539] Ibid., 29. [Robert C. Wood estimated a total of 600,000 Confederates.]

[540] Francis Springer, *War for What?* (Nashville, Tennessee: Bill Coats Ltd., 1990), 100. [Springer speculated there might have been over 800,000 Confederates, and the contributions of Blacks (an underutilized asset), for the South helped neutralize some of the manpower shortage.]

against invasion. Another often-overlooked Southern advantage was the loyalty of a large number of Blacks and American Indians.

Since Northern leadership felt their overwhelming advantages in troops, weapons, manufacturing, etc., were still not enough to subdue the South they resorted to other tactics, one being the refusal to exchange prisoners. The Union ended prisoner exchanges in April 1864 after discussions that included disagreements about Black Union soldiers and paroled Confederate soldiers from Port Hudson and Vicksburg who Grant claimed had violated their paroles. While these may well have been issues, the fact remains that it was in the North's best interest to cease the exchanges. The South did not have enough available men to win a war of attrition.

Grant testified before a Congressional committee:

> I refused to exchange prisoners because as soon as the South's soldiers are released from our prisons they rush back into the rebel ranks and begin fighting again. When Northern soldiers return from Southern prisons either they never again enter the ranks, or if they do, not until they go to their homes and have a long furlough.[541]

Another Union tactic was the draconian policy concerning medicine. From the earliest part of the war, the Lincoln Administration considered medicine and medical supplies to be contraband of war and disallowed their importation into the Confederate States.

> Even existing supplies in the hands of private physicians were destroyed when located. Not only did wounded and sick Confederate soldiers and civilians suffer terribly as a result, but so did thousands of Union

---

[541] George Edmonds, *Facts and Falsehoods Concerning the War on the South 1861-1865* (Wiggins, Mississippi: Crown Rights Book Company, 1997), 182.

soldiers held in Southern prison camps, including such
prisons as Andersonville, Libby, Belle Isle, Salisbury,
Florence, and others. It is interesting to note that such
action today would be an atrocity. (See Department of
the Army Field Manual No. 27-10 (July, 1956), The Law
of Land Warfare, Para. 234.)[542]

This practice was so detestable, that during the 1863
American Medical Association meeting in Chicago, Illinois, "Dr.
Gardner, of New York, introduced preamble and resolutions
petitioning the Northern government to repeal the orders declaring
medical and surgical appliances contraband of war..."[543] Gardner
argued that the practice was barbarous and punished Union
prisoners as well as their Confederate captors. His request was met
by hisses from the Chicago gathering, and the policy remained
unchanged throughout the war.

Declaring medicine contraband was only a part of the larger
program of total warfare. Federal armies moved beyond just
fighting Confederate Armies and began targeting civilians and
property. This plan was carried out primarily by Union generals
Sherman and Sheridan with Grant and Lincoln having full
knowledge. The standard justification for total warfare was that it
would supposedly shorten the conflict. Also, with the Emancipation
Proclamation figuratively freeing slaves in the *rebellious States*, there
appeared to be a new mindset among some in the Union that more
aggressive tactics were justified. In the process, untold suffering was
inflicted on fellow human beings, and enemies were created for
generations.

---

[542] Thomas Bland Keys, *The Uncivil War: Union Army and Navy
Excesses in the Official Records* (Biloxi, Mississippi: The Beauvoir Press, 1991),
xiii.

[543] Mildred Lewis Rutherford, *Truths of History* (Harrisonburg,
Virginia: Old South Institute Press, 2009), 22. Extracted from Dr. Gardner's
testimony.

The Official Records of the Union Army provide primary documentation of many of the outrages against Southern civilians, often in the words of the perpetrators. There are also numerous written, first hand accounts of families who were violated. No one was spared; the victims included women, children, and old men, regardless of race. With the sheer volume of outrages, much doubt is cast on the stated goal of *preserving the Union*. In 1862, Lincoln imparted to an Interior Department official, "the character of the war will be changed. It will be one of subjugation...The South is to be destroyed and replaced by new propositions and new ideas."[544] Though Lincoln was not present to witness the post-war South, his comments became a reality.

There were hundreds, if not thousands, of Union attacks on private citizens in the South. An account provided by a Louisiana lady after General Nathaniel P. Banks' army passed through is as follows:

I was watching from my window the apparently orderly march of the first Yankees that appeared in view and passed up the road, when, suddenly, as if by magic, the whole plantation was covered with men, like bees from an overthrown hive; and, as far as my vision extended, an inextricable medley of men and animals met my eye. In one place, excited troops were firing into the flock of sheep; in another, officers and men were in pursuit of the boys' ponies, and in another, a crowd were in excited chase of the work animals. The kitchen was soon filled with some, carrying off the cooking utensils and the provisions of the day; the yard with others, pursuing the poultry...They penetrated under the house, into the outbuildings, and into the garden, stripping it in a

---

[544] Kirkpatrick Sale, *Emancipation Hell* (Mt. Pleasant, South Carolina: Kirkpatrick Sale, 2012), 17. [Sale references Edgar Lee Masters' comments about the Republican goal to "plunder the South" after the war. They saw the South as a gold mine of property and resources to confiscate.]

moment of all its vegetables...This continued during the day...and amid a bewildered sound of oaths and imprecations...When the army had passed, we were left destitute.[545]

Major Ormsby Mitchel was born in Kentucky and grew up in Ohio. On May 19, 1862, with the Union's Army of Ohio, stationed near Huntsville, Alabama, he gave his observations of Federal troop activity to Secretary of War Stanton:

> The most terrible outrages—robberies, rapes, arsons, and plundering are being committed by lawless brigands and vagabonds connected with the army, and I desire authority to punish all those found guilty of perpetrating these crimes with death by hanging...In some instances, in regiments remote from headquarters, I hear the most deplorable accounts of excesses committed by soldiers.[546]

Under the direction of Union Colonel John Basil Turchin (born Ivan Basil Turchaninov in Cossack Russia), Federal soldiers terrorized Athens, Alabama, in May 1862. Many outrageous incidents were recorded during the Sacking of Athens. Union soldiers committed crimes of theft and destruction against storeowners D.H. Friend, George R. Peck, and R.C. David, as well as Allen's drugstore and John Malone's law office. Similar treatment was leveled against private citizens such as Milly Ann Clayton and Mrs. Hollingsworth.

> On the outskirts of town, the home of Charlotte Hine was ransacked for food and valuables. A blue-clad gang then invaded the slaves' quarters and raped a black girl.

---

[545] Keys, xiv. (from *The Statesmanship of the Civil War*, by Allan Nevins.)

[546] Ibid., 18.

At the plantation of John Malone, outside of town, troops went to the slaves' quarters and there, too, committed rape. When one black woman dared charge a soldier with the crime, his commanding officer tried to hush it up, commenting, 'I would not arrest one of my men on Negro testimony.' Theft, vandalism, and assault went on all day and continued for days to come.[547]

When Major General Don Carlos Buell heard of the Athens atrocities, he relieved Turchin of his command. Buell sought a court-martial of Turchin, and after being found guilty of all charges, Buell sought his removal from service. However, Union War Secretary Stanton lobbied Congress to have Turchin promoted to Brigadier General and Lincoln concurred. This coincided with pleas of mercy to Lincoln from Turchin's wife and influential politicians from Illinois where the couple had settled. Brigadier General James A. Garfield (a future president) also favored leniency. Turchin's promotion was eventually approved and his court martial voided, rendering Buell's efforts unsuccessful. "Turchin, with the blessing of Lincoln and his Republican Senate, would return to active duty as a general officer."[548] The approval of Turchin's tactics of making war on civilians was duplicated numerous times by Union forces.

A few months later, on August 12, 1862, Buell chastised Douglas A. Murray, a Lieutenant Colonel serving in the Third Ohio Cavalry, concerning activities in Woodville, Alabama, southeast of Huntsville.

Reports are made to me of the most disgraceful outrages on the part of troops along the road within ten or twelve miles of our station. Not only is property taken...but property is wantonly destroyed, negro women are debauched, and ladies insulted. Such acts are said to

---

[547] Walter Brian Cisco, *War Crimes Against Southern Civilians* (Gretna, Louisiana: Pelican Publishing Company, 2007), 60-61.
[548] Ibid., 61-62.

have been committed at Mr. Clay's place, ten miles west of you, yesterday.[549]

The frequency and severity of Union attacks on Southern civilians brought a strong rebuke from the Confederate States government. On October 3, 1862, the Confederate States Senate passed a resolution condemning such activities:

> It is notorious that many and most flagrant acts violative of the usages of war, of the rights of humanity and even of common decency, have been and still are being perpetrated by the forces of the United States upon the persons and property of citizens of the Confederate States...Such outrages cannot be fully known...whilst resting only in the oral statements of citizens in...remote States and in the hasty paragraphs of newspapers...; now...that the evidences of the said outrages may be collected and preserved in a permanent...form and the truth of history thus vindicated, and the perpetrators delivered to the just indignation of the present and future generations...Resolved, that a committee of thirteen Senators or of one from each State...take...the testimony to such outrages.[550]

As the war progressed and attacks on Southern civilians intensified, Confederate Secretary of War James A. Seddon lodged another protest on June 24, 1863:

> The war that the United States is carrying on against the Confederate States is...opposed to the fundamental principle of their own Constitution...{our enemies} have adopted a barbarous system of warfare...It is in this

---

[549] Keys, 35.
[550] Ibid., 1.

code of military necessity that the acts of atrocity and violence...have been committed by the officers of the United States and have shocked the moral sense of civilized nations...The country that adopts as allies murder, rapine, cruelty, incendiarism, and revenge is condemned by the voice of the civilized world.[551]

As Commander-in-Chief of the Union Army and micro-manager of the war, Lincoln was aware of the assaults on civilians but did not stop them, as it became official policy. As it is in war, there were violations committed by both sides, but Jefferson Davis abhorred total warfare and refused to give it legitimacy, despite encouragement by angry Southerners to respond in kind.

Southern protests fell on deaf ears. In a January 31, 1864, letter, William Tecumseh Sherman explained his view of the virtual absolute powers he felt his government possessed:

The government of the United States has in North-Alabama any and all rights which may choose to enforce in war, to take their lives, their homes, their lands, their every thing...because war does exist there, and war is simply power unrestrained by constitution or compact...To the petulant and persistent secessionists, why, death is mercy, and the quicker he or she is disposed of the better.[552]

Early in the war, many alleged Sherman to be insane, including an article published in the *Cincinnati Commercial*. Sherman had mental problems that included a nervous breakdown and bouts of depression; these issues ran in his family. Perhaps as a result of these issues, his words and actions reflect a moral void and explain his belief in an extreme form of nationalism. "For Sherman, God had long ceased to be governor of this war," observed one scholar.

---

[551] Ibid., 2.
[552] Ibid., 71.

'Sherman's religion was America, and America's God was a jealous God of law and order, such that all those who resisted were reprobates who deserved death.'"[553]

The false pretense of the Union Army being liberators was exposed on multiple occasions. On February 26, 1864, while in Huntsville, Alabama, Major-General "Blackjack" Logan sent a message to U.S. Grant who was positioned in Nashville, Tennessee: "A major of colored troops is here with his party capturing negroes, with or without their consent...They are being conscripted." [554] Another example occurred in mid-1864 when Federal soldiers robbed Allie Travis' home in Covington, Georgia. As Travis and her female servant witnessed Federal troops marching down the street, the Black servant realized the Federals had possession of her clothing. She soon realized they had broken into her house and taken her prized possessions. Travis confronted the Union soldiers, saying, "Your soldiers are carrying off everything she owns, and yet you pretend to be fighting for the Negro."[555]

On September 4, 1864, Sherman demanded the evacuation of Atlanta by everyone except his Army. Atlanta civilians were rounded up like cattle. "Eventually some 1,650 men, women and children were dumped into Confederate lines south of the city during September...Probably an equal number went north."[556] The forced expulsion of Atlanta citizens was described by historian Mary Elizabeth Massey as "the single largest forced evacuation of an entire city during the Civil War."[557]

On October 7, 1864, Union General Sheridan wrote to Grant updating him on the Shenandoah Valley Campaign in Virginia:

---

[553] Cisco, 73.

[554] Keys, 72.

[555] Cisco, 177.

[556] Stephen Davis, "Was Sherman a War Criminal?: Yes, Sherman convicted by own his words," *AJC.com*, June 13, 2014, http://atlantaforward.blog.ajc.com/2014/06/13/was-sherman-a-war-criminal/?ecmp=ajc_social_facebook_2014_sfp, (Accessed April 28, 2016).

[557] Ibid.

I have destroyed over 2,000 barns filled with wheat, hay and farming implements; over 70 mills filled with flour and wheat, and have driven in front of the Army 4,000 head of stock and have killed and issued to the troops not less than 3,000 sheep. Tomorrow I will continue the destruction down to Fisher's Mill. When this is completed, the Valley from Winchester to Stanton, 92 miles, will have little in it for man or beast.[558]

In November 1864, Sherman embarked on his infamous March to the Sea, reaching Savannah, Georgia, on December 21. Savannah's political leaders sought to be as accommodating as possible, hoping it would spare their city. Sherman's troops camped in the Savannah City Cemetery; it was fenced in, providing a means to contain their animals. While camped in the Savannah Cemetery, Union troops destroyed several headstones and moved many others from one grave to another rendering it nearly impossible to determine who was buried where. Despite such outrages, the city of Savannah was spared from complete destruction. While still in Savannah, on January 21, 1865, Sherman sent orders to General G.H. Thomas, commanding Union troops in North Alabama.

Before I again dive into the interior and disappear from view, I must give you...such instructions as fall within my province as commander of the division...With an army of 25,000 infantry and all the cavalry you can get, under Wilson, you should...march to Tuscaloosa and Selma, destroying former, gathering horses, mules (wagons to be burned), and doing all the damage possible; burning up Selma, that is the navy-yard, the railroad..., and all iron foundries, mills, and

---

[558] "Quotes from Generals William T. Sherman & Phil Sheridan," Descendants *of Point Lookout POW Organization*, October 27, 2008, http://www.plpow.com/Atrocities_QuotesFromSherman.htm, (Accessed April 24, 2016).

factories...You might reach Montgomery and deal with
it in like manner...The people of the South...see in [such
raids]...the sure and inevitable destruction of all their
property...They see in the repetition of such raids the
inevitable result of starvation and misery.[559]

As the war progressed, the Confederacy's prospects
dimmed, but the abuses directed toward Southern civilians
continued unabated. For example, Mrs. Augustus Jennings
described an event from February 1865 that her mother, Mrs. Sarah
A. Moorer, had lived through while her husband was away at war.
This letter appeared in an Orangeburg, South Carolina, paper, *The
State*, on March 7, 1906.

> While seated at breakfast they saw a squad of union
> cavalry coming from the direction of Orangeburg. They
> came yelling and screaming in the yard and house,
> frightening the ladies. In a short time they came in
> immense crowds, overrunning the yard and house, and
> terror broke loose. These soldiers acted like maniacs,
> yelling and hurrahing, breaking open doors, emptying
> the provision houses, running down all the poultry and
> at last building a bonfire, burned everything they could
> not carry off. Some of the negroes were screaming with
> fright and some were exultant. One faithful servant was
> whipped (by Yankees) until she disclosed the hiding
> place of the silver and other family treasures.
> Great hulking boors of Yankees with their soiled and
> dirty boots jumped in the lard troughs, pouring in syrup
> and vinegar, trampled it to a slush and then pouring
> syrup over the floors of the residence, emptied barrels of
> flour over it, trampled it with their feet. Numbers of
> bales of cotton were burned, which my father had
> removed from near his buildings, hoping to save it.

---

[559] Keys, 117.

Everything of value was stolen or burned, including the clothing. When my mother attempted to remonstrate with those wrecking the dwelling, she was approached by an officer from Ohio, advising her to say nothing for if the soldiers were enraged, he could not answer for her life. A squad of the marauders in the promiscuous destruction of property seized upon the old family horse, which we kept from sympathy, hitched him to an old buggy loaded with chickens, turkeys and geese and left the yard with the load. The horse reluctantly left with his load, but when they attempted to drive him past the lot gate refused to go whereupon he was beaten unmercifully.

Such meager supplies as could be raked together after the wreckage was all the provisions left on this once prosperous plantation with its bounteous stores for numerous slaves. The sun that day arose on a scene of plenty and contentment to set on a field of want and despair. This is just one of the many homes upon which fell this blackness of darkness of vandal warfare.[560]

There were many other incidents such as the destruction of Jackson and Meridian, Mississippi, despite the lack of any real resistance. The Immortal 600 consisted of 600 Confederate officers who were used by the Union as human shields at Charleston Harbor. This was supposedly in retaliation for the Confederacy placing 50 Union officers in a house on Broad Street in Charleston, (as a bluff) in a house with little danger of Union shelling. There were also outrages against the women of New Orleans at the direction of Union General *Beast* Butler. And the list goes on.

The same program of total war was directed toward American Indians, who were probably held in lower regard than secessionists. Sherman stated: "The more Indians we can kill this year the fewer we will need to kill the next, because the more I see of

---

[560] Ibid, xiv-xv.

the Indians the more convinced I become that they must either all be killed or be maintained as a species of pauper. Their attempts at civilization is ridiculous...."[561]

Sheridan was just as callous in his hatred for American Indians, with his most famous quote: "the only good Indian I ever saw were dead, as spoken to Tosawi of the Comanches."[562] Lincoln was certainly no fan of American Indians either. On December 26, 1862, he ordered the mass execution of 303 Indians in Mankato, Minnesota, after their questionable convictions by military trials. Concerned the Europeans may frown on such a large number, thirty-eight Indians were hanged, and it was discovered after the fact that two of them should not have been executed. This was the largest mass hanging in U.S. history. Lincoln revered Clay and patterned much of his politics after him, it seems including his view of Indians. When Clay served as Secretary of State, he stated, "The Indians' disappearance from the human family will be no great loss to the world. I do not think them, as a race, worth preserving."[563]

The Union government was so determined to subdue the South they abandoned civilized warfare or simply looked the other way. The destruction of the Southern States was staggering; little regard was given to the rules established by the original Geneva Convention of 1863-1864 or even the less stringent Lieber Code as established by one of the Union's own.

---

[561] "Quotes from Generals William T. Sherman & Phil Sheridan," Descendants *of Point Lookout POW Organization*, October 27, 2008, (Accessed April 24, 2016).

[562] Larry Kibby, "The Only Good Indian," *Indigenous People's Literature*, June 8, 2004, http://www.indigenouspeople.net/gooddead.htm, (Accessed April 24, 2016).

[563] Michael Gaddy, "The American Indian and the 'Great Emancipator,'" *United Native America*, http://www.unitednativeamerica.com/issues/lincoln_print.html [Also found at Sierra Times: http://www.sierratimes.com/gaddy.htm, January 9, 2003.], (Accessed April 24, 2016).

There were two main theories of warfare prevalent at the time. First, Baron Antoine Henri de Jomini was a Swiss officer who served with the French and later the Russians. His three-fold philosophy involved strategy, grand tactics, and logistics. Napoleonic strategies were generally favored, and there was a belief that senseless death and destruction should be minimized. Second, Carl von Clausewitz was a German (Prussian) general who had fought in Napoleonic and European revolutionary wars. He espoused that war was also a political tool and civilians were not off limits, stating that it is a "fallacy to disarm or defeat an enemy by moderating the violence. If the enemy was to be coerced, he had to be put into a situation that he could not endure or simply ignore and wait until things got better." [564] The Confederate States applied Jomini and Napoleonic tactics. Several of the Northern generals also used these tactics. However, Grant also incorporated "the strategy of annihilation espoused by Clausewitz as the prescription for a victory in a war of popular nationalism." [565] Sherman readily bought into this type of warfare, and in 1864, while occupying Atlanta and planning his March to the Sea, sent a letter to Lincoln suggesting this strategy would end the war sooner. Sherman had already shown his intolerance for any civilian who refused to be obedient to the U.S. government. Though Lincoln was not initially a proponent of total war, he did not veto the actions of Grant, Sherman, or Sheridan, although he had the legal right to do so.

The extremes in total warfare employed beg to question why. The war had dragged on longer than most people on both sides thought, and, although the South was reeling from shortages of men and weapons, many in the war weary North sought to end the carnage. Despite Lincoln's eagerness for reelection, he faced

---

[564] Michael T. Rean, "Shifting Strategies: Military Theory in the American Civil War," [Rean is CW03, USN Retired Professor of History, Franklin Pierce University], *MilitaryHistoryOnline.com*, http://www.militaryhistoryonline.com/civilwar/articles/militarytheory.aspx, (Accessed April 28, 2016).

[565] Ibid.

intense opposition in his own party. Not only did Lincoln face being cast into political oblivion, abolitionist Phillips claimed he and his cabinet were treasonous. As previously referenced, Lincoln genuinely feared he might lose to Democrat McClellan in the 1864 election, and his loss would likely lead to negotiations to end the war. Lincoln offered McClellan leadership of the Union Army if he would remove himself from the election; McClellan refused.

To fully accomplish his goal of wealth redistribution and tariff protection, as Commander-in-Chief, Lincoln employed the full force of the federal government and the armies at his disposal.

Chapter Twenty-Eight
Is the South Really Better Off?

"If Lincoln loved the Union, he was responsible, more than any man, for its destruction, for he consciously violated the Constitution in calling out armies for the reduction of the Cotton States. The war was not a war of slavery versus freedom; it was a war between those who preferred a federated nation to those who preferred a confederation of sovereign States....Lincoln, who had always been a Hamiltonian, saw that Hamilton's principles finally triumphed."[566]
Andrew Nelson Lytle

From a historical standpoint, a common Southern topic has been whether or not the South is better off having lost the conflict. Many Northerners and some Southerners have always said the South is better off, and, as time passes, there seem to be more Southerners who echo that peculiar position. Perhaps this is a by-product of federally influenced education. Many who previously believed that *the South is better off* change their minds once they take a serious look at the reasons for and execution of the war.

There are numerous prophetic comments from Cleburne, Davis, and many others who knew the Confederacy would be demonized and falsely propagandized if it failed to establish its independence. Cleburne's words are remarkable:

> *Surrender means that the history of this heroic struggle will be written by the enemy; that our youth will be trained by Northern school teachers; will learn from Northern school books their version of the War; will be impressed by all the*

---

[566] Andrew Nelson Lytle, "The Lincoln Myth," *Virginia Quarterly Review*, October, 1931 (Review reprinted in *Lincoln, the Man* by Edgar Lee Masters, The Foundation for American Education, Columbia, South Carolina, 1997. Original Copyright 1931 by Edgar Lee Masters.)

influences of history and education to regard our gallant dead as traitors, and our maimed veterans as fit subjects for derision.[567]

This Northern indoctrination strategy was described by former Brown University President Francis Wayland, who said the South should be "the new missionary ground for the national schoolteacher,"[568] and Harvard's President Hill added the North had the task "of spreading knowledge and culture over the regions that sat in darkness."[569] The Northern educators viewed the old States' Rights Southerners as too far gone to indoctrinate so they would just let them die out and re-educate rising generations. Southern children would be taught to revere the Puritan fathers, although they were the ancestors of New Englanders and Southern children were to be taught Lincoln was a Southern hero when, in reality, (during the war) he had been their gravest enemy. Cleburne's astute predictions and the stated goal of those in the North to re-educate Southerners explain how one of the biggest enemies of the South in this era is often her own people.

As a by-product of the unique blend of settlers, the South developed a distinctive culture, with variations within that culture. The Southern spirit and culture has historically dominant connections to the Celtic/Saxon/Norman influences brought to the region. French Huguenot, German, Cajun, Spanish, American Indian, Black, etc., have all made valuable contributions to the South, but none, however, have hitherto been the dominant culture. The South has always been a land of diverse and talented people.

---

[567] Micha Petty, "Confederate Quotes," *American Revival*, 2010, http://www.americanrevival.org/quotes/confederate.htm, (Accessed April 25, 2016). [Another version uses "Subjugation" instead of "Surrender."]

[568] Frank Lawrence Owsley, "The Irrepressible Conflict," from *I'll Take My Stand: The South and the Agrarian Tradition* (Baton Rouge, Louisiana and London, England: Louisiana State University Press, 1991), 63.

[569] Ibid.

Despite the South's legacy of accomplishment, Southern people have been routinely minimized, marginalized, and lumped into the old slur of *redneck*. A modern definition of the term conjures up images of people who are backwards, uneducated, and often bigoted; however, rednecks are (were) actually a distinct ethnic group. The term, which originated in Great Britain, was given to backcountry people because of their religious beliefs; "...historian Anne Royall in 1830...noted that 'red-neck' was a 'name bestowed upon the Presbyterians.' It had long been a slang word for religious dissenters in the north of England."[570] Redneck generally describes Lowland Scots and/or Ulster Scots (aka Scots-Irish), one of the largest groups to settle in the South. The term dates back to the largely Presbyterian Scottish Covenanters of the 1630s—the original rednecks were religious dissenters who wore red cloths around their necks and signed a pact in blood against the Anglican Church in defiance of English oppression.

The term *cracker*, "which derived from an English pejorative for a low and vulgar braggart,"[571] is a close second. *Cracker*, like *redneck*, is of British origin, and is rooted in the Scottish word *craic*, which means to talk or chat socially. The modern American stereotype is someone who is backwards, uncouth, and uneducated. Although people with this ethnic background live throughout the United States, both terms are routinely used to disparage Southern Whites, whereas ethnic slurs directed at almost any other group would be considered, in Orwellian terms, to be *hate speech*.

One method of putting a group of people on the defensive is by demonizing their ancestry, heroes, culture, symbols, etc. This form of bullying or stereotyping has been used throughout history to belittle targeted people or groups of people. For example, the U.S. Government broad-brushed American Indians as savages,

---

[570] David Hackett Fischer *Albion's Seed: Four British Folkways in America* (New York, New York: Oxford University Press, Oxford University, 1989), 758.

[571] Ibid.

relegating them to second-class status. This made it psychologically easier to forcefully move them from their native lands to Oklahoma. The Plains Indians also felt the boot heel of the federal government when the land they occupied was considered prime property for Northern corporate interests seeking railroad expansion and additional space for White settlement. Harriet Beecher Stowe fanned the flames of anti-South propaganda by stereotyping slave owners in the South (and presumably the Border States) as evil, although her knowledge of the subject was minimal. Of course, Hitler's rhetoric demonizing European Jews is universally known. Even renowned Irish flautist James Galway made a half-joking and half-serious comment years ago on *The Tonight Show*, about England's historical insistence on invading Ireland and trying to *elevate them*, although the Irish were quite capable of taking care of themselves. In a modern context, Hollywood often negatively stereotypes not only Southerners, but also Christians, gun owners, traditional families, and anything else opposed to their worldview.

The South has been accused of starting a war it did not want and desperately tried to avoid. The Northern Industrialists, essentially a nineteenth century version of the modern military industrial complex that advocates and profits from war (as identified in President Eisenhower's famous 1961 speech), were never going to let the South operate as a separate country. *War is a Racket,* written by Smedley Butler, the most decorated Marine in American history, provides details of the exorbitant corporate profits made during times of war.

The Industrial interests of the North were first promoted by Hamilton, beginning with the Tariff of 1789 that gave a small amount of protection to Northern industry (small when compared to the 1828 and 1832 tariffs) at the expense of the agricultural South. The early tariff "reduced by 10 percent or more the tariff paid for goods arriving in American craft. It also required domestic construction for American ship registry."[572] Other import taxes in that decade were established to greatly favor American ships over those that were built and owned by foreigners.[573]

The Republican Party got their man in Lincoln, and once they attained the power so long sought, they had no intentions of giving it up. The old Jeffersonian belief in limited government and States' Rights could at last be cast aside, and, in the eyes of Henry, Semmes, The *London Times*, and many others, the U.S. could finally embark on the ultimate goal of empire.

To augment the economic and political issues between North and South, some of the radical abolitionists were Unitarians, Transcendentalists, Spiritualists, social progressives, and/or socialists who were determined to use their beliefs to create social change. One example was the experiment Brook Farm, started by George Ripley, and his wife, Sophia Dana Ripley on property in West Roxbury, Massachusetts. This pre-hippie commune was based on the socialistic ideas of Charles Fourier, a French philosopher and advocate of utopianism. Brook Farm was visited and supported by Unitarian Minister Theodore Parker, Women's Rights advocate Margaret Fuller, Welsh utopian socialist Robert Owen, writer and Transcendentalist Ralph Waldo Emerson, and others of a like mind.

Another utopian commune was Fruitlands, established by abolitionist and women's rights advocate Amos Bronson Alcott of Connecticut and English-American abolitionist and transcendentalist Charles Lane. This experiment was located in Harvard, Massachusetts, on Wyman Farm. Some of their quirky beliefs included refusal to "use beef, milk or eggs, sugar, molasses, butter and fish, for 'nothing could be eaten that caused wrong or death to man or beast'...Even the canker-worms that infested the

---

[572] Slavery or Tariff?, The American Civil War, *Online Etymology*, http://www.etymonline.com/cw/economics.htm, (Accessed April 25, 2016).

[573] A valid argument can be made that such a tax could be established short term but not in perpetuity. This was the logic used when many in the South agreed to the 1816 tariff to help Northern industry pay for the costs accrued from the War of 1812.

apple trees were not to be molested: 'They had as much right to the apples as man...' [574] Coffee, tea, and salt were viewed with abhorrence and placed on the same level as liquor. Such radicalism was virtually unknown in the Bible-based culture of the South. The influential individuals promoting these movements held a near universal loathing of the South.

There were cultural differences as well since there were distinct differences in the people who settled each region of the country. Although there were examples, the brother against brother angle of the war was relatively minor. The prevalence of Hamiltonian nationalism in the Northeast versus Jeffersonian States' Rights in the South was always there. Despite theses differences, as Robert E. Lee lamented, conflict may well have been avoided if both sides had exerted more effort toward diplomacy of the points of contention. For example, had Lincoln been willing to more seriously listen to John Baldwin, the Virginia Peace Commission, Reverend Fuller or other peace seekers, the war may have been avoided.

Over 250,000 Southerners died during the war. As an example of the destruction in the South, "in the first year after the war, the state of Mississippi allotted one-fifth of its revenues for the purchase of artificial arms and legs." [575] Also, due to economic devastation caused by the war and Reconstruction, "it was not until 1911 that the taxable assets of the state of Georgia surpassed their value of 1860."[576] In Louisiana, $170,000,000.00 was lost just in slave property and at least half of the State's livestock disappeared. To illustrate the South's post war decline, the 1860 census showed the South's per capita income was ten percent higher than all States west of New York and Pennsylvania.

---

[574] Otto Scott, *The Secret Six: John Brown and the Abolitionist Movement* (Murphys, California: Uncommon Books, 1979), 148.

[575] James Ronald Kennedy and Walter Donald Kennedy, *The South Was Right!* (Gretna, Louisiana: Pelican Publishing Company, 1994), 37.

[576] Ibid.

Excessive taxes were placed on cotton. A large amount of land and property was sold because of inability to pay the inflated property taxes administered by the occupation governments. After the war, Northerners bought thousands of acres of prime Southern land at cheap prices and a discriminatory freight rate system survived well into the Twentieth Century.

Even if they are aware of the aftermath of the war and Reconstruction, many present-day Southerners refuse to discuss it. It is as though they have simply accepted the federal government-approved version of history provided through the public education system. They often dismiss these past events, perhaps not realizing or caring about the incredible hardships placed on their ancestors as well as the lingering effects felt by the entire South. The fact is, that during Reconstruction, many Southerners were forced into peonage. Confederate soldiers were disenfranchised. Tenancy and sharecropping became the rule because few people could afford their own farms as they had prior to the war.

As recently as 1960, the U.S. census provided a barometer for the post-war plight of the South. "The per capita income for all states in the Union was given. Not a single Southern State appeared in the top fifty percent!"[577] The 1960 census showed Southern States lacking in comparison to the rest of the country and even more recently, 1980 census records "stated that the South was still by far the poorest part of the country. The United States Census Bureau found that the poverty rate for the South was twenty percent higher than for the nation as a whole."[578] Northern elites looked down on the South as being educationally and economically inferior, yet it is the North that was directly responsible for many of these conditions. In light of all of these negative factors, the South's progress reflects resilience inherent in her people.

From a historical perspective, how did the invasion and subjugation of the Southern people bring any benefits? With it, the

---

[577] Ibid., 39.
[578] Ibid.

liberty-protecting advantages of States' Rights are almost entirely gone. The central government now determines the limits of its own power. The usurpation of ungranted powers changed the relationship between the central government and the States. As Henry, Mason, and other Anti-Federalists feared, the central government forced its way into areas not constitutionally delegated, especially the interpretation and exploitation of the General Welfare clause where the central government has gotten involved in education, health care, energy, and other areas outside their purview. Lincoln's precedent of bypassing Congress to declare war has also been abused on numerous occasions since. These changes not only impacted the South but the rest of the country as well. H.L. Mencken noted this with his famous quote about both sides entering the war, and in the aftermath, losing rights they have yet to recover.

It is mere conjecture to visualize what direction the South may have gone had it gained independence. A stalemate may have benefitted both regions until cooler heads prevailed. Southern victory would have probably included a time of separation, followed by negotiation, compromise, and possibly re-unification. It is possible the South would still exist as a separate nation, i.e., the North and South could certainly have existed as two American nations. The Confederate Constitution, simply an improved version of the U.S. Constitution, would have provided a strong platform for sound government. The South had ample resources and competent men to assume the roles of government and business. As advocates of free trade, the South would have been an attractive trading partner. Not only did the people of the South feel secure as to their destiny, one of the Union's top generals felt the South would have been a viable and prosperous country. In his book, *Personal Memoirs of U.S. Grant,* Grant stated the Southern States would have established "a real and respected nation."[579]

---

[579] Lyon Gardiner Tyler, *The Gray Book: A Confederate Catechism* (Wiggins, Mississippi: Crown Rights Book Company—The Liberty Reprint

Either scenario would have trumped what transpired. Compromise before the war would have spared the senseless destruction of the Southern States; it would have also accelerated the development of the country. As it was, the South started from square one about a hundred and forty years ago (when you include the twelve years of Reconstruction, occupation, and martial law).

There has been a degree of speculation as to the route the Confederate States would have taken if victorious. Much of that speculation has centered on the possibility of expansion. As early as 1805, Thomas Jefferson pondered the possibility of annexing Cuba due to its strategic location. President Polk later favored purchasing Cuba and Jefferson Davis favored annexing Northeast Mexico at the time California and New Mexico were added in 1848. President Pierce also considered adding Cuba. Tennessee-born lawyer and journalist William Walker served as first president of the Republic of Lower California and the Republic of Sonora and later as President of Nicaragua. He advocated annexation of parts of Latin America. There was support for a so-called Golden Circle by some, including South Carolinian Robert Barnwell Rhett; this called for expansion into the Caribbean. Even John Breckinridge, the Kentucky-born Vice President under President Buchanan, and one of the four Democrats who ran for President in 1860, considered possible expansion into Cuba and had actually spoken with them about annexation. Despite sentiment by some Southerners to expand, there was also strong resistance within the South based on aversion to imperialism, potential trade issues, and incorporation of cultures that did not necessarily mesh with the South. Although annexation of Cuba, Mexico, and Central America would have been a possibility, it was far from being a certainty.

The peculiar institution of slavery would have likely been short-lived under any of the possible scenarios. The Confederate Constitution expressly forbade the importation of slaves as a logical

---

Series, 1997), 8. Originally printed in *Tyler's Quarterly* in Volume 33, October and January issues, 1935.

first step toward eventual emancipation, and the free market basis of the constitution would have encouraged an end to slavery. Although slave labor was often of high quality, the laws of economics show free labor to be superior. Furthermore, an independent Southern nation with no timetable for ending slavery would have been considered a pariah (from a world trade perspective) in an anti-slavery world. A country that cannot trade is unlikely to survive. Possibly, the slaves would have been given the option of remaining in America or returning to Africa. If they chose to stay, all they needed was the opportunity to become self-sufficient.

If allowed to work unfettered, the market would have taken care of the division of labor and the changing nature of work. Technology had already begun to replace some of the manual labor, and the war had only slowed that process. In conjunction with technological advancement, the agrarian role of the South would have been placed on a more equal footing with industry. The South had begun to develop a base of small business and industry before the conflict due to raised awareness that diversification was vital to future survival and development. What actually happened was the worst-case scenario for the South.

As a means of monitoring Southern sentiment, in August 1870, Union General Rosecrans arranged a meeting of ex-Confederates. Rosecrans hoped to get positive feedback from these Confederate gentlemen about how elated they were to be back in the Union. He also encouraged General Lee to make a statement to that effect; however, no such statement was forthcoming. Lee did not feel it was his place to make broad-brush statements about the condition of the South and the sentiment of its people. He did agree to help Rosecrans assemble other ex-Confederates where they could voice opinions based on their own observations.

After a series of half-hearted endorsements for the restored Union, former Texas Governor Fletcher S. Stockdale made some blatantly honest statements about the difficult situation that his home State was facing.

Stockdale said:

> The people of Texas will remain quiet, and not again
> resort to forceful resistance against the Federal
> Government, whatever may be the measure of that
> government…The people of Texas have made up their
> minds to remain quiet under all aggressions and to have
> peace; but they have none of the spaniel in their
> composition. No sir, they are not in the least like the dog
> that seeks to lick the hand of the man that kicked
> him…They know that they resisted the Federal
> Government as long as any means of resistance was left,
> and that any attempt at resistance now must be in vain,
> and they have no means, and would only make bad
> worse…[580]

The meeting broke up and Lee spoke privately with
Stockdale:

> Governor, if I had foreseen the use those people
> designed to make of their victory, there would have
> been no surrender at Appomattox Courthouse; no, sir,
> not by me. Had I foreseen these results of subjugation, I
> would have preferred to die at Appomattox with my
> brave men, my sword in this right hand.[581]

Considering where the South was from 1865 to 1877,
recovery from war, occupation, Reconstruction, and martial law has
been remarkable. However, Southerners often remain subjects of
ridicule; they are primarily taught in public schools from books
written outside the South; and they are taught to think poorly of
their Southern and Confederate ancestors and the history associated
with them. From a broad based perspective, long lasting lessons

---

[580] Kennedy and Kennedy, 42.
[581] Ibid, 42-43.

arose from economic destruction, needless loss of life in so many Southern families, the victory of industrial interests over agricultural interests, and the infusion of many of the aforementioned radical values that originated in the North. The ideology of voluntary government has been impaired and ridiculed, if not destroyed, and allegiance to the central government and all of its machinations encouraged.

Lincoln, with significant Puritan ancestry, represented the desire for dominance that permeated portions of that unique group (many of whom had lost their true, Bible-based religion); he achieved his goal of creating a consolidated central government at the expense of a confederation of States and all regions have felt the impact since.

Chapter Twenty-Nine
Jefferson Davis—No Apologies!

"Truth crushed to the earth is truth still and like a seed will rise again."[582]
Jefferson Davis

At the close of the Constitutional Convention of 1787, Benjamin Franklin was asked what type of government we had—*a Republic or a Monarchy?* Franklin responded, "A Republic, if you can keep it."[583] Many argue that the Original Republic died at Appomattox, Virginia, when Lee surrendered the Army of Northern Virginia. One man who clearly saw the Lincoln Administration's goal of transforming the republic was Jefferson Finis Davis.

Davis was a reluctant president who preferred to serve his new country militarily as he had served his old country in the Mexican War and as Secretary of War. Nonetheless, he accepted the challenge of leading a fledgling country faced with the enormous task of creating a government, an army and navy, a postal system, and a plethora of other necessities to facilitate the proper functioning of an independent constitutional republic.

There are many ways to understand why the Southern States voted to leave the United States. Although many of the people of the Confederate States naively felt they would be left alone, they also knew there was a risk of attack and invasion as a result of their quest for independence. A concise explanation of the South's logic can be found in Davis' Inaugural Address, presented on February 18, 1861, in Montgomery, Alabama. In his address, he asked for God's

---

[582] "Quotation #37218 from Contributed Quotations," *The Quotations Page*, Michael Moncur, 1994-2015, http://www.quotationspage.com/quote/37218.html, (Accessed April 25, 2016).

[583] "Respectfully Quoted: A Dictionary of Quotations," *Bartleby.com*, 1989, http://www.bartleby.com/73/1593.html, (Accessed April 25, 2016).

blessings and expressed hope there would be no hostility. He remarked that the establishment of a Southern Nation is historically unprecedented, i.e., leaving one voluntary confederation to create another one. Davis invoked the States' Rights philosophy of Locke and Jefferson and echoed the words of the Declaration of Independence:

> It illustrates the American idea that governments rest on the consent of the governed, and that it is the right of the people to alter or abolish them at will when they become destructive of the ends for which they were established...and when, in the judgement of the sovereign States composing this Confederacy, it has been perverted from the purposes for which it was ordained.[584]

The U.S. Constitution became valid in June 1788 when New Hampshire became the ninth ratifying State and it began operation in March 1789. Davis viewed this as the beginning of a voluntary confederation (after leaving the Articles of Confederation, another voluntary agreement) and acknowledged the right of the people of the individual States to resume the powers previously delegated to the central government. In that context, Davis referenced the sovereignty of the States and their creation of a new Southern Confederacy that did not interfere with the rights of the States. "They formed a new alliance, but within each State its government has remained; so that rights of person and property have not been disturbed."[585]

---

[584] James D. Richardson, "Confederate States of America— Inaugural Address of the President of the Provisional Government, February 18, 1861," *The Avalon Project*, Yale Law School, Lillian Goldman Law Library, 2008, http://avalon.law.yale.edu/19th_century/csa_csainau.asp, (Accessed April 28, 2016).

[585] Ibid.

Davis was a product of the Southern way of life; he was born in Kentucky and spent much of his life in Louisiana and Mississippi. A Christian of the Episcopalian faith, Davis strongly supported agrarianism; he felt connected to the land and agriculture. He shared the belief with many other Southerners that rural society was superior to urban and/or industrial society. In modern vernacular, it might be phrased as being closer to God and nature.

Davis was just one of many eminent Southerners that advocated an agrarian society. Perhaps the strongest advocate was John Taylor of Caroline County, Virginia. Taylor, born in 1753, was an Anti-Federalist, Old Whig (opponent of absolute rule), who was often compared to Marcus Porcius Cato, the renowned Roman historian and senator. He was "a strong critic of central banks, an antagonist to the Money Power, supporter of the militia instead of standing armies and a firm believer in the central importance of agriculture to independence and freedom."[586] A classical liberal, Taylor began publishing the *Arator* in 1803; the publication supported and defended agrarianism. Taylor asserted agrarian societies encourage self-reliance and morality and produce more spiritually and physically complete individuals than industrial societies. In his book, *Tyranny Unmasked*, Taylor also explained how agrarian societies benefit from the peaceful exchange of goods through free trade. Taylor's friend and Davis' namesake, Thomas Jefferson, held similar beliefs. Jefferson claimed, "Those who labour in the earth are the chosen people of God, if ever he had a chosen people...."[587] In Query XIX of *Notes on the State of Virginia* (1781-1782), Jefferson echoed Taylor's contention that "Corruption of morals in the mass of cultivators is a phenomenon of which no age

---

[586] Scott M. Terry, "John Taylor of Caroline, Defender of the Agrarian Republic," *North Country Farmer*, February 23, 2012, http://www.northcountryfarmer.com/?p=295, (Accessed April 25, 2016).

[587] Jeremy Beer, "Agrarianism," *First Principles, ISI Web Journal*, December 23, 2011, http://www.firstprinciplesjournal.com/print.aspx?article=560, (Accessed April 24, 2016).

nor nation has furnished an example."[588] Jefferson also strongly advocated free trade.

Davis' words mirror Taylor, Jefferson, and other proponents of agrarianism:

> An agricultural people, whose chief interest is the export of commodities required in every manufacturing country, our true policy is peace, and the freest trade which our necessities will permit. It is alike our interest and that of all those to whom we would sell, and from whom we would buy, that there be the fewest practicable restrictions upon the interchange of these commodities.[589]

This comment underscores a major economic difference between North and South. Even the Great Seal of the Confederate States of America features George Washington on his horse surrounded by the main crops grown in the Southern States. Although agriculture was important in parts of the North, industry held greater influence and power. As previously explained, in almost every case, protectionism benefitted the North and harmed the South.

Davis recognized State sovereignty and States' Rights as being directly linked to the right of secession, an option he initially opposed and viewed only as a last resort: "My faith in that right as an inherent attribute of State sovereignty, was adopted early in life, was confirmed by study and observation of later years, and has

---

[588] Ibid.

[589] "Confederate States of America—Inaugural Address of the President of the Provisional Government, February 18, 1861," *The Avalon Project*, Yale Law School, Lillian Goldman Law Library, http://avalon.law.yale.edu/19th_century/csa_csainau.asp, (Accessed April 24, 2016).

passed unchanged and unshaken, through the severe ordeal to which it has been subjected."[590]

Davis often referenced the Declaration of Independence and the manner it laid out to correct a government that ceased to represent the consent of the governed: "That whenever any Form of Government becomes destructive of those ends, it is the Right of the People to alter or to abolish it, and to institute new Government..."[591] The Declaration goes on to add that despotic government should be thrown off and a new one instituted to include safeguards for the future.

In 1846, Davis stated his position relative to the only source of the Federal Government's powers. "I answer, it is the creature of the States; as such it could have no inherent power, all it possesses was delegated by the States."[592] Commenting further on his steadfast belief and undying commitment to the right of secession, Davis said, "the supremacy of the truths on which the Union was founded...I shall die, as I have lived, firm in the States' rights faith."[593]

Seeking peaceful separation with no malice directed toward the Northern States, President Davis said: "Actuated solely by the desire to preserve our own rights, and promote our own welfare, the separation of the Confederate States has been marked by no aggression upon others, and followed by no domestic convulsion."[594]

---

[590] Grady McWhiney, *Jefferson Davis — The Unforgiven* (Biloxi, Mississippi: The Beauvoir Press, 1989), 7.

[591] "Declaration of Independence," *The Charters of Freedom*, http://www.archives.gov/exhibits/charters/declaration_transcript.html, (Accessed April 24, 2016).

[592] McWhiney, 4.

[593] Ibid, 7.

[594] "Confederate States of America — Inaugural Address of the President of the Provisional Government, February 18, 1861," *The Avalon Project*, Yale Law School, Lillian Goldman Law Library, (Accessed April 24, 2016).

Davis echoed the Southern Christian perspective:

Reverently let us invoke the God of our fathers to guide
and protect us in our efforts to perpetuate the principles
which by this blessing they were able to vindicate,
establish, and transmit to their posterity. With the
continuance of his favor, ever gratefully acknowledged,
we may hopefully look forward to success, to peace, and
to posterity.[595]

As the Southern States worked to create an independent
republic, Davis always cast his eyes to the north. Distrust of certain
elements in the Northern States dated back to Revolutionary times.
Patrick Henry questioned the motives of certain factions in the New
England States, and he was deeply concerned about the South
entering into the new alliance (U.S. Constitution) with the North.
Henry noted, that as long as the New England States were in the
minority, they supported the rights of the States; however, it was
when they realized control was within their reach "they abandoned
their State Rights doctrines, and became consolidationists."[596] This
reflected the philosophical element in Henry's days concerning the
nature of the government—should it be federalist in the true sense
(divided sovereignty/States' Rights) or nationalist?

Davis has been harshly criticized since the War; however,
possessed with an in-depth knowledge of the U.S. Constitution and
history, he insisted the South's cause was correct. Davis imparted to
his old friend, President Pierce: "Mississippi, not as a matter of
choice but of necessity, has resolved to enter on the trial of secession.
Those who have driven her to this alternative threaten to deprive

---

[595] James Ronald Kennedy and Walter Donald Kennedy, *The South
Was Right!* (Gretna, Louisiana: Pelican Publishing Company, 1994), 326.

[596] Admiral Raphael Semmes, CSN Captain of the Alabama,
Memoirs of Service Afloat (Secaucus, New Jersey: The Blue & Grey Press,
1987), 40.

her of the right to require that her government shall rest upon the consent of the governed."[597]

The source of the schism between North and South was clear to Davis as he lamented, "Every evil which has befallen our institutions is directly traceable to the perversion of the compact of union and the usurpation by the Federal Government of undelegated powers."[598] Simply put, Davis felt the consolidationists had perverted the voluntary union.

After the war, the Union Army captured the President of the Confederate States. One fallacy surrounding his arrest dealt with his attire upon capture. "Davis was humiliated by the ridiculous rumor that spread through the North that he had been captured while wearing women's clothing. Secretary of War Stanton encouraged the rumors even though he knew them to be false."[599] In reality, in May 1865, near Irwinsville, Georgia, in his haste to escape the Union Army, Davis put his wife's waterproof raglan and a shawl on over his regular clothes. Stanton, a Radical Republican and not particularly friendly with Lincoln, made political hay from this fiction as a way to degrade Davis and imply femininity among Southern males.

After his capture, great symbolism underscored Davis' departure on the *William P. Clyde* en route to a Federal prison.

> As the tug bore him away from the ship, he stood with bared head between the files of undersized German and other foreign soldiers on either side of him, and as we looked, as we thought, our last upon his stately form and knightly bearing, he seemed a man of another and

---

[597] McWhiney, 4.

[598] Ibid., 6-7.

[599] "Aftermath & Reconstruction, 'Jefferson Davis Confined In A Dungeon,'" The War for States' Rights, *Civil War Bluegrass*, http://civilwar.bluegrass.net/AftermathAndReconstruction/jeffersondavis.html, (Accessed April 28, 2016).

higher race, upon whom 'shame would not dare to sit.'[600]

Davis was imprisoned at Fortress Monroe on May 22, 1865, and the next day manacled in irons. This humiliation lasted about a week. There was a public outcry over his treatment, as it was generally known he was in poor health. While in prison, besides being initially manacled, Davis was placed in a cold and damp cell under constant guard. The guards were ordered not to speak to him; a light burned in his cell around the clock; he rarely enjoyed over two hours of unbroken sleep; and he was not allowed to leave his cell. It was as if the Union Government placed the blame for the conflict solely upon Davis' shoulders.

In June of 1865, the U.S. Circuit Court (District of Virginia) and the District of Columbia issued indictments for treason. In May of 1866, a grand jury of the U.S. Circuit Court (District of Virginia) indicted Davis for treason. Davis knew the constitution was silent on secession; he felt a trial would validate the South's contention that the Union is voluntary and that the Ninth and Tenth Amendments meant what they said.

Even with the communication limits of the day, word spread about the ongoing poor treatment of the imprisoned Davis. Proponents of humane treatment in the North and across the world were incensed.

The May 24, 1866, edition of the New York *World,* ran an editorial criticizing his torture.

> It is no longer a matter of newspaper rumor that the treatment which Jefferson Davis has received during his incarceration in Fortress Monroe, has been to break down his constitution and to put him, after twelve

---

[600] Felicity Allen, *Jefferson Davis: Unconquerable Heart* (Columbia, Missouri: University of Missouri Press, 1999), 1.

months of protracted suffering, in imminent peril of death.[601]

Incarcerated for roughly two years and never tried, Davis firmly believed in the legality of secession and eagerly sought a trial to prove it.[602] Davis' situation caught the attention of Charles O'Conor, a Jeffersonian New York City lawyer who served as that State's Attorney General and as U.S. District Attorney. O'Conor was considered one of the top legal minds in the United States. In a June 2, 1865, note to Davis, O'Conor offered his defense services, writing "I will be happy to attend, at any time and place you may indicate, in order to confer with yourself in relation to the defense."[603] O'Conor was anxious to defend Davis, being aware of the voluntary nature of the Union (as taught at West Point from Rawles' book) and the sovereign rights of the States. Davis had support in both North and South, but the offer from such a distinguished lawyer surely provided a boost of confidence in his legal case.

Many in the North were hesitant to put Davis in front of a jury. U.S. Chief Justice Chase told Stanton that: "If you bring these leaders to trial, it will condemn the North, for by the Constitution, secession is not rebellion...His (Jeff Davis') capture was a mistake. His trial will be a greater one. We cannot convict him of treason."[604]

---

[601] Richard "Shotgun" Weeks, "The Prison Life of Jefferson Davis," *Times-Dispatch*, February 12, 1905, *American Civil War*, http://civilwarhome.com/davisinprision.htm, (Accessed April 25, 2016).

[602] Davis also felt he had already been punished by the Fourteenth Amendment that barred him from holding public office in the future.

[603] Captain John Anderson Richardson, *A Historical and Constitutional Defense of the South* (Harrisonburg, Virginia: Sprinkle Publications, 2010), 622. Originally published by A.B. Caldwell, Atlanta, Georgia, 1914.

[604] Al Benson, Jr., "Guess What Folks—Secession Wasn't Treason," Copperhead Chronicles, *Free Republic*, August 27, 2007, http://www.freerepublic.com/focus/news/1887357/posts?page=869, [From Burke Davis, *The Long Surrender*, 1985, 204.], (Accessed April 29, 2016).

Chase added that the secession issue had been settled (by military force in contravention of government by consent) and it was best to let sleeping dogs lie.

A congressional committee headed by Judge Franz Lieber concluded: "After studying more than 270,000 Confederate documents, seeking evidence against Davis, the court discouraged the War Department: 'Davis will be found not guilty,' Lieber reported, "and we shall stand there completely beaten."[605]

President Davis also received support from overseas. "Blessed Pope Pius IX was the only European Catholic prince who recognized the Confederate States government, referring to Davis as 'His Excellency, the President of the Confederate States of America.'"[606] The Pope identified with Davis' plight and shared a similar philosophy "in the sense that they believed in the world of honour, courtesy, hierarchy, chivalry and the land. For this reason, too, all Catholic bishops in the South supported the Confederacy."[607]

> As a symbol of his empathy, the Pope sent Davis *a crown of Jerusalem thorns hand-woven by the Pope's own hands which, given their sharpness, he could not have done without drawing blood. The Sovereign Pontiff also sent his own portrait self-autographed with the scriptural verse: 'If any man will come after me, let him deny himself, and take up his cross, and follow me.'*[608]

Another source of the Pope's empathy was the fact he traveled a similar path; he had been "exiled in Gaeta, fleeing the

---

[605] Ibid.

[606] "Tales from the Old South: Jefferson Davis and Blessed Pius IX," *Roman Christendom*, Saturday, November 17, 2007, http://romanchristendom.blogspot.com/2007/11/tales-from-old-south-jefferson-davis.html, (Accessed April 28, 2016).

[607] Ibid.

[608] Ibid. [Some claim Varina Davis made the crown or had it made.]

revolutionaries of Garibaldi's Roman republic, Jefferson Davis corresponded with him consoling him in his tribulation."[609]

On May 13, 1867, Davis appeared before Judge Underwood and bail was set at $100,000.00. In a remarkable gesture, Davis was freed when bond was "posted by Horace Greeley, abolitionist Gerrit Smith, a representative of Cornelius Vanderbilt, and ten Richmond businessmen; to 'deafening applause,' freed after two years of confinement."[610] Smith was one of the New England abolitionists who helped finance the activities of John Brown.

Despite the criticism during his lifetime, Davis never wavered from his beliefs. Until his dying day, he insisted the South was morally and constitutionally right, and he would do it all over again. Similar criticism has surfaced in modern times among some historians and commentators. Over the last half century, there has been a steady effort to downplay Davis as a leader, the legitimacy of the Confederacy, the tariff issue and States' Rights, laying the blame totally on slavery. Although Davis was pro-slavery, he was not fanatical about the institution and he was known to be kind to his slaves. He preferred a compromise on the slavery issue (such as the Crittenden Compromise) and realized emancipation would become a reality at some point in time.

During the latter stages of the war, Davis and Duncan F. Kenner, a large slave owner from Louisiana, worked on a plan to abolish slavery in return for recognition from Great Britain and France. This plan was not widely known about within the Confederate government. In late 1864, Davis told Kenner to put the plan in motion. "Kenner was given credentials and set out on a secret mission to Europe in January 1865. He arrived just weeks

---

[609] Ibid.

[610] "Post War Life and Career," *The Papers of Jefferson Davis, Rice University* — MS 43, Houston, Texas, 2016, http://jeffersondavis.rice.edu/PostWarLifeandCareer.aspx, (Accessed April 24, 2016).

before Robert E. Lee surrendered..."[611] Kenner met with Confederate commissioners James M. Mason, the grandson of George Mason, and John Slidell in Paris, France. They spoke with French Emperor Napoleon III who favored the proposal if the British were in agreement. The commissioners sailed to London, made their proposal and met resistance from Lord Palmerston and Prime Minister Henry John Temple. Before the Confederate commissioners could do anything to change British opinion, Lee surrendered and the point became moot. The theory that foreign powers sought to have America split in half is rendered suspect by this reality—the British could have assuredly made it happen. Lincoln was the quintessential politician with uncanny timing, whereas, Davis was committed to principle and ideology over the politics of perception.

From just after the war to modern times, one of the things that seems intolerable to anti-Confederates in both North and South is Davis' refusal to admit guilt or apologize for anything he did. He was so devoted to the principle of self-government that no amount of torture or harassment could make him change his mind. His willingness to be tried and let the judicial system rule on the constitutionality of secession is a testament to his unbending commitment.

Davis commented: "Our cause was so just, so sacred, that had I known all that has come to pass, that had I known what was to be inflicted upon me, all that my country was to suffer, all that our posterity was to endure, I would do it all over again."[612]

---

[611] Brion McClanahan, "Jefferson Davis and the Kenner Mission," *The Abbeville Blog, Abbeville Institute*, April 14, 2014, http://www.abbevilleinstitute.org/blog/jefferson-davis-and-the-kenner-mission/, (Accessed April 28, 2016). [According to McClanahan, this was recorded in 1899 by William Wirt Henry, Patrick Henry's grandson; the Library of Congress validated it in 1916; and it referenced the Joseph Brent Papers, housed at Louisiana State University. There is another contention that Kenner did not actually depart until February 11, 1865.]

[612] McWhiney, *The Unforgiven*, 7.

Like most of his Southern contemporaries, Davis loved the original Union; however, that group of Southerners understood the voluntary nature of the Union and most believed secession to be a legal option. They were adamant in their belief that the only legitimate government is by voluntary consent.

After the war, Davis lamented the ignorant attitude of some of his fellow Southerners.

> Nothing fills me with deeper sadness than to see a southern man apologizing for the defence we made of our inheritance & denying the truths on which all our institutions were founded. To be crushed by superior force, to be robbed & insulted, were great misfortunes, but these could be borne while there still remained manhood to assert the truth, and a proud consciousness in the rectitude of our course. When...I find myself reviled by Southern papers as one renewing "dead issues," the pain is not caused by the attack upon myself, but its desecration of the memories of our Fathers & those of their descendants who staked in defense of their rights—their lives, their property & their sacred honor. To deny the justice of their cause, to apologize for its defense, and denounce it as a dead issue, is to take the last of their stakes, that for which they were willing to surrender the other.[613]

Jefferson Davis, the Confederacy's only President, never wavered in his love for his country. Believing that legitimate government is one that protects life, liberty, and the pursuit of happiness, he took the words of the Declaration literally. He never surrendered in any form, but like most Southerners, he suffered greatly for his efforts to establish Southern Independence.

---

[613] Ibid.

Chapter Thirty
The Insights of Robert E. Lee and Lord Acton

"With the exception of a few honest zealots, the canting, hypocritical Yankee cares as little for our slaves as he does our draft animals. The war which he has been making upon slavery for the last forty years, is only a by-play, a device to help on his main action — Empire."[614]
Confederate Admiral Raphael Semmes

Robert E. Lee embodied all that was and is good about the Old South: Christian morality, love of family and friends, and steadfast devotion to duty. What may not be as well known is how General Lee corresponded with a like-minded individual, England's Lord Acton, the man who coined the timeless phrase: "Power tends to corrupt, and absolute power corrupts absolutely."[615]

On January 10, 1834, John Emerich Edward Acton (First Baron Acton of Aldenham) was born in Naples, Italy. Just as Lee was of noble lineage, being descended from Robert the Bruce, King of Scotland, Acton was also of proud heritage. Acton's father was Sir Richard Acton (of an established English line) and his mother was Countess Marie Louise de Dalberg, from a leading German family of the Rhineland.

Acton was an English Classical Liberal Catholic, and, in largely anti-Catholic England, his religious beliefs limited his educational options. As the son of prominent parents, Acton attended the University of Munich, where he studied history under

---

[614] Charles T. Pace, *War Between the States — Why?* (Charles T. Pace), 37.

[615] "Lord Acton in a Letter to Bishop Mandell Creighton, 1887," *Quotations by Author*, 1994-2015, http://www.quotationspage.com/quotes/Lord_Acton/, (Accessed April 25, 2016).

church historian Ignaz von Dollinger; "he was not permitted to attend Cambridge because he was a Catholic."[616]

In 1859, Acton became the co-proprietor and editor of an English periodical called *The Rambler*, a liberal Catholic journal that dealt with social, political, and theological matters. Through this publication, he became a staunch defender of religious and political freedom. He advocated that the church should promote individual liberty and encourage scientific, historical, and philosophical truths. As a member of the Irish constituency, Lord Acton entered the House of Commons in 1859 and was offered peerage by Gladstone in 1869.

Acton's life was laden with significant contributions for the betterment of humanity. In 1886, he founded the *English Historical Review*, a journal of historical scholarship that still exists. He received honorable degrees from Cambridge and Oxford in 1888 and 1889 and in 1891, Acton was appointed Queen Victoria's Lord-in-Waiting. It was in 1895 that "he was appointed Regius Professor of modern history at Cambridge (the very same institution that refused him admission, *circa* 1850)." [617] Acton's life, faith, and accomplishments closely mirrored those of Lee.

Lee's family had a long legacy of military and public service in Great Britain and America. Lee was a great lover of the original American Republic—it was literally in his blood. His grandfather, Richard Henry Lee, and his granduncle, Francis Lightfoot Lee, were both signers of the Declaration of Independence. Lee's father, Henry "Lighthorse" Harry Lee, was a renowned cavalry officer during the American Revolution. Following the established path of his ancestors, Lee chose a military career. He graduated from West

---

[616] "The History of Freedom in Christianity," from a speech by Lord John Emerich Edward Dalberg Acton, May 28, 1877, *Mondo Politico*, http://www.mondopolitico.com/library/lordacton/freedominchristianity/m pintro.htm, (Accessed April 25, 2016).

[617] Peter Landry, "Lord Acton," *Bluepete.com*, http://www.blupete.com/Literature/Biographies/Philosophy/Acton.htm, (Accessed April 25, 2016).

Point second in his class and never received a single demerit. Lee served loyally in the United States Army until Virginia voted to leave the Union.

Lee was a devout Christian of the Episcopalian faith. His life was driven by a sincere devotion to the teachings of Jesus Christ and a conscious effort to live by those convictions. It could be said, in both a figurative and a literal sense, Lee and Acton were singing out of the same spiritual hymnbook.

Acton greatly admired the Declaration of Independence, the John Locke/Thomas Jefferson view of government, and the fact that the American colonies established a constitutional government; he realized that only republics and constitutional monarchies had allowed freedom to grow.

Not only were Acton and Lee accomplished and educated men, each possessed a keen insight into history, and they shared many of the same visions about how government should work. Both men saw the dangers of centralization, and it was clear to them that the South sought to protect the Constitution while the North, based on the Republican Party Platform and Lincoln's disregard for constitutional limitations, sought to move the central government well beyond its enumerated powers. Neither Lee nor Acton felt the Constitution gave the central government the power of coercion.

Consolidated centralized power is fundamental to both the creation and perpetuation of empires, a fact not lost on Lee or Acton. For example, a king initially ruled the Roman Empire before it became a republic and eventually an empire that spread over much of Europe and Northern Africa. Though this empire made positive contributions relative to law, government, technology, architecture, etc., it eventually fell victim to moral decadence, political corruption, denial of rights, and military overextension before its demise around 476 AD. The British Empire began as a monarchy and spread its influence and control through military aggression and occupation. Centralized authority is a key component of all empires—Byzantine, Persian, Mongol, Spanish, Russian, etc. and most run through a cycle that eventually leads to moral corruption, military aggression, and often, financial ruin through over-extension. The history of the world is littered with such empires.

Acton had great admiration for the federal character of the original American government. He saw how emphasis on the liberty of the individual encouraged moral communities, "and he admired the Confederacy as the most advanced expression of such a polity. He thought the triumph of the Union was a disaster because it would encourage the trend toward consolidationism and nationalism that was transforming Europe into an order of French revolutionary-style republics."[618]

Jefferson recognized the tendency of true democracies (what he referred to as tyranny of the majority) toward consolidation and eventually dictatorship. The Founders realized this danger and thus set up a republican form of government.

Coming from a different vantage point, Karl Marx stated, "Democracy leads to Socialism."[619] Marx and Friedrich Engels (the German industrialist who supported and enabled Marx) both advocated socialism. Acton, possessing uncanny recognition of the slippery slope of consolidation, took Marx's comment a step further by saying, "Socialism is slavery."[620] The nature of command and control governments (socialism, communism, fascism, etc.) is centralization, and the people are often considered government property or subjects. States' Rights checked centralization by keeping the federal government from determining the limits of its own power. Lee echoed the sentiment of Acton.

---

[618] Thomas E. Woods, *"The Real Significance of the 'Civil War,'"* *LewRockwell.com*, November 27, 2004, http://www.lewrockwell.com/2004/11/thomas-woods/the-real-significance-of-the-civil-war/, (Accessed April 28, 2016).

[619] Austin Peterson, "Does Democracy Inevitably Lead to Socialism?" Economics of Liberty, *The Libertarian Republic — Economic Freedom — Personal Liberty*, September 6, 2013, http://thelibertarianrepublic.com/does-democracy-inevitably-lead-to-socialism/#axzz3OTxBVQGf, (Accessed April 28, 2016).

[620] Ibid.

Emory University professor Donald Livingston observed: "Had the Confederate States of America survived, the world would have had the model of a vast-scale federative polity with a strong central authority explicitly checked by the ultimate right of a state to secede. It would have shown the world that an alternative existed to the modern state."[621]

If for no other reason than economic practicality, slavery would have likely ended pretty quickly with peaceful secession. Industrialization and technological advancements were game changers; Great Britain was the birthplace of the Industrial Revolution (1760-1840), and during this time period there were improvements in manufacturing, farming technology, communications, and banking, which spread to other countries. Where the efficiency of Eli Whitney's cotton gin, patented in 1794, increased cotton production and initially the demand for slave labor, Cyrus McCormick's Virginia Reaper (patented in 1834) reduced the need for manpower because of its mechanical efficiency. Industrial and mechanical development does not remain static; it has often displaced manual labor by creating greater efficiency and increased production. For example, in the modern world, we have seen robotics replace many formerly human functions. Sans modernization in technology and equipment to keep pace with demand, the South would have suffered a competitive disadvantage in both domestic and international trade. In the Nineteenth Century, greater industrialization also increased migration from farms to the cities where slave labor was less feasible.

It would be incorrect to indict all slave labor as inefficient. As Lyon Gardiner Tyler noted, "The military system is a form of slavery in which the best results ensue when the discipline is the

---

[621] Thomas E. Woods, *"The Real Significance of the 'Civil War,'"* *LewRockwell.com*, November 27, 2004, (Accessed April 28, 2016).

strictest."[622] Despite the fact slavery can be productive, there are inherent limitations in this labor system.

Referencing Austrian economist Ludwig von Mises, he explained that slave labor could never compete in the marketplace with free labor, and added, "Servile labor could always be utilized only when it did not have to meet the competition of free labor."[623]

It is difficult to maintain morale over the long haul if there is no prospect of improving one's life. For example, the prospect of a slave having an opportunity to buy his freedom (manumission) would be a great incentive. Fixed costs are also different in that slave labor, by its nature, requires certain cradle-to-grave expenses lacking in a free labor system. Political and social attitudes were also factors. Without a plan for emancipation, an independent Southern Republic would have been short lived. The worldwide trend was anti-slavery, and the countries of Europe and South America had ended slavery peacefully, mainly by gradual emancipation and compensation.

Slavery was far from being universally supported in the South, and there was sentiment for some form of emancipation. There were several abolitionists from the South, such as Angelina and Sarah Grimke, Rev. John Rankin, Hinton Helper, and Charles Osborn. Lee described slavery as a moral evil and explained, "The best men of the South have long been anxious to do away with this institution, and were quite willing to see it abolished."[624] He also said, "So far from engaging in a war to perpetuate slavery, I am

---

[622] Lyon Gardiner, *The Gray Book* (Wiggins, Mississippi: Crown Rights Book Company, 1997), 10. Originally printed in *Tyler's Quarterly* in Volume 33, October and January issues, 1935.

[623] Robert Murphy, "Slavery Could Not Last in an (Otherwise) Free Market," *The Ludwig von Mises Institute Canada, Inc.,* quoting von Mises from page 626 of "Human Action," http://mises.ca/posts/blog/slavery-could-not-last-in-an-otherwise-free-market/, (Accessed April 25, 2016).

[624] Rod Gragg, "The Quotable Robert E. Lee," *So Good A Cause: A Decade of Southern Partisan,* ed. Oran P. Smith (Columbia, South Carolina: The Foundation for American Education, 1993), 126.

rejoiced that slavery is abolished."[625] Stonewall Jackson commented that he would like to "see the shackles struck from every slave."[626] A long list of Confederate officers had no involvement with slavery whatsoever. This list included Joseph Johnston, Patrick Cleburne, William Monaghan, A.P. Hill, Fitzhugh Lee, J.E.B. Stuart, William Montague Browne, and William Grace.

Sharing the belief in States' Rights and limited government, Lee and Acton were aware of the positive ramifications of peaceful secession. Peaceful separation would have almost certainly spared the senseless loss of over 700,000 American lives.

The main beneficiaries of consolidated government were bankers, industrialists, and corporate welfare recipients, who had long sought to implement Hamilton/Clay mercantilism. Lincoln was determined to establish federal supremacy over the States. Spooner, the Massachusetts abolitionist who supported the South's right to secede, wrote extensively about the motives of these Northern interests.

After the South's failure to establish independence, Lee and Acton lamented the damage to States' Rights and the Constitution. In his November 4, 1866, letter to Lee, Acton stated:

> I saw in States' rights the only availing check upon the absolutism of the sovereign will, and secession filled me with hope, not as the destruction but as the redemption of Democracy. The institutions of your Republic have not exercised on the old world the salutary and liberating influence which ought to have belonged to them, by reason of those defects and abuses of principle which the Confederate Constitution was expressly and

---

[625] Ibid.

[626] Chuck Baldwin, "Lee and Jackson Remembered: Robert E. Lee and Stonewall Jackson Were Anti-Slavery," *Sons of Confederate Veterans Blog Spot*, January 11, 2010, http://sonsofconfederateveterans.blogspot.com/2010/01/lee-and-jackson-remembered.html, (Accessed April 25, 2016).

wisely calculated to remedy. I believed that the example of that great Reform would have blessed all the races of mankind by establishing true freedom purged of the native dangers and disorders of Republics. Therefore I deemed that you were fighting the battles of our liberty, our progress, and our civilization, and I mourn for the stake which was lost at Richmond more deeply than I rejoice over that which was saved at Waterloo.[627]

Lee responded to Acton on December 15th:

I yet believe that the maintenance of the rights and authority reserved to the states and to the people, not only are essential to the adjustment and balance of the general system, but the safeguard to the continuance of a free government. I consider it as the chief source to our political system, whereas the consolidation of the states into one vast republic, sure to be aggressive abroad and despotic at home, will be the certain precursor of that ruin which has overwhelmed all those that have preceded it. I need not refer one so well acquainted as you are with American history, to the State papers of Washington and Jefferson, the representatives of the federal and democratic parties, denouncing consolidation and centralization of power, as tending to the subversion of state Governments, and to despotism. The New England states, whose citizens are the fiercest opponents of the Southern states, did not always avow the opinions they now advocate. Upon the purchase of Louisiana by Mr. Jefferson, they virtually asserted the right of secession through their prominent men; and in the convention which assembled at

---

[627] "The Acton-Lee Correspondence," *LewRockwell.com*, http://archive.lewrockwell.com/orig3/acton-lee.html, (Accessed April 28, 2016).

Hartford in 1814, they threatened the disruption of the
Union unless the war should be discontinued.[628]

The dangers of centralization and empire so astutely
predicted by Lee and Acton are patently obvious today. In our
world, we have a national bank acting as central planners by
manipulating interest rates and credit; corporate welfare that
includes blatant bailouts of industries that would and should
collapse under free market capitalism; industries protected from
competition; foreign interventionism, and an intrusive government
that seeks to get involved in every phase of the average person's life.

---

[628] Ibid.

Chapter Thirty-One
The Just War Theory

"War is a racket. It always has been. It is possibly the oldest, easily the most profitable, surely the most vicious. It is the only one international in scope. It is the only one in which the profits are reckoned in dollars and the losses in lives."[629]

U.S. Marine Corps Major General Smedley Butler

The origins of just war can be traced at least back to Cicero, the Roman orator who lived before the birth of Christ. The most up-to-date Christian codification of the Just War Theory is generally considered to be from the Catholic Church (or Orthodox Church), specifically with the man considered the father of the Just War Theory, St. Augustine of Hippo, who lived from 354-430. In the strictest terms, the teachings of Jesus Christ may indicate there is no such thing as just war; however, there is a right to defend oneself against an aggressor.

There are two types of justice contained within the Just War Theory. The first is known as *jus ad bellum* (justice before the war). Dutch Christian, Hugo Grotius (1538-1645), known as the Father of International Law, defined six conditions (or limitations) for *jus ad bellum* in his 1625 treatise, *De Jure Belli Ac Pacis (On the Law of War and Peace)*. They are:

1. Just cause—this includes the correct intention of self-defense along with a specific objective. The cause and intent of the war must be deemed just in God's eyes, e.g., protecting the innocent, restoring order, etc.

---

[629] Brigadier General Smedley D. Butler, *War Is A Racket* (Los Angeles, California: Feral House, 2003), 23.

2. Authorization (proportionality)—the situation is serious enough to warrant war.

3. Public declaration—there must be a fair warning given so that all means of conflict avoidance can be explored.

4. Reasonable chance of success—objectives are attainable. It is patently wrong to waste human life for causes with little or no prospects of success.

5. Declaration only by a legitimate authority—war can be waged only through the proper channels. For example, the U.S. Constitution gives Congress the power to authorize war.

6. It must be the last resort—all other options have failed. War should never be waged for frivolous, bogus or *false flag* reasons.

According to Grotius, the second type of justice is *jus in bello* (justice during the war). The three conditions exist for *jus in bello*:

1. Legitimate targets—war should be directed only at combatants, not civilians. For example, Total War is illegitimate warfare and is typically identified more with barbarism than with civilized people.

2. Proportionality—the response must be proportionate to the injury inflicted and should not be excessive.

3. Treatment of prisoners—once captured, combatants become noncombatants. Torture would never be an option in a moral society.

Going through each step of *jus ad bellum* and *jus in bello*, the South's cause mirrors this theory. The late historian and libertarian economist, Murray Rothbard, contended America had two just wars —the side of the colonists in the American Revolution and the Confederate side in the War Between the States. He said: "A just war exists when a people tries to ward off the threat of coercive domination by another people, or to overthrow an already—existing domination. A war is unjust, on the other hand, when a people try to impose domination on another people, or try to retain an already existing rule over them."[630]

Offering thoughtful insight into war in general, Christian libertarian writer Laurence Vance referenced an interesting perspective using this quote from an anonymous Baptist preacher from a 1938 issue of *The Christian Review*:

> The war spirit is so wrought into the texture of governments, and the habits of national thinking, and even into our very festivals and pomps, that its occasional recurrence is deemed a matter of unavoidable necessity...The causes of war, as well as war itself, are contrary to the gospel. It originates in the worst passions and the worst aims. We may always trace it to the thirst of revenge, the acquisition of territory, the monopoly of commerce, the quarrels of kings, the intrigues of ministers, the coercion of religious opinion, the acquisition of disputed crowns, or some other source, equally culpable; but never has any war, devised by man, been founded on holy tempers and Christian principles.[631]

To fully understand the commentary of Rothbard and Vance, we must look further into the most conspicuous example in American history—the War Between the States. While many men on the Confederate side plainly articulated the South's position, President Davis offered one of the most concise snapshots of the Southern view. A student of history and the constitution and initially an opponent of secession, Davis recognized the intent of the Radical Republicans to transform the American Republic from a voluntary confederation of States to a highly centralized

---

[630] Laurence Vance, "Christianity and War," *LewRockwell.com*, October 29, 2003, https://www.lewrockwell.com/2003/10/laurence-m-vance/christianity-and-war-2/, (Accessed April 28, 2016).

[631] Ibid.

government. He yearned for a return to the original intent of the confederation, lamenting, "I love the Union and the Constitution, but I would rather leave the Union with the Constitution than remain in the Union without it."[632] Although Davis was averse to war, he knew the financial stakes at play and saw conflict as a distinct possibility.

Davis echoed Jefferson, his namesake, and emphasized the voluntary nature of the Union, adding,

> The withdrawal of a State from a league has no revolutionary or insurrectionary characteristic. The government of the State remains unchanged as to all internal affairs. It is only its external or confederate relations that are altered. To term this action of a Sovereign a 'rebellion' is a gross abuse of language.[633]

On April 29, 1861, in Montgomery, Alabama, Davis announced the ratification of the Confederate Constitution. Within his speech, he defended the South and expressed his desire for peaceful coexistence with the Northern States:

> We feel that our cause is just and holy; we protest solemnly in the face of mankind that we desire peace at any sacrifice save that of honour and independence; we ask no conquest, no aggrandizement; no concession of any kind from the States with which we were lately confederated; all we ask is to be let alone; that those who never held power over us shall not now attempt our subjugation by arms.[634]

---

[632] "Jefferson Davis Quotes," *American Civil War Story*, 2012-2016, http://www.americancivilwarstory.com/jefferson-davis-quotes.html, (Accessed April 28, 2016).

[633] Ibid.

[634] "Confederate States of America—Message to Congress April 29, 1861 (Ratification of the Constitution)," *The Avalon Project*, Yale Law School,

Davis asserted the Union is a voluntary confederation of States, and secession is both a reserved right and a natural right based on government by consent. The central government's role is simply as an agent of the States. His emphasis on the South's just cause and desire for peace highlights the contrast between those who believe in a republic of sovereign States and those who advocate centralization.

The novice or unconcerned observer of history might suspect that Davis' view of the voluntary nature of the alliance was singularly a Southern belief; however, the words of many of the North defy such a conclusion. For example, staunch Unionist and *New York Tribune* Editor Horace Greeley stated in November 9, 1860:

> The right to secede may be a revolutionary one, but it exists nevertheless…Whenever a considerable section of our Union shall deliberately resolve to go out we shall resist all coercive measures designed to keep it in. We hope never to live in a Republic whereof one section is pinned to the residue by bayonets.[635]

The next month, in a December 17, 1860, *New York Tribune* article, Greeley expressed understanding of the South's argument by referencing the Declaration of Independence, writing:

> …if it justified the secession from the British Empire of Three Millions of colonists in 1776, we do not see why it would not justify the secession of Five Millions of Southrons from the Federal Union in 1861. If we are

---

Lillian Goldman Law Library, http://avalon.law.yale.edu/19th_century/csa_m042961.asp, (Accessed April 25, 2016).

[635] David M. Kennedy and Lizabeth Cohen, *The American Pageant* (Boston, Massachusetts: Wadsworth Cengage Learning, 2013), 413.

mistaken on this point, why does not some one attempt to show wherein and why?[636]

Here Greeley points out how no one on the Union side had legitimately repudiated the South's position. Although Lincoln communicated with the abolitionist Greeley on several occasions, at least in the beginning, they clearly expressed contrasting views.

Philadelphia anti-slavery lawyer William Rawle was one of the founders of the Historical Society of Pennsylvania, a trustee to the University of Pennsylvania, Chancellor of the Law Association of Philadelphia and a major contributor to the Code of Pennsylvania. In Rawle's view, "It will depend upon the State itself whether it will continue to be a member of the Union...If the States are interfered with they may wholly withdraw from the Union"[637] Lee specifically cited Rawle's 1825 book, *A View of the Constitution*, as being instrumental in his West Point teaching as to the voluntary nature of the Union and the right of a State or States to leave it.

Though Rawle's opinion is generally considered Jeffersonian, Hamilton echoed similar sentiment in *The Federalist*. This view of the alliance was also acknowledged by the commentary of John Codman Ropes, a Russian-born, Massachusetts military historian and pro-Union lawyer:

> The States which seceded held, it must be remembered, the theory that the United States was not a single nation, but a collection of nations, which had for many years

---

[636] "New York Daily Tribune December 17, 1860, Monday," *Dilemmas of Compromise*, Tulane University, http://www.tulane.edu/~sumter/Dilemmas/Tribune17Dec.html, (Accessed April 28, 2016).

[637] Mildred Lewis Rutherford, *Truths of History* (Harrisonburg, Virginia: Old South Institute Press, 2009), 3.

acted for certain purposes through an agency known as the Government of the United States.[638]

Ironically, Ohio Senator Benjamin Wade, a Radical Republican, devout Unionist, and known foe of the South, questioned the merits of using force to subdue the Southern States. In 1858, Wade asked, "Who is the final arbiter—the government or the States—why, to yield the right of the States to protect its own citizens would consolidate this government into a miserable despotism."[639] Even this devoted enemy of the South saw the danger of forced consolidation and the government being the judge of its own powers.

Some Northerners agreed with Lincoln's indivisible Union theory by claiming the States were not sovereign. One such person was George Comstock, a founder of Syracuse University and Chief Judge of the New York Court of Appeals. Comstock felt if the States were indeed sovereign, the North was committing a crime against civilization and Christianity. As a proponent of the war, Comstock mused about the possibility of the South being right:

> If Mr. Davis is right as to all circumstances and results flowing from separation, then the seceded states are rightful possession of a perfect sovereignty...[the Civil War then] was a war of possession and conquest, for which there is no warrant in the Constitution, but which

---

[638] John Codman Ropes, *The Story of the Civil War, Part 1: Chapter II: The Question of the Southern Forts* (New York, New York and London, England: G.P. Putnam and Sons, The Knickerbocker Press, 1894), 17, https://archive.org/stream/storyofthecivilw015812mbp#page/n3/mode/2up, (Accessed August 20, 2016).

[639] Rutherford, *Truths of History*, 4.

John M. Taylor

is condemned by the rules of Christianity, and the law
of the civilized world.[640]

Prior to his Inauguration, Lincoln made plans to initiate
conflict with the Confederate States. Sending a message to General
Scott through Illinois Whig turned Republican Congressman and
attorney Elihu B. Washburne, Lincoln wrote: "Please present my
respects to the General and tell him, confidentially, that I shall be
obliged to him to be as well prepared as he can to either hold, or
retake the forts, as the case may require, at and after my
inauguration."[641]

Despite Lincoln's opposition to the Mexican War earlier in
his political career, he let it be known in his First Inaugural Address
that there would be no compromise. "The determination expressed
by Lincoln in his Inaugural Address to hold, occupy and possess the
property and places belonging to the United States, precipitated the
war."[642] Lincoln's emphasis on collecting duties and imposts was
tantamount to a threat of war and U.S. Secretary of State Seward,
part of the inner circle, observed, "The attempt to reinforce Sumter
will provoke war. The very preparation of such an expedition will

---

[640] Charles Adams, *When in the Course of Human Events—Arguing the Case for Southern Secession* (Lanham, Maryland: Rowman & Littlefield Publishers, Inc.), 182.

[641] Robert Dickinson Sheppard D.D., *Abraham Lincoln: A Character Sketch* (Chicago, Illinois: Frederick J. Drake & Company, by H.G. Campbell Publishing Company, 1903), 63. (Original Copyright by The University Association, 1898 and digitized by Indiana State University.), https://archive.org/details/abrahamlinc2788shep, (Accessed August 21, 2016).

[642] James Kendall Hosmer, *The American Nation: A History, The Appeal to Arms: Volume 20, 1861-1863* (New York, New York and London, England: Harper and Brothers Publishers; Edited by Albert Bushnell Hart, L.L.D., 1907), 26. [Hosmer was a Massachusetts educator, writer, and Union soldier.]

precipitate war. I would instruct Anderson to return from Sumter."[643]

Regarding the forts in the South, they were considered to be "partnership property; and each of the States was an equal party in the ownership. The Federal Government, strictly speaking, was not a party in this ownership at all, but was only the general agent of the real parties, that is, the several States composing the compact of the Union."[644] The forts "were designed each for the protection of the States where they were located, it was held that such forts necessarily went with the withdrawing States to which they belonged." [645] The numerous offers extended by the South to financially settle the issue with the forts were ignored by the Lincoln Administration.

In his book, *Died for Their State*, Lowell, Massachusetts, author Benjamin Williams wrote: "The South was invaded and a war of subjugation was begun by the Federal government against the seceding States in amazing disregard of the foundation principle of its existence...The North had no Constitutional right to hold Fort Sumter in case the States seceded and to hold it meant war."[646]

Even after the war, the Supreme Court echoed the contention of an indissoluble union despite overwhelming evidence to the contrary. In his 1888 work, *The American Commonwealth*, renowned British author and politician James Bryce questioned the logic of a Union that could not be broken, describing such reasoning as "a mass of subtle, so to speak, scholastic metaphysics regarding the nature of government."[647] It was as though the case was somehow different from all other federations in the history of the world, that

---

[643] Rutherford, *Truths of History*, 9.

[644] R.G. Horton, *A Youth's History of the Great Civil War in the United States, 1861-1865* (New York, New York: Van Evrie, Horton and Company, 1867), 71.

[645] Ibid.

[646] Rutherford, *Truths of History*, 10.

[647] Adams, *When in the Course of Human Events*, 182.

"the American federation was not a compact between commonwealths 'but an instrument of perpetual efficacy.'"[648]

Using basic rules of the Just War Theory, beginning with *Jus ad bellum*, the first question concerns whether or not there was proper criteria to wage war. Did the North have a just cause by acting in self-defense, fearing the South would invade the Northern States? Was the situation serious enough to warrant a war? Were all measures taken to avoid war? Would war bring on senseless loss of life? Did the Congress of the United States declare war? Were all options extinguished before engaging in war?

Now, looking at just war through *jus in bello*, did the North only make war against military combatants and not on civilians and property? Was proportionality exhibited, collateral damage minimized and property rights respected? Did the North treat their captured prisoners as non-combatants, refrain from torture, and respect due process of law?

The written words of the participants on both sides as well as the Official Records of the War Between the States answer all of these questions.

---

[648] Ibid.

Chapter Thirty-Two
Northern Disapproval of the War

"If our sister States must leave us, in the name of Heaven let them go in peace."[649]
Edward Everett, Massachusetts Whig politician, educator, and pastor

Lysander Spooner was one of the strongest critics of Lincoln and the war. Spooner, born in Athol, Massachusetts, was so independent–minded, he was often characterized as an "individualist anarchist,"[650] meaning he only recognized his right to rule himself and considered all other forms of government to be tyrannical. His career included the study of law under lawyer/politicians John Davis and Charles Allen of Massachusetts. Spooner was an uncompromising abolitionist and his 1845 book, *The Unconstitutionality of Slavery*, drew considerable praise in abolitionist circles.

Spooner adhered to the Jeffersonian philosophy, believing the people of the South had a right to secede and choose the government that suited them. He was a severe critic of the Republican Party, realizing their primary interest was not eradicating slavery but rather keeping the South in the Union for economic reasons.

---

[649] Mildred Lewis Rutherford, *Truths of History* (Harrisonburg, Virginia: Old South Institute Press, 2009), 5. Original source: George Lunt, *Origin of the Late War*, 435.

[650] Carl Watner and Steve J. Shone, "Lysander Spooner — American Anarchist," *The Foundation for Economic Education*, August 11, 2011, http://fee.org/freeman/detail/lysander-spooner-american-anarchist/, (Accessed April 25, 2016).

In *The Lysander Spooner Reader,* he wrote:

The principle, on which the war was waged by the North, was simply this: That men may rightfully be compelled to submit to, and support, a government that they do not want; and that resistance, on their part, makes them traitors and criminals....No principle, that is possible to be named, can be more self-evidently false than this; or more self-evidently fatal to all political freedom. Yet it triumphed in the field, and is now assumed to be established. If it really be established, the number of slaves, instead of having been diminished by the war, has been greatly increased; for a man, thus subjected to a government that he does not want, is a slave.[651]

Spooner was skeptical of the nature and critical of the content of the U.S. Constitution, but he recognized, at least in theory, it was intended to strike a balance between State and Federal power. He did not believe the Federal government had been granted the authority to force States to remain within the Union. Noting before the war, the government was at least theoretically based on free consent and post-war based on force, Spooner said: "If that principle be *not* the principle of the Constitution, the fact should be known. If it *be* the principle of the Constitution, the Constitution itself should be at once overthrown."[652]

When it came to the subject of slavery, Spooner held a no compromise position, even to the point of sympathizing with slaves

---

[651] Thomas J. DiLorenzo, "Lysander Spooner, Neo-Confederate," *LewRockwell.com,*
Posted on February 23, 2012, https://www.lewrockwell.com/lrc-blog/lysander-spooner-neo-confederate/, (Accessed April 25, 2016).

[652] Wendy McElroy, "Lysander Spooner," *LewRockwell.com,* Feb. 11, 2006, https://www.lewrockwell.com/2006/02/wendy-mcelroy/lysander-spooner/, (Accessed April 25, 2016).

who committed acts of violence against their owners. He believed in government by consent, realizing that forcing individuals to live under a government they did not want is in itself a form of slavery.[653] When the war broke out in 1861, Spooner did not join the pro-Union abolitionists, despite his intense hatred of slavery.

In the eyes of Spooner, the war and the true intent of the North had nothing to do with freedom or justice. Unaffected when hostilities began, Spooner remained an unapologetic supporter of the South's right to govern itself. Even after the war, Spooner did not deviate from his view of why the war was fought. In his 1867 essay entitled *No Treason No. 1*, Spooner wrote:

> On the part of the North, the war was carried on, not to liberate slaves, but by a government that had always perverted and violated the Constitution, to keep the slaves in bondage; and was still willing to do so, if the slaveholders could be thereby induced to stay in the Union.[654]

Spooner was alarmed at the corruption associated with the military occupation of the Southern States. He saw Reconstruction as just another phase of a plan enacted by the individuals determined to destroy the South. Within his *No Treason* pamphlets of 1867 and 1870, Spooner was not only critical of the occupation of the South; he mocked the phony declarations of the victors.

Spooner wrote: "All these cries of having 'abolished slavery,' of having 'saved the country,' of having 'preserved the union,' of

---

[653] Spooner's logic was echoed by Paul S. Whitcomb, the post-war writer from Gladstone, Oregon, referenced in earlier text, i.e., Spooner believed, in matters of principle, the South's right to govern itself paralleled the slave's natural right to be free.

[654] "No Treason, No. 1," Lysander Spooner, *Mises Daily*, March 22, 2011, https://mises.org/library/no-treason-no-1, (Accessed April 25, 2016).

establishing a 'government of consent,' and of 'maintaining the national honor,' are all gross, shameless, transparent cheats."[655]

Even the complete title of his pamphlets, *No Treason—The Constitution of No Authority*, reflected Spooner's belief that the Constitution carried no obligation to the present and essentially died with the generation that adopted it. Spooner insisted the fact that there *was* a crisis indicated the government was dysfunctional and should be ended or replaced.

Spooner made enemies on both sides of the conflict, but his greatest sense of anger was directed at Lincoln, his administration, and his supporters in their invasion of the Southern States.

Nathaniel Hawthorne, of Salem, Massachusetts, was one of the elite authors in American history, having penned classics such as *The Scarlet Letter* and *The House of the Seven Gables*. Hawthorne, a Democrat and close friend of President Pierce, was a loyal Unionist who was ambivalent toward slavery and apparently baffled by the entire schism between the North and the South. In a May 26, 1861, letter to his classmate, Commodore Horatio Bridge, Chief of the Navy's Bureau of Provisions and Clothing, Hawthorne wrote:

> Meantime, though I approve the war as much as any man, I don't quite see what we are fighting for or what definite result can be expected...Whatever happens next, I must say that I rejoice that the old Union is smashed. We never were one people and never really had a country since the Constitution was formed.[656]

---

[655] "The Constitution of the United States, Chapter 8, No. VI," 58, *lysanderspooner.org,* http://www.lysanderspooner.org/works/#, (Accessed April 25, 2016).

[656] "The Project Gutenberg EBook of The Complete Works of Nathaniel Hawthorne," 543, Appendix to Volume XII: Tales, Sketches, and other Papers by Nathaniel Hawthorne with a Biographical Sketch by

In an October 12, 1861, letter to Bridge, Hawthorne continued to express his confusion about the war but reiterated his support for his region of the country:

> For my part, I don't hope, nor indeed wish, to see the Union restored as it was. Amputation seems to me the much better plan, and all we ought to fight for is the liberty of selecting the point where our diseased members shall be lop't off. I would fight to the death for the Northern Slave States and let the rest go.[657]

Almost a year later, in February 1862, Hawthorne revealed his Jeffersonian inclinations by stating, "It would be too great an absurdity... to spend all our Northern strength, for the next generation, in holding on to a people who insist on being let loose."[658] Later that same year, referencing a trip to the White House in a March 16, 1862, letter to his wife, Hawthorne stated "I have shaken hands with Uncle Abe."[659] The Uncle Abe reference was supposedly meant as a term of kindness. Although Hawthorne held Lincoln in high regard, he failed to see the logic of the U.S. President's insistence on the use of force against the Southern States.

George Parsons Lathrop; Release Date: August 18, 2012 [EBook #40529] *Gutenberg.org*, http://www.gutenberg.org/files/40529/40529-h/40529-h.htm, (Accessed April 25, 2016).

[657] Horatio Bridge, *Personal Recollections of Nathaniel Hawthorne, Chapter XV*, 1893, *eldritchpress.org*, http://www.eldritchpress.org/nh/hb15.html, (Accessed April 24, 2016).

[658] Peter Carlson, "Nathaniel Hawthorne disses Abe Lincoln," American History 46.4 (2011): 16+. *U.S. History in Context*, Web, http://ic.galegroup.com/ic/uhic/AcademicJournalsDetailsPage/DocumentTo olsPortletWindow?jsid=5695e7d082f14b46ea38ec334e313ee8&action=2&catI d=&documentId=GALE|A264270626&userGroupName=tricotec_main&zid =449b4c01cf5ddab365960c7a1fd856f6, (Accessed April 24, 2016).

[659] Ibid.

The Lincoln Administration sought to meld together a variety of factions in the North. Although Northerners, in general, and Republicans, in particular, were not generally friendly to Irish and German immigrants (especially Catholics), the Republicans courted and welcomed the Germans who were thrown out of power in 1848. Even the Know Nothings who created the nativist American Party before becoming Republicans, managed to accept them. These Germans, who settled heavily in the Midwest, were known as Forty-Eighters, and many were adamantly socialistic/communistic in their view of government. Along with the pro-protection manufacturers and New England intellectuals, the Forty-Eighter Germans/Europeans were among Lincoln's most loyal supporters.

As history has repeatedly shown, the Irish—specifically Irish Catholics—were considered to be expendable as cannon fodder. (Also, the fact the Irish were traded as slaves seems to get lost in most historical discussions.) The Enrollment Act of 1863 was just one more example. Whereas wealthy Northerners had the option to fight or pay the $300.00 exemption from the draft, the Irish, mostly coming from extremely meager circumstances, lacked the funds to buy an exemption. A large number of wealthy Southerners fought, but few wealthy Northerners did. Even Sherman referenced and lamented this fact when he said, "that without conscription there would have been no way to 'separate the sheep from the goats and demonstrate what citizens will fight and what will only talk.'"[660] Few wealthy Northerners passed the Sherman test. Furthermore, Blacks were not considered citizens and were thus exempt from the draft, making them an even greater target for Northern anti-war factions. It was known within the federal government who supported the war and who did not and the draft reflected it; John

---

[660] Commander Douglas G. Cooper, U.S. Navy, USAWC Class of 1997, "Stumbling Toward Total Civil War: The Successful Failure of Union Conscription 1862-1865," *U.S. Army War College*, Carlisle Barracks, PA, 23; quoted from: Eugene C. Murdock, Ohio's Bounty System in the Civil War (Ohio State University Press, 1963), 111.

Chodes, the New York playwright and historian, noted that about four times more men were drafted from New York than from Massachusetts.

In July 1863, many Irish and German immigrants in New York City violently protested the implementation of the first Federal military draft. The first day (Saturday, July 11) started as organized resistance and was relatively incident free; however, when the list of names of those conscripted for war began to spread, the anger intensified. By Monday, protests became violent with destruction of property, including the draft equipment used by the locals. Attacks were made on Horace Greeley's *New York Tribune* office. Even the Colored Orphan Asylum was attacked—the children were removed in time but toys, clothing and supplies were destroyed, and then the building was set on fire.

The rampage continued on Tuesday with looting and destruction of businesses, including military uniform supplier Brooks Brothers. Mob attacks became more intense, and at least two Blacks were lynched.

On Wednesday, at least four more Blacks were killed. Over a five-day period, New York City was disrupted by the destruction of property—both public and private, factory closings, violence against law enforcement, and brutal violence against Black Northerners. "The long term damage to New York's black population was significant: In the aftermath of the riots, the city's black population plummeted by more than 20 percent, to below 10,000 (the lowest number since the 1820s), as blacks fled the city in droves."[661]

Prior to the Draft Riots, racial tension had been fueled by the issuance of the Emancipation Proclamation and the fear that more Black people would move to New York and compete in the labor market. By the end of the draft riots, over 100 civilians had been

---

[661] Barbara Maranzani, "Four Days of Fire: The New York City Draft Riots," History in the Headlines, *History.com*, July 5, 2013, http://www.history.com/news/four-days-of-fire-the-new-york-city-draft-riots, (Accessed April 24, 2016).

killed and at least eleven Blacks had been lynched. The *New York Times* reported: "No period in the history of this city will be more memorable than the riot week. It will not be forgotten by this generation, and the stories of it will be transmitted to the generation that follows us."[662]

The story of the New York Draft Riots does not figure prominently in most discussions of the war. Generally treated as a footnote in history, the riots were extremely violent and deadly. Lasting almost a week, the riots were finally suppressed by the appearance of several thousand troops, including New York State Militia and Union troops from New York, Michigan, and Indiana.

★ ★ ★

William Archibald Dunning, the son of a wealthy manufacturer, was born in Plainfield, New Jersey, in 1857. His father possessed an interest in the events of the day, especially the sectional rancor, and he openly discussed these issues when William was a child. Dunning's father was concerned with the problems that would arise with forcing the South back into the Union. Intrigued by his father's concerns, William focused much of his historical research on this subject as an adult.

Dunning attended Columbia University and the University of Berlin. He used logic and objectivity rather than emotion in evaluating the situation with the South. Dunning developed a strong distrust for many Republicans, especially Radicals such as U.S. Representative Stevens from Pennsylvania and U.S. Senator Sumner from Massachusetts. It was Stevens who believed the post-war South should be treated as a conquered province. Dunning detested

---

[662] "New Publications; The Draft Riots in New-York: The Honorable Record of the Metropolitan Police During Riot Week, by David M. Barnes. New York: Baker & Godwin, Publishers, October 23, 1863," The *New York Times*, http://www.nytimes.com/1863/10/23/news/new-publications-draft-riots-new-york-honorable-record-metropolitan-police.html, (Accessed April 28, 2016).

slavery, but he also knew there were some alternatives to escape the system, such as manumission policies in the South and Border States. Gauging the prevailing sentiments toward the institution, Dunning felt slavery would perish without outside interference.

Dunning's writing style was elegant with a touch of dry humor. He directed some of his most descriptive verbiage toward characters such as Stevens, whom he described as "'truculent, vindictive, and cynical' with 'a total lack of scruple.'"[663] He had similarly strong comments about Sumner, claiming, "His forte was exalted moral fervor and humanitarian idealism...He was the perfect type of that narrow fanaticism which erudition and egotism combine to produce, and to which political crises alone give the opportunity for actual achievement."[664]

Critics of the Southern point of view often label Dunning as an apologist, but he simply possessed the temerity to identify the instigators of the *Union At All Costs* side of the schism. He also understood the invasion of the Southern States and eventual Reconstruction were both unnecessary. Dunning offered an astute analysis of the general mood of Southerners during Reconstruction:

> The necessity of submission to force had been thoroughly learned, and no organized resistance was attempted to the few thousand troops that were scattered over the ten states but the mere consciousness that the center of authority was at military headquarters, and not at the state capital, disheartened the most moderate and progressive classes. It soon appeared, moreover, that military government was not to be simply nominal; the orders of the commanders

---

[663] Gail Jarvis, "The Dunning School," *LewRockwell.com*, https://www.lewrockwell.com/2004/02/gail-jarvis/the-dunning-school/, (Accessed April 28, 2016).

[664] Ibid.

reached the commonest concerns of everyday life, and created the impression of a very real tyranny.[665]

Dunning was aware of the massive corruption connected to the occupation of and martial law imposed on the post-war South. State treasuries were raided, and taxes were set so high that many Southerners could not pay them. Not only did Southerners risk losing their property because of high taxes, if they were ex-Confederates, due to The Reconstruction Acts, they were disenfranchised and had no voice in government. Although the much ballyhooed Fourteenth Amendment gave Black men the right to vote, no such right was given to American Indians, women, or ex-Confederate soldiers.

During the election that put Grant in office, Northern States debated whether or not to give Blacks the right to vote. If equality were a valid reason for the war, there would have been no debate on this matter, i.e., granting voting rights to Blacks would have simply been part of the drive toward equality. Observers such as Dunning were aware of the inconsistencies and realized the Union had only been preserved in a geographical sense, and in reality a new forced Union had been instituted in contravention of the principles of the Original Republic.

William Lloyd Garrison was born in Newburyport, Massachusetts, in 1805. His father was a merchant sailing master who had been hit hard financially by the 1807 Embargo Act, signed by President Jefferson in an effort to stop exports from the American Colonies. The Act's goal was to establish American neutrality in the war between Britain and France and resulted from French seizure of American ships and British seizure of ships and impressment of

---

[665] Ibid.

American captors into service. Garrison's father eventually deserted his family and left them to survive as best they could.

Garrison joined the abolitionists at age twenty-five and became part of the American Colonization Society. After becoming disgruntled with the society, he began publishing his anti-slavery newspaper, the *Liberator*, on January 1, 1831, and continued to push an anti-slavery agenda throughout his life. He advocated immediate, uncompensated emancipation, an unpopular stance in the South and much of the North.

Garrison was an outspoken enemy of the Constitution and initially an advocate for peace, preferring to let the Southern and Border States separate. He criticized Lincoln's stated war goal of preserving the Union, preferring the goal to be ending slavery. It was Garrison who belligerently referred to the Constitution as follows: "The compact which exists between the North and the South is a covenant with death and an agreement with hell..."[666] For good measure, Garrison also publicly burned a copy of the U.S. Constitution. Lincoln, however, felt his nebulous *higher law*, overrode the fact that the people created sovereign independent States who voluntarily authorized the Federal Government to perform only their enumerated tasks.

As the war progressed, Garrison eventually joined the pro-war faction, but his hatred of the U.S. Constitution remained. Despite the constitutional and moral concerns from thousands of Northerners about the war, the eventual Union victory cast those reservations into mere footnotes of history.

---

[666] "William Lloyd Garrison Quotes and Quotations," Famous Quotes and Authors, http://www.famousquotesandauthors.com/authors/william_lloyd_garrison_quotes.html, (Accessed April 28, 2016).

Chapter Thirty-Three
Lincoln, Democracy and Secession

"If the Constitution is adopted the Union will be in fact and in theory an association of States or a Confederacy."[667]
Alexander Hamilton

It does not seem to matter which television channels you watch or radio stations you listen to, when someone mentions Abraham Lincoln the subsequent commentary will usually be filled with praise and adoration. These commentaries appear locally, regionally or nationally. For example, a few years ago a national sports talk-radio program (the Paul Finebaum Show) featured banter between Finebaum and co-host Neal Vickers where they exchanged praises of Lincoln. I emailed Finebaum, referencing and carefully documenting several facts about Lincoln. He graciously responded to my email by letting me know, that in the future, he *would pick another hero*. Perhaps a close reading of this text will have a similar effect on others.

The public education system tends to elevate historical figures like Lincoln, the Kennedys, the Roosevelts, etc., to a lofty status. Most people do not question these characterizations; however, a comment from one of America's most accomplished men raised an eyebrow early on. It was none other than Henry Ford who proclaimed in the May 25, 1916, edition of the *Chicago Tribune* that "History is more or less bunk."[668]

---

[667] Mildred Lewis Rutherford, *Truths of History* (Harrisonburg, Virginia: Old South Institute Press, 2009), 2. Original source: *Volume LX of The Federalist.*

[668] "This Day in History,"*telegram.com*, Worcester, Massachusetts, May 25, 2010,
http://www.telegram.com/article/20100525/DIGESTS/5250418/1102/RSS01, (Accessed April 26, 2016).

The prevailing historiography was written in favor of the victor, and the victor typically does whatever is required to ensure the *official* government version is taught. From the outset, one of the goals of this project has been to examine the validity of ongoing efforts to continue the Lincoln Mythos. The Lincoln depicted in the modern world is the post-war creation of those who had much to gain by such a portrayal.

★ ★ ★

Did Abraham Lincoln and democracy have anything in common? *The Real Lincoln*, written by Charles L.C. Minor in the early 1900s, investigated this and other relevant questions. Minor was born December 3, 1835, and lived in Edgewood, Hanover County, Virginia. Minor held a Masters of Arts Degree from the University of Virginia (1858). At the outset of the war, he taught in Albemarle County, Virginia at Bloomfield, LeRoy Broun's School. After Virginia seceded, he volunteered for service in the Confederate Army. At the end of the war, Minor resumed his teaching career and ultimately became the first president of Virginia Agricultural and Mechanical College, now Virginia Polytechnic Institute. Minor possessed impressive academic credentials, a keen intellect, and a devout Christian faith.

The Real Lincoln covers a large amount of fact and fiction about the sixteenth president.[669] To minimize personal bias, in his text, Minor used the views and commentary of individuals who held Lincoln in high regard. In Appendix C there is even more thought-provoking information provided by Paul S. Whitcomb of Gladstone, Oregon. Whitcomb's article, entitled *Lincoln and Democracy*, was first published in the July 27, 1927, edition of *Tyler's Quarterly Magazine*.

An understanding of Mr. Whitcomb's teaching and perspective is in order. A native of New England, Whitcomb moved

---

[669] Minor's meticulously documented book, *The Real Lincoln*, has been an important resource for this project.

to the Northwest in 1852. Imbued with the standard teaching about Lincoln, a historical inconsistency aroused Whitcomb's curiosity, and he decided to dig deeper into the subject.

> I do not know when I was attracted to the critical study of Lincoln, but that study was intensified subsequent to the late war by the fact that DeValera, the Irish leader, used the principles of the Declaration of Independence as a basis for argument tending to show Ireland's right to complete independence and, in rebuttal, (Welsh-born, British Prime Minister) Mr. Lloyd-George quoted Lincoln's arguments against secession. Only a bigot acting in bad faith could fail to see that Lincoln's position did not square with the principles of the Revolution and of Democracy.[670]

★ ★ ★

Lincoln's early political career provided nothing spectacular relative to the controversies surrounding slavery and secession. He did, however, make early impressions as a proponent of the Whig agenda, especially in the area of internal improvements. Lincoln ballyhooed a nebulous higher law relative to the slave's legal status but denied the right of secession, which the South asserted as their right of self-government. He either failed to see or intentionally ignored the fact that the principles were the same—"the right of secession was absolute and unqualified and no more required oppressive acts to justify it than did the right of the slave to secede from his master."[671]

The same arguments that denied freedom to the South also denied freedom to everyone and undermined the foundation of a free society. Although Lincoln did not hold Blacks in particularly

---

[670] Charles L.C. Minor, *The Real Lincoln* (Harrisonburg, Virginia: Sprinkle Publications, 1992), 246.
[671] Ibid., 253.

high regard, when it was politically advantageous to trumpet freeing the slaves, he cleverly used abolitionist rhetoric to mask his goal of consolidating power within the central government. It has been shown through words and actions that Lincoln was an effective advocate of the protectionist Whig/Republican agenda. As has been the case *ad infinitum*, he let others, such as abolitionist Phillips, Garrison, etc., stir the pot emotionally and divert attention away from other parts of his agenda. Though he disagreed with them in many ways, their efforts aided his overall agenda. For example, unlike many of the abolitionists, Lincoln maintained a strong desire to relocate Blacks to other parts of the world. On October 16, 1854, in Peoria, Illinois, he commented: "My first impulse would be to free all the slaves, and send them to Liberia, to their own native land."[672] Lincoln maintained this goal into the early part of 1865; this included efforts to send Blacks to Guyana and Belize.[673] He also felt Blacks and Whites could not co-exist lest one destroy the other. On June 26, 1857, during a speech voicing his opposition to the Kansas-Nebraska Act, Lincoln said, "There is a natural disgust in the minds of nearly all white people to the idea of indiscriminate amalgamation of the white and black races…A separation…is the only perfect preventative of amalgamation, but the next best thing is to keep them apart where they are not already together."[674] Lincoln

---

[672] Robert Morgan, "The 'Great Emancipator' and the Issue of Race — Abraham Lincoln's Program of Resettlement," *Institute for Historical Review*, 2013-2016, http://www.ihr.org/jhr/v13/v13n5p-4_Morgan.html, (Accessed April 26, 2016).

[673] The book, *Colonization After Emancipation: Lincoln and the Movement for Black Resettlement*, by Magness and Page documents Lincoln's negotiations with Great Britain to deport Blacks from the U.S. to other locations.

[674] Robert Morgan, "*The 'Great Emancipator' and the Issue of Race — Abraham Lincoln's Program of Resettlement*," Institute for Historical Review. (Accessed April 26, 2016). [Though it occurred, racial amalgamation was frowned upon in the North and the South. This sometimes extended to intermarriage between different ethnicities within the same race.]

reasoned that simply keeping Blacks out of Kansas would solve what he perceived as a potential problem.

Lincoln's war against the South lacked necessity in that there was no imminent catastrophe manifest in the right of secession. Reducing the number of States by eleven would not have literally destroyed the Union; it would have simply decreased its geographical size. Even the headlines in Southern newspapers claiming the Union to be dissolved was mainly in the context that the departed Southern States were simply no longer part of the compact. Each section had competing economic interests and social structures. It would have made more sense for Lincoln to acknowledge the grievances and meet with Southern representatives to at least have an opportunity to work out a peaceful resolution.

War is destructive in a multitude of ways and leaves physical and emotional scars for generations. Perhaps the regions would have prospered as separate republics instead of enduring the war years (1861-1865) and the senseless deaths of over 700,000 Americans. Despite the claims of post-War prosperity being derived from the forced re-unification of the country, real prosperity was primarily generated by the economic reality of the development of the West, technological advancements, the abolition of the Lincoln Administration's income tax, and a reduction in government spending.

Lincoln's actions show he viewed coercion as a viable way to govern. Regarding those who opposed him, he said: "their idea of means to preserve the object of their affection would seem to be exceedingly thin and airy."[675] Lincoln's belief that force is a sound basis of government is contradictory to the principle that legitimate government is administered by consent. Is it any mystery why many authoritarians have cited the words and deeds of Lincoln whereas they tend to never defend States' Rights or quote Jefferson Davis?

---

[675] Minor, 255.

Chapter Thirty-Four
A Different View of Mr. Lincoln's Faith

"Lincoln told me a thousand times that he did not believe the Bible was a revelation from God as the Christian world contends...And that Jesus was not the Son of God."[676]

William H. Herndon

One of the many myths included in the Lincoln historiography is the contention that he was a Christian. Another largely suppressed school of thought repudiates this assertion, using Lincoln's words and commentary from the people closest to him.

Herndon, like Lincoln, a Kentuckian by birth, was Lincoln's friend and law partner for over twenty years. He said:

> Lincoln was a deep-grounded infidel. He disliked and despised churches. He never entered a church except to scoff and ridicule. On coming from a church he would mimic the preacher. Before running for any office, he wrote a book (The Chronicles of Reuben) against Christianity and the Bible. He showed it to some of his friends and read extracts.[677]

The Chronicles of Reuben, in reality a prose narrative followed by a poem, was written somewhere around the year 1830 and was partially based on actual events. On the same day, Reuben Grigsby married Elizabeth Ray and Charles Grigsby married Matilda

---

[676] Hon. George L. Christian, *The Life and Character of Abraham Lincoln — Monster or Messiah?* (Birmingham, Alabama: Society for Biblical and Southern Studies, 1999), 15. Original source: William H. Herndon, *Life of Lincoln*, 489.

[677] George Edmonds, *Facts and Falsehoods* (Wiggins, Mississippi: Crown Rights Book Company, 1997), 52-53. Original source: William H. Herndon, *Life of Lincoln*.

Hawkins in Spencer County, Indiana. A reception for both couples was held the next day at the home of Reuben Grigsby, Sr., but the Lincolns were not invited. Lincoln resented being shunned. There was another troubling incident involving Lincoln's sister Sarah Lincoln Grigsby, who had married Aaron Grigsby. Sarah died in childbirth and Lincoln blamed her death on Grigsby's tardiness about calling a doctor.

These incidents were catalysts for Lincoln's retaliation. *The Chronicles of Reuben* was patterned after scripture and contained a message of implied homosexuality toward Aaron's brother, Billy Grigsby, claiming females had rebuffed him so he married a man named Natty. With a touch of vengeance, it appears to have been crudely satirical and dealt openly with controversial subject matter for the time period. It fell in the category of vulgar tales and stories that Lincoln enjoyed. The following is from *The Chronicles of Reuben*:

> *I will tell you a Joke about Jewel and Mary*
> *It is neither a Joke nor a Story*
> *For Rubin and Charles has married two girls*
> *But Billy has married a boy*
> *The girlies he had tried on every Side*
> *But none could he get to agree*
> *All was in vain he went home again*
> *And since that he's married to Natty.*
> *So Billy and Natty agreed very well*
> *And mama's well pleased at the match*
> *The egg it is laid but Natty's afraid*
> *The Shell is so soft it never will hatch*
> *But Betsy she said you Cursed bald head*
> *My suitor you never Can be*
> *Beside your low crotch proclaims you a botch*
> *And that never Can answer for me.*[678]

---

[678] "The Chronicles of Reuben," Presidential Poetics II, *The Speak Easy*, March 6, 2012, http://thespeakeasy.bandcamp.com/track/the-chronicles-of-reuben, (Accessed April 26, 2016).

Herndon related how Lincoln's friend, New Salem merchant and fellow non-believer, Samuel Hill, at the urging of his son, expressed concern that the contents of the book would be politically damaging and he strongly discouraged its publication. Herndon claimed Hill got his hands on the book and threw it into a stove whereupon it went up in flames. (It seems Redmond Grigsby of Rockport, Indiana, had a copy of the manuscript that was discovered in 1865.) As time went on, Lincoln became more discreet about his anti-Christian verbiage when running for office. He used carefully chosen words and phrases that inferred to others that he was a Christian or at least sympathized with Christian teachings. However, Herndon offers numerous first hand accounts and quotes in support of his claim Lincoln never changed his true feelings and remained a non-believer to his death.

According to Lamon, Lincoln "never denied or regretted its composition; on the contrary, he made it the subject of free and frequent conversations with his friends in Springfield, and stated with much particularity and precision the origin, arguments, and object of the work."[679] In addition, "Herndon describes the 'essay' or 'book' as 'an argument against Christianity, striving to prove the Bible was not inspired, and therefore not God's revelation, and that Jesus Christ was not the Son of God.'"[680]

Lincoln's intention to have the essay published was also noted by New Salem associate and friend, John Matthews, who "testified that he 'attacked the Bible and the New Testament.'"[681] He

---

[679] Charles L.C. Minor, *The Real Lincoln* (Harrisonburg, Virginia: Sprinkle Publications, 1992), 28. Original source: Ward Hill Lamon, *Life of Lincoln*, 157.

[680] Ibid.

[681] Greg Loren Durand, "The Cult of Lincoln," *America's Caesar: The Decline and Fall of Republican Government in the United States of America*, Sourced from John Matthews, quoted by George Edmonds, *Facts and Falsehoods*, 56, and Minor, *The Real Lincoln*, 28-29,

added that Lincoln would come to the clerk's office, obviously proud of his composition, read chapters out of the Bible, and then argue against what he had just read.

Widespread knowledge of such belligerence toward Christianity in the nineteenth century would have caused severe political backlash if not career suicide. Perhaps this is one reason Hill's name and observations rarely come up in most modern discussions about Lincoln.

In 1848, in a contest for the Illinois House of Representatives against the Reverend Peter Cartwright, Lincoln was labeled an infidel, atheist, and other disparaging names, but never responded to the charges; because there was a good chance the accusations could be validated. A well-documented letter (February 18, 1870) from Herndon to Lamon contained the following sentence: "When Lincoln was a candidate for our Legislature, he was accused of being an infidel; of having said that Jesus Christ was an illegitimate child. He never denied the opinions or flinched from his religious views."[682] Herndon continued, "I know when he left Springfield for Washington he had undergone no change in his opinion on religion...He held that God could not forgive sinners. The idea that Mr. Lincoln carried a Bible in his bosom or in his boots to draw on his opponent is ridiculous."[683]

Both a cousin and tutor, Dennis Hanks, reflected on some of Lincoln's youthful antics.

> At an early age, Abe began to attend the preachings about...with a view to catching anything that might be ludicrous in the preaching...and making it a subject of mimicry...He frequently reproduced a sermon with nasal twang, rolling his eyes, and all sorts of droll aggravations, to the great delight of the wild fellows

---

http://www.americascaesar.com/etext/cult_of_lincoln.htm, (Accessed April 26, 2016).

[682] Minor, 29. Original source: Ward Hill Lamon, *Life of Lincoln*, 499.
[683] Edmonds, 55.

assembled. Sometimes he broke out with stories passably humorous and invariably vulgar.[684]

Hanks also wrote, "When he went to New Salem he consorted with free thinkers and joined them in deriding the gospel story of Jesus."[685] Hanks stated Lincoln's religious opinions did not change as he got older, but he became more discreet about sharing them. Given their close relationship, Hanks knew Lincoln more intimately than most. As with Hill, this may explain the dearth of references to Hanks' commentary, especially from modern writers. Lamon recalled:

> Mr. Lincoln was never a member of any church, nor did he believe in the inspiration of the Scriptures in the sense understood by evangelical Christians ...Overwhelming testimony out of many mouths, and none stronger than out of his own, place these facts beyond controversy...When he went to church at all, he went to mock, and came away to mimic.[686]

John Hay was Lincoln's private secretary and later served as Secretary of State under McKinley and Roosevelt; John G. Nicolay was also Lincoln's private secretary. Both moved from Springfield, Illinois, to Washington with the president. Nicolay said, "Mr. Lincoln did not, to my knowledge, in any way change his religious views, opinions or beliefs from the time he left Springfield to the day of his death."[687]

David Davis, one of Lincoln's closest friends, was born into a wealthy Maryland family, and eventually settled in Illinois to practice law. After John Archibald Campbell resigned in disgust

---

[684] Ibid., 55.

[685] Ibid., 54.

[686] Christian, 14. Original source: Ward Hill Lamon, *Life of Lincoln*, 486-487.

[687] Ibid., 15. Original source: John G. Nicolay, *Abraham Lincoln*, 492.

over Lincoln's insistence on going to war, Lincoln promptly appointed Davis to take Campbell's place as associate justice of the Supreme Court. The U.S. Senate quickly confirmed Davis. Judge Davis, the final executor of Lincoln's estate, said: "He had no faith, in the Christian sense of the term."[688]

Referencing the comments of Mary Todd Lincoln, Lamon wrote: "Mr. Lincoln had no hope and no faith, in the usual acceptance of those words." [689] After their son Willie died, the Lincolns allowed séances in the White House. Though Spiritualism is scorned in the Christian faith and often connected to Satanism, it is unclear that these séances reflected any long-term commitment to this practice by either of the Lincolns.

Author James Ford Rhodes said Lincoln was "an infidel, if not an atheist...and...When Lincoln entered political life he became reticent upon his religious opinions."[690]

Lincoln himself provides the summary comment: "The Bible is not my book, and Christianity is not my religion. I could never give assent to the long, complicated statements of Christian dogma." [691] Certainly, if the Bible was not his book, Christianity could not be his religion. Following the same theme, Lincoln provided an interesting response after an inquiry from Judge James N. Nelson about his Thanksgiving messages being replete with religious undertones in contradiction to his own beliefs. Lincoln responded: "Oh! This is some of Seward's nonsense and it pleases the fools!"[692]

---

[688] Ibid.

[689] Ibid.

[690] Minor, 27. Original source: William Ford Rhodes, *History of the United States, Vol. IV*, 13.

[691] Abraham Lincoln Quote, *QuoteDB*, http://www.quotedb.com/quotes/2140, (Accessed April 19, 2016).

[692] Joseph Lewis, "Lincoln, the Freethinker," *Atheism And Other Addresses*, 1924, *Positive Atheism*, http://www.positiveatheism.org/hist/lewis/lewis07.htm, 1995-2016, (Accessed April 26, 2016).

As Lincoln's career developed, he exercised discretion, and having read and memorized a good bit of the Bible, developed skills to use religion for his political benefit.

Based on the statements of his close friends and his wife, Mr. Lincoln's alleged Christianity appears to be purely mythical. History is laden with scoffers and unbelievers, but not all have openly shared their feelings. Lincoln's utterances about religion were often aggressive and vindictive as though he felt Christianity was an enemy of mankind. Truly knowing what lies in the innermost thoughts of an individual is difficult at best; however, abundant evidence indicates Lincoln lacked a true faith in the Christian sense of the word.

What then would be considered his religious motivation? According to Edgar Lee Masters, Andrew Lytle, and others from the old Jeffersonian, agrarian tradition, Lincoln was a proponent of a spiritual ideology known as Hebraic-Puritanism. "Hebraic-Puritanism, according to Masters, is the use of Christian morality for political effect."[693] If anyone could effectively use such a technique, it was Lincoln, the master of the political game, who had a knack for using words and phrases to captivate his audience and steer the conversation in the direction he desired to take it. One example is his House Divided Speech; "Lincoln used the words of Christ in order to 'cast a spell over the moral force of the electorate.'"[694]

Lincoln has been portrayed as a *Godly man*, a *Christian*, *Christ-like*, etc. yet it was the sophistry of Hebraic-Puritanism and his faith in centralized power and union where he flourished. Going back as far as 1832, while running for election in Illinois, he explained his political beliefs. Whether he called himself a Whig or a

---

[693] Matthew D. Norman, "An Illinois Iconoclast: Edgar Lee Masters and the Anti-Lincoln Tradition," Volume 24, Issue 1, Winter 2003, *Journal of the Abraham Lincoln Association,* http://quod.lib.umich.edu/j/jala/2629860.0024.105/--illinois-iconoclast-edgar-lee-masters-and-the-anti-lincoln?rgn=main;view=fulltext, (Accessed April 26, 2016).

[694] Ibid.

Republican, his beliefs never changed and both parties possessed strong elements that supported his core ideologies.

Though overwhelming evidence refutes it, the writers of history took it upon themselves to recreate Lincoln as a Christian man. To better fit the narrative, the mythical Lincoln was preferable to the actual man.

Chapter Thirty-Five
The Apotheosis of Abraham Lincoln

"Abraham Lincoln...has almost disappeared from human knowledge. I hear of him, I read of him in eulogies and biographies, but I fail to recognize the man I knew in life."[695]

Union General Don Piatt

The initial episode involving South Carolina illustrated Lincoln's uncanny political ability. By making it appear South Carolina initiated the conflict instead of reacting to an act of war, Lincoln gained the advantage he earnestly sought. He could have called Congress back in session to discuss the possibility of war but chose not to follow the proper constitutional route. By overstepping his power, Lincoln's actions set precedents many future presidents were eager to follow.

Lincoln authorized the invasion of Maryland—a State still in the Union—to make sure they did not vote to secede. The only government oath required is to obey and uphold the constitution; there is no oath to preserve the Union, and there is no constitutional authority to invade a State.

Lincoln was concerned with the survival of the Republican Party and its agenda, as well as his own political career. The party was anti-Jeffersonian, anti-States' Rights, and advocates of strong centralized government. They represented the economic, largely protectionist interests of the North and Midwest. As noted by M.E. Bradford, "Thousands of Northern boys lost their lives in order that the Republican Party might experience rejuvenation, to serve its partisan goals. And those were 'party supremacy within a Northern

---

[695] George Edmonds, *Facts and Falsehoods* (Wiggins, Mississippi: Crown Rights Book Company, 1997), 37. Original source: General Donn Piatt's *Memories of the Men Who Saved the Union.*

dominated Union.'"[696] On April 4, 1861, Lincoln made it clear to Baldwin of Virginia that he could not allow the South to leave because he felt the lost tariff revenue would put him out of business.

The contention that the North invaded the South to free the slaves was refuted by Lincoln's own words. Framing a war around the slavery issue sounds more palatable than saying it was an invasion to collect import duties, centralize power, and keep Blacks confined to the South and Border States. There has been a steady drumbeat claiming the poor Whites of the South were duped and fought to protect the interests of wealthy slave owners, yet slavery was a detriment to poor Whites by taking work away from them and skewing the value of labor. This argument undermines the intelligence of White Southerners, who were simply fighting to defend their homes against an invading army. Imagine the outcry if the poor Whites of the North had realized their efforts to *preserve the Union* were largely for the benefit of wealthy Northern manufacturers, railroads, and bankers. Even suggesting such often draws an angry response. Massachusetts abolitionist Spooner said as much; he not only saw through the façade of slavery, he also recognized the South's God-given right to govern itself and said so:

> The pretense that the "abolition of slavery" was either a motive or justification for the war is a fraud of the same character with that of "maintaining the national honor." ...And why did these men abolish slavery? Not from any love of liberty in general...but only "as a war measure," and because they wanted his assistance, and that of his friends, in carrying on the war they had undertaken for maintaining and intensifying that political, commercial, and industrial slavery, to which

---

[696] M.E. Bradford, *Remembering Who We Are—Observations of a Southern Conservative* (Athens, Georgia: The University of Georgia Press, 1985), 151.

they have subjected the great body of the people, both black and white.[697]

Despite the Emancipation Proclamation, slavery was not legally abolished until the Thirteenth Amendment was ratified on December 6, 1865, approximately eight months after Lincoln's death.

It is human nature to seek a silver lining after years of death and destruction; the victor has to have some solace that the war was worth it. Once satisfied the effort was worthwhile, hero status is typically assigned to the leader, deserved or not. The losing side does not typically share that view nor do those who voice an objective view. Commenting on Lincoln's Gettysburg Address, H.L. Mencken observed:

> The doctrine is simply this: that the Union soldiers who died at Gettysburg sacrificed their lives to the cause of self-determination—"that government of the people, by the people, for the people," should not perish from the earth. It is difficult to imagine anything more untrue. The Union soldiers in that battle actually fought against self-determination; it was the Confederates who fought for the right of their people to govern themselves. What was the practical effect of the battle of Gettysburg? What else than the destruction of the old sovereignty of the States, i.e., of the people of the States? The Confederates went into battle free; they came out with their freedom subject to the supervision and veto of the rest of the country—and for nearly twenty years that veto was so effective that they enjoyed scarcely more

---

[697] Lysander Spooner, "No Treason—The Constitution of No Authority," reprinted at *LewRockwell.com*, https://www.lewrockwell.com/1970/01/lysander-spooner/no-treason-the-constitution-of-no-authority/, (Accessed April 28, 2016).

liberty, in the political sense, than so many convicts in the penitentiary.[698]

The post-war occupation of the South was rife with theft, oppression, disenfranchisement, and martial law. Fulfilling the desires of many Radical Republicans, the South was treated as a conquered territory. This fact is rarely mentioned; it does not fit the narrative of the politically correct version of America's history. Reconstruction has been sanitized; instead of being the military occupation and denial of rights it was documented to be, it has been portrayed by some as a benevolent effort to reform or elevate the South. Since the Original Republic was born out of secession, voicing support for the South's efforts to govern itself paints the union by force agenda to be anti-American at its core.

It has often been written how Lincoln assembled a cabinet composed of political rivals and men who possessed varying views of the South and sectional issues. That was a wise political move by Lincoln, who possessed remarkable shrewdness and cunning. Nonetheless, a steady theme among his subordinates was their ridicule and disrespect for him. For example, Union General McClellan wrote about Stanton's low regard for Lincoln: "Stanton never speaks of the President in any way other than as 'that original gorilla.' He often says: 'DuChaillie was a fool to wander all the way to Africa in search of what he could have found in Springfield, Illinois.'"[699] After his initial meeting with Lincoln, Sherman "left the mansion…silenced and mortified…I was sadly disappointed, and

---

[698] "H.L. Mencken on Abraham Lincoln," From "Five Men at Random," *Prejudices: Third Series*, 1922, 171-76. First printed, in part, in the Smart Set, May, 1920, 141, Posted by H.R. Gross on June 20, 2002, *freerepublic.com*, http://www.freerepublic.com/focus/news/703308/posts, (Accessed April 28, 2016).

[699] Edmonds, 18.

remember that I broke out on John, damning the politicians generally, saying 'you have got things in a hell of a fix.'"[700]

Union General Piatt opined that "Lincoln was believed by contemporaries secondary in point of talent...Lincoln as one of fame's immortals does not appear in the Lincoln of 1861, whom men...likened to the 'original gorilla.'"[701] However, after his death, Lincoln was elevated to virtual martyrdom by those who despised or disrespected him during his life. Indeed, many former skeptics and critics—Stevens, Wade, Sumner, Henry Winter Davis, etc., led the charge and became some of Lincoln's greatest eulogizers.

Around 1904, author George Edmonds noticed a trend in an unlikely place. "Even in the South the real Lincoln is lost sight of in the rush and bustle of our modern life, and many Southerners accept the opinion of Lincoln that is furnished them ready made by writers who are either ignorant, or else who purposely falsify plain facts of history."[702] Less than forty years after the war's end, the apotheosis had taken root in the areas he helped destroy.

It is common practice to paint a positive picture when most people die, and this human tendency applied to Lincoln. Referencing the departed Northern hero, Union General Piatt stated, "With us, when a leader dies, all good men go to lying about him, and, from the monument that covers his remains to the last echo of the rural press, in speeches, sermons, eulogies and reminiscences, we have naught but pious lies."[703]

Lincoln's reputation likely benefitted more after his assassination than any other person in history and Booth's deadly shot at Ford's Theater may have been the most poorly timed event

---

[700] Charles L.C. Minor, *The Real Lincoln* (Harrisonburg, Virginia: Sprinkle Publications, 1992), 3. Original source: James Schouler, *History of the United States, Vol. VI*, 23.

[701] Ibid, 10. Original source: General Don Piatt, *Reminiscences of Abraham Lincoln*, 477.

[702] Edmonds, 1.

[703] Ibid, 36. Original source: General Don Piatt, *Reminiscences of Abraham Lincoln*.

in American history. It made peaceful reconciliation more difficult by enraging the citizens of the North, who had violently lost their president. The ill-timed and tragic assassination added fodder to the purveyors of the apotheosis by adding fuel to their effort to make him the standard bearer for the new Union or the so-called Second Founding, complete with the modern phenomenon of *exceptionalism*. It is unlikely that anyone in history has been remade and lionized to the level of Abraham Lincoln.

Beginning April 15, 1865, members of the Republican Party enacted a post-war plan to sanitize and deify Lincoln. Though the arrogant and often stubborn Union Secretary of War Stanton had a mixed relationship with Lincoln, after his death, Stanton made the lofty proclamation, "Now he belongs to the ages."[704]

Lamon went into greater depth and summed up the effectively executed plan of adulation:

> The ceremony of Mr. Lincoln's apotheosis was planned and executed by men who were unfriendly to him while he lived. The deification took place with showy magnificence; men who had exhausted the resources of their skill and ingenuity in venomous detractions of the living Lincoln were the first, after his death, to undertake the task of guarding his memory, not as a human being, but as a god.
>
> There was the fiercest rivalry as to who should canonize Mr. Lincoln in the most solemn words; who should compare him to the most sacred character in all history. He was prophet, priest and king, he was Washington, he was Moses, he was likened to Christ the Redeemer, he was likened to God. After that came the ceremony of apotheosis. For days and nights after the President's death it was considered treason to be seen in public

---

[704] "Memory," *American Treasures of the Library of Congress*, July 27, 2010, http://loc.gov/exhibits/treasures/trm210.html, (Accessed April 28, 2016).

with a smile on your face. Men who ventured to doubt the ineffable purity and saintliness of Lincoln's character, were pursued by mobs of men, beaten to death with paving stones, or strung up by the neck to lamp posts until dead.[705]

---

[705] Greg Loren Durand, "The Cult of Lincoln," *America's Caesar: The Decline and Fall of Republican Government in the United States of America*, Originally from Ward H. Lamon, *Life of Abraham Lincoln*, Boston: James R. Osgood and Company, 1872, http://www.americascaesar.com/etext/cult_of_lincoln.htm, (Accessed April 28, 2016).

Conclusion

"The Union was formed by the voluntary agreement of the states; and these, in uniting together, have not forfeited their nationality, nor have they been reduced to the condition of one and the same people. If one of the states chose to withdraw its name from the contract, it would be difficult to disprove its rights to do so, and the Federal government would have no means of maintaining its claims directly, either by force or by right."[706]
Alexis de Tocqueville

The truth can be controversial; however, controversy is often a good thing if it stimulates individuals to question what they have been taught. The willingness and ability to examine, reexamine, and readjust one's beliefs is a mature and admirable human quality.

From the beginning of the American experiment there were different views as to what type of country this would be. Even the interpretation of the Declaration of Independence was not universal. Many in the South, especially those of the Jeffersonian persuasion (Democratic Republicans), saw it as a secession document. However, Lincoln had a different view, going so far as to make the ahistorical claim the Union began with the 1774 Articles of Association.

Natural links to the Declaration were basic to the beliefs in States' Rights and secession. Under the system of dual sovereignty created by the Constitution, States' Rights are simply the rights retained by the States and not granted to the central government. In the context of a voluntary union, secession is a reserved right, reflected in the Ninth and Tenth Amendments to the U.S. Constitution. The majority in the South and many in the North believed the Union was/is voluntary. Again, Lincoln disagreed, claiming the Union is not voluntary, that it could not be divided, and a State or States could not physically separate from it.

---

[706] Alexis de Tocqueville, *Democracy in America* (New York, New York: Alfred A. Knopf, Ninth Edition, September 1963), 387-388.

The economic structure of each region played a large part in their respective political ideologies. The South was overwhelmingly agricultural; meaning certain crops, such as cotton and tobacco, were labor intensive. Agrarian-dominated societies also require the freest possible trade, especially when a high percentage of their products are exported. High tariffs punish heavy exporters. The North was somewhat agricultural, but industrial and corporate interests drove the bulk of its economy. These interests generally favored high import duties to protect their products from foreign competition. This disparate view existed from the earliest days of America.

Abraham Lincoln was descended from a first class family with admirable accomplishments dating back to 1600s Hingham, England. Thomas, his father, seemed to have lost something in the genealogical line. As a young man, Lincoln was known for his love of vulgar and bawdy stories and mocking the Bible. Also, from an early age, he was highly motivated and stated his goal was to be President of the United States. To reach his goal it was necessary to exercise more discretion when voicing his beliefs. He reveled in the political world and his ascent up the ladder began in the 1820s and 1830s as he proclaimed to the world his three-pronged belief in the Whig philosophy and his belief in a higher law that he said transcended the Constitution. In 1848, Lincoln offered a classic pro-secession comment that would make a Jeffersonian proud, but he did an about face with his 1860 stance that the union is indivisible.

The astute Lincoln realized early on that great wealth and influence was tied to the Whig Party. They were connected to the iron and steel industry, railroads, and various corporate interests in the North and Upper Midwest. From his early support of river travel to his support of the railroads, Lincoln was steadfast in his advocacy of internal improvements. Many influential individuals noted his excellent service as a lawyer serving the Illinois Central and other railroads. He built a reputation that fit the protectionist Whig and later the Republican agenda. His support of central banking and protective tariffs provided the hat trick needed to reach his presidential goal.

A combination of groups—Wide Awakes, Free Soilers, Marxists, Abolitionists, etc.—gravitated with intense loyalty to the Republican Party. In a four-way race, Lincoln secured the 1860 presidential election with under forty percent of the vote. He was now in place to institute the agenda of his most adamant supporters.

From the outset, Lincoln and radicals in the Republican Party set a no-compromise position with the Confederacy. Unless the South got in line and accepted the Republican agenda there would be no peace. The South's numerous attempts at peace were fruitless. Lincoln sought capitulation, not compromise. From the South's thwarted attempts at sending representatives to meet with Lincoln, to the actual meeting between Colonel Baldwin and Lincoln just prior to the enactment of hostilities, the South exhausted all avenues in their attempts to avoid conflict.

The Southern States not only did not want a war, they were ill prepared for it. They had to establish a functioning government as well as an army, navy, postal service, manufacturing base, etc. With such a tight time constraint, it is miraculous they accomplished as much as they did. Though all the odds were stacked against them in every measurable manner, they were charged with trying to create a new republic literally out of thin air. Given the political climate of the day, the South saw two options: complete surrender to the Lincoln Administration or departure from the Union.

The South's many efforts to maintain constitutional government within the old Union failed. Abraham Lincoln was elected to represent the industrial and banking interests of his constituency and he represented them well. To accomplish this goal, the Lincoln Administration repeatedly violated the U.S. Constitution and the rule of law, often by his own admission.

The people of the North and South, though culturally different, lacked sufficient reasons to go to war so the politicians resorted to creating them. The only way the South would have been allowed to leave peacefully was if "protection money" (*double entendre* intended) was paid. Of course, this would have only been a superficial departure from the Union since Lincoln told the South they would be invaded if they did not pay duties and imposts.

In a 2007 edition of *Meet the Press*, Congressman Ron Paul gave the late Tim Russert a quick history lesson. Paul explained how slavery could have been ended peacefully in America as it had in virtually every other civilized country. A war over slavery was out of the question as evidenced by Lincoln's conciliatory position. If slavery were the real issue, letting the South go would have settled the fugitive slave question and fear of the spread of the institution to U.S. territories. Colonel Baldwin also stated Virginia had no intentions of fighting over the issue. Lincoln sloughed it off during his conversation with Baldwin but responded with great emotion about the possible loss of tariff revenue. Lincoln consistently admitted the North had as big of a hand in slavery as the South.

Not only did the South aggressively seek a resolution to the quarrel, there were many in the North who wished to avert war such as the outspoken abolitionist Spooner, who saw through Lincoln. Even Hawthorne, the great Northern author, mused about why a war was necessary to keep the States in the Union when they wanted to leave it.

Lincoln played fast and loose with the Constitution. The use of coercion not only violated the spirit of being an American, coercive government was what most Americans had escaped from in the Old World. The use of force did not faze Lincoln nor did the violation of International Law during the *Trent Affair*. His suspension of *habeas corpus* violated the very basis of old English, and, ultimately, American law. The attack on Fort Sumter was planned to make it appear the South initiated hostilities though reinforcement was considered an act of war. Lincoln admitted the Emancipation Proclamation was a strategically worded war measure that had no legal basis.

The election of Lincoln left ripples that are felt to this day. Once in office, Lincoln established the basic Hamiltonian principles of Clay's American System with a central bank, trade protection for favored industries, and those dreaded internal improvements to benefit those north of the Mason-Dixon Line who were in political favor. The dubious creation of West Virginia helped cement the newly increased tariffs and made them virtually irreversible via veto. The arrest and banishment of Vallandigham for exercising his Free Speech rights in opposition to Lincoln's war illustrate lack of enforcement of the legitimate rule of law.

Blockades are considered acts of war, yet Lincoln never hesitated to use this aggressive measure. Like modern-day sanctions, such tactics disproportionately harm those who can least withstand them. The Lincoln Administration's attacks on the press were unprecedented. These attacks included shutting down newspapers and arresting those who disagreed with Lincoln's war. In Maryland, legally elected political leaders were arrested and imprisoned because they dared to oppose his regime. Popular sovereignty was antithetical to Lincoln's agenda and had to be stifled. Lincoln even had the audacity to blame God for the war.

One of the ironies of the Fugitive Slave Law is the use of nullification by some of the Northern States (such as Wisconsin). Although this was a constitutionally valid law, the Northern States' use of States' Rights was noteworthy and shows that the use of "nullification" makes perfect sense under a federal system. Nullification is a great equalizer when used to stop unjust laws.

On the Southern side of the issue, one has to ask, were such measures practical if the real goal was preserving the Union? Making war on combatants is understood but making war on noncombatants—civilians, animals, and property creates long-term, generational hatred of the aggressor. The post-war martial law era was largely an extension of the war itself. Rebuilding the South and attempting to heal the war's wounds would have hastened reunification. Honoring some degree of Confederate money would have helped, instead of destroying its value and impoverishing virtually all Southerners. Why heap more punishment on people who committed the "sin" of believing the Union is voluntary? Why was the South not rebuilt in the same manner as Japan, Germany, etc.? Who benefitted financially from the occupation of the Southern States?

President Davis was steadfast in his belief in the doctrine of States' Rights and government by consent. Not once did Davis back down; he stated he would do it all over again if necessary. Davis operated on a set of principles, which made him more of a statesman than his chief rival, who was the quintessential politician.

When Lincoln was elected, many in the South were aware of what was coming. Symbolically and literally, his election represented the culmination of all of the grievances the South held against the Northern States dating back to the late 1700s. Just as Patrick Henry had warned, the New England States used their numerical majority to forge legislation detrimental to the South.

The Confederate Constitution, which emphasized free trade, patterned itself after the U.S. Constitution and addressed all of these issues. Southerners were renowned experts on constitutional government, and they were also overwhelmingly Christian. The age-old Christian Just War Theory applies to the Southern side of the conflict. The Southern States fought a defensive war in their effort to protect life, liberty, and property against an aggressor.

It is difficult to measure the after-effects of the invasion and destruction of the Southern States. As Patrick Cleburne predicted, the Southern point of view is rarely taught in history books; it does not fit the federal government narrative. Post-war, there were twelve years of martial law, disenfranchisement of Confederate soldiers, and the installation of pseudo State governments with an array of individuals with bad intent who made a mockery of legitimate government. Not only was Confederate money not redeemed, tax laws were established to further rob the Southern people. Many had no way to pay the taxes and subsequently lost their property to the questionable governments and their friends.

President Davis suffered through the post-war years. This included imprisonment, torture and eventual release—but never the trial for "treason" that he desired. Famed New York lawyer Charles O'Conor was anxious to defend Davis should it ever go to trial. Despite the suffering, Davis was adamant that the South's assertion of governing itself was both valid and quintessentially American. Only a fool apologizes for being right and Davis was no fool.

The Lee-Acton correspondence simply mirrored the stance of Davis. They lamented the destruction of States' Rights would lead to government aggression thence centralization of power resulting in predicted aggression abroad and despotism at home. When a government is allowed to define its own powers, the danger is immense. States' Rights provide the critical bulwark that kept the central government in check. It leads to undeclared war, wars to profit those with a vested interest in conflict, intrusion into the daily lives of everyday citizens, and a seemingly endless stream of violations and usurpations that requires dramatic action to slow down. Their predictions ring true, and it is with these results that we must live and ultimately decide which measures have to be taken to restore true constitutional government.

In the dystopian classic *1984*, George Orwell famously observed: "Who controls the past, controls the future; who controls the present controls the past." [707] The modern era of political correctness (Cultural Marxism) is filled with misleading information, half-truths and complete fabrications, yet this practice is not unprecedented in American history. The plan to deify Lincoln began immediately after his death. The plan has worked to near perfection. Portraying him as a virtuous Christian man and savior of the Union was the narrative those in charge felt was best suited for post-war America and themselves. With this deification the goals of the Radicals in the Republican Party have been largely hidden from view. An apotheosis of Lincoln was virtually mandatory to mask the real cause of this unnecessary war. Lincoln's new founding—his forced *Union At All Costs*—is central to his legacy and marks the genesis of the modern leviathan state.

---

[707] George Orwell, *1984* (New York, New York: Signet Classic, published by the Penguin Group, 1984), 32.

Bibliography

[1] "Abraham Lincoln: Another Look—The Republican Party." *House of Paine.* http://www.houseofpaine.org/Abraham_Lincoln/Abraham%20Lincoln%20main.htm Original source: John W. Starr, *Lincoln and the Railroads.* (Accessed April 18, 2016).

[2] "Abraham Lincoln and the Election of 1864." Referencing Jennifer Weber's book *The Rise and Fall of Lincoln's Opponents in the North*, Oxford Press, *Abraham Lincoln's Classroom*, The Lehrman Institute. http://abrahamlincolnsclassroom.org/abraham-lincoln-in-depth/abraham-lincoln-and-the-election-of-1864/ Sourced from Stephen W. Sears, editor, *Civil War Papers of George B. McClellan.* (Accessed April 24, 2016).

[3] "Abraham Lincoln, First Inaugural Address—Monday, March 4, 1861." *Bartleby.com.* http://www.bartleby.com/124/pres31.html. (Accessed April 19, 2016).

[4] "Abraham Lincoln's Health." *Lincoln Financial Foundation Collection.* Published in 1861. http://archive.org/stream/abrahamlincolnsx00linc/abrahamlincolnsx00linc_djvu.txt. (Accessed April 17, 2016).

[5] "Abraham Lincoln and Iowa." *Abraham Lincoln's Classroom.* The Lehrman Institute, 2016. http://abrahamlincolnsclassroom.org/abraham-lincoln-state-by-state/abraham-lincoln-and-iowa/ Original source: J.R. Perkins, *Trails, Rails and War: The Life of General G.M. Dodge.* (Accessed April 18, 2016).

[6] "Abraham Lincoln Quote." *QuoteDB.* http://www.quotedb.com/quotes/2140. (Accessed April 19, 2016).

[7] "Absolutely shocking facts about the GOP." Deny Ignorance. Above Top Secret. *The Above Network*, January 15, 2012. http://www.abovetopsecret.com/forum/thread797646/pg1. (Accessed April 18, 2016).

[8] "The Acton-Lee Correspondence." *LewRockwell.com.* http://archive.lewrockwell.com/orig3/acton-lee.html. (Accessed April 28, 2016).

[9] Adams, Charles. *For Good and Evil: The Impact of Taxes on the Course of Civilization.* Lanham, Maryland: Madison Books, 1993.

[10] Adams, Charles. *Those Dirty Rotten Taxes: The Tax Revolts That Built America.* New York, New York: The Free Press, 1998.

[11] Adams, Charles. "The Warrant to Arrest Chief Justice Roger B. Taney: 'A Great Crime, a fabrication or Seward's Folly?'" *LewRockwell.com*, March 18, 2002. https://www.lewrockwell.com/2002/03/charles-adams/the-warrant-to-arrest-chief-justice-roger-b-taney-a-great-crime-a-fabrication-or-sewards-real-folly/. (Accessed April 23, 2016).

[12] Adams, Charles. *When in the Course of Human Events—Arguing the Case for Southern Secession*. Lanham, Maryland: Rowman & Littlefield Publishers Inc., 2000.

[13] "Aftermath & Reconstruction, Jefferson Davis Confined In A Dungeon." The War for States' Rights. *Civil War Bluegrass*. Civil War Heritage Ring owned by Kevin Eisert. http://civilwar.bluegrass.net/AftermathAndReconstruction/jeffersondavis.html. (Accessed April 28, 2016).

[14] Alexander, General E.P. *Fighting for the Confederacy*. Chapel Hill, North Carolina: The University of North Carolina Press, 1989.

[15] Alexander, Holmes. "Virginia's 'Lost Counties.'" in *So Good A Cause: A Decade Of Southern Partisan*, edited by Oran P. Smith, 90-95. Columbia, South Carolina: The Foundation for American Education, 1993.

[16] "All-Seeing Eye." *Crystalinks.com*. http://www.crystalinks.com/allseeingeye.html. (Accessed April 18, 2016).

[17] Allen, Felicity. *Jefferson Davis: Unconquerable Heart*. Columbia, Missouri: University of Missouri Press, 1999.

[18] "American System." *United States History*. http://www.u-s-history.com/pages/h278.html. (Accessed April 20, 2016).

[19] Angle, Paul M. "Freeport Doctrine." *Encylopedia.com - Dictionary of American History*, The Gale Group, 2003. http://www.encyclopedia.com/doc/1G2-3401801612.html. (Accessed April 18, 2016).

[20] "Another Newspaper Suppressed; Missouri in Doubt; Kentucky in Turmoil." Saturday, August 24, 1861, *Civil War Daily Gazette*. http://civilwardailygazette.com/2011/08/24/another-newspaper-suppressed-missouri-in-doubt-kentucky-in-turmoil/. (Accessed April 23, 2016).

[21] "Archibald Campbell: A Champion for West Virginia." *WVWeb*, June 6, 2013. http://wvweb.com/page/content.detail/id/500125/Archibald-Campbell--A-Champion-for-West-Virginia.html?nav=5032. (Accessed April 24, 2016).

[22] "The Arrest of Vallandigham." *Montgomery County, Ohio Genealogy and History, Genealogy Trails*.

http://genealogytrails.com/ohio/montgomery/news_crime.html. (Accessed April 24, 2016).

²³ Ashe, Captain S.A. *A Southern View of the Invasion of the Southern States and War of 1861-1865.* Crawfordville, Georgia: Ruffin Flag Company. Published from the 2ⁿᵈ (1938) edition, 1997.

²⁴ Ashwood, Samuel. "The Corwin Amendment—The Forgotten Amendment." *dixieoutfitters.com,* October 1, 2008. http://dixieoutfitters.com/pages/blog/corwin-amendment/. (Accessed April 28, 2016).

²⁵ Baldwin, Chuck. "Lee and Jackson Remembered: Robert E. Lee and Stonewall Jackson Were Anti-Slavery." *Sons of Confederate Veterans Blog Spot,* January 11, 2010. http://sonsofconfederateveterans.blogspot.com/2010/01/lee-and-jackson-remembered.html. (Accessed April 25, 2016).

²⁶ Beard, Rick. "The Pirate Sumter." *The New York Times,* June 29, 2011. http://opinionator.blogs.nytimes.com/2011/06/29/the-pirate-sumter/?_php=true&_type=blogs&_r=0. (Accessed April 23, 2016).

²⁷ Beer, Jeremy. "Agrarianism." *First Principles, ISI Web Journal,* December 23, 2011. http://www.firstprinciplesjournal.com/print.aspx?article=560. (Accessed April 24, 2016).

²⁸ Benson, Al, Jr. "Guess What Folks—Secession Wasn't Treason." Copperhead Chronicles, in *Free Republic,* August 27, 2007. http://www.freerepublic.com/focus/news/1887357/posts?page=869 (Accessed April 28, 2016).

²⁹ Bovard, James. "Ethnic Cleansing, American-Style." Explore Freedom. *The Future of Freedom Foundation,* October 1, 1999. http://fff.org/explore-freedom/article/ethnic-cleansing-americanstyle/. (Accessed April 24, 2016).

³⁰ Bradford, M.E. *Remembering Who We Are—Observations of a Southern Conservative.* Athens, Georgia: The University of Georgia Press, 1985.

³¹ Bridge, Horatio. "Personal Recollections of Nathaniel Hawthorne." Chapter XV, 1893, *eldritchpress.org.* http://www.eldritchpress.org/nh/hb15.html. (Accessed April 24, 2016).

³² "A Brief History of U.S. Banking." "http://www.factmonster.com/ipka/A0801059.html" Fact Monster. © 2000–2013 Sandbox Networks, Inc., publishing as *Fact Monster.* 18 Apr. 2016 <http://www.factmonster.com/ipka/A0801059.html>. (Accessed April 18, 2016).

³³ Brown, Dee, *Hear That Lonesome Whistle Blow*. New York, New York: Holt, Rinehart and Winston, 1977.

³⁴ Buchanan, Patrick J. "Mr. Lincoln's War: An Irrepressible Conflict?" *Patrick J. Buchanan—Official Website*, February 13, 2009. http://buchanan.org/blog/pjb-mr-lincolns-war-an-irrepressible-conflict-1440. (Accessed April 19, 2016).

³⁵ Bulla, David W. & Gregory A. Borchard. *Journalism in the Civil War Era*. New York, New York: Peter Lang Publishing, Inc., 2010.

³⁶ Burgwyn, Colonel Henry King. *Confederate War Poems*. Nashville, Tennessee: Bill Coats, Ltd., 1990.

³⁷ Butler, Brigadier General Smedley D. *War Is A Racket*. Los Angeles, California: Feral House, 2003.

³⁸ Cajun Huguenot. "Thomas Jefferson and Secession." *As I See It*, Sunday, August 3, 2008. http://cajunhuguenot1.blogspot.com/2008/08/thomas-jefferson-and-secession-thomas.html. (Accessed April 23, 2016).

³⁹ Carlson, Peter. "Nathaniel Hawthorne disses Abe Lincoln." *American History* 46.4 (2011): 16+. *U.S. History in Context*. http://ic.galegroup.com/ic/uhic/AcademicJournalsDetailsPage/DocumentToolsPortletWindow?jsid=5695e7d082f14b46ea38ec334e313ee8&action=2&catId=&documentId=GALE|A264270626&userGroupName=tricotec_main&zid=449b4c01cf5ddab365960c7a1fd856f6. (Accessed April 24, 2016).

⁴⁰ Carman, Ezra. *The Maryland Campaign of 1862—Volume I, South Mountain*, Edited and Annotated by Thomas G. Clemens. New York, New York: Savos Beatie LLC, 2010.

⁴¹ Christian, Hon. George L. *The Life and Character of Abraham Lincoln—Monster or Messiah?* Second Printing. Birmingham, Alabama: Society for Biblical and Southern Studies, 1999. An address delivered before Robert E. Lee Camp No. 1 by Christian on October 29, 1909.

⁴² "The Chronicles of Reuben." Presidential Poetics II. *The Speak Easy*, March 6, 2012. http://thespeakeasy.bandcamp.com/track/the-chronicles-of-reuben. (Accessed April 26, 2016).

⁴³ Cisco, Walter Brian. *War Crimes Against Southern Civilians*. Gretna, Louisiana: Pelican Publishing Company, 2007.

⁴⁴ "Civil War Tested Lincoln's Tolerance for Free Speech." *First Amendment Center*. February 11, 2009. http://www.firstamendmentcenter.org/civil-war-tested-lincolns-tolerance-for-free-speech-press. (Accessed April 24, 2016).

⁴⁵ "Confederate States of America—Inaugural Address of the President of the Provisional Government, February 18, 1861." Yale Law

School, Lillian Goldman Law Library. *The Avalon Project.* http://avalon.law.yale.edu/19th_century/csa_csainau.asp. (Accessed April 24, 2016).

46 "Confederate States of America—Message to Congress April 29, 1861 (Ratification of the Constitution)." Yale Law School, Lillian Goldman Law Library. *The Avalon Project.* http://avalon.law.yale.edu/19th_century/csa_m042961.asp. (Accessed April 25, 2016).

47 "Constitution of the Confederate States; March 11, 1861." Yale Law School, Lillian Goldman Law Library. *The Avalon Project.* http://avalon.law.yale.edu/19th_century/csa_csa.asp. (Accessed April 20, 2016).

48 "The Constitution of the United States, Chapter 8, No. VI." *Lysander Spooner.org.* http://www.lysanderspooner.org/works/#. (Accessed April 25, 2016).

49 Cooper, Commander Douglas G. U.S. Navy, USAWC Class of 1997. "Stumbling Toward Total Civil War: The Successful Failure of Union Conscription 1862-1865." *U.S. Army War College.* Carlisle Barracks, PA, 23; quoted from: Eugene C. Murdock, Ohio's Bounty System in the Civil War. Columbus, Ohio: Ohio State University Press, 1963.

50 Corliss, Carlton J. *Abraham Lincoln and the Illinois Central Railroad: Main Line of Mid-America.* Champaign, Illinois: University of Illinois Library, Compliments of the Illinois Central, 1901. https://archive.org/details/abrahamlincolnil00corl. (Accessed April 18, 2016).

51 "Corwin Amendment." Slavery and the Secession Crisis. *Harp Week,* 2001-2008. http://13thamendment.harpweek.com/HubPages/CommentaryPage.asp?Commentary=02CorwinAmend. (Accessed April 19, 2016).

52 "Clement L. Vallandigham." *National Park Service Quick Facts.* http://www.nps.gov/resources/person.htm?id=111. (Accessed April 28, 2016).

53 Cox, Dale. "Fort Barrancas, Florida – First Hostile Shots of the Civil War." *Explore Southern History Blog,* April 20, 2010. http://southernhistory.blogspot.com/2010/04/fort-barrancas-florida-first-hostile.html. (Accessed April 23, 2016).

54 Curtis, Michael Kent. "Lincoln, Vallandigham and Anti-War Speech in the Civil War." *William and Mary Bill of Rights Journal, Volume 7, Issue 1, Article 3,* (1998).

http://scholarship.law.wm.edu/cgi/viewcontent.cgi?article=1428&context=wmborj. (Accessed April 24, 2016).

55 Dabney, Robert L., D.D. *The Origin & Real Cause of the War, A Memoir of a Narrative Received of Colonel John B. Baldwin, Reprinted from Discussions, Volume IV*. Collins, Mississippi: Homestead Printing.

56 Davis, Martha F. "To Promote the General Welfare." American Constitution Society for Law and Policy, *ACS Blog*, September 15, 2011. http://www.acslaw.org/acsblog/to-promote-the-general-welfare. (Accessed April 20, 2016).

57 "The Declaration of Independence." *ConstitutionFacts.com*. http://www.constitutionfacts.com/us-declaration-of-independence/read-the-declaration/. (Accessed April 17, 2016).

58 DiLorenzo, Thomas J. "Abraham Delano Messiah Obama?" *FourWinds10.com*, January 19, 2009. http://www.fourwinds10.net/siterun_data/history/american/news.php?q=1232403799. (Accessed April 28, 2016).

59 DiLorenzo, Thomas J. "The Economics of Slavery." *LewRockwell.com*. http://www.lewrockwell.com/2002/09/thomas-dilorenzo/the-economics-of-slavery/. (Accessed April 24, 2016).

60 DiLorenzo, Thomas J. "The Lincoln Cult's Latest Cover-Up." *Information Liberation*, July 24, 2006. http://www.informationliberation.com/?id=13613.(Accessed April 19, 2016).

61 DiLorenzo, Thomas J. *Lincoln Unmasked—What You're Not Supposed to Know About Dishonest Abe*. New York, New York: Crown Forum, 2006.

62 DiLorenzo, Thomas J. "Lysander Spooner, Neo-Confederate." *LewRockwell.com,* Posted on February 23, 2012. https://www.lewrockwell.com/lrc-blog/lysander-spooner-neo-confederate/. (Accessed April 25, 2016).

63 DiLorenzo, Thomas J. *The Real Lincoln—A New Look at Abraham Lincoln, His Agenda, and an Unnecessary War*. Roseville, California: Prima Publishing, 2002.

64 DiLorenzo, Thomas J. "The Real Reason Why Lincoln Imprisoned and Deported a Democratic Congressman." *LewRockwell.com*, September 16, 2010. http://www.lewrockwell.com/lrc-blog/the-real-reason-why-lincoln-imprisoned-and-deported-a-democratic-congressman/. (Accessed April 24, 2016).

65 DiLorenzo, Thomas J. "Rewriting History, American Style." From L.M. Schwartz. *The Virginia Land Rights Coalition*, March 1, 2002. http://www.vlrc.org/authors/59.html. (Accessed April 17, 2016).

66 DiLorenzo, Thomas J. "Traitors to the American Revolution." *LewRockwell.com*, September 12, 2006. https://www.lewrockwell.com/2006/09/thomas-dilorenzo/traitors-to-the-american-revolution/. (Accessed April 20, 2016).

67 Davis, Stephen. "Was Sherman a War Criminal?: Yes, Sherman convicted by own his words." *AJC.com*, June 13, 2014. http://atlantaforward.blog.ajc.com/2014/06/13/was-sherman-a-war-criminal/?ecmp=ajc_social_facebook_2014_sfp. (Accessed April 28, 2016).

68 "Declaration of Independence." *The Charters of Freedom*. http://www.archives.gov/exhibits/charters/declaration_transcript.html. (Accessed April 24, 2016).

69 "Definition of Petit Mal." MedicineNet.com. http://www.medicinenet.com/script/main/art.asp?articlekey=4854. (Accessed April 17, 2016).

70 Donald, David Herbert. *Lincoln Reconsidered*. New York, New York: Vintage Books, A Division of Random House, Inc., 2001.

71 Draper, Sharon. "Timeline of Slavery in America 1501-1865." *SharonDraper.com*. https://sharondraper.com/timeline.pdf. (Accessed April 2016).

72 Durand, Greg Loren. "The Cult of Lincoln." *America's Caesar: The Decline and Fall of Republican Government in the United States of America*. http://www.americascaesar.com/etext/cult_of_lincoln.htm Sourced from John Matthews. (Accessed April 26, 2016).

73 Edmonds, George, *Facts and Falsehoods Concerning the War on the South 1861-1865*. Wiggins, Mississippi: Crown Rights Book Company Liberty Reprint Series, 1997. Originally published by Spencer Hall Lamb, 1904.

74 "1848 Free Soil Party Platform." *Angelfire*. http://www.angelfire.com/indie/ourcampaigns/1848.html. (Accessed April 18, 2016).

75 "1860 Lincoln v. Douglas v. Breckinridge v. Bell." John Bell. *HarpWeek Explore History*. http://elections.harpweek.com/1860/bio-1860-Full.asp?UniqueID=1. (Accessed April 18, 2016).

76 "The 1860 Presidential Vote in Virginia." [extracted from *The Tribune Almanac and Political Register for 1861* (New York: The Tribune Association)], *West Virginia Division of Culture and History*. http://www.wvculture.org/history/statehood/1860presidentialvote.html. (Accessed April 24, 2016).

77 "Election of 1864." *Georgia's Blue and Gray Trail present American Civil War*, November 8.

20http://blueandgraytrail.com/event/Election_of_1864. (Accessed April 24, 2016).

[78] "The Election of 1864." U.S. History Online Textbook. *ushistory.org*. 2016, http://www.ushistory.org/us/34e.asp. (Accessed Sunday, April 24, 2016).

[79] Ely, James W., Jr. "Abraham Lincoln as a Railroad Attorney." *Indiana History.org*. http://www.indianahistory.org/our-services/books-publications/railroad-symposia-essays-1/Abe%20Lincoln%20as%20a%20Railroad%20Attorney.pdf. (Accessed April 18, 2016).

[80] Farrow, Anne, Joel Lang, and Jenifer Frank. "The Myth Of Northern Innocence: Before Emancipation, The North Perpetuated And Profited From Slavery." *Hartford Courant*, September 25, 2005. http://articles.courant.com/2005-09-25/news/0509230479_1_civil-war slaves-cotton/2. (Accessed April 20, 2016).

[81] Fazio, John C. "Intrepid Mariners: John Winslow & Raphael Semmes of the CSS Alabama." *The Cleveland Civil War Roundtable*. http://clevelandcivilwarroundtable.com/articles/naval/intrepid_mariners.htm. (Accessed April 23, 2016).

[82] "First Session of the Second Wheeling Convention, June 11-25, 1861, Chapter Seven." A State of Convenience—The Creation of West Virginia. *West Virginia Division of Culture and History*. http://www.wvculture.org/history/statehood/statehood07.html. (Accessed April 24, 2016).

[83] "First Tariff Act, Approved July 4, 1789." Impact of Congress. *The Center on Congress at Indiana University*. http://tpscongress.indiana.edu/impact-of-congress/key-impacts.html. (Accessed April 17, 2016).

[84] "First Wheeling Convention. The Bar: October 1913," *West Virginia Division of Culture and History*. http://www.wvculture.org/history///statehood/sayre.html. (Accessed April 24, 2016).

[85] Fischer, David Hackett. *Albion's Seed: Four British Folkways in America*. New York, New York: Oxford University Press, Oxford University, 1989.

[86] Fishman, Dr. Ronald. "Abraham Lincoln had a Lopsided Face and Strabismus–Development defect or horse kick?" *Softpedia.com*. http://archive.news.softpedia.com/news/Abraham-Lincoln-Had-a-Lopsided-Face-And-Strabismus-62674.shtml. (Accessed April 17, 2016).

[87] "Foreign Influences: Trent Affair. One War at a Time, November 8, 1861," The War for States' Rights. *Civil War Bluegrass.* http://civilwar.bluegrass.net/ForeignInfluences/trentaffair-onewar.html. (Accessed April 24, 2016).

[88] "Fort Sumter—April 12-14, 1861." *US CivilWar.com.* http://www.us-civilwar.com/sumter.htm. (Accessed April 23, 2016).

[89] "The Fortress Monroe Conference; An Inside History-What was done and What was Said-The Terms Offered the South-Mr. Lincoln's Suggestions." New York Times, June 26, 1865, *Marshall University.edu.* http://www.marshall.edu/special-collections/hampton_roads/pdf/NYT-article.pdf. (Accessed April 24, 2016).

[90] Foster, William Z. *History of the Communist Party of the United States. Chapter Three: Marxists in the Struggle Against Slavery.* http://williamzfoster.blogspot.com/2013/01/chapter-three-marxists-in-struggle.html. (Accessed April 18, 2016).

[91] "Freedom of the Press? The Suppression of the Christian Observer and the Evening Journal." *Historical Society of Pennsylvania.* https://hsp.org/education/unit-plans/civil-liberties-and-the-civil-war-in-pennsylvania-0/freedom-of-the-press-the-suppression-of-the-christian-observer-and-the-evening-journal. (Accessed April 23, 2016).

[92] "Free-Soil Party." *United States History.* http://www.u-s-history.com/pages/h139.html. (Accessed April 18, 2016).

[93] Gaddy, Michael. "The American Indian and the 'Great Emancipator.'" *United Native America,* January 9, 2003. http://www.unitednativeamerica.com/issues/lincoln_print.html Also found at Sierra Times: http://www.sierratimes.com/gaddy.htm. (Accessed April 24, 2016).

[94] Garrison, Webb. *The Lincoln No One Knows.* Nashville, Tennessee: Rutledge Hill Press, 1993.

[95] "German Revolution of 1848." Quote from Rudolph Cronau. *The Activists.* http://comminfo.rutgers.edu/~dalbello/FLVA/activists/48rev.html. (Accessed April 18, 2016).

[96] Gienapp, William E. "Abraham Lincoln and the Border States." *Journal of the Abraham Lincoln Association,* Volume 13, Issue 1 (1992). http://quod.lib.umich.edu/j/jala/2629860.0013.104/--abraham-lincoln-and-the-border-states?rgn=main;view=fulltext. (Accessed April 23, 2016).

[97] Gorham, George C. *Life and Public Services of Edwin M. Stanton.* Boston and New York: Houghton, Mifflin and Company, 1899, Volume I, 193, University of California.

http://babel.hathitrust.org/cgi/pt?id=uc1.$b539234;view=1up;seq=231. (Accessed April 23, 2016).

[98] Gottfried, Paul. *Through European Eyes, So Good A Cause: A Decade of Southern Partisan*, edited by Oran P. Smith, 57-62. Columbia, South Carolina: The Foundation for American Education, 1993.

[99] Gourley, Bruce. "Baptists and the American Civil War: April 23, 1861." *In Their Own Words*, April 23, 2011. http://www.civilwarbaptists.com/thisdayinhistory/1861-april-23/ (As reprinted in the *Memphis Daily Avalanche*, May 8, 1861, p. 1, col. 4). (Accessed April 21, 2016).

[100] Gragg, Rod. "The Quotable Robert E. Lee." *So Good A Cause: A Decade of Southern Partisan*, edited by Oran P. Smith, 120-127. Columbia, South Carolina: The Foundation for American Education, 1993.

[101] Graham, Paul C. "How The War Was About Slavery." *The Abbeville Institute Blog*, January 26, 2015. http://www.abbevilleinstitute.org/blog/how-the-war-was-about-slavery/. (Accessed April 19, 2016).

[102] Griffith, Michael T. "The Smearing of General George B. McClellan." *miketgriffith.com*, 2014. http://miketgriffith.com/files/smearingmcclellan.htm. (Accessed April 23, 2016).

[103] Grinspan, John. "Young Men for War: The Wide Awakes and Lincoln's 1860 Presidential Campaign." *The Journal of American History*, 96 (September 2009), 357–78. http://archive.oah.org/special-issues/lincoln/contents/grinspan.html. (Accessed April 18, 2016).

[104] Grissom, Michael Andrew. *Southern By The Grace Of God*. Gretna, Louisiana: Pelican Publishing Company, 1990.

[105] Guernsey, Alfred H. and Henry M. Alden. *Harper's Pictorial History of the Civil War*. McLean, Virginia: The Fairfax Press, 1987. From Florida International University Libraries. http://dpanther.fiu.edu/dpService/dpPurlService/purl/FI11081206/#dvFileP anel. (Accessed July 24, 2016).

[106] Gutzman, Kevin R.C., J.D., Ph.D. *The Politically Incorrect Guide to the Constitution*. Washington, D.C.: Regnery Publishing, Inc., 2007.

[107] "H.L. Mencken on Abraham Lincoln." From "Five Men at Random." *Prejudices: Third Series*, 1922, 171-76. First printed, in part, in the Smart Set, May, 1920, 141. Posted by H.R. Gross on June 20, 2002, *freerepublic.com*. http://www.freerepublic.com/focus/news/703308/posts. (Accessed April 28, 2016).

[108] "H.L. Mencken Quotations." *FreedomWriter.com.* http://www.freedomwriter.com/quotes.htm. (Accessed April 17, 2016).

[109] "Habeas Corpus." The American Civil War. *Online Etymology.* http://www.etymonline.com/cw/habeas.htm. (Accessed April 23, 2016).

[110] Harper, Douglas. "American Colonization Society." *Slavery in the North.* http://slavenorth.com/colonize.htm. (Accessed April 17, 2016).

[111] Harper, Douglas. "Northern Profits from Slavery." *Slavery in the North.* Lorenzo Johnston Greene quote from *The Negro in Colonial New England, 1620-1776.* http://slavenorth.com/profits.htm. (Accessed April 17, 2016).

[112] Harper, Douglas. "Slavery in Massachusetts." *Slavery in the North.* http://slavenorth.com/massachusetts.htm. (Accessed April 28, 2016).

[113] Harrison, Lowell. *The Civil War in Kentucky.* Lexington, Kentucky: The University of Kentucky Press, 1975.

[114] "Hartford Wide-Awakes." Today in History: July 26. *ConnecticutHistory.org.* http://connecticuthistory.org/hartford-wide-awakes-today-in-history/; See more at: http://connecticuthistory.org/hartford-wide-awakes-today-in-history/#sthash.M1sdDybs.dpuf. (Accessed April 18, 2016).

[115] Harwell, Richard B. *The Confederate Reader.* New York, New York: Barnes & Noble Books, 1992.

[116] Hawes, Robert. "Fort Sumter, the Untold Story: Failed Negotiations." *The Jeffersonian,* January 5, 2012. http://jeffersonian73.blogspot.com/2012/01/fort-sumter-untold-story.html. (Accessed April 18, 2016).

[117] "The History of Freedom in Christianity." from a speech by Lord John Emerich Edward Dalberg Acton on May 28, 1877, *Mondo Politico.* http://www.mondopolitico.com/library/lordacton/freedominchristianity/mpintro.htm. (Accessed April 25, 2016).

[118] Holcombe, Randall G. "The Confederate Constitution." Volume 10, Number 6, *The Free Market,* Mises Institute, June 1992. https://mises.org/library/confederate-constitution.(Accessed April 20, 2016).

[119] Hornberger, Jacob. "Writ of Habeas Corpus as the Lynchpin of Freedom." *The Future of Freedom Foundation,* October 12, 2006. https://www.lewrockwell.com/2006/10/jacob-hornberger/the-linchpin-of-freedom/. (Accessed April 28, 2016).

[120] Horton, R.G. *A Youth's History of the Great Civil War in the United States, From 1861-1865.* New York, New York: Van Evrie, Horton and Company, 1867. https://archive.org/details/youthshistoryofg01hort. (Accessed May 18, 2016).

[121] Hosmer, James Kendall. *The American Nation: A History, The Appeal to Arms: Volume 20, 1861-1863*, New York, New York and London, England: Harper and Brothers Publishers; Edited by Albert Bushnell Hart, L.L.D., 1907.

[122] Hough, Joan. "The 48'ers, Part 1 of a Critique of Hochbruck's 'Actundvierziger.'" *The Confederate Society of America*, October 22, 2013. http://www.deovindice.org/1/post/2013/10/the-48ers.html. (Accessed April 18, 2016).

[123] "Independence Hall." Lincoln, February 22, 1861. *ushistory.org*. http://www.ushistory.org/independencehall/history/lincoln.htm. (Accessed July 14, 2016).

[124] "Interview Between President Lincoln and Col. John B. Baldwin, April 4th, 1861, Statements and Evidence," *Stanton Speculator*. Staunton, Virginia: Spectator Job Office, D.E. Strasburg, Printer, 1866. https://ia800301.us.archive.org/5/items/interviewbetween00bald/interviewbetween00bald.pdf. (Accessed April 21, 2016).

[125] Jarvis, Gail. "The Dunning School." *LewRockwell.com*. https://www.lewrockwell.com/2004/02/gail-jarvis/the-dunning-school/. (Accessed April 28, 2016).

[126] "Jefferson Davis' Farewell Address." Senate Chamber, U.S. Capitol, January 21,1861. From *The Papers of Jefferson Davis, Rice University*. https://jeffersondavis.rice.edu/Content.aspx?id=87. (Accessed April 17, 2016).

[127] "Jefferson Davis Quotes." *American Civil War Story*, 2012-2016. http://www.americancivilwarstory.com/jefferson-davis-quotes.html. (Accessed April 28, 2016).

[128] "Jefferson Davis Quotes." *AZ Quotes*. http://www.azquotes.com/quote/658598. (Accessed April 17, 2016).

[129] "Jefferson Davis Quotes." *Thinkexist.com*. http://thinkexist.com/quotes/jefferson_davis/. (Accessed April 17, 2016).

[130] Jefferson, Thomas. "The Declaration of Independence." *ushistory.org*. http://www.ushistory.org/declaration/document/. (Accessed April 17, 2016).

[131] Jefferson, Thomas. "Democracy is nothing more than mob rule…" Thomas Jefferson Foundation. *The Jefferson Monticello*. https://www.monticello.org/site/jefferson/democracy-nothing-more-mob-rule. (Accessed April 18, 2016).

[132] Johnstone, H.W. *Truth of the War Conspiracy of 1861*. Wake Forest, North Carolina: The Scuppernong Press, 2012.

[133] Jordan, Ervin L. *Black Confederates and Afro-Yankees in Civil War Virginia*. Charlottesville, Virginia: University of Virginia Press, 1995.

[134] Kantor, Myles. "Getting Right with Lincoln as a Libertarian." *LewRockwell.com*. Dec. 14, 2000. https://www.lewrockwell.com/2000/12/myles-kantor/getting-right-with-lincoln-as-a-libertarian/. (Accessed April 23, 2016).

[135] Kelly, Martin. "Compromise of 1850." *About Education*. http://americanhistory.about.com/od/beforethewar/g/compromise1850.htm. (Accessed April 28, 2016).

[136] Kennedy, David M. and Lizabeth Cohen. *The American Pageant*. Boston, Massachusetts: Wadsworth Cengage Learning, 2013.

[137] Kennedy, James Ronald and Walter Donald Kennedy. *The South Was Right!* Gretna, Louisiana: Pelican Publishing Company, 1994.

[138] Keys, Thomas Bland. *The Uncivil War: Union Army and Navy Excesses in the Official Records*. Biloxi, Mississippi: The Beauvoir Press, 1991.

[139] Kibby, Larry. "The Only Good Indian." *Indigenous People's Literature*, June 8, 2004. http://www.indigenouspeople.net/gooddead.htm. (Accessed April 24, 2016).

[140] Landry, Peter. "Lord Acton." *Bluepete.com*. http://www.blupete.com/Literature/Biographies/Philosophy/Acton.htm. (Accessed April 25, 2016).

[141] Latner, Richard B. "Compromise Efforts." *Tulane University*. http://www.tulane.edu/~latner/Background/BackgroundCompromise.html. (Accessed April 18, 2106).

[142] Lee, Susan Pendleton. *Lee's New School History of the United States 1907 Edition*. Boise, Idaho: Grapevine Publications, 1995. Original Copyright 1899 and 1900, Susan Pendleton Lee.

[143] "Lee Supports Slave Soldiers, Gradual Emancipation." *Civil War Daily Gazette*, January 11, 1865 (Wednesday). http://civilwardailygazette.com/2015/01/11/lee-supports-slave-soldiers-gradual-emancipation/. (Accessed April 19, 2016).

[144] Leidner, Gordon. "Lincoln Outfoxed Seward for the Nomination." How Lincoln Won the 1860 Republican Nomination. *Great American History*, September 3, 2015. http://www.greatamericanhistory.net/nomination.htm. (Accessed April 18, 2016).

[145] "Letter to Abraham Lincoln, Horace Greeley, July 07, 1864." *TeachingAmericanHistroy.org*. http://teachingamericanhistory.org/library/document/letter-to-abraham-lincoln/. (Accessed April 24, 2016).

[146] Lewis, Joseph. "Lincoln, the Freethinker." Atheism And Other Addresses, 1924, *Positive Atheism.* http://www.positiveatheism.org/hist/lewis/lewis07.htm 1995-2016. (Accessed April 26, 2016).

[147] "Lincoln's Call for Volunteers." Civil War's *Harpers Weekly,* April 27, 1861, *Son of the South.* http://www.sonofthesouth.net/leefoundation/civil-war/1861/april/call-for-volunteers.htm. (Accessed April 23, 2016).

[148] "Lincoln's New Salem 1830-1837." *National Park Service—Lincoln Home National Historic Site.* http://www.nps.gov/liho/learn/historyculture/newsalem.htm. (Accessed April 18, 2016).

[149] "Lincoln Provoked the War." Reflections. *Tulane University.* Information sourced from Stephens, *Constitutional View,* 2: 35-41; Davis, *Rise and Fall,* 1: 289-95; Ramsdell, "Lincoln and Fort Sumter," 259-88. http://www.tulane.edu/~sumter/Reflections/LinWar.html. (Accessed May 28, 2016).

[150] "Lincoln on Secession in 48 and 61." This Sacred Right will Liberate the World, Richmond Times Dispatch—July 10, 1861, *Civil War Daily.*http://dlxs.richmond.edu/cgi/t/text/textidx?c=ddr;cc=ddr;type=simple;rgn=div2;q1=july%2010%2C%201861;view=text;subview=detail;sort=occur;idno=ddr0214.0020.009;node=ddr0214.0020.009%3A6.1. (Accessed April 23, 2016).

[151] "Lord Acton in a Letter to Bishop Mandell Creighton, 1887." *Quotations by Author,* 1994-2015. http://www.quotationspage.com/quotes/Lord_Acton/. (Accessed April 25, 2016).

[152] Lytle, Andrew Nelson. "The Lincoln Myth." the *Virginia Quarterly Review,* October, 1931. Review reprinted in *Lincoln, the Man* by Edgar Lee Masters, The Foundation for American Education, Columbia, South Carolina, 1997. Original Copyright 1931 by Edgar Lee Masters.

[153] "Magna Carta, #39." Historic Documents. *ushistory.org.* http://www.ushistory.org/documents/magnacarta.htm. (Accessed April 23, 2016).

[154] Magness, Phillip W. "Abraham Lincoln and the Corwin Amendment." Phillip W. Magness-Historian. *philmagness.com.* http://philmagness.com/?page_id=398. (Accessed April 19, 2016).

[155] Magness, Phillip W. and Sebastian N. Page. *Colonization After Emancipation: Lincoln and the Movement for Black Resettlement.* Columbia, Missouri: University of Missouri Press, 2011.

[156] Malone, J.D. "June 10, 1863: Arrest of Copperhead angers The Allentown Democrat." Lehigh Valley's Newspaper *The Morning Call*, June 6, 2013. http://articles.mcall.com/2013-06-06/news/mc-pa-153rd-pennsylvania-volunteers-gettysburg-150-20130606_1_allentown-democrat-copperheads-war-effort. (Accessed April 24, 2016).

[157] Maranzani, Barbara. "Four Days of Fire: The New York City Draft Riots." History in the Headlines. *History.com*, July 5, 2013. http://www.history.com/news/four-days-of-fire-the-new-york-city-draft-riots. (Accessed April 24, 2016).

[158] Masters, Edgar Lee. *Lincoln The Man*. Columbia, South Carolina: The Foundation for American Education, 1997. Reprinted from 1931 original and 1959 renewal by permission of Hilary Masters.

[159] McClanahan, Brion. "Jefferson Davis and the Kenner Mission." The Abbeville Blog. *Abbeville Institute*, April 14, 2014. http://www.abbevilleinstitute.org/blog/jefferson-davis-and-the-kenner-mission/. (Accessed April 28, 2016).

[160] McClarey, Donald R. and Paul Zummo. "Breckinridge Platform 1860." *Almost Chosen People, A blog about American History, and the development of a great Nation*, October 6, 2010. http://almostchosenpeople.wordpress.com/2010/10/06/breckinridge-platform-1860/. (Accessed April 18, 2016).

[161] McElroy, Wendy. "Lysander Spooner." *LewRockwell.com*, Feb. 11, 2006. https://www.lewrockwell.com/2006/02/wendy-mcelroy/lysander-spooner/. (Accessed April 25, 2016).

[162] McManus, Edgar J. and Tara Helfman. *Liberty and Union: A Constitutional History of the United States, Concise Edition*. New York, New York: Routlegde, an Imprint of the Taylor & Francis Group, 2014.

[163] McNamara, Robert. "Barnburners and Hunkers." *About Education*, November 26, 2014. http://history1800s.about.com/od/1800sglossary/g/Barnburners-And-Hunkers.htm. (Accessed April 18, 2016).

[164] McWhiney, Grady. *Jefferson Davis — The Unforgiven*. Biloxi, Mississippi: The Beauvoir Press, 1989.

[165] "Memory." *American Treasures of the Library of Congress*, July 27, 2010. http://loc.gov/exhibits/treasures/trm210.html. (Accessed April 28, 2016).

[166] Miller, Donald W., Jr. MD. "A Jeffersonian View of the Civil War." *LewRockwell.com*. https://www.lewrockwell.com/2001/09/donald-w-miller-jr-md/a-jeffersonian-view-of-the-civil-war/.(Accessed April 23, 2016).

[167] Minor, Charles L.C. *The Real Lincoln.* Harrisonburg, Virginia: Sprinkle Publications, 1992. Originally published by Everett Waddey Company in 1904 and by Atkins-Rankin Company in 1928.

[168] Mitchell, Charles W. *Maryland Voices of the Civil War.* Baltimore, Maryland: The Johns Hopkins University Press, 2007.

[169] Moore, Craig. "A Guide to the Francis H. Pierpont Restored Government Executive Papers, 1861-1865." A Collection in the Library of Virginia, Accession Number 36928. *Library of Virginia,* 2002. http://ead.lib.virginia.edu/vivaxtf/view?docId=lva/vi00167.xml. (Accessed April 28, 2016).

[170] Morgan, Robert. "The 'Great Emancipator' and the Issue of Race—Abraham Lincoln's Program of Resettlement." *Institute for Historical Review,* 2013-2016. http://www.ihr.org/jhr/v13/v13n5p-4_Morgan.html. (Accessed April 26, 2016).

[171] Munroe, John A. *History of Delaware.* Cranbury, New Jersey: Associated University Presses, 2006.

[172] Murphy, Robert. "Slavery Could Not Last in an (Otherwise) Free Market." *The Ludwig von Mises Institute Canada, Inc.,* quoting von Mises from *Human Action.* http://mises.ca/posts/blog/slavery-could-not-last-in-an-otherwise-free-market/. (Accessed April 25, 2016).

[173] Napolitano, Andrew P. *The Constitution in Exile.* Nashville, Tennessee: Thomas Nelson, Inc., 2006.

[174] "New Publications; The Draft Riots in New-York: The Honorable Record of the Metropolitan Police During Riot Week, by David M. Barnes. New-York: Baker & Godwin, Publishers, October 23, 1863." The *New York Times.* http://www.nytimes.com/1863/10/23/news/new-publications-draft-riots-new-york-honorable-record-metropolitan-police.html. (Accessed April 28, 2016).

[175] "New York Daily Tribune December 17, 1860, Monday." Dilemmas of Compromise. *Tulane University.* http://www.tulane.edu/~sumter/Dilemmas/Tribune17Dec.html. (Accessed April 28, 2016).

[176] "No Treason, No. 1." Lysander Spooner. *Mises Daily.* March 22, 2011. https://mises.org/library/no-treason-no-1. (Accessed April 25, 2016).

[177] Norman, Matthew D. "An Illinois Iconoclast: Edgar Lee Masters and the Anti-Lincoln Tradition." Volume 24, Issue 1, Winter 2003, *Journal of the Abraham Lincoln Association.* http://quod.lib.umich.edu/j/jala/2629860.0024.105/--illinois-iconoclast-edgar-lee-masters-and-the-anti-lincoln?rgn=main;view=fulltext. (Accessed April 26, 2016).

[178] North, Gary. "Abraham Lincoln and the Federal Reserve System: A Forgotten Connection." *Gary North's Specific Answers*, September 24, 2013. http://www.garynorth.com/public/11585print.cfm. (Accessed April 18, 2016).

[179] Norton, Roger J. "Lincoln's Brush with Death!" *Abraham Lincoln Research Site*, December 29, 1996. http://rogerjnorton.com/Lincoln19.html. (Accessed April 17, 2016).

[180] Norton, Roger J. "A Very Brief View of the Legal Career of Abraham Lincoln." *Abraham Lincoln Research Site*, December 29, 1996. http://rogerjnorton.com/Lincoln91.html. (Accessed April 18, 2016).

[181] Nunes, Bill. "The longest and shortest railroads in the world." *Suburban Journals of Greater St. Louis*. St. Louis Dispatch, October 10, 2007. http://www.stltoday.com/suburban-journals/the-longest-and-shortest-railroads-in-the-world/article_6a5885f2-ae9d-5ed0-b77d-59207fce9acf.html. (Accessed April 18, 2016).

[182] Orwell, George. *1984*. New York, New York: Signet Classic, published by the Penguin Group, 1984.

[183] Owsley, Frank Lawrence. "The Irrepressible Conflict" in *I'll Take My Stand: The South and the Agrarian Tradition*, 61-91. Baton Rouge, Louisiana and London, England: Louisiana State University Press, 1991.

[184] Pace, Charles T. *War Between The States—Why?* Published by Charles T. Pace.

[185] Padgett, Vernon R., Ph. D. Division Adjutant, California Division, Sons of Confederate Veterans. "Did Blacks Serve in the Confederate Army as Soldiers?" *CaliforniaSCV.org*. http://californiascv.org/Did%20Blacks%20Serve%20in%20the%20Confederate%20Army%20as%20Soldiers%20PDF.pdf. (Accessed April 24, 2016).

[186] "Patrick Henry, Virginia Ratifying Convention." *The Founder's Constitution*, Volume 2, Preamble, Document 14, 4 June 1788—Elliot 3:22—23. http://press-pubs.uchicago.edu/founders/documents/preambles14.html. (Accessed April 20, 2016).

[187] Pearson, Richard. "Former Ala. Gov. George C. Wallace Dies." *Washington Post*, Monday, September 14, 1998; Page A1. http://www.washingtonpost.com/wp-srv/politics/daily/sept98/wallace.htm. (Accessed April 18, 2016).

[188] Peterson, Austin. "Does Democracy Inevitably Lead to Socialism?" Economics of Liberty. *The Libertarian Republic—Economic Freedom—Personal Liberty*, September 6, 2013. http://thelibertarianrepublic.com/does-democracy-inevitably-lead-to-socialism/#axzz3OTxBVQGf. (Accessed April 28, 2016).

[189] Petty, Micha. "Confederate Quotes." *American Revival*, 2010. http://www.americanrevival.org/quotes/confederate.htm. (Accessed April 25, 2016).

[190] Pinsker, Matthew, "Letter to Horace Greeley (August 22, 1862)." Dickinson College, Carlisle, Pennsylvania. *House Divided Project.* http://housedivided.dickinson.edu/sites/lincoln/letter-to-horace-greeley-august-22-1862/. (Accessed April 24, 2016).

[191] Pollard, E.A. *The Lost Cause,* A Facsimile of the Original 1886 Edition. Avenel, New Jersey: Gramercy Books, 1994.

[192] "Post War Life and Career." *The Papers of Jefferson Davis — Rice University — MS 43*, Houston, Texas, 2016. http://jeffersondavis.rice.edu/PostWarLifeandCareer.aspx. (Accessed April 24, 2016).

[193] "The Pratt Street Riot." *National Park Service.* http://www.nps.gov/fomc/historyculture/the-pratt-street-riot.htm. (Accessed April 24, 2016).

[194] "The Preachers: James Jaquess." *Mr. Lincoln & Friends*. http://www.mrlincolnandfriends.org/inside.asp?pageID=100&subjectID=10. (Accessed April 24, 2016).

[195] "Proclamation of Blockade Against Southern Ports, April 19, 1861." *Angelfire*. http://www.angelfire.com/my/abrahamlincoln/Blockade.html. (Accessed April 23, 2016).

[196] "The Project Gutenberg EBook of The Complete Works of Nathaniel Hawthorne.", Appendix to Volume XII: Tales, Sketches, and other Papers by Nathaniel Hawthorne with a Biographical Sketch by George Parsons Lathrop; Release Date: August 18, 2012. EBook #40529. *Gutenberg.org.* http://www.gutenberg.org/files/40529/40529-h/40529-h.htm. (Accessed April 25, 2016).

[197] "Protective Purpose of the Tariff Act of 1789." Early Journal Content on JSTOR. *Internet Archive.* http://archive.org/stream/jstor-1819831/1819831_djvu.txt. (Accessed April 17, 2016).

[198] "The Protector, 70, U.S. 12 Wall 700 700, 1870." Justia, *US Supreme Court.* https://supreme.justia.com/cases/federal/us/79/700/. (Accessed April 23, 2016).

[199] Quigley, Carroll. *Tragedy and Hope.* New York, New York: The MacMillan Company and London, England: Collier-MacMillan, 1966. In Collection Community Texts, Uploaded by TrimbleScottish on 6/29/2009. https://archive.org/details/TragedyAndHope_501. (Accessed June 12, 2016).

[200] "Quotation #37218 from Contributed Quotations." *The Quotations Page*. Michael Moncur, 1994-2015. http://www.quotationspage.com/quote/37218.html. (Accessed April 25, 2016).

[201] "Quotes from Generals William T. Sherman & Phil Sheridan." Descendants *of Point Lookout POW Organization*. October 27, 2008. http://www.plpow.com/Atrocities_QuotesFromSherman.htm. (Accessed April 24, 2016).

[202] Rand, Clayton. *Sons of the South*. New York, New York: Holt, Rinehart and Winston, 1961.

[203] Rawle, William, LL.D. *A View of the Constitution — Secession as Taught at West Point*. Edited and annotated by Walter D. Kennedy and Ronald R. Kennedy. Baton Rouge, Louisiana: Land and Land Publishing Division and Simsboro, Louisiana: Old South Books, 1993.

[204] Rean, Michael T. "Shifting Strategies: Military Theory in the American Civil War." *MilitaryHistoryOnline.com*, March 16, 2008. http://www.militaryhistoryonline.com/civilwar/articles/militarytheory.aspx. (Accessed April 28, 2016).

[205] "A Rebel Newspaper in Iowa Suppressed; The Keokuk Constitution Destroyed." Chicago, Friday, February 20. Published February 21, 1863, *The New York Times*, 2014. http://www.nytimes.com/1863/02/21/news/a-rebel-newspaper-in-iowa-suppressed-the-keokuk-constitution-destroyed.html. (Accessed April 23, 2016).

[206] Reese, Charley. "We Are Revolutionaries." *LewRockwell.com*, September 19, 2005. https://www.lewrockwell.com/2005/09/charley-reese/were-revolutionaries/ - September 19, 2005. (Accessed April 17, 2016).

[207] *Resolutions*, Volume 12 of *United States at Large*, Edited by George P. Sanger, Counsellor at Law, Little, Brown and Company, Boston, Massachusetts, 1863. Reprinted by Dennis & Co., Buffalo, New York in August 1961. https://www.loc.gov/law/help/statutes-at-large/36th-congress/c36.pdf. (Accessed April 19, 2016).

[208] "Respectfully Quoted: A Dictionary of Quotations." *Bartleby.com*, 1989. http://www.bartleby.com/73/1593.html. (Accessed April 25, 2016).

[209] Richardson, James D. "Confederate States of America — Inaugural Address of the President of the Provisional Government, February 18, 1861." *The Avalon Project*. Yale Law School. Lillian Goldman Law Library, 2008. http://avalon.law.yale.edu/19th_century/csa_csainau.asp. (Accessed April 28, 2016).

[210] Richardson, Captain John Anderson. *A Historical and Constitutional Defense of the South.* Harrisonburg, Virginia: Sprinkle Publications, 2010. Originally published by A.B. Caldwell, Atlanta, Georgia, 1914.

[211] "Robert E. Lee Quotes." *Brainy Quote.* http://www.brainyquote.com/quotes/quotes/r/robertele169541.html. (Accessed April 18, 2016).

[212] Ropes, John Codman. *The Story of the Civil War, Part 1: Chapter II: The Question of the Southern Forts.* New York, New York and London, England: G.P. Putnam and Sons. The Knickerbocker Press, 1907. Original from New York Public Library. *Hathi Trust Digital Library.* https://babel.hathitrust.org/cgi/pt?id=nyp.33433113859874;view=1up;seq=39 (Accessed May 8, 2016).

[213] Rumberg, Dr. H. Rondel. *Was Lincoln a Christian?* Spout Spring, Virginia: SBSS (Biblical and Southern Studies), 2006.

[214] Rutherford, Mildred Lewis. *A True Estimate of Abraham Lincoln & Vindication of the South.* Wiggins, Mississippi: Crown Rights Book Company, 1997. Rutherford's original book appeared in March 1923 under the title, *The South Must Have Her Rightful Place in History.*

[215] Rutherford, Mildred Lewis, *Truths of History.* Harrisonburg, Virginia: Old South Institute Press, 2009. Reprinted from statements of prominent men and gathered by Mildred L. Rutherford, concerning the early years of the American Republic to the War Between the States and beyond.

[216] Sale, Kirkpatrick. *Emancipation Hell.* Mt. Pleasant, South Carolina: Kirkpatrick Sale, 2012.

[217] *Savant Noir. You Thought we Had a Two Party System? Recycle Washington, out with the old, in with the new. Posted by Savant Noir, May 15, 2010.* http://recyclewashington.wordpress.com/2010/05/15/1-2/. (Accessed April 18, 2016).

[218] Scharf, John Thomas. *History of the Confederate States Navy from its Organization to the Surrender of its Last Vessel.* New York, New York: Crown Publishers, 1977. Originally published in Baltimore, Maryland by Fairfax Press, 1887.

[219] Scott, Otto, The Secret Six: John Brown and the Abolitionist Movement. Murphys, California: Uncommon Books, 1979.

[220] Scruggs, Mike. "Understanding the Causes of the Civil War: A Brief Explanation of the Impact of the Morrill Tariff." *The Tribune Papers,* June 4, 2005. http://ashevilletribune.com/archives/censored-truths/Morrill%20Tariff.html. (Accessed April 18, 2016).

[221] "Secession Crisis: States' Rights—'Powers Reserved To The States.'" The War for States' Rights. *Civil War Bluegrass.* http://civilwar.bluegrass.net/secessioncrisis/statesrights.html. (Accessed April 17, 2016).

[222] "Secession Crisis: U.S. Constitution—'The Right to Secede'—March 4, 1789." The War for States' Rights. *Civil War Bluegrass.* http://civilwar.bluegrass.net/secessioncrisis/890304.html. (Accessed April 23, 2016).

[223] "Secession Crises: Ships, Blockades and Raiders." The War for States' Rights. *Civil War Bluegrass.* http://civilwar.bluegrass.net/ShipsBlockadesAndRaiders/theblockade1.htm l . (Accessed April 23, 2016).

[224] "Secession Crises: Ships, Blockades and Raiders, Blockade Running 'Profits Worth the Risk." The War for States' Rights. *Civil War Bluegrass.* http://civilwar.bluegrass.net/ShipsBlockadesAndRaiders/blockaderunning-profits.html. (Accessed April 23, 2016).

[225] "Second Session of the Second Wheeling Convention, August 6-21, 1861, Chapter Nine." A State of Convenience—The Creation of West Virginia. *West Virginia Division of Culture and History.* http://www.wvculture.org/history/statehood/statehood09.html. (Accessed April 24, 2016).

[226] Semmes, Admiral Raphael, CSN Captain of the Alabama, *Memoirs of Service Afloat.* Secaucus, New Jersey: The Blue & Grey Press, 1987.

[227] Shaw, Robert Gould. *Blue-Eyed Child of Fortune: The Civil War Letters of Colonel Robert Gould Shaw.* Edited by Russell Duncan. Athens, Georgia: The University of Georgia Press, 1992.

[228] Sheppard, Robert Dickinson, D.D. *Abraham Lincoln: A Character Sketch.* Chicago, Illinois: Frederick J. Drake & Company, by H.G. Campbell Publishing Company, 1903. Original Copyright by The University Association, 1898 and digitized by Indiana State University. https://archive.org/details/abrahamlinc2788shep. (Accessed August 21, 2016).

[229] Sheriff, Derek. "The Untold History of Nullification: Resisting Slavery." *Tenth Amendment Center.* http://www.tenthamendmentcenter.com/2010/02/10/the-untold-history-of-nullification/. (Accessed April 24, 2016).

[230] "Signers of the Confederate Constitution." Hargrett Rare Book & Manuscript Library. *University of Georgia Libraries,* August 26, 2013.

http://www.libs.uga.edu/hargrett/selections/confed/signers.html. (Accessed April 20, 2016).

231 "Slavery, the Economy, and Society." *Cliffs Notes*. Houghton, Mifflin, Harcourt, 2016. http://www.cliffsnotes.com/study-guides/history/us-history-i/slavery-and-the-south/slavery-the-economy-and-society. (Accessed April 20, 2016).

232 Slavery or Tariff? The American Civil War. *Online Etymology*. http://www.etymonline.com/cw/economics.htm. (Accessed April 25, 2016).

233 Sophocleus, John P. "Emancipation Proclamation Sesquicentennial (Slavery? Bah, Humbug!)." *The Alabama Gazette*, January 2013.

234 "A Southern View of History: The War for Southern Independence, Part III: Servitude, Slavery, Abolitionists." *Sons of Confederate Veterans*. http://www.scv.org/curriculum/part3.htm. (Accessed April 28, 2016).

235 Spooner, Lysander. "No Treason—The Constitution of No Authority." Reprinted at *LewRockwell.com*. https://www.lewrockwell.com/1970/01/lysander-spooner/no-treason-the-constitution-of-no-authority/. (Accessed April 28, 2016).

236 "Spotty Lincoln." Today's Document. *National Archives*. http://todaysdocument.tumblr.com/post/14622684113/spotty-lincoln-congressman-abraham-lincoln. (Accessed April 17, 2016).

237 Springer, Francis W. *War For What?* Nashville, Tennessee: Bill Coats, Ltd., 1990.

238 Starr, John W., Jr. *Lincoln & the Railroads*. New York, New York: Dodd, Mead & Company, 1927. From *Hathi Trust Digital Library*. https://babel.hathitrust.org/cgi/pt?id=uc1.$b68226;view=1up;seq=1. (Accessed May 16, 2016).

239 "A State of Convenience: The Creation of West Virginia." Opinion of Abraham Lincoln on the Admission of West Virginia from the Lincoln Papers, Library of Congress, *West Virginia Division of Culture and History*. http://www.wvculture.org/history/statehood/lincolnopinion.html. (Accessed April 24, 2016).

240 Stowe, Charles Beecher. "Honest Confession Good for the Country." *Confederate Veteran Magazine*. (Publication of the United Confederate Veterans), Volume 19, Number 7, July 1911. http://www.usgennet.org/usa/ga/county/macon/newspapers/CV/cv1911pg12.htm. (Accessed April 23, 2016).

241 Symonds, Craig L. *The Naval Institute Historical Atlas of the U.S. Navy*. Annapolis, Maryland: Naval Institute Press, January 15, 2013.

242 "Tales from the Old South: Jefferson Davis and Blessed Pius IX." *Roman Christendom*, Saturday, November 17, 2007. http://romanchristendom.blogspot.com/2007/11/tales-from-old-south-jefferson-davis.html. (Accessed April 28, 2016).

243 Taylor, John. *New Views of the Constitution of the United States.* Washington, D.C.: Regnery Publishing, Inc., 2000. First published in 1823 by Way and Gideon, Washington, D.C.

244 Terry, Scott M. "John Taylor of Caroline, Defender of the Agrarian Republic." *North Country Farmer.* February 23, 2012. http://www.northcountryfarmer.com/?p=295. (Accessed April 25, 2016).

245 "This Day in History."*telegram.com.* Worcester, Massachusetts, May 25, 2010. http://www.telegram.com/article/20100525/DIGESTS/5250418/1102/RSS01. (Accessed April 26, 2016).

246 "Thomas Jefferson, on Politics & Government." Foreign Commerce—Eliminating International Duties and Regulations, Jefferson to Marquis de Lafayette, 1786. ME 5:346. *famguardian.org.* http://famguardian.org/Subjects/Politics/ThomasJefferson/jeff1450.htm. (Accessed May 8, 2016).

247 Thornton, Mark. "The Quotable Mises." *Ludwig von Mises Institute,* July 27, 2007. Quoted from Human Action, 626; 630-31. http://mises.org/quotes.aspx?action=subject&subject=Slavery. (Accessed April 19, 2016).

248 Thornton, Mark and Robert B. Ekelund, Jr. *Tariffs, Blockades and Inflation: The Economics of the Civil War.* Wilmington, Delaware: A Scholarly Resources Inc. Imprint, 2004.

249 Tilley, John Shipley. *Facts The Historians Leave Out.* Twenty-Second Printing. Nashville, Tennessee: Bill Coats, Ltd., 1991.

250 Tilley, John Shipley. *Lincoln Takes Command.* Nashville, Tennessee: Bill Coats, Ltd., 1991.

251 Tocqueville, Alexis de. *Democracy in America.* New York, New York: Alfred A. Knopf, Inc. Ninth Edition, September 1963.

252 Tokarick, Steven. "How large is the bias against exports from import tariffs?" Research Department. *International Monetary Fund.* http://www.dartmouth.edu/~rstaiger/lerner.symmetry.theorem.evidence.pdf. (Accessed April 20, 2016).

253 "Towards Confederation—Influence of the American Civil War: The Trent Affair." *Library and Archives Canada.* https://www.collectionscanada.gc.ca/confederation/023001-2400.03-e.html. (Accessed April 24, 2016).

254 Towne, Stephen E. "*Killing the Serpent Speedily: Governor Morton, General Hascall, and the Suppression of the Democratic Press in Indiana*, 1863." https://scholarworks.iupui.edu/bitstream/handle/1805/696/Killing%20the%20Serpent%20Speedily.pdf?sequence=1. (Accessed April 23, 2016).

255 "The Trent Affair; Opinion of the Law Officers of the Crown." The *London Globe* (Reprint), December 19, 1861, The *New York Times*. http://www.nytimes.com/1861/12/19/news/the-trent-affair-opinion-of-the-law-officers-of-the-crown.html?pagewanted=2. (Accessed April 24, 2016).

256 "The Trent Affair; Opinion of the Law Officers of the Crown." The *London Herald*, December 19, 1861, *New York Times Reprints*. http://www.nytimes.com/1861/12/19/news/the-trent-affair-opinion-of-the-law-officers-of-the-crown.html. (Accessed April 24, 2016).

257 "The Trent Affair; Opinion of the Law Officers of the Crown." The *London Times*, December 19,1861, *New York Times Reprints*. http://www.nytimes.com/1861/12/19/news/the-trent-affair-opinion-of-the-law-officers-of-the-crown.html. (Accessed April 24, 2016).

258 "The Trent Affair." *U.S. Department of State*. http://future.state.gov/when/timeline/1861_timeline/trent_affair.html. (Accessed April 24, 2016).

259 "Tsar Alexander II Pledges support for the Union." *Reformation.org*. Excerpted from his autobiography, *Memoir of Thurlow Weed, Vol. II*, Boston, Massachusetts: Houghton-Mifflin Co., 1884. http://www.reformation.org/czar-alexander.html.(Accessed April 24, 2016).

260 Tyler, Lyon Gardner. *The Gray Book: A Confederate Catechism*. Wiggins, Mississippi: Crown Rights Book Company, 1997. Originally printed in Tyler's Quarterly, Volume 33, January and February, 1935, and Volume 33, January and October, 1935.

261 Vallandigham, Rev. James Laird. *A Life of Clement L. Vallandigham*. Baltimore: Turnbull Brothers, 8 North Charles Street, 1872. *The Library of Congress Internet Archive*, https://archive.org/stream/lifeofclementlva00vall#page/106/mode/2up, (Accessed April 24, 2016).

262 Vance, Laurence. "Christianity and War." *LewRockwell.com*, October 29, 2003. https://www.lewrockwell.com/2003/10/laurence-m-vance/christianity-and-war-2/. (Accessed April 28, 2016).

263 von Drehle, David. "Lincoln's Reluctant War: How Abolitionists Leaned on the President." *The Atlantic*, October 26, 2012. http://www.theatlantic.com/national/archive/2012/10/lincolns-reluctant-war-how-abolitionists-leaned-on-the-president/264125/. (Accessed April 18, 2016).

264 "The War of the Rebellion: A Compilation of the Official Records of the Union and Confederate Armies: Reports: - No. 1: Maj. Robert Anderson, First U.S. Artillery, of the evacuation of Fort Moultrie." Prepared under the direction of the Secretary of War, by Bvt. Lieut. Col. Robert N. Scott, Third U.S. Artillery and published pursuant to Act of Congress approved June 16, 1880, (Washington: Government Printing Office, 1883). *http://www.simmonsgames.com/research/authors/USWarDept/ORA/TOC.html.* (Accessed April 23, 2016).

265 Watner, Carl and Shone, Steve J. "Lysander Spooner—American Anarchist." *The Foundation for Economic Education,* August 11, 2011. http://fee.org/freeman/detail/lysander-spooner-american-anarchist/. (Accessed April 25, 2016).

266 "Web Field Trip." *U.S. History—Abolitionism.* http://tdl.org/txlor-dspace/bitstream/handle/2249.3/617/04_abolitionism.htm. (Accessed April 18, 2016).

267 Weeks, Richard "Shotgun." "The Trent Affair," excerpted from *The Confederate Military History, Volume I, Chapter XV. Shotgun's Home of the American Civil War.* http://civilwarhome.com/trent.htm. (Accessed April 24, 2016).

268 Weeks, Richard "Shotgun." "The Prison Life of Jefferson Davis." *Times-Dispatch,* February 12, 1905, *American Civil War.* http://civilwarhome.com/davisinprison.htm. (Accessed April 25, 2016).

269 Weeks, Richard "Shotgun." "Election of 1864." Excerpted from *The Civil War and Reconstruction,* by J.G. Randall and David Herbert Donald. *Shotgun's Home of the American Civil War.* http://civilwarhome.com/elections1864.htm. (Accessed April 24, 2016).

270 "West Virginia." *Hometown USA.* http://www.hometownusa.com/wv/index.html. (Accessed April 28, 2016).

271 Whitehead, John. "Habeas Corpus." *The Rutherford Institute—Dedicated to the Defense of Civil Liberties and Human Rights.* https://www.rutherford.org/constitutional_corner/habeas_corpus/. (Accessed April 23, 2016).

272 "THE WIDE-AWAKES; Fear of the Wide-Awakes at the South Idle Apprehensions." *New York Times,* September 29, 1860, excerpted from the *Columbia (S.C.) Guardian.* http://www.nytimes.com/1860/09/29/news/the-wide-awakes-fear-of-the-wide-awakes-at-the-south-idle-apprehensions.html. (Accessed April 18, 2016).

[273] "William Lloyd Garrison Quotes and Quotations." Famous Quotes and Authors. http://www.famousquotesandauthors.com/authors/william_lloyd_garrison _quotes.html. (Accessed April 28, 2016).
[274] Williams, Frank J. "Abraham Lincoln, Civil Liberties and the Corning Letter." Rhode Island Superior Court. *Roger Williams University Law Review*, Volume 5, Issue 2, Article 1, Spring 2000. http://docs.rwu.edu/cgi/viewcontent.cgi?article=1132&context=rwu_LR. (Accessed April 24, 2016).
[275] Williams, Frank J. "When Albany Challenged the President." *New York State Archives*, Winter 2009. http://nysa32.nysed.gov/apt/magazine/archivesmag_winter09_Williams.pdf. (Accessed April 24, 2016).
[276] Williams, Michael G. "Baltimore Riot of 1861." *Weider History, History.net*, August 8, 2011. Originally published by *Civil War Times*. http://www.historynet.com/baltimore-riot-of-1861.htm. (Accessed April 24, 2016).
[277] Wilson, Clyde. "The Republican Charade: Lincoln and His Party." Clyde Wilson Library. *Abbeville Institute*, November 19, 2014. http://www.abbevilleinstitute.org/clyde-wilson-library/the-republican-charade-lincoln-and-his-party/. (Accessed April 17, 2016).
[278] Wood, Robert C. *Confederate Hand-Book*. Falls Church, Virginia: Sterling Press, 1982.
[279] Woods, Thomas E., Jr. *The Politically Incorrect Guide to American History*. Washington, DC: Regnery Publishing, Inc., 2007.
[280] Woods, Thomas E., Jr. *"The Real Significance of the 'Civil War.'"* *LewRockwell.com*. November 27, 2004. http://www.lewrockwell.com/2004/11/thomas-woods/the-real-significance-of-the-civil-war/. (Accessed April 28, 2016).

Index

Union At All Costs
From Confederation to Consolidation
John M. Taylor

"[T]he contest is really for empire on the side of the North, and for independence on that of the South, and in this respect we recognize an exact analogy between the North and the Government of George III, and the South and the Thirteen Revolted Provinces. These opinions...are the general opinions of the English nation." -- London Times, November 7, 1861

"All that the South has ever desired was that the Union as established by our forefathers should be preserved and that the government as originally organized should be administered in purity and truth." -- Robert E. Lee

"With her immense staples, [the South] has furnished near three-fourths of the entire exports of the country. Last year she furnished seventy-two per cent. Of the whole . . . It is almost impossible to estimate the amount of money realized yearly out of the South by the North." -- Daily Chicago Times, December 10, 1860

"These holders of the debt are to be paid still further—and perhaps doubly, triply, or quadruply paid—by such tariffs on imports as will enable our home manufacturers to realize enormous prices for their commodities; also by such monopolies in banking as will enable them to keep control of, and thus enslave and plunder, the industry and trade of the great body of the Northern people themselves." -- Lysander Spooner, abolitionist from Athol, Massachusetts and a supporter of the South.

"There is no mystery why lovers of big government strongly loathe the Confederacy and worship Lincoln. The Confederate soldier represents the last true defense of consensual constitutional government and they were the last real threat to the omnipotent leviathan state." -- John M. Taylor

CPSIA information can be obtained
at www.ICGtesting.com
Printed in the USA
BVHW071347031019

560132BV00001B/16/P

9 781634 916462